PRAISE FOR ELIZABETH M. NORMAN
AND

We Band of Angels

"This is a gripping book. Elizabeth Norman presents a war story in which the main characters never kill one of the enemy, or even shoot at him, but are nevertheless heroes. . . . First on Bataan, then moved to Corregidor, they were under almost constant shell fire, were always hungry, close to starvation, had horrendous diseases to deal with despite a shortage or even a complete lack of proper medicines, getting little or no sleep, nothing in the way of recreation—yet they were a true band of angels, inspiring all the men whom they were there to help. In a squalid prison camp, they remained giants, despite their small size. . . . They were the bravest of the brave, who endured unspeakable pain and torture. Americans today should thank God we had such women."

—Stephen E. Ambrose

"Compelling . . . engrossing . . . suspense-filled. . . . Terrific reading."
—*Austin American-Statesman* (TX)

"The most comprehensive account ever told of the capture and captivity of the ninety-nine nurses known as the 'Angels of Bataan'. . . . The vivid details of their actions, taken from interviews, journals, letters, and government testimony . . . prove to be the real gems of the book."

—*The Philippine Inquirer*

"One cannot help but be impressed by their courage in the worst of circumstances. . . . An incredible piece of research."

—*Richmond Times-Dispatch*

"Harrowing . . . well-written."

—*Library Journal*

"Packs an emotional wallop."

—*San Antonio Express-News*

"Gripping. . . . Norman's touching and stirring narrative makes a fitting tribute to these women's courage and dedication."

—*Kirkus Reviews*

"Makes excellent use of extensive quotations from diaries and interviews. . . . Norman also captures moments of great courage. . . . But the true highlights come in the evocation of tears and sweat that went into the nurses' daily struggle . . . in the face of overwhelming adversity."

—*Publishers Weekly*

"Captures [war's] gritty, surreal texture with as much eloquence as the best writers on the Balkan front lines. . . . Norman tells the story of Bataan with authority, compassion, and an unusually clear-sighted view of the American military. She hooks readers from the start."

—*The Boston Globe*

"Required reading for anyone who thinks women cannot stand up to the rigors of combat."

—*U.S. Naval Institute Proceedings*

"From diaries, letters, and interviews with aging survivors, Elizabeth Norman has filled in a vital but missing chapter in the history of World War II: the stunning heroism of women. Bombing raids. Malaria. Starvation. Capture. Survival. Here is the little-known story of the Army and Navy nurses caught in the brutal retreat of U.S. forces from Manila to Bataan to Corregidor, and eventually to three years in a Japanese prisoner-of-war camp. It is as inspiring as it is horrific."

—Linda Bird Francke

"Vivid details and . . . precise narration make this a bracing read."
—*The San Diego Union-Tribune*

"Elizabeth Norman brings a powerful new voice to the nonfiction literature of war, combining first-rate reportage with a lyrical narrative style to present an unforgettable story of courage and character. *WE BAND OF ANGELS* is at once a terrific read and a classic study of human behavior under extreme duress, seen from the perspective of women nurses held captive under the harshest conditions imaginable in the jungles of the Philippines during World War II. These nurses were independent, professional, and fearless long before American society encouraged such behavior in women. They saw the worst of war, and, thanks to Norman's masterpiece, their heroism can be forgotten no more."

—David Maraniss

Elizabeth M. Norman

POCKET BOOKS

New York London Toronto Sydney Singapore

We Band of Angels

The Untold Story of American Nurses Trapped on Bataan by the Japanese

POCKET BOOKS, a division of Simon & Schuster Inc.
1230 Avenue of the Americas, New York, NY 10020

ISBN: 0-671-78718-7

First Pocket Books trade paperback printing May 2000

20   19   18   17   16

Cover design by Tom McKeveny
Front cover photo courtesy of U.S. Signal Corps

To Michael, Joshua and Benjamin

Also by Elizabeth M. Norman

Women at War: The Story of
Fifty Military Nurses
Who Served in Vietnam

Contents

Foreword

I CANNOT SAY where or when, exactly, this story really began. Sometimes, I think it started with my mother.

Dorothy Riley Dempsey served as a SPAR in the Coast Guard in World War II. Growing up, my four sisters and I heard a lot about our mother's days in uniform, holding down Stateside duties to free the men to go to sea, but it was hard to think of Mom as a "military woman." The term always seemed an oxymoron to me. In fact, it was hard to think of any woman in such a "man's world," a domain I thought was antithetical to everything a woman was, or was supposed to be: wife, mother, sister, friend.

Then early in my academic career I interviewed fifty women who had served as military nurses in Vietnam. As a registered nurse I became fascinated by their stories, stories of dying soldiers and wounded children, of exhaustion, frustration and fear. They said their experiences—caring for the sick and wounded, sorting out mass casualties, suffering rocket and artillery attacks—changed them. War, they told me, was their life's dividing line.

I wondered: Was it the bizarre and tragic nature of Vietnam that made these women seem so different from the other nurses I had worked with across the years, or was the difference the result of women trying to live and work in a domain almost exclusive to men, women trying to adapt to what has always been a man's enterprise, war?

During my research on Vietnam I kept coming across references to a small group of women who had "fought" in World War II, a group commonly referred to as the Angels of Bataan and Corregidor. To follow up I called Brigadier General Lillian Dunlap, a retired chief of the Army

Nurse Corps. What she said that morning started me on a search that has taken me eight long years to complete.

THE SAME DAY the Imperial Japanese Navy launched its surprise attack on the United States naval base at Pearl Harbor in Hawaii it also struck American naval and army bases, airfields and ports in the Philippine Islands—December 8, 1941.[1]

Caught in the air raid and the murderous invasion that followed were ninety-nine army and navy nurses. Without any formal combat training or wartime preparation, most found themselves on Bataan with their backs to the sea, retreating from a well-trained, well-supplied and relentless army. They were hungry and scared, jumping into trenches during bombing raids, caring for thousands of casualties. Before the enemy finally caught up with them on Corregidor, a handful of the women— some two dozen—escaped on ships or small aircraft that managed to slip through the enemy blockade. The main body, however—seventy-seven women, a group in many ways representative of American womanhood in the era between the great wars—were captured by the Japanese and held behind concrete and barbed wire for three years in prison camps.

As a unit the nurses of Bataan and Corregidor represent the first large group of American women in combat and the first group of American military women taken captive and imprisoned by an enemy.

Thinking of my mother, a strong purposeful woman, and thinking of the nurses of Vietnam, a group struggling to reconcile their notions of women's identity with their experience in war, I knew the Angels' story would be compelling and decided to go after it.

General Dunlap had given me phone numbers for two of the Angels, and in the spring of 1989 I called them, offered my background and explained my purpose. At length they agreed to sit down and talk. Their willingness to cooperate came, I'm sure, from our sorority—nurse talking to nurse—but I also got the sense that these women were painfully aware that their ranks were dying, and that if they did not speak out now, if they did not attempt to preserve their dark but wonderful story, it would disappear. In short they did not want their legacy folded into the larger story of World War II and lost in the often indiscriminate pages of history.

So I set out to visit the two women the general had recommended to see if there was a story I could tell. At first I wondered about their ability to recall in detail events and relationships some fifty years old. To my surprise, and embarrassment, both women, Mary Rose Harrington Nelson, a former navy nurse in her late seventies, and Ruby Bradley, a retired army nurse in her mid-eighties, were often encyclopedic in their accounts, and I sat there rapt as they took me back to their war and the trials of their survival.

Each woman also supplied me with names and addresses of her comrades, but told me to hurry because time was taking them. Old and enervated by their long captivity, the group was dying. At the time, January 1990, only forty-eight of the original seventy-seven captured in 1942 and repatriated in 1945 were still alive.

I quickly began to arrange visits. Several times my fears about the Angels' advancing age and ill health proved true. In January 1992 one of them, Bertha Dworsky of Sunnyvale, California, apologized and said she could not see me. "I'm eighty-one years old," she wrote, "and it's all I can do to take care of myself."[2] A month later, she was dead. Another woman, Ruth Straub from Colorado Springs, went into a hospital the day before I was scheduled to sit down with her. After that I rushed to find Josephine Nesbit, a senior army nurse and a central figure in the story. Her husband, Bill Davis, called to say his wife was too weak from a recent heart attack to talk. Then I wrote a letter to Inez McDonald Moore in San Marcus, Texas. A week or so passed and an envelope arrived bearing her return address. I opened it to find a note from her husband and a clipping—Inez's obituary. Nine other women died before I could find and contact them.

Three of the forty-eight refused to see me. "It was too long ago and too hard to remember," one said.[3] Another wrote, "I regret that I am not able to assist you. I do not want to live in the past."[4]

About a dozen were simply impossible to locate, lost to time or circumstance.

In the end I spoke with twenty of the women, all generous with their time and their memories. We talked in their homes or in the retirement centers they called home. I filled out these personal accounts with scores of additional interviews—other veterans, government officials, the Angels' children and relatives.

Early in my search I noticed that the interviews seemed to take on a pattern. They always began with humor—something I had noticed in my interviews of the women from Vietnam. I have spoken with other war writers about this, why those who have seen heavy combat mask their grim vitae with jokes and rhetorical slapstick. I think it is a way for them to introduce the idea of living with the absurd or of taking part in the unthinkable. Or perhaps the jokes are a way to keep the loss and the savagery from overwhelming them. Several nurses, for example, told me the same raucous prewar story about a particularly self-possessed nurse in a bar who became so angry at the soldier interrupting her quiet beer, she slugged him and knocked him out.

When we finally got past the "fun" and turned to the real fighting, many found it extremely painful to talk about their losses—the loss of their youth, health, patients, battlefield husbands and boyfriends. A few broke down and wept as they recalled the helplessness they felt watching the enemy pull the wounded from their hospital beds and cart them to certain death in a military prison. Nothing, nothing at all, is more devastating to a nurse than to be pulled away from the patients in her charge, the lives entrusted to her.

The more I studied the women, the more I realized I was dealing not with individuals but with a collective persona. The women often answered my questions using the pronoun "we" rather than "I." They were some of the least egocentric people I've met and as such were difficult interviews. Many simply did not want to talk about themselves. They did not have the habit of self-reflection that seems to drive the conversation of our era, the need to dwell on identity, to indulge the ego and see all stories as memoir. Rather they insisted on emphasizing their connections, their relationships with one another—a turn of mind made familiar to the modern woman by the research of social psychologists. And so their individual stories were sketchy, too sketchy for full-length profiles or portraits, but when those stories were put together, the Angels seemed to come to life. So I let them teach me the way, and the way was to consider their experience as a group, an identification of their own making.

They learned this—the notion of strength in numbers—as military women. In the ranks nothing is more important than "unit cohesiveness." Masses of arms and men win wars, not the impulsive deeds of heroes. As it turned out, the "group" saved their lives. Their collective sense of mission, both as nurses and as army and naval officers, allowed them to survive when stronger people faltered. In prison not one of the nurses died of disease or malnutrition, while more than four hundred other internees perished. In that context their survival as a group was extraordinary.

IN SOME WAYS the women in this book are typical of their time—they were born, most of them, in the early twentieth century, the daughters of immigrants and farmers and shopkeepers, obedient girls who studied long and hard in school, then came home to hours of chores and house-work. In other ways, however, they were distinct, for early on they learned or perhaps were taught the virtue of independence and the au-tonomous life.

In some the ethos of independence bred ambition, in others rebel-lion. As teenagers they started to reject the roles society had set for them. They had watched their mothers struggle—long hours cooking, sewing, washing, hoeing and milking cows—and they decided they wanted something more, something different than an early marriage, a house full of babies and a life over a cast-iron stove.

Teaching and office work held little appeal—the former meant tak-ing care of someone else's children, the latter someone else's man—so they entered the only other profession open to them, nursing.

After nursing school and a stint on a ward, they joined the army or the navy. No subculture in American society was more intolerant of women than the military, but signing on to a life of restrictions and reg-ulations seemed to make a strange kind of sense for these noncon-formists. In a time of economic depression, when thousands were standing on breadlines, the nurses had jobs, and good ones. More to the point, the military gave the women a way to get what each really wanted—adventure. And no post was more exotic, more filled with the possibility for encounters, escapades and romance than the lush, tropi-cal islands of the Philippine archipelago.

The dazzling flowers, the sprawling white stucco haciendas and pris-tine beaches of Manila seemed almost dreamlike set against the frugal venues of their youth. And a light workload in a sleepy military hospital left plenty of time for play—afternoons on the golf course or the tennis courts, evenings waltzing under an Oriental sky. All they needed was the right wardrobe (a uniform, a bathing suit and an evening gown), the right dance steps, a little dinner-table riposte and repartee, and they were ready for their tour in paradise.

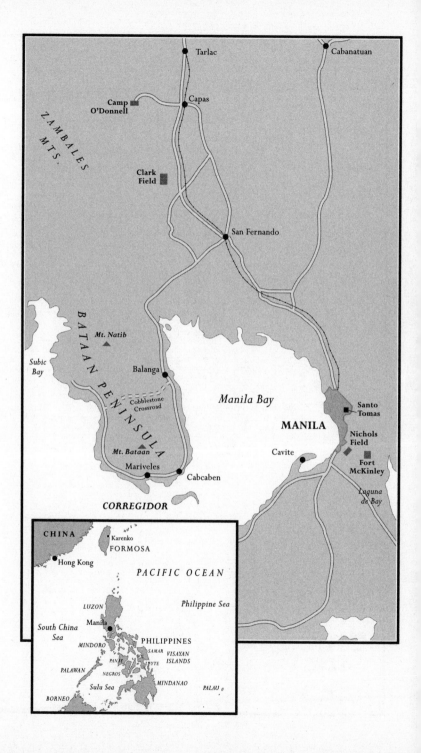

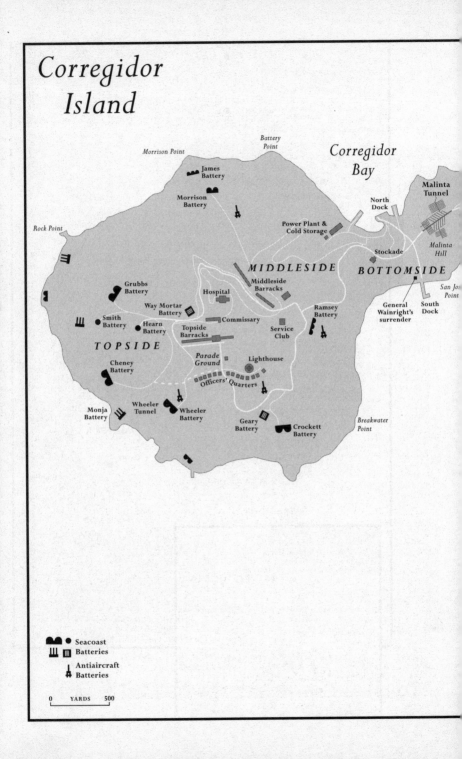

Corregidor Island

Morrison Point

Battery Point

Corregidor Bay

James Battery

Morrison Battery

Power Plant & Cold Storage

North Dock

Malinta Tunnel

Rock Point

Malinta Hill

Stockade

MIDDLESIDE

BOTTOMSIDE

San Jos Point

Grubbs Battery

Hospital

Middleside Barracks

Way Mortar Battery

Commissary

Ramsey Battery

General Wainright's surrender

South Dock

Smith Battery

Hearn Battery

Topside Barracks

Service Club

TOPSIDE

Parade Ground

Lighthouse

Cheney Battery

Officers' Quarters

Monja Battery

Wheeler Tunnel

Wheeler Battery

Geary Battery

Crockett Battery

Breakwater Point

● Seacoast Batteries

Antiaircraft Batteries

0   YARDS   500

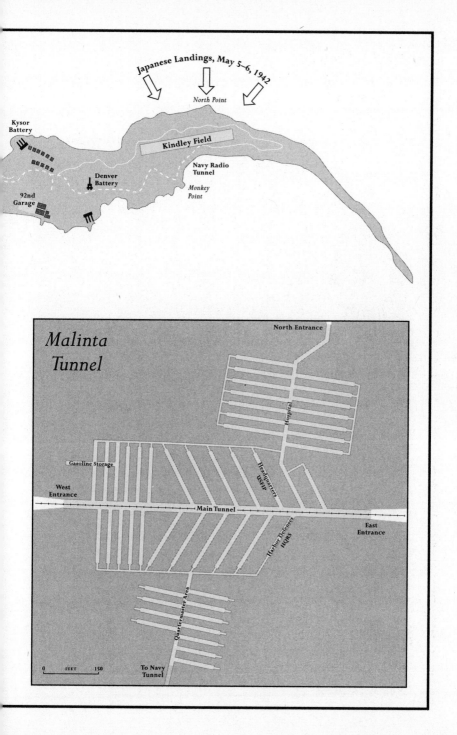

Japanese Landings, May 5–6, 1942

North Point

Kysor Battery

Kindley Field

Denver Battery

Navy Radio Tunnel

Monkey Point

92nd Garage

Malinta Tunnel

North Entrance

Gasoline Storage

Hospital

Headquarters USFIP

West Entrance

Main Tunnel

East Entrance

Harbor Defense HQS

Quartermaster Area

To Navy Tunnel

0   FEET   150

We Band of Angels

Chapter 1

Waking Up to War

I N THE FALL of 1941, while the Imperial Japanese Army and Navy secretly stockpiled tons of materiel and readied regiments of troops to attack American and European bases in the Pacific, the officers of General Douglas MacArthur's Far East Command in the Philippines pampered themselves with the sweet pleasures of colonial life.

For most, war was only a rumor, an argument around the bar at the officers club, an opinion offered at poolside or on the putting green: let the bellicose Japanese rattle their swords—just so much sound and fury; the little island nation would never challenge the United States, never risk arousing such a prodigious foe.

The Americans had their war plans, of course—MacArthur had stockpiled supplies and intended to train more Filipino troops to fight alongside his doughboys—but most of the officers in the Far East Command looked on the danger with desultory eyes. They were much too preoccupied with their diversions, their off-duty pastimes and pursuits, to dwell on such unpleasant business. To be sure, there were realists in the islands, plenty of them, but for the most part their alarms were lost in the roar of the surf or the late-afternoon rallies on the tennis court.

Worry about war? Not with Filipino houseboys, maids, chefs, gardeners and tailors looking after every need. And not in a place that had the look and sweet fragrance of paradise, a place of palm groves, white gardenias and purple bougainvillea, frangipani and orchids—orchids everywhere, even growing out of coconut husks. At the five army posts and one navy base there were badminton and tennis courts, bowling alleys and playing fields. At Fort Stotsenberg, where the cavalry was based, the officers held weekly polo matches. It was a halcyon life, cocktails and bridge at sunset, white jackets and long gowns at dinner, good gin and Gershwin under the stars.

Word of this good life circulated among the military bases Stateside, and women who wanted adventure and romance—self-possessed, ambitious and unattached women—signed up to sail west. After layovers in Hawaii and Guam, their ships made for Manila Bay. At the dock a crowd was often gathered, for such arrivals were big events—"boat days," the locals called them. A band in white uniforms played the passengers down the gangplank, then, following a greeting from their commanding officer and a brief ceremony of welcome, a car with a chauffeur carried the new nurses through the teeming streets of Manila to the Army and Navy Club, where a soft lounge chair and a restorative tumbler of gin was waiting.

Most of the nurses in the Far East Command were in the army and the majority of these worked at Sternberg Hospital, a 450-bed alabaster quadrangle on the city's south side. At the rear of the complex were the nurses quarters, elysian rooms with shell-filled windowpanes, bamboo and wicker furniture with plush cushions and mahogany ceiling fans gently turning the tropical air.

From her offices at Sternberg Hospital, Captain Maude Davison, a career officer and the chief nurse, administered the Army Nurse Corps in the Philippines. Her first deputy, Lieutenant Josephine "Josie" Nesbit of Butler, Missouri, also a "lifer," set the work schedules and established the routines. For most of the women the work was relatively easy and uncomplicated, the usual mix of surgical, medical and obstetric patients, rarely a difficult case or an emergency, save on pay nights or when the fleet was in port and the troops, with too much time on their hands and too much liquor in their bellies, got to brawling.

For the most part one workday blended into another. Every morning a houseboy would appear with a newspaper, then over fresh-squeezed papaya juice with a twist of lime, the women would sit and chat about the day ahead, particularly what they planned to do after work: visit a Chinese tailor, perhaps, or take a Spanish class with a private tutor; maybe go for a swim in the phosphorescent waters of the beach club.

The other posts had their pleasures as well. At Fort McKinley, seven miles from Manila, a streetcar ferried people between the post pool, the bowling alley, the movie theater and the golf course. Seventy-five miles north at Fort Stotsenberg Hospital and nearby Clark Air Field, the post social life turned on the polo matches and weekend rides into the hills where monkeys chattered like children and red-and-blue toucans and parrots called to one another in the trees. Farther north was Camp John Hay, located in the shadow of the Cordillera Central Mountains near Baguio, the unofficial summer capital and retreat for wealthy Americans and Filipinos. The air was cool in Baguio, perfect for golf, and the duffers and low-handicappers who spent every day on the well-tended fairways of the local course often imagined they were playing the finest links this side of Scotland. South of Manila, a thirty-mile drive from the capital, or a short ferry ride across the bay, sat Sangley Point Air Field, the huge Cavite Navy Yard and the U.S. Naval Hospital at Canacao. The hospital, a series of white buildings connected by passageways and shaded by mahogany trees, was set at the tip of a peninsula. Across the bay at Fort Mills on Corregidor, a small hilly island of 1,735 acres, the sea breezes left the air seven degrees cooler than in the city. Fanned by gentle gusts from the sea, the men and their dates would sit on the veranda of the officers club after dark, staring at the glimmer of the lights from the capital across the bay.

Even as MacArthur's command staff worked on a plan to defend Manila from attack, his officers joked about "fighting a war and a hangover at the same time." A few weeks before the shooting started, nurse Eleanor Garen of Elkhart, Indiana, sent a note home to her mother: "Everything is quiet here so don't worry. You probably hear a lot of rumors, but that is all there is about it."[1]

In late November of 1941, most of the eighty-seven army nurses and twelve navy nurses busied themselves buying Christmas presents and new outfits for a gala on New Year's Eve. Then they set about lining up the right escort.

MONDAY, DECEMBER 8, 1941, just before dawn. Mary Rose "Red" Harrington was working the graveyard shift at Canacao Naval Hospital. Through the window and across the courtyard she saw lights come on in the officers quarters and heard loud voices. What, she wondered, were all those men doing up so early? And what were they yelling about? A moment later a sailor in a T-shirt burst through the doors of her ward.

They've bombed Honolulu!

Bombed Honolulu? What the hell was he talking about, Red thought.[2]

Across Manila Bay, General Richard Sutherland woke his boss, General Douglas MacArthur, supreme commander in the Pacific, to tell him that the Imperial Japanese Navy had launched a surprise attack on the U.S. Naval Base at Pearl Harbor, Hawaii. Later they would learn the details: nineteen American ships, including six battle wagons, the heart of the Pacific fleet, had been scuttled, and the Japanese had destroyed more than a hundred planes; through it all, several thousand soldiers and sailors had been killed or badly wounded.

After months of rumor, inference and gross miscalculation, the inconceivable, the impossible had happened. The Japanese had left the nucleus of the U.S. Pacific fleet twisted and burning. America was at war and the military was reeling.

Juanita Redmond, an army nurse at Sternberg Hospital in Manila, was just finishing her morning paperwork. Her shift would soon be over. One of her many beaus had invited her for an afternoon of golf and she planned a little breakfast and perhaps a nap beforehand. The telephone rang; it was her friend, Rosemary Hogan of Chattanooga, Oklahoma.

The Japs bombed Pearl Harbor.

"Thanks for trying to keep me awake," Redmond said. "But that simply isn't funny."

"I'm not being funny," Hogan insisted. "It's true."[3]

As the reports of American mass casualties spread through the hospital that morning, a number of nurses who had close friends stationed in Honolulu broke down and wept.

"Girls! Girls!" Josie Nesbit shouted, trying to calm her staff. "Girls, you've got to sleep today. You can't weep and wail over this, because you have to work tonight."[4]

Some slipped off alone to their rooms while others rushed to a bank to cable money home. Two women, apparently resigned to whatever fate was going to bring, shrugged their shoulders and strolled over to the Army and Navy Club to go bowling.

At Fort Mills Hospital on the island fortress of Corregidor, Eleanor Garen and the rest of the night-shift nurses headed for the post restaurant for a cup of coffee or a glass of Coke. Their custom was to sit and relax after work, but on this particular morning they were chatty and impatient. Would war come to the Philippines? they wondered.

The news so concerned Eleanor that she took out a pencil and slip of paper and started a shopping list—supplies she considered important in case of an emergency: Noxema face cream, tooth powder, a comb, bath towel, shampoo, Kleenex, chocolate candy and another pair of lieutenant's bars.

At Fort McKinley Hospital just outside Manila, the day-shift nurses, doctors and medical staff were issued steel helmets and gas masks. Two women coming off the night shift stuffed their helmets and masks in their golf bags and headed for the links.

None of the nurses knew it, of course, but the war was already on its way to them.

Two HUNDRED MILES north of the capital, in the cool mountain air of Baguio, Ruby Bradley, a thirty-four-year-old career army nurse on duty at Camp John Hay Hospital, was busy sterilizing the instruments she would need for her first case, a routine hysterectomy.

All at once a soldier appeared at the door and summoned her to headquarters. No surgery that morning, she was told; the Japs had attacked Pearl Harbor, the high command was convinced the Philippine Islands would be next, and Baguio, the most important military and commercial center in northern Luzon, might be one of the enemy's first targets.

Bradley stood there stunned, almost unable to move. What did it mean? she asked herself. Was the hospital truly in danger? Surely the Japanese would not waste their ordnance on such an up-country post. She reported to the surgeon's office for further instruction.

Then the bombs began to fall.

The first hit so close the explosion left their ears ringing. Nurse and doctor ran to the window. Airplanes with big red circles on their wings and fuselage were coming in low, so low Bradley was sure she could see the pilots staring down at her. By instinct she glanced at her watch—it was 8:19 A.M., December 8, 1941. Scuttlebutt was now substance; war had come to the Philippines.

A few minutes later the first casualties started to crowd the wards and hallways at John Hay Hospital. A civilian dependent named Susan Dudley and her year-old son had been out walking and were severely wounded in the attack. A Filipino passerby snatched up the wounded boy and rushed him to the receiving room. Bradley could see that the child was in bad shape; his face was blue—clearly something was wrong with his heart—and his kneecap seemed to be shattered. Bradley felt herself starting to flinch. She was a sturdy and experienced clinician, but even years of practice had not prepared her for something like this. Her heart raced, her stomach started to tighten.

The doctor on duty tried giving the boy oxygen, then he and Bradley took turns at mouth-to-mouth resuscitation, but nothing worked, and it was clear that the child was slipping away.

Leave him, the doctor ordered. The wounded were beginning to mount, he said, and they had no time to linger over a dying child.

Bradley balked. "How about a stimulant in the heart?" she said, imploring him.

The doctor thought for a moment; it was probably hopeless, he said, but if Bradley wanted to try it, she should do it herself.

The needle was six inches long; if she plunged it into the wrong place in the baby's heart she would instantly kill him. Meanwhile the boy was turning a deeper shade of blue, and the nurse, watching him wane, was growing angry and afraid. Then, looking around the room, she hit on an idea. In the medicine cabinet she spotted a bottle of whiskey and, remembering that liquor was sometimes effective as a heart stimulant, she took a piece of gauze, laced it with some sugar, soaked it in whiskey, and stuck it in the boy's mouth. At first the baby did nothing. Then, slowly, he started to suck, harder, and harder, until, at last, blue gave way to white, white to pink, pink to crying.

"Where's my baby? Where's my baby?" his mother yelled from her bloody gurney. Bomb fragments had shattered the woman's legs and she faced certain amputation.

"You hear him in there yelling?" said the nurse, bending over her. "Well, he's . . . he's all right now."[5]

AFTER BAGUIO, THE Japanese attacked their primary target, Clark Air Field and Fort Stotsenberg, the main base of the Army Air Corps in the western Pacific. There on the runway sat scores of American fighters and bombers, lined up wingtip to wingtip, fully armed, unmanned, a perfect target.

The Japanese pilots probably could not believe their luck. They had approached cautiously from the South China Sea at 25,000 feet, hoping to elude radar and observers on the ground. The Japanese high command had been convinced that the Americans at Clark Field, having heard the news of Pearl Harbor, would be waiting to repel them, but through a series of communication and command blunders, American air chiefs and MacArthur's staff had left their airplanes like so many sitting ducks for the Zeros Mitsubishis now coming in from the sea.[6] In fact, as the enemy approached, almost everyone at Clark Field was enjoying Monday lunch.

At 12:35 P.M. a tight group of twenty-seven Japanese aircraft making a low moaning sound appeared suddenly from the Zambales Mountains and startled the Americans at their noon repast. American pilots scrambled to their planes, but it was too late—the bombs were already falling. And the ground shook from the shock of the attack.

Some of the startled soldiers and airmen took potshots at the attackers with Springfield rifles, antiquated firearms from an earlier war. In a matter of minutes the diving, screaming attackers reduced the squadrons of planes at Clark to seven aircraft, seven.

A second wave of twenty-six Zeros followed, machine-gunning the field. By 1:37 P.M. the raid was over, and the once beautiful and tranquil Fort Stotsenberg and Clark Field were littered with shrapnel and thousands of pieces of mangled, twisted and burning aircraft. The oil dump was ablaze. The enlisted men's barracks, officers quarters, aircraft hangars and machine shops were leveled. A flash fire was raging in the tall grass around the perimeter. And everywhere, everywhere, lay the wounded, and the dead.

Off-duty nurses sprinted to the hospital and found themselves almost overwhelmed by the slaughter. Some of the women filled large syringes with morphine dissolved in sterile water, then walked among the wounded administering injections to kill the pain and quiet the screaming. Others performed triage, literally deciding who might live and who might die, a practice they had read about in their textbooks but never imagined they would have to employ.

Many of the wounded had dived head first into holes and ditches and were lying facedown during the raids, and the concussions from the bombs and strafing runs had blown dirt and cinders into their faces, lacerating their eyes. Using bath towels soaked in cool water, the women tried to wipe the debris from the faces of the blind.

By mid-afternoon, three hours after the raid ended, the doctors and nurses at Fort Stotsenberg were so overwhelmed with work, they put in an urgent call to Sternberg Hospital in Manila. Send help, they pleaded. Send it now!

*E*ARLY ON THE morning of December 8, army nurse Helen Cassiani, "Cassie" to her friends, reported for her regular shift at the ear, nose and throat clinic at Sternberg Hospital in Manila. At twenty-four she was pretty and bright, with dark, curly hair down to her neck, a round face and an inviting smile. She had been in paradise only some six weeks, but already she was taken with the place—the exotic trips, the spectacular landscape, the impassioned encounters. Now suddenly "public events and private lives had become inseparable,"[7] crowding out a future she had been planning for a long time.

When word of the bombings at Baguio, Stotsenberg and Clark reached Manila, the nurses at Sternberg Hospital began to wonder whether the capital would be next. And now someone came through the wards spreading word that an invasion force had been spotted; General Masaharu Homma's 14th Army was streaming toward the Philippines to launch a ground attack.

Headquarters tried to reassure everyone that Manila was safe, but the assurances sounded empty, and Cassie, a bit stunned by the turn of events and somewhat bitter that her tour in paradise was about to turn into an exercise in anxiety and distress, went about her tasks like an automaton, shifting without thinking from one little job to the next. Soon her feet began to hurt and she got a helluva headache.

At 2:00 P.M. the thirty-five doctors and thirty-seven nurses at Sternberg were ordered to a meeting with their commanding officer, Colonel Percy Carroll. Aides passed out gas masks and issued instructions on their use. The Japanese, the colonel explained, were known to use a variety of poison gases. Cassie, listening carefully, began to feel a little dizzy.

At that point an aide rushed into the room and summoned the colonel to a telephone. A few minutes later he returned; Cassie thought he looked pale and seemed to be struggling to maintain his self-control.

The commanding officer at Fort Stotsenberg had just called him, the colonel said. It seemed the attack there had been a disaster for the Americans, and the medical staff desperately needed more nurses, preferably women with surgical skills. The colonel said that he and Maude Davison had decided to send five army nurses from Sternberg and fifteen Filipino nurses from local hospitals north to Stotsenberg. Were there any volunteers?

The room was quiet. All at once, a nurse whose fiancé was stationed at Clark Air Field raised her hand. Then came another, and another, and one more after that. Davison waited; she needed a fifth. Who would it be? Cassie looked around the room, studying the faces of her colleagues. She wanted to go, wanted to be part of what was unfolding, this great historical convulsion. But she was afraid. Then, as if acting on its own, her hand went up, and before she had time to think, she was collecting her helmet and gas mask and heading toward a bus that would take her to war.

S<small>HE WAS, AT</small> heart, a farm girl, and like many farm girls, she had a capacity for hard work and a curiosity about the ways of the world.

Her parents, Sarah, a diminutive woman, and Peter, well over six feet, had left their Tuscany village as newlyweds and arrived in Bridgewater, Massachusetts, with plans to build a new life. Peter Cassiani worked in a foundry at first, then saved enough money to buy a five-acre chicken farm at 54 High Street, a plot of ground surrounded by two-story houses filled with Irish immigrants. The Irish, of course, resented the newcomers—"the wops on High Street," the neighborhood called the Cassianis—but as Peter and Sarah began to have children, and as those four children exposed the family to the neighborhood and brought the ways of the new world into the family's house, the Italian Cassianis and their Irish neighbors made peace.[8]

Born on January 26, 1917, Helen, or "Eleana," as her mother liked to call her, was an outgoing girl with dark brown hair, deep brown eyes and an easy laugh. As the youngest of the four, she had the benefit of her siblings' experience and the gift of their attention. Her older sister, Rose, for example, once bought Cassie a doll with money Rose earned selling soap bars door to door, and one of her brothers, Louis, a minor-league shortstop, taught her to play baseball and gave her a lifelong love of the game.

When her siblings were grown and gone, Cassie spent part of each day helping her father with the farm chores. She loved her father and flourished in his company. They built chicken coops together, repaired fences, fixed farm implements. "I learned the busy end of a hammer," she said.

Her father was not an educated man but he tried to turn his farmyard into a kind of school for his daughter. To be a farmer, he taught her, was to learn to deal with the unpredictable and unexpected. A farmer, he said, had to know how to size up a problem and quickly find a solution. She listened closely and learned well; it was a skill that would later help her survive.

Cassie found pleasure in the hauling and hard labor and often used the work as an excuse to ignore her studies. She was smart enough, curious too, but no one had ever taught her how to study, and, untutored as she was, school work was often overwhelming, and her lack of skill left her feeling embarrassed. Then one day two friends from the neighborhood sat her down in the library and showed her how to study. Soon she acquired the habit of reading—history, science, stories. Somewhere in all those books an idea took hold of her. "I became fascinated with illness and taking care of people," she said. And after high school, with some money she had saved and a little help from her parents, she moved to Boston and entered the Massachusetts Memorial Hospital School of Nursing.

Then tragedy struck. Her father, in a freak accident, died of carbon monoxide poisoning and, concerned for her mother, she considered leaving school and returning to the farm. She wrote home often that semester, always in Italian, reassuring her mother that she would not forget the family or her roots.

After graduation Cassie joined the Red Cross. That winter, January 1941, the army, desperate for nurses, invoked a provision of the mandatory national military service law that allowed it to mobilize Red Cross professionals, and Helen Cassiani became a twenty-four-year-old second lieutenant in the Army Reserves.

She was assigned to the hospital at Camp Edwards in Hyannis, Massachusetts. It was routine duty, too routine for someone so self-possessed, someone who "was out to experience as much as I could." So she put in for a transfer.

A week or so later she went home to tell her mother. She had to deliver her news cautiously, for Sarah Cassiani had just had a heart attack.

So Cassie laid it out a bit at a time. She had put in for a transfer, she said . . . a transfer overseas . . . the transfer had been approved . . . she would be going soon, going overseas . . . overseas to the Pacific . . . to the Philippines . . . the Philippine Islands.

"You're going where?" her mother said. She looked bewildered. Why was her daughter going half a world away?

Cassie tried to reassure her. "Let's face it, Mom—did you know what was going to happen to you when you left Italy and came to this country? Did you know what was in store for you? No, but you came."

Sarah sat in silence for a while, and Cassie was sure her mother would try to persuade her to stay, plead loneliness, perhaps, or invoke her ill health.

At length she leaned forward.

"I'll pray for you," she said.

And that was that.

In August 1941, less than four months before the first bombs fell on paradise, Sarah Cassiani kissed her daughter good-bye and bid her bon voyage. It was to be their last embrace; they would never again set eyes on each other.

THE RELIEF BUS, loaded with five army nurses, fifteen Filipino nurses, two doctors and a few dozen enlisted men, left Manila around 4:00 P.M. and crept along without lights for five hours before the driver finally arrived at his destination.

Stotsenberg, a shambles, was still burning, and the runways at Clark Field were destroyed. Almost every aircraft had been stripped of its skin, either blown off or burned down to the frame. The twisted hulks reminded one of the nurses of "dinosaur bones."

In the darkness the medical team had trouble locating the hospital, and it was only when they heard the moans and cries of the wounded that they knew they were in the right place.

The nurses tried to set to work, but nothing in their experience had prepared them for the wanton slaughter of war, the sights, sounds and smells that make the heart race, leave the mouth dry, buckle the knees.

Cassie had never seen so many broken bones, so much scorched flesh, and the groaning and sobbing and wailing unnerved her. At one point she happened upon a large pile of discarded uniforms covered with dirt and blood. In the middle of this detritus lay a helmet, twisted like so much tin. What, Cassie wondered, had happened to the head inside it?

She tried to keep her bearing, hold on to her assurance. Stay in control, she told herself as she headed for surgery. No mistakes, no slipups. Be quick but be careful. Watch the sutures, check for shock, manage the bleeding.

Nearby, Phyllis Arnold was working on a sergeant who had bullet wounds in both feet. He was anxious to get back to the fighting, he said, and wondered how quickly he would heal. Arnold put him off; rest easy, she told the man, then she turned to the surgeon, who was standing behind her, waiting to amputate the man's legs.

The last surgical case left the operating room at 5:30 A.M. During the long night, the surgical team lost only seven patients, a remarkable record for peacetime clinicians, inexperienced with such trauma. But no one stopped to pat themselves on the back. At that point the number of dead at Stotsenberg totaled eighty.

In a daze of exhaustion the doctors and nurses wandered over to a makeshift mess hall for breakfast. Afterward some dragged themselves to temporary quarters for showers and sleep, but a few of the women, worried that the enemy might mount another raid, returned to the hospital and huddled in a concrete bunker under the pharmacy.

The chamber was small, putrid and cramped. Cassie looked around for a moment, then stepped outside for some fresh air. Just then, the enemy came roaring back.

Again the Zeros came in strafing. Cassie dashed across the compound and jumped into the deep end of an empty swimming pool, pressing herself against one of its walls. In minutes the raid was over, and she made her way to the shallow end and climbed out.

The base was burning again and thick black smoke from the fires filled the tropical sky, casting a dark veil on the green mountains beyond.

A<small>MONG THE OTHER</small> volunteers at Stotsenberg was Ruth Marie Straub, a quiet, square-faced woman who had joined the army in 1936 after graduating from Mount Sinai Hospital School of Nursing in Milwaukee, Wisconsin, her hometown.

Ruth was somewhat of a mystery to her comrades. They remembered her as a quiet woman who spent hours writing letters to her mother, Elsie Straub.

On a troop transport to Manila, Ruth had met Glen M. Adler, an army pilot and a graduate of the University of California at Los Angeles. Across the months that followed, she and Adler, both twenty-four years old at the time, fell in love and planned to marry. Adler, convinced that war was at hand and hoping to take advantage of an army regulation that allowed officers to send their wives home, was eager to wed right away. "But I wanted to wait until he could go with me," Straub said. So they delayed. Then the bombs started falling.

Adler was stationed at Clark Field, and when word reached Manila that the field had been hit, Straub was the first to raise her hand to go. That night, she also began to keep a diary.

The document shows her to be a sentimental and, at times, fragile woman. Some people by temperament are ill-equipped for war—they feel it too deeply—and Ruth Straub was one of these. At one point she suffered a nervous breakdown and had to be hospitalized and sedated. Often in the face of such savagery the psyche simply shatters.

Still, Ruth, the nurse, did her job, and every evening wrote in her little book.

[Straub Diary, December 8, 1941] News that Pearl Harbor had been bombed is here today. During a meeting of nurses and doctors Colonel Carroll announced that Clark Field had been bombed and that nurses and doctors were needed badly up there.

I had to volunteer. Thought I couldn't wait to get there. Arrived at Stotsenberg at nightfall. The hospital was bedlam—amputations, dressings, intravenouses, blood transfusions, shock, death . . . Worked all night, hopped over banisters and slid under the hospital during raids. It was remarkable to see the medical staff at work. One doctor, a flight surgeon, had a head injury, but during the night he got up and went to the operating room to help with the other patients.

[December 9] Reported off duty tonight and several of us crawled into a cement enclosed cubicle under a hospital ward. It was damp, and the air was putrid, but we really slept. Pure exhaustion. The girls are taking this beautifully.[9]

Chapter 2

Manila Cannot Hold

*F*OR THE NEXT six days the Japanese pounded the islands. By December 14, the end of the first week of the war, the U.S. naval base at Canacao, Fort Stotsenberg–Clark Field and Fort McKinley all lay in ruins.

Sleepy little hospitals before the war, the army and navy clinics were now packed with wounded and dying men, and the military nurses and doctors in the islands were quickly becoming experts in trauma and triage, the medicine of war.

The enemy kept up the raids. With each drone of an airplane engine, the nurses looked skyward to see enemy bombers flying in large V formations, like the wings of a giant bird of prey.

In a sense the men had an easier time controlling their terror and dread; at least they could shoot back. The women, however, were left to manage the damage and loss, the awful inventory that battle always leaves.

The casualties overflowed the wards and spilled into the corridors, then into lobbies and onto the verandas. When the hospitals ran out of room and out of beds and canvas cots, they put the wounded out on the lawns and nearby tennis courts, laying them on old doors and scraps of wood and corrugated roofing.

There was so much trauma—so many wounds, so many dismembered limbs—that at one point, the nurses came to look on their labor with a dark irony: the bloody dressings, they said, made them think of the bright poinsettias that so typified their paradise.

With each raid the nurses were made to work harder and longer, and soon they were so tired, so enervated by the surgeries and rounds of duty, they turned numb with fatigue. A young navy nurse, looking up from an operating table into the darkness at the fires consuming the once beautiful naval base at Canacao, told herself, "If the Japanese would just come over and drop another load, this suffering would be over, mine included."[1]

The ranking medical officers in Manila, Colonel Wibb Cooper and Dr. Percy Carroll, annexed the Saint Scholastica Girls School, the Jai Alai Club and other places and turned them into dispensaries and aid stations, creating what they called the Manila Hospital Center, with Sternberg at the hub.[2]

[*Straub Diary, December 10*] This A.M. the commanding officer sent me to Manila on a special ambulance detail. Took four patients. Tried again to reach Glen before I left, but no success. Left word with the chaplain to tell Glen I would be back later in the day. Left about 11:15 A.M. Caught in an air raid alarm as we reached Clark Field. The patients, driver and I hid in some tall, dry grass. Wondered if the message I left for Glen had been delivered.

Arrived at Sternberg late P.M. Air raid sounded just as we came in. Saw 77 planes overhead on way to port area which they bombed. During the raid, Colonel Carroll called me to the office: "You're not to go back to Stotsenberg. Your fiancé has been seriously injured." Dead? No. Thought I would lose my mind. Later Major Hubbard came down from Stotsenberg and told me Glen had suffered a basal skull fracture [at the base of the skull where the basic function of breathing is located], but that he'd be all right. Wonderful news! NO sleep tonight. UP and down stairs during several alarms.[3]

On the day before Christmas the army nurses at Fort Stotsenberg prepared to evacuate the battered base. As they rushed to ready their patients and pack a few belongings, Cassie was told to report to a sergeant waiting for her in front of the hospital.

The soldier was standing beside an ambulance. He smiled politely and told her he had been ordered to prepare her for a "special assignment." Then he held out a pistol and a green army sock filled with cartridges. "Take them," he said, climbing into the ambulance and motioning for Cassie to get in next to him.

"What's going on?" she demanded.[4]

A few minutes later, the sergeant stopped the vehicle in the middle of the jungle and hopped out. He was going to teach Cassie how to fire the weapon, he told her, and for the next few minutes he went through the basics, then he pointed at a clump of large banana blossoms and told her to start shooting.

This is movie stuff, she thought, but went along with it all even though "I didn't believe I could do much damage."

When they got back to the base, she discovered the reason for the dramatics: she'd been put in charge of a hospital train that was to ferry the wounded from Fort Stotsenberg to Sternberg Hospital in Manila, and "they told me I had to be armed to defend myself and the patients."

Defend the patients? To hand a pistol to a healer was a desperate step for a desperate army, and Cassie was afraid. The nurse in her would do her job, no question of that, but she did not know whether she could play the soldier too and pull the trigger.

As she boarded the train "carrying this gun and bullets in a sock," she felt a little "stupid," so she set the weapon aside, checked her thirty patients, then settled in for the ride. The windows were open and the cool sea air filled the car.

As the train approached the city, she looked intently out the window, surveying the side streets for signs of trouble. She was looking as well for the three ambulances that were supposed to be waiting somewhere along that stretch of track to ferry the patients to Sternberg.

Suddenly the train jerked to a stop. Out the window she could see people fleeing. Then came the wail of an air-raid siren. Overhead appeared a large formation of enemy aircraft, another bird of prey, this one bearing down on the train.

The patients, many of them still in shock from earlier attacks, heard the drone of the planes and panicked. They began to yell and shout and struggled to free themselves from their bloody litters. One man with a tightly bandaged stump of a leg was struggling to right himself. Another recovering from multiple shrapnel wounds in both legs was pleading with the others to drag him to safety. An officer who had been diagnosed with shell shock and had been quiet now began to sob and laugh like a madman.

Cassie shoved her way through the panicked car and positioned herself at the exit. No one, she yelled, was going anywhere! And she ordered the men back to their seats and litters and told her orderly that if anyone tried to leave the car he was to use his weapon to stop them.

The bombers, as it turned out, had another target. When the danger had passed, Cassie checked the wounded to make sure their sutures were intact, quieted the shell-shock patients and settled the car down for the rest of the trip.

When they finally reached Manila, she happily turned in her pistol and sockful of bullets, and in the weeks that followed, the war pushed the incident from her mind. Then one day in the field a month or so later, her supervisor approached, holding a piece of paper.

HEADQUARTERS PHILIPPINE DEPARTMENT
IN THE FIELD

February 6, 1942

SUBJECT: Commendation
TO: *Second Lieutenant Helen M. Cassaino [sic], ANC*

The commanding General has directed me to commend you and to express to you sincere thanks for your courageous conduct and unfailing attention to duty at Fort Stotsenburg [*sic*], P.I., on December 24, 1941, during a Japanese air attack. By your conduct and fearless example you calmed a number of litter patients . . . on a hospital car . . . when the air alarm was sounded and a number of enemy planes passed overhead. The litter patients had become panic stricken and tried to leave the car causing great confusion which might have resulted in serious injury to a number of patients . . . but you remained at your post. . . .

Allan C. McBride
Brigadier General, G.S.C.,
Chief of Staff[5]

Manila could not hold. The enemy controlled the sky and sea, and the allies had neither the men nor the materiel to defend the city. By the end of December MacArthur knew he would have to retreat south in advance of the enemy attack.

In Washington, Generals Dwight Eisenhower and George Marshall met with Secretary of War Henry Stimson and President Roosevelt to analyze the situation in the Philippines. America was fighting a two-front war, and the two theaters of battle, Europe and the Pacific, were vying for the scant resources Washington could provide. Making matters worse, the Pacific fleet was in ruins and incapable of running the Japanese blockade in the Philippines. Stimson insisted that America's top priority should be to keep open the North Atlantic sea lanes, and Roosevelt agreed. So on December 23, at a conference with top American and British leaders, the president announced that the primary theater of war for the United States would be Europe.[6] MacArthur was told that he would have to use the forces at hand to stop the Japanese offensive.

American commanders in the Philippines decided to implement a decades-old strategy called War Plan Orange 3: to avoid massive civilian casualties and the destruction of property, Manila would be declared an open, neutral city; all military personnel, with their equipment, would retreat to the Bataan peninsula and Corregidor Island, a fortress known as "the Rock," and from these two positions the Americans and their Filipino allies would try to defend Manila Bay until Washington could send help.

It was a doomed plan and everyone knew it. MacArthur and his generals were, literally, bottling up their army, tens of thousands of troops, on a small peninsula, fighting a holding action without air cover or any assurance of resupply. All the Japanese had to do was to press their attack until the Americans and their Filipino allies lost the capacity, or will, to fight.

On December 22, 1941, forty-three thousand well-trained, well-equipped enemy soldiers, many of whom had already seen action in other campaigns, came ashore through the turbulent waters of the Lingayen Gulf, a bay in northern Luzon Province that lay at the mouth of a wide valley between two ranges of mountains, a natural corridor from the sea south to the city of Manila.

The next day General MacArthur, his family and his staff left Manila to join top Filipino and American politicians in the underground fortress of Malinta Tunnel on the island of Corregidor. From this command center across the bay from the capital, they would direct the retreat of their forces and the defense of the Bataan peninsula. On December 24, the Japanese landed another seven thousand infantrymen, this time at Lamon Bay, to the southeast, at Manila's back door, closing the trap.

MANILA HAD LONG since lost its shimmer. It was hit first on December 10, two days after the bombings at Baguio. Seventy-seven warplanes attacked Manila's port area, sinking ships and setting the docks afire. More raids quickly followed. When gasoline stocks were hit, the city ran short of fuel, and people took to riding bicycles and hauling things in horse-drawn carts. Blackouts were the rule at night and many of the clubs shut down. Antiaircraft crews took over the once beautiful parks and patches of greensward, trampling the flowers and tearing up the grass with their tents and trenches.

[Straub Diary, December 13] Ordered to go out as acting chief nurse to set up 590 bed hospital in the Holy Ghost school across from Malacanan [*sic*] palace. It has become an emergency hospital as Sternberg is overflowing. (We are burying the dead in sheets.) The Catholic nuns are grand and have helped us put up beds in empty classrooms. Work, work, work. I keep going back to Sternberg to find out about Glen.

Every day the bombs fell, destroying churches in the old, walled city, warehouses at the waterfront, office buildings in the business district, the homes of the rich, the shanties of the poor.

At Sternberg Hospital, the jewel of the army's medical facilities, military and civilian casualties were stretched out on floors, waiting for treatment. The workload began to wear on the staff. For them each bombing raid meant another rush of casualties, another chorus of suffering. When the bombs fell the heavy crystal chandeliers in the dining room began to sway; windows shattered and sprayed glass on the ward; patients cried out in terror. "The feeling," said Madeline Ullom of O'Neill, Nebraska, "pierced our hearts."[7]

[Straub Diary, December 14] Worked all A.M. but couldn't keep my mind on my work. Finally I got Lieutenant Brown to take me to Sternberg. Perhaps someone would know about Glen. Searched all over the hospital. So many of our friends who lived at Clark Field are in it now, but no one can tell me a thing. Had dinner at Sternberg and then drove back to Holy Ghost. I found myself alone in the receiving office, so I made an official call to the hospital at Fort Stotsenberg. Captain Kege answered. He hesitated a long time and finally said: "I am sorry to be the one to tell you. Glen was admitted on the tenth and died shortly thereafter." The world tumbled around my ears.

Meanwhile, the bombing went on and on. An ominous mood came over the capital and a deep cynicism and dark humor crept into daily conversation. "If you see [only] one plane flying in formation," the nurses joked, "you know it is ours."[8] Someone hung a sign in the hospital hallway that read DON'T BE A DEFEATIST. But the declaration did little to improve morale.[9]

The nurses at Sternberg and the other army hospitals tried to focus on their work. Were there enough bandages? Which patients would be transferred where? Would there be time to eat a meal before the next rush of broken bones and mangled limbs? What had happened to their friends elsewhere, the women they had worked with, the men they had loved?

[Straub Diary, December 16] It doesn't seem to be true. They took me back [to Sternberg] as a patient. Luminal [another name for the sedative phenobarbital] every four hours. Why, why, why . . . Others have carried on bravely, and I must too. Glen would want it. "Everything is all right," he said that last time he called. Air raid signals were frightening at first. I hardly think of them now. . . .

During one bombing raid Maude Davison was knocked to the floor, injuring her lumbar vertebrae, and Josie Nesbit took her place as chief nurse. Nesbit and the other nursing supervisors quickly adapted standard nursing practice to meet the needs of war. They shifted schedules, stretched supplies, looked for new ways to manage their patients' pain. They also gave up a garment that had long been the symbol of their profession—starched white uniforms.

The long dresses were ludicrously impractical, especially when nurses were bending over bloody stretchers or jumping into open trenches, so army quartermasters issued each woman two pairs of standard olive-drab coveralls. The new gear, as it turned out, came in one size, men's 44, and the women joked that two of them could easily fit into one.

Some tried to cinch up the slack with safety pins or a few stitches, but they soon drafted some Chinese tailors to cut the coveralls down to size. As it turned out, these green cotton suits became a short footnote in nursing history: the nurses of the Philippines became the first American military women to wear fatigues, as field uniforms were called, on duty. The angels in white had learned to dress for the dirty business of war.

[Straub Diary, December 17] They brought me Glen's personal effects today. Now I know he is dead.

Even to this day, some Manilans call December 25, 1941, "Black Christmas." Enemy aircraft repeatedly bombed the city and suburbs, and patients at all the hospitals ate their Christmas dinners under their beds. The Filipino cooks who ran the American mess halls and galleys had originally planned elaborate meals. One menu, for example, included oyster stew, mixed olives, celery sticks, roast American turkey, mushroom dressing, cranberry sauce, giblet gravy, snowflake potatoes, creamed peas, vanilla ice cream with chocolate sauce, candy, mixed nuts, bread, butter, coffee, cream and sugar and cigarettes.[10] Instead, the nurses, doctors and patients at Sternberg celebrated the season of peace with cold turkey sandwiches.

[Straub Diary, December 24] The Japs continue to bomb the port area. Christmas eve. The girls milling around, no music, no lights, no greetings. Sent a note to Miss MacDonald [chief nurse at Stotsenberg]. Asked her to put some flowers on my darling's grave for Christmas.

With Manila declared an open city, the army nurses were ordered to evacuate the hospitals, and Josie Nesbit set about moving her eighty-seven-member staff from Manila to field hospital sites on Bataan and Malinta Tunnel on Corregidor. Between Christmas and New Year's Eve, she slipped her women out two dozen or so at a time.

[Straub Diary, December 25] Christmas. We hardly realized it. Sent more nurses out today to Bataan and Corregidor. Only 14 left now. Orders say we are all to evacuate by the first.

Most of the women were under the impression they were headed for hospitals—buildings with red-tile roofs and whitewashed walls—so they packed their white shoes, alabaster stockings, makeup, curlers and nursing school pins. But the Angels of Bataan, as they would soon become known around the world, were about to become the first group of American military nurses sent onto the battlefield for duty.[11]

Those that left the city by truck were frequently attacked from the air, and the women had to jump for cover often along the way. The roads were clogged with refugees fleeing the fighting, and as they walked past the lumbering convoys, they often smiled at the sight of women in the trucks and held up two fingers in the sign of victory.

The nurses evacuated from Manila by ferry had a panoramic view of the fires engulfing the capital. At night the light from the holocaust was so bright, the women could sit on the deck of the ferry and read their newspapers in the orange glow. When a boat entered a minefield or a squadron of enemy planes was spotted, the women quickly removed their heavy army shoes and combat boots in case they ended up in the water. (One ferry, in fact, the *Mc E. Hyde,* was attacked off the Bataan coast and sank as the nurses watched from the bushes onshore.)

As the New Year approached, Sternberg held only those patients too crippled or mangled to move. Eleven nurses, along with Josie Nesbit, had volunteered to stay behind with the bed-bound to care for them. The army, given the rush and confusion, assumed it would not be able to get the final eleven out of the city in advance of the enemy and issued them identification cards naming them noncombatants, cards the women were to present to the enemy when they surrendered.

"Surrender?" said Madeline Ullom. "The only surrender which entered my mind . . . was [the name of] a favorite perfume."[12]

A few days later, headquarters reversed itself and ordered all army nurses to Bataan. (The last army nurse to leave Manila was Floramund Fellmuth, who had agreed to take charge of the Filipino Red Cross nurses aboard a makeshift hospital ship, the inter-island steamer the *Mactan.* The little ship was the last chance for many of the wounded. Its skipper had agreed to try to reach Australia, and he took on enough supplies for thirty days. Then three hundred wounded were loaded on the *Mactan*'s decks. Heavy rains and rough seas left most of them ill and miserable, a fire in the boiler almost panicked the ship's company, and the Japanese often seemed close to catching and sinking them, but with incredible luck and some deft seamanship, the *Mactan*'s crew brought their cargo to safety, one of the few surface ships to slip through enemy lines.)

By New Year's Eve all eighty-seven army nurses had been safely evacuated from the city. But there were still American women in uniform in Manila, nurses of the United States Navy.

No one can say for sure why the navy nurses were left behind. Perhaps in the haste and jumble of the evacuation they were an oversight, simply forgotten. Or maybe some myopic commander failed to calculate their value in the battle that was to come. Whatever the case, Josie Nesbit knew the navy women were there, and years later, a bit abashed, said that these sisters in arms, her professional kin, had been abandoned, "left," in her words, "holding the bag."[13]

Navy nurse Red Harrington, fair and freckled with hazel eyes and alabaster skin, was, at twenty-eight, an Irish beauty. Her real name was Mary Rose, but after one look at that auburn mien everyone called her "Red."

Standing in a hallway of the Saint Scholastica Girls School just after New Year's, Red was angry. Three weeks earlier the navy had turned the school into a makeshift hospital and had staffed the facility with navy doctors, corpsmen and the twelve navy nurses from its destroyed bases at Canacao and Cavite on the south side of Manila Bay. Since there were so few of them, the navy nurses were, for command purposes, folded into the army, and even though they had their own supervisor, Laura Cobb, they were put under the iron hand of Maude Davison.

One of the navy nurses, Ann Bernatitus, had managed to slip out of the threatened city in the company of a navy surgeon and corpsman and had joined the army on Bataan. A few days later the other eleven navy nurses were told to prepare themselves to flee the city. They watched the army pack to leave, and they patiently waited their turn. Waited . . . and waited . . . and waited.

What was happening? Red asked Laura Cobb. When was the army going to get the navy out?

"We have no orders to leave," Cobb said. So "we stay put."[14]

Then the navy nurses began to notice that the army was sending them the most critically ill and injured patients, soldiers who obviously could not be moved any significant distance. The navy wards at Saint Scholastica Girls School began to fill with these hopeless cases. And Red and the ten other navy women began to wonder if they too were considered expendable.

Of all the Angels, Red Harrington was the only one who could look on abandonment with a certain irony.[15]

Born August 10, 1913, at a home for unwed mothers, she was immediately deserted and sent to St. Monica's Orphanage in Sioux City, Iowa.

One day not long thereafter, in walked Petra Harrington, a childless farm wife from Elk Point, South Dakota. Mrs. Harrington quickly fixed on a cute little boy, but every time she looked at him or tried to pick him up, the child began to cry. Then she noticed an infant girl lying quietly on her back, holding a bottle. Here was the child for her, she told the director. And she wrapped the redheaded infant in a comforter and took her home to meet her husband, Maurice.

Elk Point was a quiet place to grow up. Maurice, who took up the life of a salesman, was on the road a lot, and as a child Red trailed after Petra like a puppy, and soon mother and daughter grew close. In the winter, Petra took her skating on the frozen town pond, in the summer to the banks of the Sioux River for a swim. A firm but fair woman, Petra determined to give her daughter a moral foundation that would last. "When the Lord gives you [a child], you don't have any choice. But I went out and adopted one," she said. "And I'm going to raise one right." A skilled seamstress, Petra dressed her red-haired daughter well and, as the girl got older, let her roam a bit. On Tuesdays and Fridays in the summer, Red and her friend Dorothy would go down to the local dance hall and listen to the latest traveling band.

In school Red studied hard, worked on the school newspaper and dreamed of being a reporter, but with the Great Depression, newspapers were closing, and after she graduated, jobs were scarce, so Red Harrington decided to become a nurse.

When she entered the job market, however, the economy was still depressed. Instead of hiring new graduates, hospital administrators, looking for cheap labor, were staffing their wards with student nurses. Just then, Red's father died and, knowing she would have to help support her mother, Red decided to join the navy.

The service, she reasoned, was her only escape from a hardscrabble life. She could marry, move in with some lonely farmer or grizzled rancher and bring her mother with her, but Petra had taught her to be independent and self-reliant, so in January 1937 she entered the Navy Nurse Corps and moved Petra from the cold gray landscape of Elk Point to the pink stucco, blue water and warm breezes of San Diego.

Red quickly took to navy life, and her supervisors at Balboa Naval Hospital were delighted with her work. Her mother settled in easily as well, and after a while Red decided that she could risk leaving Petra on her own and indulge her wanderlust. She put in for a transfer, requesting either the Brooklyn Navy Yard in New York or the navy base at Canacao in the Philippine Islands. In January 1941, she said good-bye to her mother and boarded the boat for Manila.

She loved the nightlife—dining at the clubs and dancing under the stars, riding horses, playing tennis, walking under the moon by the seawall with lights on the water. Bright, independent and beautiful, she was soon sought by a number of men, among them a handsome physician. They were together all the time and before long Red was in love and dreaming of marriage. One day, a season after their affair began, he came to her sober-faced. He was headed Stateside, he said, going home . . . to his wife. Later, much later, Red looked back and smiled. Never mind, she told herself. In three months with him, "I lived a lifetime."

O N NEW YEAR'S Day, 1942, a sign on the front of Manila City Hall announced: OPEN CITY, BE CALM, STAY AT HOME, NO SHOOTING. The *Manila Bulletin* warned its readers to "Stay where you are located. . . . You are as safe where you are as you would be at the place where you plan to move."[16]

In a shortwave-radio message to the islands, President Roosevelt told his countrymen and the Filipinos, "I give to the people of the Philippines my solemn pledge that their freedom will be redeemed and their independence established and protected."[17]

Red Harrington and the ten other navy nurses stood by calmly as an enlisted man slowly lowered the American flag in the front of Saint Scholastica.

The women were worried. Most had visions of being overrun by a wanton conquering hoard. Red was sure the enemy was bent on murder, not pleasure, and would just walk in and gun them down. "I wondered, were they just going to come in and shoot up the place or take us all out and shoot us?"[18] Someone showed her a leaflet the Japanese had dropped on Manila the day before. The illustration was a caricature of Uncle Sam with a severed head. Underneath was the word DESTINY.

On January 2, 1942, General Homma and his victorious troops marched smartly into the capital. From their porch at Saint Scholastica, the navy nurses had a front-row seat on the welcoming celebration at the nearby Japanese embassy. They watched Homma's car, flying miniature flags with the Rising Sun, pass in review. Out front, cheering and yelling support, were hundreds of ecstatic Japanese residents. The next day, uniformed Japanese officers arrived at Saint Scholastica and accepted the surrender of twenty-seven physicians and dentists, eleven American nurses, a Filipino nurse, a Red Cross director, a Catholic priest and several dozen enlisted men. The enemy ordered the sailors to string barbed wire around the building, then the Japanese politely began to loot the place, "confiscating" the contents of the school safe, radios, knives, flashlights and anything else they wanted and could carry off. They ransacked every room in the building—every room, that is, save the quarters of the American nurses.

As it turned out, the Japanese were baffled by the presence of women in uniform. In their country, women did not join the military. When a Japanese woman wanted to help the war effort, she would volunteer for one of three patriotic societies: Joshi Teishen Tai, or the "Women's Benevolent Force," which encouraged volunteer war work; Joshi Hokotu Tai, the "Women's National Service," which organized working parties to help rural families, especially farm families with men in the military; and Aikoku Fujin Kai, or the "Women's Patriotic Society," which prepared "comfort bags" and other packages for soldiers overseas.[19]

At Saint Scholastica the Japanese at first maintained the status quo, and the nurses simply continued to care for their badly wounded patients. From time to time enemy officers would come through the wards, but there were few incidents. When they ordered Laura Cobb and her nurses to catalog their store of supplies, the women became convinced that their captors meant to filch their precious serums, painkillers and other medications, so they shrewdly mislabeled things. Valuable antimalarial drugs, like quinine, became "bicarbonate of soda" and were passed over when the looters came back through.

The women, disgusted by the looting and the harassment, started to utter epithets at the guards, then they discovered that a few of their captors spoke English, so they bowdlerized their invective. Now, for example, instead of calling the guards "yellow-bellied bastards," the nurses would smile and say, "There go the yellow bees."

Then the humor stopped. Four Filipino patients escaped and the guards posted a notice: for every patient that turned up missing, two other patients—and the *nurse on the ward*—would be shot.

Soon the enemy was pressing the sick and injured into work gangs, forcing patients who could barely stand to spend the day at hard labor.

Laura Cobb reacted to all this by insisting that her nurses maintain good order and military discipline. She assigned each woman to a ward and coordinated shifts to make sure every ward was adequately covered. The nurses worked from 7:00 A.M. till 9:00 P.M., then, because Cobb was afraid to leave her women alone at night with the Japanese, corpsmen took over.

They lived thus for weeks and weeks. Finally, in early March 1942, the enemy shipped most of the patients and the doctors and corpsmen to Bilibid Prison, a civilian penitentiary in Manila used to hold American prisoners of war and a place that soon became known for its barbarism and cruelty.

Laura Cobb, Red Harrington and the others—Mary Chapman of Chicago, Illinois; Bertha Evans of Portland, Oregon; Helen Gorzelanski of Omaha, Nebraska; Margaret Nash of Wilkes-Barre, Pennsylvania; Goldia O'Haver of Hayfield, Minnesota; Eldene Paige of Lomita, California; Susie Pitcher of Des Moines, Iowa; Dorothy Still of Long Beach, California; and C. Edwina Todd of Pomona, California[20]—all were ordered to pack their belongings and were shipped across town to the grounds of Santo Tomas University, a large suburban campus that the enemy had turned into an internment camp for foreign nationals.

Meanwhile west of the city and across the bay, the American army was bottled up on the peninsula of Bataan in a desperate struggle for survival. Back home newspapers and magazines carried accounts of the battle, portraying the defenders as brave and resolute. And indeed they were. In truth, however, the Philippines were falling.

Chapter 3

Jungle Hospital #1

THE PENINSULA OF Bataan, located on Luzon's southwest coast, is twenty-five miles in length and, at its widest point, twenty miles across, twice as long and ten times as wide as the island of Manhattan.

On a simple map Bataan looks like a lone fat toe extending south from the mainland foot into the South China Sea. The tip of the toe bends back slightly east forming a body of water, Manila Bay. In the mouth of the bay, between the tip of the peninsula and the mainland, lies the tiny island fortress of Corregidor, "the Rock," guarding the entrance to the bay and Manila, the capital city, on the bay's eastern shore.

In 1941 Bataan, named for the Bata, or diminutive Negritos that once lived there, was an untamed place, part jungle, part mountain preserve, with small towns and barrios of nipa and wooden huts, holding no more than thirty thousand Filipinos, a land of monkeys and snakes, wild pigs and quail.[1]

Bataan was so infested with mosquitoes that health authorities considered it the worst malarial breeding ground in the islands. In 1930 a large lumber company abandoned its logging and milling operations there and fled the disease-ridden land.[2] The lumberjacks were through with the mosquitoes, the dengue fever, amoebic and bacillary dysentery, the flatworms and roundworms, the skin fungus, the open supperating sores.

Most of the peninsula was covered by the slopes and foothills of two extinct volcanoes. Only the land along the coasts was passable, and these narrow corridors were mostly marsh and thick, tropical forest. Bataan was so wild and unsettled that the military referred to its various en-campments by kilometer posts—kilometer 143.5 or kilometer 162.5, numbers in the middle of nowhere, places where no one wanted to go.

Densely wooded ravines, malarial swamps, heavily vegetated jungle—that was Bataan, as uninspired a piece of geography as anywhere in the world, but it was there, in that thick and tangled terrain, that the United States of America, along with its Filipino allies, fought its first major land battle of World War II.

The plan was simple: pull all allied forces onto the big toe, set up a line of defense at the top, and hold on for 180 days, time enough, so military planners thought, for Washington to send help. During the year the American command in the Philippines had established supply depots and dumps on Bataan, but instead of stocking them to capacity, MacArthur, who wanted to meet the enemy upland, had moved much of his food, ammunition, spare parts and equipment north off the peninsula.

And now, with the Japanese invasion force moving fast, as it had since December 22, when it landed, MacArthur's infantry, cavalry, artillery and tank units were forced into fighting a retreat, leaving behind them on Luzon the stores their commander had so unwisely repositioned. To make matters worse, thousands of refugees, many more than military planners had anticipated, were streaming onto the Bataan peninsula along with the retreating troops, putting an even greater demand on the depleted stores.

Senior military staff estimated that on January 7, 1942, when the allied retreat was completed, Bataan held 102,000 people—14,000 American troops, 72,000 Filipino troops, and 16,000 refugees from Manila and northern Luzon—three times as many people as envisioned in War Plan Orange 3.[3]

With so much untamed land, Bataan had only three roads. East Road and West Road ran north to south along the coasts; about halfway down the peninsula, connecting the two, was a cobblestone crossroad that cut the peninsula in half. In late December these roads, and the routes out of Manila leading to them, were jammed night and day by columns of soldiers, some of them barefoot recruits carrying ancient bolt-action rifles, and by long queues of cannons, tanks, trucks, scout cars, two-wheeled carts drawn by horses frothing at the bit, carabao laden with chicken coops and torn mattresses, and processions of weary, frightened women, children and men.

Soaked in sweat and covered with yellow dust, the columns of combatants and refugees extended for miles, and the grinding and clanking of the massive equipment created a kind of mechanical thunder that rumbled from dawn to dawn without stopping.

Meanwhile, dug in at the neck of the peninsula and ready to make their stand were American and Filipino soldiers. It was a brave defense. The American air force had only a handful of planes, perhaps twenty at any one time, including training aircraft. The American navy's Philippine "fleet" consisted of only three gunboats, three minesweepers, four tugboats, two converted yachts and six torpedo boats. (The crew from the U.S.S. *Canopus*, a submarine tender tied up at Mariveles on the southern tip of Bataan, had rigged their ship to look as if she were abandoned; they deliberately tilted her, placed her cargo boom askew, and started smudge fires on deck. The ruse worked, and Japanese pilots left the *Canopus* alone while belowdecks her crew forged weapons so the infantry could continue the fight.)

On DECEMBER 24, 1941, twenty-five army nurses, one navy nurse (Ann Bernatitus) and twenty-five Filipino nurses boarded trucks on a convoy bound for Bataan.

As part of War Plan Orange 3 the army had stockpiled enough equipment at Camp Limay on the peninsula's East Road to set up a one-thousand-bed hospital, including a fifty-kilowatt generator powered by a diesel motor to pump water and provide electricity. Army planners envisioned this battlefield clinic, named Hospital #1, as a surgical facility, a place to reset shattered bones, suture gaping wounds, repair perforated organs, dress burns, resection intestines and perform amputations.

The senior physician at Hospital #1 planned to set up a surgical pavilion with nine operating tables, each staffed by a team of surgeons, nurses and medics specializing in a specific area of the body—arms and legs, the abdomen, the brain, the kidney and bladder, the chest. A central table in the operating pavilion would hold all the equipment; nurses would decide what they needed for each operation and put it on a small stand next to their operating tables. Surrounding the operating pavilion would be a complete military hospital: emergency station, registration room, fifteen post-operative wards, a dental clinic, pharmacy, staff quarters, laundry and mess.

Bouncing in the back of a truck as it made its way west around the bay, then south down Bataan's East Road toward their new assignment, several of the nurses told one another they would probably be working in a redbrick building with all the amenities. Many still had not accepted the reality of war, or, to give it the proper perspective, they likely could not envision the deprivations, hard labor and primitive living that war forces on those who wage it. They were accustomed to their comforts, and they had hope, hope that no matter how bad things got, they would always find some respite, some relief. A few, in fact, were convinced that the war would soon be over. It was only a matter of weeks, they told themselves, months at the most before everyone would be back in Manila in long dresses, dancing under the stars.

Instead of neat red brick, of course, their trucks pulled up to twenty-nine rough-hewn buildings, long sheds really, with walls of woven bamboo and roofs of thatched nipa grass.

"This is a hospital?" Leona Gastinger said, wide-eyed.[4]

The day before, a handful of officers, physicians and medics had arrived to begin setting up. One of the men had spread a bunch of bedsheets on the ground in the middle of the compound and on them had painted a huge red cross. Now some of the crew stepped forward to greet the fifty-one women.

The convoy had been delayed and it was too dark to work, so Rosemary Hogan, a well-liked Oklahoman and the senior nurse in charge, walked her nurses down to the beach to cool off.

It was a clear night, the stars were shimmering on the water, and the women, slipping off their shoes and shaking the road dust from their hair, sat in small clusters on the pristine sand. Most remember the quiet of that moment; they spoke in hushed voices and listened to the waves break on the beach. Then someone realized the date—it was Christmas Eve.

Back at the compound they rummaged in a warehouse for footboards, headboards, frames, braces and springs, which they hauled across the dusty compound to their new quarters, a screened hut, then knocked the parts together into beds and, finally, exhausted, slipped into sleep.

Christmas Day was "hotter than any August Day in Kansas City," Dorothy Scholl remembered.[5] The quartermaster issued each woman tropical-weight khaki slacks, shirts, socks and army shoes, a uniform much cooler and more comfortable than their air-corps coveralls, then they headed back to the warehouse to unpack cartons of bedpans, steel trays and tin basins. The operating-room nurses discovered that their equipment had been coated in Cosmoline, a viscous petroleum preservant that only ether would dissolve; one nurse spent so many hours stooped over a bucket with an ether rag cleaning the equipment that by nightfall she was almost anesthetized. The rest of the crew filled pails with water pumped from an artesian well and began to wash down tables and stands, beds and cabinets, doorways and walls. An enlisted man jerry-rigged a sterilizer from steel pressure cookers and a multijet Bunsen burner. (The women did a bit of jerry-rigging themselves; when they discovered a dearth of operating-room caps, they took a carton of white chef's hats and cut them down to size.) That night a group of exhausted doctors and nurses sat down to enjoy a Christmas dinner of roasted pig, but the war interrupted their holiday meal; an ambulance rolled into the compound with eight wounded, two of whom needed immediate surgery.

On December 26 Cassie and six other army nurses joined the group at Limay. She and Rosemary Hogan were friends and Hogan gave her pal the assignment she wanted, the operating pavilion. A few hours after Cassie met her surgical team, the hospital received 212 casualties. The Japanese were bludgeoning the retreating American and Filipino troops, catching them as they withdrew over the roads and bridges leading to Bataan. Cassie worked for hours that afternoon, handing a surgeon the instruments he needed to cut and suture. The work went well, she thought, as clean and efficient as any redbrick operating room Stateside. But they weren't Stateside, not with flights of bombers overhead, the drone of their engines an alarm that sent the doctors and nurses to their knees, squatting under the operating tables with their hands raised above their heads, trying to keep their gloves sterile in the surgical field. "It was strange to see these poor patients lying there with all these hands hovering over their bellies," Cassie said. "When the bombers passed, everybody stood up, looked around and continued with their work."[6] (As Cassie surveyed the room, she happened to glance toward the refrigerator that held the OR's supply of blood and noticed two feet protruding from the bottom shelf; Ann Bernatitus had decided to turn the icebox into a one-woman bomb shelter.)

Between rounds of casualties, the off-duty nurses at Hospital #1 would sometimes stroll down the road to a local bodega for a bottle of Coca-Cola and a few minutes of rest on the bodega's front porch. The rural market reminded some of the women of country stores back home, and sitting there on a bench with their feet propped up on a rail, they would chat about their lives before the war and wonder if they would ever get back to them.

Shortly after New Year's Day 1942, Japanese dive bombers attacked a barrio some one hundred yards from Hospital #1, but the Americans and their patients were lucky. Shrapnel fell harmlessly onto the sheds and pathways. Still the bombing worried James W. Duckworth, the senior physician, and he decided to move the hospital west and inland to the cover of the jungle and away from its exposed position on Manila Bay.[7]

During the first weeks in January, General Homma's soldiers punched holes in the allied line at the neck of the peninsula and began to push their way down the East Road toward Limay. When the enemy reached Abucay barrio, the first major town on the road and thirteen miles from Hospital #1, the allies regrouped for a fight. For twelve days Japanese artillery lobbed volley after volley on Abucay while Japanese pilots strafed the beaches. Then came the infantry. The fighting was fierce, often hand to hand, and the casualties came pouring into Hospital #1 on trucks and buses and mules and horse carts.[8] In one twenty-four-hour period on January 16, the OR teams performed 187 major surgical procedures, four to five times the average number of cases at the largest Stateside hospital. So many men were so badly wounded that as they were lined up for their operations, the staff set them on sawhorses— angled head down to prevent shock—to wait.[9] When the generator went out, or during a blackout, orderlies took up kerosene lanterns and the doctors cut and stitched in the narrow beams of light. Some men came in with multiple wounds received across several days of fighting; they'd get hit, a field medic would patch them up at a battalion aid station, and they would head back to battle, only to be wounded again. There were so many critical injuries at the hospital, chaplains were on permanent duty in the operating room, stepping carefully around the tables, whispering last rites and anointing the foreheads of those on their way to the morgue.

In some ways, war is at its ugliest, its most grotesque, in an operating room. Alfred Weinstein, a surgeon from Georgia, was never able to leave behind memories of

> the zzz-zzz-zzz of a saw as it cut through bone . . . the plop of an amputated leg dropping into a bucket, the grind of a rounded burr eating its way through a skull, the tap, tap, tap of a mallet on a chisel gouging out shell fragments . . . the hiss of the sterilizer blowing off steam, the soft patter of the nurses' feet scurrying back and forth, the snip of scissors cutting through muscle, the swish of a mop on the floor cleaning up blood . . . the gasp of soldiers with chest wounds . . . the snap of rubber gloves on outstretched hands, the rustle of operating gowns being changed. Rivulets of sweat washed away the nurses' rouge and powder, leaving only lipstick to match the ruby-red blood.[10]

After hours of this, time lost all meaning. Was it noon or near dusk? Who could tell? One patient began to look like another, there were so many of them. The operating tables became a kind of assembly line, torn limb following torn limb, sucking chest wound after sucking chest wound. The utility rooms were piled high with bloody linen, detritus that measured the surgeons' work.

Cassie and her surgical team simply kept at it, sometimes kidding one another to break the tension at the table. Now and then between cases they might grab a quick doughnut or cup of coffee. Mostly they tried to concentrate on the job in front of them. "I was thankful for the hard physical labor," she remembered. "The work gave me . . . the weariness to put [my mind] to sleep."[11]

General MacArthur was forced to order his troops back from their initial line of defense and set up a secondary position farther down the peninsula, but the relentlessness of the enemy was only one of the general's problems.

The officer in charge of food and supplies informed MacArthur that without relief supplies, Bataan would run out of provisions in less than sixty days, so the general ordered his command to cut its diet to fewer than two thousand calories a day, less than half the amount of food a soldier needed to carry the fight to his enemy. At Hospital #1 the order meant that everyone would now live on two meals a day, even as those days got longer and longer.

In mid-January MacArthur sent a message to his forces on Bataan from his headquarters in Malinta Tunnel on Corregidor, two miles across the bay.

HEADQUARTERS
UNITED STATES ARMY FORCES
IN THE FAR EAST FORT MILLS P.I.

January 15, 1942

Help is on the way from the United States. Thousands of troops and hundreds of planes are being dispatched. The exact time of arrival of reinforcement is unknown as they will have to fight their way through Japanese attempts against them. It is imperative that our troops hold until these reinforcements arrive.

No further retreat is possible. We have more troops in

Bataan than the Japanese have thrown against us; our supplies are ample; a determined defense will defeat the enemy's attack.

It is a question now of courage and of determination. Men who run will merely be destroyed but men who fight will save themselves and their country.

I call upon every soldier in Bataan to fight in his assigned position, resisting every attack. This is the only road to salvation. If we will fight we will win; if we retreat we will be destroyed.

MacArthur[12]

So they waited for relief because their commander told them relief would come, and they believed him, or wanted to believe him, hope being what it is, the only antidote to desperation. Some historians think that MacArthur meant what he said. They point to a January 3 message from Washington in which General George C. Marshall, the army chief of staff, told MacArthur

Our definitely allocated air reinforcements together with British should give us an early superiority in the Southwest Pacific. Our strength . . . should exert a decisive effect on Japanese shipping and force a withdrawal northward. . . . Every day of time you gain is vital to the concentration of the overwhelming power necessary for our purpose. . . . The current conferences in Washington . . . are extremely encouraging in respect to accelerating speed of ultimate success.[13]

In other words, help seemed on the way, but other historians say MacArthur knew that Washington had at its disposal only limited resources; he also knew well the extent to which the Japanese had crippled the Pacific fleet. Two days after MacArthur promised his troops that help was on the way, two days after they began lining up on the beach scanning the horizon for the relief convoys their commander had promised were coming, he sent the following radiogram to the War Department:

The food situation here is becoming serious. For some time I have been on half rations and the result will soon become evident in the exhausted condition of the men. . . . I asked for blockade running ships. No reply has been received. . . . The strategic problem involving an advance from the south will not relieve the food situation here in time. . . . No attempt yet seems to have been made along this line. This seems incredible to me. . . . I cannot over emphasize the psychological reaction that will take place here unless something tangible is done in this direction. . . . I repeat that if something is not done to meet the general situation which is developing the disastrous results will be monumental.[14]

The nurses at Hospital #1 began to look out at Manila Bay for relief ships stuffed with food and medicine. They told one another the supplies would arrive soon, and soon after that the war would be over.

Dr. James Duckworth, their commanding officer, seemed to sense the fatuousness in MacArthur's memoranda. He continued with his plan to move Hospital #1 inland, out of the range of the Japanese big guns. At night now the nurses could see the flashes of gunfire in the distance and hear the rumble of tanks.

An officer sent to scout a new location for the hospital reported back with two possible sites, and Duckworth picked kilometer post 155, a cool, green mountainous area where military engineers were carving out a camp. Here was running water and three large wooden buildings that could be converted into staff quarters, wards and operating rooms. The location reminded a number of staff of the cool, green summer capital of the Philippines, Baguio, so people took to calling the new Hospital #1 "Little Baguio." On the roofs of the buildings they painted large red crosses on white backgrounds. Some of the huts nearby were turned into supply sheds, laboratories and a pharmacy. Down the road were an engineers' headquarters, a quartermasters' food storage unit, an ordnance supply depot, a motor pool and an antiaircraft battery. It took the staff at Limay two days and nights to pack their equipment and gear. Surgeons put protective plaster casts around the broken bones of the traction patients, nurses boxed up medicines, bandages and instruments and the patients were readied for transport in buses that had been converted into large ambulances.

About 9:00 A.M. on January 25, Cassie and the others boarded trucks for Little Baguio. On their way out of camp they passed sixty-four white crosses in the hospital cemetery. During its twenty-nine days at Limay, the staff at Hospital #1 had treated twelve hundred casualties. Not long after everyone had cleared the camp, Japanese pilots came in low with incendiary bombs and burned the hospital to the ground.

Chapter 4

The Sick, the Wounded,
the Work of War

*B*EFORE THE BUCKETS of bloody limbs and the white crosses on the
jungle floor, the women of the Army Nurse Corps did not really think
themselves part of the profession of arms. Yes, they were in the army—
they wore their country's uniform and the insignia of military rank—but
they were healers, not soldiers. They had no interest in siegecraft and
strategy. Theirs was a culture of care, not nodding plumes and bugles
and battle cries. The army was an arena for men, and women were on
the periphery of that domain, that place of male passage.

Then the shooting started, and they found themselves confronting as
much danger and deprivation as any dogface in the field. The men who
worked with them—doctors, medics, orderlies and attendants—were no
longer "colleagues" and "staff," they were comrades in arms now, and
"the girls," as so many referred to them, were no longer anomalies in the
ranks, they were a military unit in the middle of a battle.

They were women at war.

*F*ROM THE FIRST day of the war the allies did much of their medical
planning on the fly, improvising as exigencies arose. Hospital #1 had
been part of War Plan Orange 3, but the idea for a second hospital on
Bataan seems to have evolved not long after the fighting started, and during Christmas week, nineteen army nurses from Sternberg set out by
boat across Manila Bay to Bataan and a point inland on the peninsula,
kilometer 162.5, to establish General Hospital #2.

The moment they arrived on the shores of the peninsula, they found trouble. Their ship, the ferry *Mc E. Hyde,* negotiated the bay safely, but not long after it tied up at a wharf off the East Road, enemy planes appeared overhead. The nurses scrambled for cover, some to foxholes, some behind bushes, some just flattened themselves in the dirt. When they finally looked up, the *Mc E. Hyde* was sinking, and with it many of the hospital supplies and basic equipment the women had carried with them.

Somewhat stunned and disheveled, they brushed themselves off and found a small water pipe at the side of the road. Here they were, some of them told themselves, headed for a hospital that did not exist and their supplies now lay at the bottom of Manila Bay. Just then a medical officer appeared with trucks to take them inland. They spent the night at a staging area, and the next morning, after linking up with seventeen doctors and thirty medics and orderlies, headed for kilometer 162.5. They arrived at the medical depot there just in time for dinner. The troops at the depot stood by in disbelief as the trucks rolled to a stop and nurses—*nurses?*—climbed down to the ground. "What in the hell are we going to do with *women* here!" one dogface growled.[1]

What, indeed.

Since the Civil War, when a relatively large number of nurses began working in military hospitals, women in uniform or serving as civilian nurses in the ranks have had to endure the disaffection and raw culture of men—men's behavior, men's ethos, men's appetites—and the army, for its part, was aware of the difficulty. In a memo to his command in the spring of 1941, H. C. Michie, an army colonel in charge of a military hospital in Louisiana, noted, "Except in the hospital, hostess house, post office, on the highways, and except by invitation, the presence of women may be embarrassing and may deny officers and enlisted men privileges due them in their areas." In other words, women in the ranks were denying men the freedom to be men. "Prior to 1920," the colonel continued, "nurses occupied a difficult and awkward status. They were in the military establishment and had the status of civilians. Growing out of the considerable work and effort, in which the undersigned played a part, nurses were given the relative rank [as opposed to permanent rank and title] of officers in order that their military and social status would be clearly defined. When this status is properly practiced by the nurses, it had materially bettered her [*sic*] position and solved many of her social and military problems." To put it plainly, when women acted like officers, male officers, and not women, they were safe. "It must be kept in mind that, where there are large groups of men removed from the restraining influences of home many things are liable to occur that would not occur under the usual and normal conditions."[2]

The army had not prepared its nurses for war—provided no training in the field or in weapons or even in battlefield medicine—and during their first days on Bataan, they seemed out of place.

The evening the women arrived at the site for Hospital #2, a detail of men was assigned to set up cots for them and dig a women's latrine. As she watched the men swinging their picks and sweating in the heat and dirt, Sally Blaine of Bible Grove, Missouri, thought to herself, We're so much trouble here . . . we shouldn't be here. We're nothing but a burden. Clara Mae Bickford also remembered the men grumbling and the way the nurses "really took it on the chin."[3]

That night after supper the women found a cool creek in a secluded area and stripped down for a bath. The roiling water restored them, made them feel like "glamour girls." Too bad their combs and toothbrushes were at the bottom of Manila Bay, they thought. Later, under mango and acacia trees hard by the Real River, they settled on their cots and fell asleep to the shrieks of birds and the soft creak of bamboo.

Many of the women were strangers to one another, but danger has a way of driving people together, and no human enterprise is more dangerous than combat. In combat people need one another, need to know who can think clearly and who can be counted on when things start to go wrong. So like fighting men, the nurses closed ranks, and within a day or two these strangers were calling one another by their nicknames, "Hatch" and "Blackie" and "Bickie" and "Shack." Soon they were teasing one another too, poking fun at the peculiar way someone held a cigarette or said "y'all." In the late afternoon they would set their cots together on a level spot next to the creek and talk for hours about their families and their men.

THE SITE FOR Hospital #2 had been selected for its dense jungle canopy, its level ground and the availability of water—the swift, clear Real River. The only "roads" were a carabao trail connecting the site with the rest of the peninsula and a footpath that ran east to west. There were no open fields and no buildings. Just jungle, a canopy of acacia and mahogany and bamboo, draped with thick vines.

Everything had to be brought in or built. Quickly the medical crew found tools and transportation, and engineers cut a one-lane dirt road to carry patients in and out. Two bands of intrepid officers and enlisted men commandeered some trucks and, before the Japanese occupied the city and established a siege line on Bataan, dashed back to Manila in advance of the invaders to scrounge for surgical supplies, medicine, generators, tools and food. (One surgeon led another group north to Stotsenberg and, with the enemy closing in fast there, he snuck into the base hospital and made off with a critical piece of equipment—an operating-room sterilizer.)[4]

Of all the early efforts, however, nothing was more important than setting up the kitchens. Napoleon is believed to have said that his army marched on its stomach, and every military commander since has at one time or another echoed that assertion. Nothing, say those who have been to war, not the stifling sun or monsoon rain, not the mud, mosquitoes or maggots, not even the relentless enemy, affects the morale and performance of a fighting force as much as its food.

War is hard labor and no one works well without being fed. Bad food, monotonous food or severely reduced rations only add to the numbing fatigue of combat or the labor of tending the sick, the injured and the dying. Sometimes the only act of ego, save sleep, that the nurses and doctors were allowed was their meal. For them, as for all soldiers, mess call was a ritual, a time when comrades gathered together for a few moments of peace and, by breaking bread shoulder to shoulder, reaffirmed their community, their identity as a group. The mess hall—in their case a jungle clearing—became a kind of sanctuary, a formal break in the hard routine of war, a break too from the continual discomfort, unease and self-denial that began at first light and ended only with sleep.

The nurses helped set up the first kitchen at Hospital #2 and pitched in to serve one of the first meals: tea, biscuits and slumgullion stew, a concoction of meat and whatever other edible ingredients the cooks could find. Helping out on KP ("kitchen police") put the nurses shoulder to shoulder with ordinary soldiers. None of these men, of course, were accustomed to working alongside women, and a few of the grizzled sergeants were unsettled by the idea of "soldiers in skirts." One day on KP one of them told Sally Blaine that he "didn't want any damn woman in my kitchen."[5]

After the kitchen was established, the staff had to find the furnishings basic to any hospital, especially beds. Hospital #2 started with five chairs found in the brush, eight refrigerators and thirty tables, then a local planter loyal to the Americans hired carpenters to build what the Americans needed, and they fashioned almost everything from bamboo: mess and dining tables, medicine cabinets, nurses' desks, chairs, beds, trays, brooms, fly swatters, laundry baskets, wastebaskets, serving spoons, urinals, storage cabinets, benches, linen closets, ashtrays and floor mats.[6]

The staff stuffed rice straw into mattress covers, which made surprisingly comfortable beds. Chinese and Filipino civilians caught in the retreat volunteered to set up a laundry on the Real River. They boiled the linens in oil drums and strung several hundred feet of clothesline along the riverbank. At another spot along the river, engineers built a dam to divert water to a 3,000-gallon high-pressure filter and chlorination system.

Sanitation, a problem for any army, was particularly difficult in the tropics. With a high water table the open-pit latrines did not drain well, and without chemicals to kill insects, these privies became breeding grounds for flies. Almost everyone suffered from diarrhea until a new sanitary officer reported to the unit and had his men build wooden latrine boxes with removable seats. He accommodated the women with their own private facility, and they were so pleased with this small convenience, they lined up in front of it to pose for a photograph.

The most difficult task, of course, was to set up the open-air wards. After bulldozers cleared the ground of stumps and rocks, Filipino laborers swinging long bolos cleared out the underbrush. (Their crew bosses had strict orders not to remove climbing vines or tall brush that could serve as air cover.) Once the construction was done, the nurses and their assistants set up the beds and desks and medicine cabinets. One of the few available pup tents was reserved for a records room. "We had a tent over the records, but no tent over the patients," said Sally Blaine. "I guess the army thought the patients would dry out quicker than the records."[7]

Some of the open-air wards were square, some round, some with no identifiable shape at all, just a sprawl of old iron beds or rickety wooden cots under clumps of bamboo or acacia. Here and there between the al fresco wards, the staff hung canvas Lister bags filled with water. The medical supply depot sent over blankets, sheets, pajamas, pillows, morphine, quinine, sulfa and vitamins. (Drugs were enclosed in tins and bottles and buried in deep trenches to protect them from bombardment.)

One of the last tasks was to number each ward with small wooden signs nailed to the trees. In the end there were seventeen wards, each with between two hundred and five hundred patients—bed after bed after bed spread out on the jungle floor in the open under a canopy of branches and vines, literally as far as the eye could see.[8]

With so many patients, each day seemed endless. And, according to one of the surgeons assigned to the hospital, the danger of the work only added to the fatigue.

> Hospital No. 2 had a peculiar and uncomfortable location. It is probably the first Army hospital of such size located near installations that were constantly being bombed. It was certainly in the zone of action. When the enemy air ships approached these installations they almost invariably do so directly over the hospital. This was disconcerting for two reasons: (1) It always drew fire from our anti aircraft guns. fragments [sic] of shells were constantly falling in the hospital area. Fifty calibre [sic] bullets also fell in the hospital area. (2) We were never certain that an enemy bomb, by accident, might not fall in one of the wards. On one occasion a 50 calibre bullet went through the only empty bed in one ward. Another 50 calibre bullet went through the [h]ead of a civilian kitchen police and the foot of one of our soldiers. One of our cooks heard the anti aircraft guns begin firing, jumped from his cot and fell flat on the ground 3 feet away just in time for an unexploded 3 inch shell to go through his chest and 3 feet into the ground. [The man eventually recovered.] Various sizes of shrapnel and or shell fragments fell in every mess and ward and twice in the dental clinic in our quarters. Only the operating room escaped. Several 155 shells fell in one mess, killing 5 and injuring 12 other persons. Every ward was riddled with fox holes which men often used. This was hard on the poor bed patients who could not get out of bed.[9]

On January 2, a week or so after it began receiving patients, the hospital recorded its first death. The body was buried in a rice paddy near the south end of the complex. There were no caskets on Bataan, so they covered the deceased with a sheet and lowered him into a hole. Later, when sheets were in short supply, the dead were simply covered with a blanket of damp earth. Soon there would be a graves registration unit and a cemetery on a hill to the southeast.

That first week of the new year, 150 military patients who had been part of the final exodus from Sternberg Hospital in the Christmas retreat arrived after a journey that took them from Manila to Corregidor by one boat, then by another to Bataan. An admitting physician looked at these travel-worn stretcher cases with a strange kind of awe; it was the first time, he said, that someone had decided to evacuate patients toward the front line instead of away from it.

Accompanying the group were five doctors, two dentists, two supply

Prewar view of the nurses' quarters at Sternberg Hospital, Manila.

ARMED FORCES
INSTITUTE OF
PATHOLOGY

Living room of the nurses' quarters at Sternberg. "The nurses' quarters, elysian rooms with shell-filled windowpanes, bamboo and wicker furniture with plush cushions, and mahogany ceiling fans gently turning in the tropical air."

ARMED FORCES
INSTITUTE OF
PATHOLOGY

En route to the Philippines,
October 1941, U.S.S. Holbrooke.
Front: Eleanor Garen, Phyllis Arnold,
Imogene (Jeanne) Kennedy.
Standing: Millie Dalton, Grace
Hallman, Leona Gastinger. "Women
who wanted adventure and romance—
self-possessed, ambitious and
unattached women—signed
up to sail west."

ELEANOR GAREN

Eleanor Garen and Winifred
Madden on duty at Station Hospital
Corregidor, fall 1941.

ELEANOR GAREN

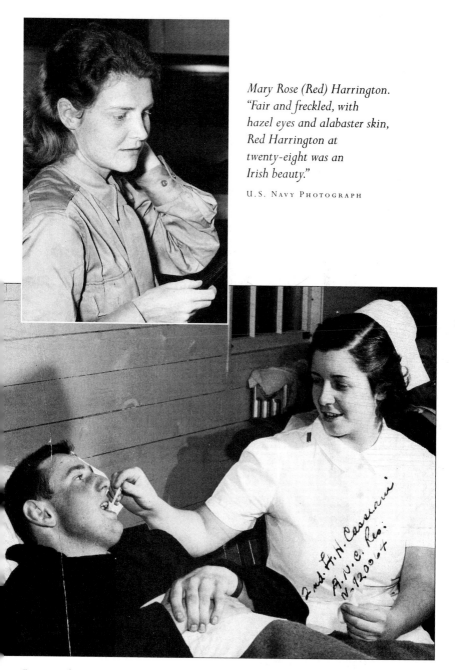

Mary Rose (Red) Harrington. "Fair and freckled, with hazel eyes and alabaster skin, Red Harrington at twenty-eight was an Irish beauty."

Cassie with a patient at Camp John Edwards, Hyannis, Massachusetts, fall 1941. "Routine duty, too routine for someone so self-possessed, someone who 'was out to experience as much as I could.' So she put in for a transfer."

HELEN CASSIANI NESTOR

Jungle Hospitals, Bataan

Lifting the lids on the nurses' latrine at Hospital #2. The nurses "were so pleased with this small convenience, they lined up in front of it to pose for a photograph."

JEANNE KENNEDY
SCHMIDT

Hospital #2, Bataan. Clara Mae Bickford at the hospital chapel. "Some of the nurses found solace in religion . . . the chapel at Hospital #2 [was called] the Church of All Faiths."

JEANNE KENNEDY
SCHMIDT

Hospital #2 nurses' quarters, Bataan. "They grew accustomed to falling asleep with monkeys chattering in the stumps overhead. Tree branches served as their valets, jungle vines as clothes hangers."

JEANNE KENNEDY SCHMIDT

Patient ward at #2. "'We had a tent over the records, but no tents over the patients.'"

SALLY BLAINE
MILLETT

Jeanne Kennedy mending her coveralls in the nurses' quarters. "The angels in white had learned to dress for the dirty business of war."

JEANNE KENNEDY
SCHMIDT

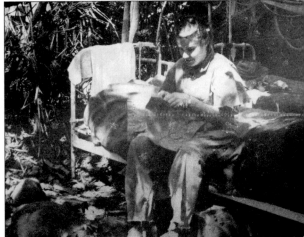

Hospital #2 nurses in their quarters. Standing: Rose Rieper, Mary Moultrie. Kneeling: Edith Corns, Beth Veley. "Nurses, doctors, and medical staff were issued steel helmets and gas masks."

Hospital #2. Rose Rieper in the nurses' quarters. "I would hear girlish giggles coming across the Real River from the burlap confines [of the nurses' quarters]."

ROSE RIEPER, EDITH CORNS LLOYD

"There were seventeen wards, each with between two hundred and five hundred patients—bed after bed after bed, spread out on the jungle floor in the open under a canopy of branches and vines, literally as far as the eye could see."

ROSE RIEPER, EDITH CORNS LLOYD

"*For a few moments away from the eyes of men, the women could be women with themselves. . . . Sometimes together in the water . . . they would break into song.*"

JEANNE KENNEDY SCHMIDT

Civilian dietitian Vivian Weisblatt (left), Josie Nesbit (middle) and another army nurse at a Hospital #2 mess. "The mess hall became a kind of sanctuary, a formal break in the hard routine of war."

ROSE RIEPER, EDITH CORNS LLOYD

A 1931 nursing school photo of Rosemary Hogan, one of the nurses wounded in the Hospital #1 bombing, April 1942.
" 'I saw Rosemary Hogan being helped from her ward. Blood streamed from her face and her shoulder; she looked ghastly. She managed to wave her good arm at me. "Just a little nose bleed," she said cheerfully. . . . "How about you?" ' "

A square of cloth taken from a rough muslin bedsheet signed the day of surrender, May 6, 1942. "'We wanted to leave a record in case we disappeared.'"

"Malinta Tunnel was so well built, the hospital staff could continue to work during raids, interrupted only by the muffled thuds of bombs and shells landing above."

Corregidor and Surrender

After Surrender

Japanese photograph taken outside Malinta Tunnel, May 1942. Left to right: civilian dietitian V. Weisblatt, army nurses A. Foreman, J. Kennedy, P. Greenwalt, E. Young, D. McCann, E. Garen. "While the Japanese photographer was setting up his equipment, the women had a chance to look around . . . amid twisted girders and splintered trees, were scores of bloated . . . corpses covered by swarms of . . . flies."

U.S. ARMY MILITARY HISTORY INSTITUTE

Santo Tomas Internment Camp. Foggy Bottom Shantytown in the foreground, Main Building in the background. "To relieve the oppression of such tight quarters, the prisoners soon took to building small outdoor sheds, or 'shanties,' as they liked to call them." TERRY MYERS JOHNSON

Red Cross ceremony honoring the nurses who escaped from Corregidor, July 1942. Standing (left to right): F. McDonald, Surgeon General Magee, M. Lohr, H. Lee, E. Hatchitt, D. Daley, J. Redmond, Eleanor Roosevelt, Red Cross Chairman Norman Davis. "The first American women decorated for bravery in World War II." AMERICAN RED CROSS

Santo Tomas Internment Camp, Manila

Main Building, Santo Tomas Internment Camp, date unknown. "With its giant clock and towering crucifix, [it] stood solidly as a source of power and authority. For the internees it was also a compass point, the place against which all other places on the sixty-acre campus were measured."

TERRY MYERS JOHNSON

Japanese photograph. Arriving at Santo Tomas Internment Camp, date unknown. "Some people came into the camp with money, a lot of it, others with only the clothes they had on their backs." TERRY MYERS JOHNSON

Japanese photograph. Nurses wearing their handmade uniforms, 1942.
Main Building in background. Back row, left to right: Navy nurse
L. Cobb, army nurses E. Francis, E. Shacklette, A.Wurts, R. Palmer,
S. Durrett, I. McDonald and "Albert," a child internee. Front: J. Kennedy,
H. Gardner, A. Foreman, E. Thor. TERRY MYERS JOHNSON

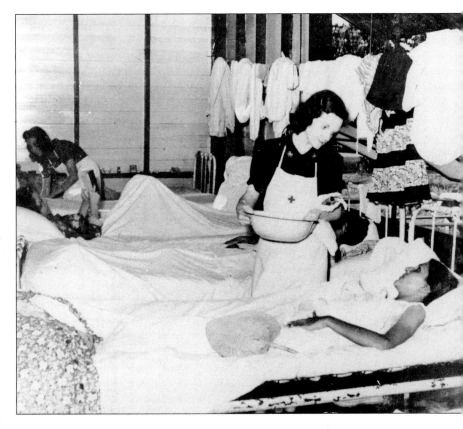

Japanese photograph, 1943. Camp hospital. Navy nurse Peg Nash speaking with "Gladys," a British internee. After the Japanese published this photo, U.S. naval personnel saw it, identified Nash, contacted her mother and verified that her daughter was alive.

U.S. NAVAL HOSPITAL, OAKLAND, CALIFORNIA

officers and Josie Nesbit, the perfect choice to lead the staff of nineteen nurses at Hospital #2. Even before the shooting started, Nesbit, who had been working in an underground hospital on Corregidor, had proven herself an agile administrator and leader and had won the respect of almost every woman under her command.

Nesbit was handed her assignment on Corregidor by Colonel Wibb Cooper, the chief medical officer in the Philippines. "Colonel," she said, "if you want to send me out there to be in charge of a hospital, don't you think I should be promoted?"[10] Indeed he did, and Josie Nesbit arrived in the jungle a newly minted first lieutenant.

Privately, however, she doubted herself and worried whether, at the age of forty-seven, she had enough endurance to organize the care of thousands in a jungle hospital. "Admittedly," she said, "I tired more quickly and much of the stamina I had in the past may have been somewhat lacking when we withdrew to the combat zone on Bataan, but . . . there was absolutely no time for self-pity."[11]

JOSEPHINE NESBIT, SECOND in command of the army nurses in the Philippines in 1941, was as resolute and uncompromising as her superior, Maude Davison, but no two women could have been more different.

Everyone, from the most junior nurse to the most senior surgeon, called Lieutenant Nesbit "Josie." A formidable-looking woman from Missouri, she was tall and large-framed with brown hair, wire-rimmed glasses and a size thirteen shoe. But her bearing hardly matched her demeanor. She had an almost maternal affinity for the women under her— "my girls," she called them in a voice of reassurance and understanding. Indeed the Filipino nurses referred to her as "Mama Josie."

Born on December 23, 1894, on a farm near Butler, Missouri, Josie was the seventh of ten children. It was a hard life that took its toll. Her parents died early, and by the age of twelve, Josie was an orphan living first with a grandmother and later with a cousin in Kansas.

She left high school at sixteen, went into nurse's training with a sister and in early 1914 became a registered nurse. Four years later, an army recruiter traveled to Kansas City, hoping to recruit nurses to help with an influenza epidemic that was decimating the ranks of the military, and on October 1, 1918, Josie Nesbit became Reserve Army Nurse N700665.

She was first stationed at Camp Logan Hospital near Houston, Texas, and in the years that followed she lived the life of a military nurse, a good life free from want and filled with interesting work and adventure.

She hiked the American Rockies, worked in Hawaii, rode a camel in Egypt through the Valley of the Kings. She did two tours in the Philippines. During the first, on maternity duty, she befriended the wife of an officer, who persuaded her "to go on a 12-day hike with them from Baguio up through Ifugao country to the region of the famous rice terraces. Those RICE TERRACES were such a beautiful sight when we arrived at the top of them at sunset, that tears came to my eyes!"[12]

When she returned to the Philippines in the summer of 1941, she was named Maude Davison's assistant. She was a well-traveled forty-six-year-old second lieutenant with twenty-two years of military service.

On Bataan she worked herself to exhaustion, roaming Hospital #2 from one end to the other and back, but every day she took the time to make herself presentable, always gathering her dark brown hair in a bun or a turban. She believed that a woman should look like a woman, even—or as she would argue, "especially"—in combat: "We were the first Nurses in the United States Army to be subjected to actual combat; on Bataan there simply were no 'rear areas.' Although we worked around the clock, we were careful to ensure that when our troops saw a woman Nurse, that Nurse had to look as much a woman as circumstances would permit. In light of our situation, this was not easily accomplished."[13]

When her nurses, her "girls," needed something personal—underwear or shoes, for instance—she would beg pilots who might be flying to the other islands to ferry the gear back. If she came upon a woman at work burning with fever or in a malarial ebb, she would relieve her of duty and put her to bed. She did not suffer slackers, or fools, either. But if a woman had a problem, Josie helped her work it out, always in private. She took care of her charges, and in return they gave her their loyalty, their labor, their love.

BY THE END of January 1942 the initial wards at Hospital #2 were full and the staff were preparing to open additional wards. At first they had tried to group patients by their condition or injury, but so many people had a combination of problems, usually wounds on top of tropical diseases, each ward became a hospital within a hospital, housing patients with a wide variety of medical and surgical problems. Indeed, many wards had more patients than the whole of Sternberg Hospital before the war. Overall, counting the hundreds of patients sent over from Hospital #1 when that facility moved from Limay to Little Baguio, Hospital #2 had a census at the end of the month of 2,160 patients.[14]

Some wards looked like tropical greenhouses, with beds set between trees and under palm fronds, a tangle of vines hanging close overhead. Other wards looked like hobo camps, with clothes hanging from tree limbs or bushes, and with pieces of poncho or shreds of canvas stretched between stalks of bamboo. The mess hall resembled a scout-camp dining hall without a roof, its long, picnic-style tables and benches stacked row after row under the acacias.

By February 1, Hospital #2 had a nursing staff of forty-three army officers, twenty-one Filipinos and eight civilian nurses.[15] Despite the withering workload, morale was high. Many of the women had grown up on farms or in towns like Bible Grove, Missouri, and Prairie Lea, Texas. They had labored in the fields, made their own clothes, and read by lamplight, and they knew how to live lean, without amenities, and were accustomed to hard work. The army had given them luxuries and a new life, and now it was time to pay the army back.

Each day they carried out the banal duties of battlefield nursing. They washed their patients down, scrubbing off the dirt and sweat of war with water from the Real River. Then they cleaned out the abrasions and lacerations, scrubbing the men with green soap before they sprinkled sulfa powder on their open wounds. They changed thousands of dressings, often giving morphine shots beforehand to ease the pain they would inflict when they lifted bandages from incisions and burns, bandages bound to raw flesh by blood and pus dried hard as glue.

At night they worked under blackout conditions, using flashlights or kerosene lamps painted blue. After a few hours of stumbling around, their eyes would become accustomed to the night, and they learned to recognize light and dark spots on the jungle floor. Sometimes animals wandered around in the darkness. Wild pigs would brush against their legs, and geckos, those small lizards with suction-cup feet, came diving out of the trees. A large carabao appearing in the dark like an apparition was beast enough to frighten anyone. One night a nurse hiking between beds was smacked in the forehead by a snake swinging from a branch.

On their way to work on the night shift, the women would stop by the mess hall and grab a packed lunch—cold salmon, corned beef hash, cheese or jam sandwiches with cups of cold cocoa or coffee—to eat later, usually around midnight. Soon, however, the rations they had set aside began to disappear. Monkeys and rats were carrying them off, so the women learned to eat on the run, right away, before the jungle left them hungry.

Living in a world of men, the women tried to achieve some seclusion, some separation. Josie Nesbit begged and borrowed as many canvas shelter halves as she could find so her women could section off the area of jungle where they slept. She also screened off part of a stream where the nurses bathed, a kind of elysian water garden where, for a few moments away from the eyes of men, the women could be women with themselves. The younger nurses would strip naked and sit on the cool wet rocks and slowly let the water rush over them. The older nurses, raised with a sense of Victorian discretion, were too shy to peel off everything and bathed in their panties and bras. Sometimes together in the water, for a rare moment they would break into song:

> *"You are my sunshine, my only sunshine*
> *You make me happy, when skies are gray*
> *You'll never know dear, how much I love you*
> *So don't take,*
> *My sunshine away."*[16]

And sometimes they would wade over to a tree that had a massive root growing from the bank into the stream, a natural water slide that set them laughing and giggling, even as the sounds of gunfire echoed down the road.

Quickly the women learned the ways of the jungle. In their al fresco quarters they put tins of water under each leg of their beds to keep the ants from migrating up and under their sheets. They grew accustomed to falling asleep with monkeys chattering in the stumps overhead. Tree branches served as their valets, jungle vines as clothes hangers.

Everyone hated the rats. War seemed to make them especially avaricious. At night the rats would come out in force, crawling over the recumbent bodies asleep under the trees. One night Josie Nesbit was awakened by a blood-curdling scream from the nurses quarters. The Japs have finally broken through, she thought. As it turned out, a mammoth rat had worked its way into a nurse's bed and had nuzzled her.

*E*VERY VENUE IN the large hospital had its own routine.

In the operating room two nurse-anesthetists poured a potent barbiturate, pentobarbital sodium, onto pieces of cotton, then held the cloth over a patient's nose to sedate him. Other women assisted at surgery, managing the instruments, irrigating the wounds, sopping up the blood. In the moments between patients, they would roll bandages or patch surgical gloves and resterilize them. As they worked they listened to the sounds of war—the bombs falling, the artillery and antiaircraft guns firing, the moans and cries of the wounded. Ethel Thor, a redhead from Tacoma, Washington, was assigned to circulate among the operating tables to make sure the pace of the surgery kept up with the flow of patients. Sometimes, however, the surgery became frenzied and Ethel would intervene to stop a doctor from cutting. In their eagerness, it seemed, some physicians had a habit of trying to debride—or slice away—dead tissue from burns and shrapnel wounds before the Novocain had taken hold. Even for Thor, an experienced nurse, the screaming was too much to bear.

At the eye, ear, nose and throat clinic, nurses worked with doctors to repair broken eyeglasses so the troops could see to shoot. At the dental clinic they helped reconstruct mouths torn and shattered by bullets and shrapnel or, when the fighting was hand to hand, as it often was, by rifle butts or bayonets.

Everyone—doctors, nurses, orderlies and attendants—often worked all day and all night.

"I heard not a single complaint about long hours and I cannot recall a single instance where there was any personal grievance among the officers, nurses or enlisted men," wrote Colonel Duckworth. "Many of us felt that the best work of our lives had been done here."[17]

Chapter 5

Waiting for the Help That Never Came

Tʜᴇ ᴀʟʟɪᴇꜱ ꜰᴀᴄᴇᴅ two enemies on Bataan, the Japanese with their bombs, bullets and long bayonets, and a second adversary, more powerful and unforgiving than any army that has ever taken the field, Nature.

If Nature had not opposed them, the men and women of the United States Armed Forces Far East might have been able to hold the desolate and forlorn Bataan peninsula much longer than they did, stalemating General Homma's army and making the Japanese pay a heavy price in blood for their imperial dream of conquest. But Nature, in the form of hunger and disease, helped the enemy, and after that the battle for Bataan became a crying game.

Nᴀᴛᴜʀᴇ ᴄᴀᴍᴇ ᴀᴛ them in the night, an army of female anopheline mosquitoes carrying a host of deadly parasites. When a mosquito punctures the skin of her victim with her teeth, she pumps saliva into the puncture wound, and in that saliva is the parasite called plasmodium, commonly known as malaria. An anopheline may have as many as 5,000 to 100,000 malaria sporozites in her salivary glands. Once in the human bloodstream the parasites invade the red blood cells, reproducing inside the cells again and again until the cell membranes burst, spilling the disease into the bloodstream and sending the victim into paralyzing paroxysms of fever and chills. One species of plasmodium, falciparum malaria, causes blood cells to adhere to one another and clog the capillaries, and it is this clogging that deprives parts of the body of oxygen. If this takes place in the brain, as it often does, the victim falls into a coma, and if the clogging paralyzes an internal organ like the kidneys or the liver, death often follows.[1]

On Bataan, malaria was epidemic. In a postwar report, Colonel Wibb Cooper, chief medical officer in the Philippines, found that malaria

soon became the primary cause of admission to clearing stations and its incidence rose steadily until by March 1st it reached 500 cases per day. By April 1st the rate was approaching 1,000 cases per day and the shortage of quinine [the only drug then available to treat the disease] was so acute that the issue of the drug was based on an allowance of but eight grams per case [hardly enough to effect a cure].[2]

At first, the doctors and nurses on Bataan took preventative doses of quinine, but when supplies began to dwindle, they stopped and soon came down with the disease. The commander of Hospital #2 estimated that half his personnel had malaria. (To Josie Nesbit, everyone looked ill.) A surgeon standing over a patient with a scalpel might suddenly start to shake violently with malarial chills. A nurse dressing a wound might begin to swoon with malarial fever. When Sally Blaine became bedridden with malaria, she set herself on a cot in the middle of her ward and directed the work of her staff from there. Lucy Wilson, an operating room nurse dizzy and weak with the disease, found a way to wedge an arm in a space near her operating table to steady herself during surgery. "It was with great reluctance that the nurses reported off duty ill," wrote Josie Nesbit. "They knew the need . . . to care for the hundreds of sick and wounded men."[3] It wasn't long, in other words, before the nurses were nursing one another.

Dysentery was also endemic. Flies from the open pit toilets were contaminating the food and water. "We had to eat when the air was thick with flies, usually waving with one hand while eating with the other," said John R. Bumgarner, a doctor at Hospital #2.[4]

The effects of malaria, dysentery, dengue fever and half a dozen other conditions were aggravated by the growing problem of malnutrition. The troops were hungry and every day, Colonel Cooper watched them grow weaker and less able to resist the diseases that were consuming them.

[By the end of February 1942, two months after the fall of Manila, the army on Bataan was down] to only about 1,000 calories [per person] per day. The operation of a defense in a mountainous jungle terrain which re-

quired hand carrying of supplies over difficult trails and the preparation of positions required a high energy output per man that can be conservatively estimated at not less than 4,000 calories per day. [The men's body fat dropped to dangerously low levels and their muscle mass shrank] with attendant weakness, loss of endurance, and nutritional edema [grotesque and painful swelling]. There was a serious shortage of both protein and vitamins. . . . All livestock on Bataan, including horses and ponies, were slaughtered and issued. Clinical and incipient beriberi was not only universal by April 1st but in combination with malnutrition and nutritional edema was the cause of the hospitalization of thousands of cases. On April 9th . . . there was in Bataan only enough food to make one issue of a half-ration [a few mouthfuls and all the food was gone].[5]

Curiously, through all this—the malaria, the amoebic dysentery, the starvation diet, the intense combat—through it all there was only a handful of men who suffered from battle fatigue, "shell shock," as it was known in World War I, or, as it is called today, post-traumatic stress disorder. Wibb Cooper was convinced these "cases were few in number [six or eight] because . . . there was no haven for retreat," no safe place to get away from the fighting "and everyone knew that."[6]

*I*N LATE JANUARY 1942, the Japanese launched two new offensives. One, from the South China Sea, was intended to capture the port of Mariveles on the tip of Bataan and cut off supplies from Corregidor. Meanwhile one thousand Japanese infantrymen tried to sneak through a gap in the allied line that stretched across the peninsula. The fighting was fierce, from the bamboo thickets near the coast to the thickly wooded foothills of the interior. For a while American and Filipino troops managed to hold their positions, but casualties on both sides were high.

To the Americans, the captured or dead Japanese soldiers looked robust; the enemy carried individual water filters, medical kits, ample supplies of food. This apparent plenty galled the deprived dogfaces. Frank Hewlett, a United Press reporter covering the Bataan campaign, summed up the mood of the troops in a poem he titled "The Battling Bastards of Bataan":

We're the battling bastards of Bataan:
No momma, no poppa, no Uncle Sam,

No aunts, no uncles, no nephews, no nieces,
no rifles, no guns, no artillery pieces,
And nobody gives a damn.[7]

The nurses, showing both solidarity and a sense of humor, began to refer to themselves as the "Battling Belles of Bataan."[8]

The Japanese offensives left hundreds dead and wounded, and since the battles had taken place in remote areas of jungle and on inaccessible slopes, the allied casualties were slow to reach the jungle hospitals, often lying for days not far from where they fell. By the time they were carried into the receiving wards, their wounds were suppurating with infection, crawling with maggots or, worst of all, bubbling with the scourge of gas gangrene.

Bacillus Welchii, the bacteria that causes gas gangrene, has ravaged every army. The contagious organism, which thrives in dirt contaminated with the manure of domestic or wild animals, finds its way into open wounds and works its way deep into the muscles where its enzymes devour blood and tissue, giving off a sickeningly sweet odor and leaving tiny gas bubbles in their wake. If these wounds are not drained quickly, the infection spreads, and when that happens, limbs swell to an enormous size and surgeons are forced to amputate the bloated extremities or lose the patient to systemic shock.[9]

At both field hospitals there were so many cases of gas gangrene the staff set up separate facilities to deal with the infection, and no one was eager to work there.

"The gangrene ward [was] on a low hill away from the hospital sheds," said Juanita Redmond. "The putrid odor, the ugly exposed wounds, the monstrous limbs where the infection had not yet been cut out, the agonized moans of 'Take it off, please take it off,' made it a place to avoid when one could."[10]

Short on bacillus antitoxin, the only effective cure, the medical staff tried to improvise. Nurses would double their efforts to keep the wounds clean and free from flies. At first they used sulfa powder to control the infection, but that too soon became scant. Then, a surgeon from Hospital #1 pioneered a new treatment: he made deep incisions in the infected muscle, debrided dead tissue, removed pieces of bone and metal fragments, then swabbed the area with hydrogen peroxide; afterward he left the incisions open but covered the wounds with mosquito netting and ordered patients to be set in direct sunlight. He guessed that oxygen in the air would destroy the anaerobic bacteria consuming the patient. And he was right. Within twenty-four hours nurses were reporting pulse rates and blood pressure readings near normal. This sun cure, wrote correspondent Melville Jacoby in *Time* magazine, "saved a large number of arms and legs."[11]

MELVILLE JACOBY AND his wife, Anna Lee Jacoby, a former Metro-Goldwyn-Mayer scriptwriter, covered the Bataan campaign for *Time* and *Life*. In some ways their reports were typical of the early news coverage of the war. The country needed heroes and the press needed melodrama, so in World War II, as in all other wars, truth became the first casualty.

One of their accounts from Bataan had all three thousand patients at Hospital #2 living in tents, when in fact the men were out in the open, often on the ground. In another account, Jacoby reported "doctors probe wounds for bullets and shell fragments . . . and also bet on the type of fragments they will dig out of wounds. Among their finds (all made in the U.S.): parts of Ford automobiles; nuts and bolts. Out of one soldier's body came a Singer sewing machine screw-driver."[12] There are no records, testimony or firsthand accounts to validate Jacoby's report, but likely such inventions found their way into print as a message to all those prewar pacifists who had supported the sale of scrap metal to the Japanese.

Often the journalistic errors were glaring. "One night when the doctors and nurses had amputations on every table, they donated their own blood,"[13] the Jacobys wrote. In fact most of the staff had malaria and thus their blood was contaminated and never used for transfusions.

Of all these fictions, however, the most revealing were the stories about the nurses. In combat women were a novelty, and no one, including the press, was quite sure what to think of them.

In many ways the modern debate about the role of women in combat can be traced back to those bleak early days of 1942 when fivescore nurses traded their hospital whites for battle dress. War is an exercise in raw animus and fifty years ago it was almost unthinkable that women would have a part in it.

In the middle of the twentieth century American women were still thought of primarily in terms of their relationships to men—girlfriends or wives, sisters or mothers, not self-contained individuals bent on careers or in search of adventure. To be sure there were anomalies—tough, resourceful, accomplished women: Isadora Duncan, Dorothy Parker, Georgia O'Keeffe, Amelia Earhart, Gertrude Ederle, Helen Wills, to name a few. But once the shooting started, once men went to war, the American press—the mostly male press—naturally "feminized" women, softened them and made them a metaphor for home, for safety and comfort, for desire and love. Women served by waiting—Mom in her apron at the stove, Betty in her bathing suit—for men to finish the fight and come home to them. The best way, the American way, for a woman to help the cause was to look and behave like a woman.

So when Brunetta Kuehlthau, a physical therapist assigned to Hospital #2, sent a letter to her mother, a letter she likely slipped to a pilot or officer on a boat running the blockade, it was not surprising to see the text of it in *The New York Times* under the headline: NURSE ON CORREGIDOR FINDS IT "NOT TOO BAD": LETTER SAYS HAIRPIN SHORTAGE CAUSES WOMEN TO CUT HAIR. "We are comparatively safe here," Kuehlthau wrote, a fiction of a different kind and for a different reason. "If we have to stay long food may be a problem but so far we have done very well. . . . Could bring very little [when evacuated]. . . . Did have the sense to bring the diamond bracelet and rings, but that is all in that line. . . . Finally had to have my hair cut. Impossible to buy hairpins. . . . Haven't had to work very hard. . . . Don't worry too much. Things are not too bad and I'm sure I'll get back safely."[14]

DURING THE FIRST week in February, five nurses were transferred from the tunnel fortress on Corregidor to Hospital #2 on Bataan, among them Ruth Straub.

[*Straub Diary, February 5, 1942*] This is a place of another world. The only covering is the sky. It is jungle land and everyone lives under the trees. Rows of beds snuggled under the trees with narrow winding paths between them and the night sky overhead. It is eerie and fantastic. I found a cot, no mattress, beside a brook, but not far from the latrine. Can look up from my cot and watch the moon and stars.

[*February 6*] They call this a Jungle hospital and it is. I am assigned to ward 17, a new 300 bed ward a mile away which we are to open. I walk there through sinuous paths. We take five grains of quinine a day as prophylaxis. Had carabao stew at supper. Couldn't eat it. O[h], O[h], it's bombing again.

[*February 7*] More bombing this morning. It seemed awfully close. I have taken a turn or two at chopping trees. The food is dreadful. Carabao, rice and tomatoes with hot tea, no cream. I have a bed now, a pleasant surprise. If I get a head shelter to keep the mosquitoes, moisture, and leaves out, I'll be all set.

[*February 8*] Two months since the war began. Rumor of the day: We're being evacuated to Australia. That is a joke. What will we sail in? Attended church services tonight at 5:30. Seats are made of bamboo. There is a little bamboo altar, and many of the boys sit on the ground. The preacher pointed out two foxholes to be used by the ladies and admonished the men to scatter about in case of bombing.

[*February 9*] Today I was transferred to a busy surgical ward up on the hill where the operating room was moved. At 12:15 P.M. several of our P-40's zoomed back and forth just above the treetops. A little later they opened their machine guns against Jap planes. We were terrified. I kept working to keep from thinking. The fighting was hot and heavy, we shot down five. Worked until 8 P.M.

[*February 10*] Started out early this morning doing dressings and kept at it until 3:40. I was so tired I could hardly stand. . . . Thought I was hungry tonight but I just can't swallow food. . . . No dogfighting today, thank goodness. The Japs are still trying to land troops on the west coast. . . . I have a real delicacy tonight, a doughnut. I fill my canteen with cold water and have a feast. . . . More of the nurses are coming down with malaria. Others have dysentery.

[*February 11*] They got us out of bed at sunrise. More dogfighting overhead. Our main danger—O[h], just as I was writing, the Japs dropped bombs nearby. Much more of this and we'll all be nervous wrecks. To continue, our main danger is shrapnel from our own anti-aircraft. Yesterday, a piece went through a mattress. Fortunately, the patient had just left his bed. . . . Here they come again. Whew! Where is all the bravery I thought I possessed.

[February 12] Jap planes flew low and bombed near here again. We ducked under patient beds, patients and all. What a helpless sensation. . . . Rations are to be cut again, but we had beef for supper. Rice, rice, rice . . . Didn't sleep again last night. A huge iguana kept prowling through the underbrush by my bed. Sounded like it might be a sniper. They are hideous things with tails, like a snake. The creaking of the bamboo adds to the weird atmosphere at night. . . . It's becoming very damp. Our clothes are sticky.

[February 13] Japs overhead about 11:30 bombing Cabcaben again. Many women and children killed, injured and burned. What will become of all of us? One soldier brought in a four-month-old Filipino baby. Both parents were killed during the bombing. . . . I am so hungry—rice, cold salmon, tomatoes. Couldn't eat any of it. Found a heel of bread and some jam.

[February 15] Am so tired and hungry I just scribble along. Surely help must be on its way, but when will it arrive?

[February 16] Another busy day. Don't feel badly until 1 P.M. when it gets hot. Washing hair at night and while it was frowzy with soap the Japs came back. Scared? We just huddled near a tree and sat. . . . Eight of us jumped into a small foxhole in a raid today and nearly killed each other. One of the cooks was shot through the head. . . . Rats are chewing up our clothes. Iguanas every night. Food progressively worse. More malaria. All in all, we are pretty low. . . . We nurses look very strange in our air corps dungarees. Mine are size 42. All of us have long hair now. We part it and tie it in two braids, fastening the braids with the flannel we found around the hospital. . . . Lately I have been having nightmares. I am always stealing heads of fresh lettuce from dead men.[15]

THE GENERALS IN Tokyo were angry. Their plan for the Philippines had called for total victory by the end of January, but General Homma was still stuck on Bataan. What is more, he had suffered massive casualties, seven thousand killed and wounded. And now he was calling for re-inforcements.

While Tokyo debated his request, there was a lull in the fighting, six weeks of relative quiet from mid-February until the end of March, and General MacArthur's staff used the lull to regroup.

Worried about the monsoon rains, Josie Nesbit got permission to transfer twelve 1926 and 1928 Dodge buses from a nearby motor pool to Hospital #2, where enlisted men removed the seats to create makeshift barracks, or "improvised apartments" as Nesbit dubbed them, space that allowed roughly half the nurses to get off the wet ground.[16]

Also during the lull Maude Davison came over from her command post on Corregidor to inspect the two jungle hospitals, but her visit ended abruptly. Walking the seventeen wards of Hospital #2—five difficult miles—exhausted the fifty-seven-year-old commander and aggravated her injured back. She saw enough, however, to convince her that the medical staff was overwhelmed and she transferred some additional women from the tunnel hospital on Corregidor.

Even during the lull, work in the jungle hospitals was long and hard. The weather was either hot and humid or just plain hot. Clouds of dust and whorls of dirt blew through the open wards, covering the beds and patients with grime. The nurses began the day by bathing the bedridden, then leading the ambulatory men to the river. Afterward they made their rounds, changing dressings and administering medications and treatments. Later they checked their stores and equipment, sharpening dulled needles on rocks, boiling glass syringes and dissolving morphine tablets in solution. In the afternoon they worked with men newly disabled, teaching amputees how to shave or guiding the blind on walks over the uneven jungle floor.

A few of the women volunteered for shifts in the prison ward, some five dozen cots encircled by barbed wire where captured Japanese were recuperating. It was the women's duty, of course, to minister to these men—medicine's oaths and ethics make no distinction between enemy and ally—but in truth it was more curiosity than duty that made them volunteer. They wanted to get a good look at the "sons of Nippon," the vaunted imperial troops that had been spilling so much American blood and causing the Allies so much suffering. To the women's surprise, many of the enemy were just boys, and when they spoke—a few knew English—they sounded just like the young Americans they had been trying so hard to kill. They too wanted to know about the latest movies; they too longed for the day they could go home.

As the lull wore on, everyone, medical staff and patients alike, discovered something new in their day: a bit of free time. One group of patients transformed a marshy area near their ward into a scenic rock garden. Another patient, obviously a comedian, took to hanging signs on the jungle trees. One read: FREE SHAVES FOR JAPS: NOT RESPONSIBLE FOR MISTAKES![17]

Some of the men caged a bit of cardboard and cut it into jigsaw puzzles and playing cards. Others made marbles for Chinese checkers out of plaster of Paris dyed violet with gentian and blue with methylene or took pennies and painted them red and black for checkers. Old Tarzan comic books were the literature of the day. And the patients who could manage it even tried playing a bit of baseball, volleyball and badminton on fields marked out in clearings.

A Red Cross official evacuated from Manila with the army started a two-page mimeographed newsletter, "The Jungle Journal." Written on a manual typewriter, the little sheet had an amateurish look, but the troops and the staff eagerly awaited each ribald issue.

FOXHOLE FORECASTS: Hottest rumors of the week. [A] B-19 flew over Japan and dropped a bomb in Fujiyama volcano and now there's 2 inches lava all over Japan! . . . [B] The U.S. Navy steamed toward Japan so fast that they created a tidal wave which completely swamped the island. Well, after all that the Japs can't help but lose.

BATAAN REPAIR SHOP

Come in for an overhaul.
We remove everything and anything. If you have any old tonsils, appendix or shrapnel, let us remove it. Reasonable prices.

Col. SCWARTZ, Shop Foreman

ROOMS FOR RENT

Newly built Nurses home. Beautiful location—overlooking Bataan river. Clean airy rooms with southern exposures. With or without bath. Meals extra.

Miss NESBIT, Landlady.[18]

At Hospital #2, Josie Nesbit converted her bamboo shack into a nurses recreation room, and at night the women gathered around her radio to listen to the Voice of Freedom transmission from Corregidor or the news broadcast from station KGEI in San Francisco.

With a coal-oil lantern casting a cheerless yellow glow, the group would sit in Nesbit's shed drinking cups of watered-down coffee, longing for news of the outside world. Sometimes the news cheered them, sometimes it brought a cruel reality to their door. In late January they learned that the convoy they had desperately been awaiting had been routed to Northern Ireland instead.[19] And in February they heard news of the Japanese conquests of nearby Java and Singapore.

Meanwhile at Hospital #1 in Little Baguio nurses and doctors delivered a baby—Victoria Bataana Sullivan, so named for her Irish-American father, her birthplace and the spirit of those fighting there—a healthy girl with big blue eyes. A few of the nurses scrounged a skein of twine and knit sweaters and booties and some of the Filipino patients wove the little girl a rattan bassinet. A birth amid all the suffering and death seemed to renew everyone. As a nurse carried the little girl through the wards to her mother for a feeding, the bedridden soldiers propped themselves up on their elbows to look at the child. Soon word of the delivery spread beyond the hospital, and it was not long before seasoned infantrymen were stopping by as well. Eventually mother and daughter left Hospital #1 for a refugee camp deep in the jungle. That afternoon the wards seemed more cheerless than they'd been in weeks.

The lull also gave all the nurses time to unwind. After three months of unremitting work; three months of gunshot and shrapnel wounds, malaria, dysentery, jungle fever, gangrene, concussions, infections, chronic illness and death; three months, in short, of living with the awful inventory of battle, the nurses needed a rest. And the men fighting in the field, eager for a woman's company, eager to be near an emblem of home, if only for a few moments, were only too happy to oblige them.

"There were a lot of spur-of-the-moment parties," Cassie said. "People would say, 'Come on up to such-and-such a location; we're gonna have a party.' At this one party I met a group of navy men who told me they were going to try to get to Australia by commandeering a PT [patrol-torpedo] boat. They even offered me a seat. Of course it meant going AWOL [absent without leave] and I wasn't ready to do that. I never found out what happened to those guys."[20]

A few days later an engineering officer asked Cassie if she wanted to take part in an unusual outing. "He was on a burial detail and he asked me to go with him to a couple of towns to pick up some of the bodies. We went through one little barrio that was really deserted and we decided to investigate. In one hut we found an old piano, an upright, and I sat down to play. But the keys wouldn't move so the engineer opened the lid. And you know what? Someone before evacuating had hidden their best dishes in there!"[21]

All the nurses had a standing invitation to dinner aboard the U.S.S. *Canopus,* the ship the navy had camouflaged to look derelict. The ruse had fooled Japanese pilots, and belowdecks the men secretly turned out weapons. Down there out of sight they were also hoarding a store of treasures taken from the Cavite naval base during the first week of the war. Their mess tables were covered with white linen, silver cutlery and navy china, and their galley was stocked with canned meats and vegetables. Hungry nurses eagerly accepted the captain's invitation to dine at his officers table, and the women marveled at the place settings and the sumptuous, by Bataan's standards, bill of fare. They also never forgot their dessert.

"When the Chaplain said good night," Juanita Redmond wrote, "he handed each of us a lollypop [*sic*]; we could hardly believe our eyes. The very word 'candy' belonged to a dead language."[22]

A motor transport battalion at Mariveles also invited the women to dinner. The men had bartered with the locals for meat, milk and coffee, then set up outdoor tables with tin plates and handprinted menus bearing the message WELCOME TO THE VICTORY HOTEL. After dinner, the nurses sat back and enjoyed an old-fashioned musical revue staged by Filipino singers and performers.

Birthdays were always a great excuse for a party, and when Cassie turned twenty-five in late January, she dug out a bottle of Johnny Walker Red she had been hoarding, unscrewed the cap and threw herself and her friends at Hospital #1 in Little Baguio a celebration.

Sometimes in the evening the male doctors and medics at the hospitals would tack old army blankets over a bamboo floor, crank up a vintage phonograph and create an ad hoc dance hall. A few of the nurses still had a dress or two in their wardrobe, and they would put on makeup, from what was left, slip on a pair of mended socks and, in the arms of a doctor, glide over the tightly stretched blankets, pretending all the while that they were back in Manila dancing under the peacetime stars.

One morning during the lull, a group of nurses and doctors from Hospital #1 packed up some caraboa sandwiches and lime juice, piled into a couple of trucks and headed for Manila Bay where they parked on a bluff, changed clothes in the underbrush and walked down a footpath to a pretty little cove with a white sand beach. From their vantage point they could see Japanese planes bombing Corregidor across the bay, but the war did not spoil their mood. They swam in the blue water and lazed on the beach. (One woman had fashioned a makeshift bathing suit out of a white-and-red flannel bedspread, and as she emerged from the water she quickly discovered, to the delight of her male companions, that when flannel gets wet it is practically transparent.) One of the doctors offered to teach the nurses to swim, but a few of the women thought that his lessons "looked more like Swedish massage" than swimming instruction.[23] But no one put up a fuss. With war all around, there was a sense of carpe diem in the air, a feeling that everyone should make every moment count.

And so during those quiet days no one was surprised when three couples announced they wanted to get married. It did not matter that the military expelled women who wed—there was nowhere for them to go and no way for them to get there—and it did not matter that the brides sometimes stood before the chaplain in combat boots instead of wedding slippers. Marriage represented a beginning in a place where most people were thinking only of the end.

Nurse Rita Palmer of Hampton, New Hampshire, married navy Lieutenant Edwin Nelson of Huntington, West Virginia (her wedding band was a jade ring the groom had bought in Hong Kong for his mother); dental nurse Earleen Allen of Chicago, Illinois, married dentist Garnet Francis; and on February 19, 1942, ward nurse Dorothea Mae Daley married an artillery officer, Emanuel "Boots" Engel, Jr., of New Orleans, Louisiana.

Daley and Engel had long been lovers. They became engaged in the fall of 1941, then when war broke out, events separated them. In early January, Captain Engel, who was assigned to a beach defense unit at Mariveles, got word that his fiancée was in Hospital #1, roughly twenty miles away, and he quickly hitchhiked north to find her. When Daley set eyes on her man, she nearly swooned.

> We were both in khaki, tired and discouraged, feeling like trapped animals, yet when his arms were around me I felt as if the reality of war was merely a nightmare. . . . When he did find me in the midst of that living hell it gave me the conviction that always he would find me.
>
> Boots hitched a ride to see me as often as possible, and during January and part of February we were as happy as an engaged couple can be who are fighting a losing war. Perhaps we appreciated those moments more because they were so rare and unexpected. . . .
>
> Boots had decided we would be married while we were still together on Bataan. We are both Catholics, and we consulted with several chaplains as to how a ceremony could be performed on a jungle battlefield. Father

William Thomas Cummings, who had been director of a boys' school in
civilian life, agreed to perform the ceremony. He said that in the presence
of death he would give us the spiritual blessing that he knew we wanted.

And on February 19, I, Dorothea Mae Daley, took Emanuel Engel Jr.,
to be my wedded husband, for better, for worse, in sickness or in health, till
death do us part. Everybody in the wedding party, including the bride, was
in khaki. I had covered my khaki pants with a khaki skirt which one of the
nurses had concocted and which she loaned to me for my wedding night.

There was no ring, no license, no bouquet, no veil, no Mass. It was
Lent, a season during which Catholics are forbidden to wed. The chaplain
had no time to get a license to marry in the Philippines. Sounds of bombs
were in the distance, and my feet, encased in huge army boots, felt awkward
as I stood in an army hospital, the like of which had never been seen before.
Two male witnesses heard us exchange vows. But there was a solemnity and
a sacredness about the ceremony, performed in the midst of so much tragedy,
that made us both feel that ours was no ordinary marriage.[24]

B Y ALL AVAILABLE accounts the presence of women on the battlefield
boosted the morale of the men. And the more the men watched the
women suffer war's deprivations and danger, the more determined they
were to carry the fight.

In a memoir composed after the war, surgeon John R. Bumgarner
was convinced that

One of the most remarkable things coming out of our experience in Bataan
was the presence and performance of the army nurses. In retrospect I believe
that they were the greatest morale boost present in that unhappy little area
of jungle called Bataan. I was continually amazed that anyone living and
working under such primitive conditions could remain as calm, pleasant,
efficient and impeccably neat and clean as those remarkable nurses.

. . . Some of the men in the combat area who had a moment of quietness
would steal away to the hospital to spend a short while in the company of a
woman. Often in the evening hours Jack [his barracks-mate] and I would
hear girlish giggles coming across the Real River from the burlap confines [of
the nurses quarters] accompanied by male voices speaking in low tones. . . .

In my mind, however, and in the minds of others, there lurked the fear
that we would be unable to protect the nurses should the Japanese combat
troops overrun the hospital. We had all heard the stories out of China
about the atrocities committed against the female population of Nanking

[the so-called Rape of Nanking]. Even today, in spite of all the efforts to maintain that women properly belong in combat situations, I must admit that the thought of placing women in the front lines in a situation such as existed in Bataan offends me. There is something ingrained and inbred in man, though he may laugh at the idea, which persuades him that he is the protector.[25]

Maybe it was the false security of the lull or maybe just the natural tendency of human beings, as well-known sociobiologist Edward O. Wilson might argue, to be born enthusiastic and full of hope—whatever it was, many, many of the men and women fighting on Bataan believed they would be rescued.

Some of the nurses took to greeting one another with a refrain popular among the patients: "Don't save for tomorrow. . . . We may be out of here!"[26] The staff started an informal betting pool, with wagers of scotch (to be paid when they were safely repatriated), on the hour and day the relief convoy would arrive. A few people took turns climbing a pine tree in the middle of Little Baguio to scan the horizon for a mast or a hull. At Hospital #2 a few of the nurses hiked up a hill every morning, looking for the same thing.

Of course there were never any sightings because there were never any ships. "It sounds ludicrous," Cassie wrote, "these rumors, these optimisms, these assurances . . . but at the time they helped us to live. I cannot, indeed, imagine how long we should have succeeded living without them."[27] Helen Summers of Queens, New York, wrote a song reflecting the fantasy of hope that sustained them.

A.N.C. [Army Nurse Corps] ON BATAAN
[Sung to the strains of the "Missouri Waltz"]

When we were in Bataan, in the good old ANC
We ate twice a day and drank diluted ginger tea.
We sweat out the chow line, after a day's grind
And caraboa stew was our daily menu.

Sitting on a rock and bathing in a babbling brook
Is not the kind of life by choice we would have took
But for the duration
We'll pretend it's a vacation
And see it through.[28]

Meanwhile at night in her little book, Ruth Straub carefully recorded the details of the nurses' difficult days.

[*Straub Diary, February 18*] Ash Wednesday [beginning of Lent] Whenever two or more people gather, there is talk of food. Corned beef, rice and tea for breakfast. Salmon or Carabao (water buffalo), tomatoes, rice and tea for supper.

[*February 19*] The men now are picking up cigaret [*sic*] butts and smoking them in little holders made of bamboo twigs or rewrapping the tobacco in newspaper.

[*February 25*] We ran into a huge cobra tonight. It was ready to spring when one of the fellows shot at it. . . . Latest fantastic rumor: we may go to Siberia. . . . The Japs are dropping propaganda leaflets telling the Filipinos to surrender and making all sorts of promises to them. . . . Had [mango] beans—sickly looking green pellets—and macaroni and an incredible thing, custard for supper.

[*February 26*] A rat got into the bed of Rita Palmer and bit her. . . . Wrote notes [home]. Wonder if they'll ever get to the States. We have had no mail since we left Manila.

[*February 28*] Rumor of the day: Santa Barbara Cal. has been bombed. Latest story, radiogram we sent to the commanding officer of the Ninth Corps area—"If you hold out 30 days we'll send reinforcements" . . . Almost three months now since we heard that same promise.

[*March 3*] We should rename our ward "medical dump." In addition to our surgical cases, 20 new medical cases including tuberculosis, malaria, dysentery, and asthenia were dumped on us. . . . We have to sign in and out and [state our] destination now when leaving the hospital area.

[*March 4*] Hotter every day. Rats more numerous. More snakes have been killed in the vicinity. Flies are here in droves.

[*March 5*] I guess we are self-imposed prisoners-of-war. All we're doing is protecting our own lives. Almost three months now and help has not arrived.

[*March 8*] Rain drenched the beds and all our things under the trees this afternoon. Now it is sticky. . . . Cases of malaria increase day by day. . . . Several new rumors: One that a convoy has arrived; the second, that our fleet is waging a fight with the Japs somewhere between Guam and the Philippines. . . . Our quinine is running low. Wonder how much longer we'll be able to carry on.

[*March 11*] The song "The Old Gray Mare" keeps buzzing through my head. We had horse meat for supper.

[*March 12*] The food is becoming worse. Caraboa stew. . . . Last night a group of us got together and had coffee and toast.

[*March 14*] Malaria continues to claim the nurse corps. . . . We carry kerosene lamps painted blue through the wards at night.

[*March 15*] Found worms in my oatmeal this morning. I shouldn't have objected because they had been sterilized in the cooking and I was getting fresh meat with my breakfast. . . . I'm still losing weight and so are most of us. . . . I only have two pieces of underwear left. . . . Drugs are rapidly being used up. No new supplies have arrived. We need quinine terribly.[29]

Chapter 6

"There Must Be No Thought of Surrender"

*E*VEN IN PEACETIME when its ranks are filled with self-selecting volunteers, the military still serves as a kind of mirror of American society. Here in uniform are all kinds—the emotive pessimist (someone like Ruth Straub wearing her heart on her sleeve), the stoic (a Maude Davison, as unemotional as her male counterparts, focused only on the job at hand), the sentimentalist (Dorothea Mae Daley, swept up as much in the melodrama of war as its actuality), and the clear-eyed realist, impatient with daydreams and self-delusions, a woman like Eleanor Garen.

Single-minded and smart, Garen was an avid reader who understood the basics of politics, interservice rivalries and the hard choices that resulted from fighting in a two-front war. For months before Pearl Harbor Garen had been studying articles on foreign policy and the tenuous American position in the Far East. She knew that her country had been grossly unprepared for war and now would never be able to mount a rescue.

After the fall of Manila, Garen was assigned to the tunnel hospital on Corregidor where, almost every day, she and her fellow nurses received reports about the plight of their sisters on Bataan. When Maude Davison asked the women on Corregidor to help at the overburdened field hospitals across the bay, Garen immediately volunteered.

She landed on Bataan the first week in February, and when she saw the thousands of sick and wounded patients out in the open at Hospital #2, she knew she was right—the end was inevitable.

She kept her opinions to herself, of course—she was no Cassandra—pasted a smile on her face and set to work. But in a letter home that first week in February, it was easy to read between the lines and discover her true mind, easy, in fact, to feel her worry.

Feb. 7, 1942

Dear Lauretta and Bill [her sister and brother-in-law]:

Write Mother and tell her I am fine. In fact I am in the best of health with all this fresh air, sunshine and plain wholesome diet. Although we can't go swimming yet we have a marvelous creek in which to bathe. However I do sleep under a mosquito net but as yet I haven't found a mosquito. . . . Please check with Mother about my car, whether the sale of it will pay off all my insurances, annuity and the Metropolitan Life. Have made my allotment out to you so if more money is needed for the insurance use it, otherwise bank it for me to have when I come back. Unless Mother needs it. . . . For goodness sake don't feel sorry for me or worry. I'll do OK by the Garens . . . if needs be.

Love to all
Eleanor[1]

A plain woman, roughly five feet seven inches with a round face and big blue eyes, Eleanor Garen was born March 7, 1909, in Elkhart, Indiana. She had three brothers, Dana, Reese and Paul, and one sister, Lauretta.

Eleanor was the brightest and most adventurous of the Garens. She learned to read early and became such a bookworm she would fill up her own library card, then take out books on her brothers' accounts. She loved to read history and was so good at Latin that her classmates pushed her forward to recite the day's declensions and conjugations while they sat secretly trying to catch up.

Outside of school she was a tomboy who liked to play baseball and fish for trout and bass on Lake Wawasee. Her brothers were her pals, and the four of them were usually in trouble. Once they tried to dig a swimming pool in the backyard. When that failed they took it into their heads to become parachutists and were perched in the family cherry tree with umbrellas, ready to leap into the void, when their father rushed out to stop them.

John Garen worked for the railroad and Lulu Garen ran a restaurant and boardinghouse. Sometimes Eleanor would help her mother and soon became friendly with the waitresses and chambermaids. These women, mostly working class, talked often and freely of their lives—lives dominated by hard work, too many children and drunken husbands with heavy hands. Their utter dependency and their red welts and bruises left young Eleanor determined to lead an autonomous life. She wanted to be a nurse, self-possessed and, above all, self-reliant.

After she graduated from Chicago's Wesley Hospital School of Nursing in 1931, she enrolled part-time as an undergraduate at the University of Chicago while she worked as a nurse in the university clinics. At first she saved her money to buy a car, but all that reading across all those years had given her an incurable case of wanderlust, and she set out for Europe to attend the International Council for Nurses convention in London. When she got home, she bought her car, but the payments, along with other bills, left her in debt. So in January 1941, hoping for a higher salary and another ticket overseas, she joined the Army Nurse Corps.

Her first post was Fort Benning, Georgia, where she worked in a surgical ward and tried to pay off some of her obligations.

July 29, 1941

Dear Mother,

Well, here it is the first of the month again and as usual I am broke and need help. Don't you get tired of me bothering you? . . . Perhaps it may be the last time if this situation goes on into war. . . . Never again will I buy a car on time. . . . I believe I have learned my lesson and never again . . . will I incurr [sic] any more debts.

Have been swimming in the officers swimming pool. It is swell. In fact I have been so busy doing things I haven't had time to think. This one Major that I met is lots of fun and for the last 2 weeks he had been taking me to dinner every night. . . . Last week we drove 90 miles just to go swimming in a natural spring and to have dinner in another place.

You must think that I am doing a lot of running around but then the truth is that I never know but what some day there will be orders for me and I will have to sweat it out at some hot army post in South America. Or there is the Philippines also and I would not be surprised to find myself there some day in the future. I don't mean to alarm you but . . . you read the paper more than I do . . . so you know the situation.

I will write to you when I [am transferred] to [Camp Livingston, Louisiana]. Don't worry, for it is too late now unless you want to go insane. We are in for some trouble with Japan.

> *Your daughter*
> *Eleanor*

A short time later she got the news that one of her colleagues at the hospital had been injured in a riding accident and that Eleanor was to take her assignment—in Manila.

On October 4, 1941, Garen boarded the U.S.S. *Holbrooke* in San Francisco to set sail for Manila Bay.

Dear Mother,

Well today is the day of sailing. We are leaving at noon. . . . I will write you my next letter from Hawaii. There are to be two ships going to the Philippines with over 20 nurses and many troop[s]. Give my love to all.

The voyage was filled with rumors of war, but most of her shipmates soon discounted such talk. Japan would never challenge American might, they said. The United States had won the Great War and overcome the Great Depression. Certainly they could face down a small island nation with its ancient codes and backward ways. For her part, Eleanor was preoccupied by the adventure ahead, the excitement of a new and exotic place.

> *Oct. 25, 1941*

Dear Mother,

Well the ships made it into the Manila Bay and we docked about 7 P.M. on Thursday. The weather is warm and the . . . streets dirty. Cabs cost only 5 cents and 10 cents for a ride. Clothes are about the same price.

> *Love*
> *Eleanor*[2]

Then came war and in early February 1942 Eleanor Garen found herself in the middle of a sprawling jungle hospital.

She worked nights, in charge of Ward 14—some three hundred patients with tropical diseases.

During the lull she passed her off-duty hours sitting on a wooden box with her back against a tree at the crossroads between the nurses' latrine and the creek where they bathed.

She was popular with her colleagues, a cheerful woman who wore her brown pigtails tied with red ribbons, so happy-go-lucky, they said. She watered the flowers that grew outside the nurses quarters, or liked to stand around the stove in the shed drinking coffee and chatting with her bunkmates.

What she knew of politics and foreign policy she kept to herself, choosing to mask her concern with cheerfulness, her intelligence with small talk. Years later she told an interviewer that more than anything else, she wanted to be part of the group, and in the way women sometimes have with one another, she played the part of the cooperative optimist and kept her doubts and growing melancholy to herself.

THE JAPANESE WERE well aware of the shortages in the allied ranks and the deteriorating condition of the American and Filipino army. Japanese intelligence officers knew that MacArthur's troops could barely hold their positions at the lower end of the peninsula. Captured GI's revealed that they were down to one solid meal a day, and Japanese patrols spotted American soldiers foraging for carabao, bananas, rice—anything to eat.[3]

Meanwhile General Homma's army grew stronger and stronger. Fresh troops from Shanghai, new squadrons of planes and artillery pieces from Japan had reached the Japanese 14th Army that spring. And now they were ready to renew their attack. A quartermaster officer on Corregidor, sensing the peril, warily looked across the two-mile channel at Bataan and wrote in his diary, "It looks like something may happen over there. It's been too damn quiet to be comfortable."[4]

By March malaria was epidemic. (On March 9 alone, 290 malaria patients were admitted to one of the field hospitals.) Stocks of quinine were low, and with the food ration reduced to less than one thousand calories a day, malarial patients had tremendous difficulty fighting the disease. Hundreds of men with dysentery and nutritional edemas showed up every day for treatment. The staff began to notice that the soldiers' muscle tissue was shrinking and atrophying, a sign of severe protein loss.

The desperate battle in the Philippines captured the country's attention. After Pearl Harbor, America needed a victory, or at least evidence that the country could mount a decent defense. And that fight was being waged on Bataan.

Life and *Newsweek* magazines carried headlines declaring, STILL HOLDING and BATTERED BATAAN. The editors of the *Saturday Review* published a ringing tribute to the beleaguered force.

> *Bataan! The world is but an island.*
> *This the brave knew . . .*
> *They fought and fell, not for our promises,*
> *Not for victory, but for the day*
> *That would give the future, and kill the enemy.*[5]

MacArthur turned out his own brand of propaganda, trying to convince his troops all was not lost:

10 March 1942

. . . All elements of the Philippine Department, operating under conditions that imposed the utmost hardship upon officers and men, under continuous aerial bombardment, performed prodigies far beyond reasonable expectations, in the execution of its mission . . . making possible the magnificent resistance of the I and II Philippine Corps on the battle positions.

By Command of General MacArthur[6]

Nevertheless a kind of fatalism crept into the ranks. Even Josie Nesbit, who fussed and brooded about every nurse and every patient in the seventeen wards under her charge, remembered a moment in March when she accepted the inevitable. Quit worrying! she told herself. Just accept what comes.[7]

In the late evening of March 11, a day after his communiqué exhorting his troops to keep up the fight, General MacArthur, along with his wife, Jean, their son, Arthur, and the boy's Cantonese amah boarded patrol torpedo boat 41 at Corregidor's north dock and, along with other key members of MacArthur's staff, began their escape to Australia.

The general had been ordered off the rock by Washington, but many felt he could have refused his orders and stayed with his command. On March 18 *The New York Times* announced the news with the headline: MACARTHUR IN AUSTRALIA AS ALLIED COMMANDER; MOVE HAILED AS FORE- SHADOWING TURN OF TIDE.[8]

In fact there were those on Bataan, some nurses among them, who believed that MacArthur would now be able to rally Washington policy makers and the War Department to the cause of saving the Philippines. But, for the most part, the brave defenders of Bataan and Corregidor felt betrayed. "We were just about as down as we could get when MacArthur left," said Ann Mealor, the assistant chief nurse in Corregi- dor's Malinta Tunnel.[9]

One soldier, whose name has long since been lost to history, coined the phrase "Dugout Doug" and offered some new lyrics to the melody of "The Battle Hymn of the Republic":

> *Dugout Doug's not timid,*
> *He's just cautious, not afraid.*
> *He's carefully protecting*
> *The stars that Franklin made.*
> *Four-star generals are as rare as good food on Bataan*
> *And his troops go starving on.*[10]

MacArthur's successor, General Jonathan "Skinny" Wainwright, as- sumed command of the sixty thousand troops on Bataan, then quickly estimated that their combat efficiency was less than 20 percent. Wain- wright also guessed that facing him were 250,000 well-fed, well- equipped, well-supported Japanese infantry.

The nurses, doctors and fighting men admired Skinny Wainwright, an angular man who always wore a red kerchief tied around his neck and always seemed to have time for his troops. Before he left Bataan for the main command post on Corregidor, he visited the field hospitals and tried to raise the spirits of the nurses and their patients. Later he spoke to the entire army:

March 22, 1942

To all American and Filipino Troops in the Philippines
  . . . I am proud to have been given this opportunity to lead
you, whose gallantry and heroism have been demonstrated on

the field of battle and who have won the admiration of the world. We are fighting for a just cause and victory shall be ours. I pledge the best that is in me to the defense of the Philippines. Assisted by your courage and by your loyalty we shall expel the invader from Philippine soil.

> J. M. *Wainwright*
> Commanding General[11]

On March 18, the same day word reached the Philippines that MacArthur had arrived safely in Australia, thousands of tomato-sized cans tied with red and white ribbons fell from the sky onto Bataan and Corregidor.

At first, the allies thought the cans were a new trick explosive and poked and prodded them with sticks. As it turned out each can held a neatly folded note. One enlisted man looked at the contents and quipped that the troops had finally received some mail.

[To] His Excellency Major Jonathan Wainwright:

We have the honor to address you in accordance with Bushido— the code of the Japanese warrior. . . . You have already fought to the best of your ability. What dishonor is there in following the example of the defenders of Hong Kong, Singapore, and the Netherlands East India. . . . Your duty had been performed. Accept our sincere advice and save the lives of those officers and men under your command. . . . if a reply to this advisory note is not received . . . by noon March 22, 1942 we shall consider ourselves at liberty to take any action whatsoever.[12]

Homma had already moved his reinforced troops into the front line and now Japanese warships appeared on the horizon. Shortly after noon on March 22, the bombers reappeared, the warships began a barrage and the Imperial Army attacked. The lull was over.

Whole areas of Bataan were leveled and the field hospitals were overwhelmed with casualties. Now most of the nurses worked from daybreak till dark, stacking patients on triple-tiered bamboo bunks in the wards. When these ran short, a blanket on the jungle floor became a man's hospital bed. One evening Sally Blaine happened to look around her ward and, as if for the first time, noticed that there were patients lying everywhere, so many it reminded her of the railway panorama in *Gone With the Wind,* thousands of sick and bleeding men spread out on the ground in the jungle as far as the eye could see.

Supplies were critically short. An average ward of three hundred patients shared six medicine glasses, fifteen thermometers and a single teaspoon. The nurses were so busy they changed only the most bloody and foul of dressings. They stopped taking routine temperatures. A man literally had to shake with fever to draw their attention and treatment. In the operating room, nurse-anesthetists administered only minimal amounts of anesthetics and muscle relaxants, trying to husband their ether until the very last moment before the surgeon lowered his scalpel.

By late March, Hospital #1 at Little Baguio had grown to 1,500 patients, Hospital #2 to more than 3,000. Caring for this huge population were 67 officers, 83 nurses, 250 enlisted men and 200 civilian employees. (The civilians came from refugee camps located just outside the hospital.)

The Bataan doctors and nurses pleaded with their commanders on Corregidor for help. The rainy season, just six weeks away, would bring with it a whole new set of illnesses, pneumonia among them. Doctors at Hospital #2 estimated that they would need five thousand beds to house everyone. How would they feed these people? Keep the drinking water safe? Collect and dispose of garbage?

Colonel Wibb Cooper, the chief medical officer, could only listen and sympathize. Along with the other commanders at the USAFFE headquarters in Malinta Tunnel on Corregidor, he knew that attrition from hunger and disease would soon leave the allied fighting force defenseless.

In the admitting wards of the hospitals, men were arriving barefoot, dressed in rags and limping from foot drop, a classic sign of malnutrition. Even the youngest and most able were faltering. Their skin hung loosely from their bones, they had no muscle mass, their gums bled, their faces were puffy, their hands numb. The wounded wanted food, not treatment for their wounds. They surrendered their rifles and begged for something to eat.

On Thursday, March 26, as the assault continued and as his troops wasted away, General MacArthur, safely in Australia, received the Congressional Medal of Honor from the U.S. minister there. General Wainwright, learning of the news, radioed his congratulations from Corregidor, even as the bombs were falling on top of him. He also reported on the desperate state of his supplies.

Surveying his losses and the mounting casualties, Wainwright was forced to order limited access to the Bataan field hospitals. Henceforth only men who could not get the necessary treatment at medical aid stations on the combat line, or those who needed long hospitalization and were unlikely to return to duty, would be allowed a hospital bed—or a spot on the jungle floor. The others would have to survive on first aid.

Skinny Wainwright and his staff knew well that soon the Japanese would wear them down. For all practical purposes, they had been abandoned by their country, their supreme commander fleeing to safety. They fought on, in part because there was still plenty of fight in them and because they simply had no choice.

"The Defenders of Bataan," as the War Department called them in all its public communiqués, stood in sharp contrast to the "victims" of Pearl Harbor and the quick devastating defeat the country suffered that December Sunday. The ability of the Defenders "to hold the line" (another War Department phrase) against an overwhelming force was offered as an example of American valor. Wrote Hanson Baldwin of *The New York Times,*

> These men of Bataan have done their country valiant service . . . service far greater than that which can be counted merely in military terms. . . . On Bataan they redeemed the American soul. There had been doubt: our men were soft, it had been said. It may have been so. But not on Bataan. . . . They found and they proved that courage does not die and that the American soldier need yield to no man.[13]

BY NOW THE nurses were as seasoned and weathered as any front-line trooper. They too had struggled to survive on less-than-survival rations. They too were tired and weary from a long day's fight. They worked through fever and through chills, through the heat and the driving rain. Most of all, they had learned to live with death.

The battlefield philosopher John Glenn Gray has written that combatants often become so accustomed to death, they soon lose their fear of it: "As a consequence of temperament and experience, some soldiers can learn to regard death as an anticipated experience among other experiences, something they plan to accept when the time comes for what it is."[14]

The surgical staffs began witnessing ghastly sights. Outside their tents were piles of shrapnel removed from bodies. Anesthetists, now without nitrous oxide, sodium Pentothal or curare, were putting men to sleep with ether, a drug that filled the operating room with an eerily sweet odor. Toward the end of one long workday, a surgeon was removing shrapnel from a belly wound when an eight-inch worm crawled from the patient's stomach. Some on the surgical team thought it was going to hiss.

At the end of March quartermasters shot the last cavalry horse, and the troops began to forage along their own lines. At Hospital #2, a monkey adopted by a number of people as a pet—Tojo, they called him, after the notorious Japanese militarist—mysteriously disappeared and everyone suspected he'd become someone's dinner. Food was so much on everyone's mind, the chief nurses at both hospitals gathered their staffs to discuss the situation. With bombers constantly overhead, they explained, no supplies could get through. "We've got to make what we have last," Edith Shacklette told her nurses at Hospital #1. "If necessary we'll have one meal every two days. I know you won't complain."[15] At Hospital #2 Josie Nesbit said simply, "Look, all of us are starving."[16]

The night shift no longer got sandwiches and tea when it reported for work, so Eleanor Garen and a friend who shared night duty began to save crusts from their breakfast bread. Each night they arranged to take their work breaks together so they could toast their crusts over a small fire built in a hollow. Nothing, Garen thought, exposed the false glory of war more than a stale crust of bread.

No one talked about a relief convoy anymore. Optimists became realists, realists pessimists. "I put my cards on the table," Cassie said. "We were losing on Bataan. There was no convoy. We were indeed expendable. You'd have to be pretty dumb not to know that this was it, buddy."[17]

One day when flak started flying through the trees, Sally Blaine threw herself on the ground. When she looked up at the bed nearest her, she saw a sergeant who had earlier lost both his legs. I'm a coward to protect myself and not him, she thought, and thereafter when among her charges she never again took cover.[18]

The battle reminded Ruth Straub of Christ's forty days in the wilderness "because by that time I had been in the jungle for more than 40 days."

[*Straub Diary, March 23*] Japs active again today. Formation of nine planes flew back and forth about eight times. With planes overhead and shrapnel flying with such terrible force, there comes a fright I cannot express in words. . . .

[*March 27*] Patients are being admitted in droves, all medical cases. Had to clear another section of the jungle for beds. Casualties of the day's bombing are still coming in, and the operating room staff has been called back to work.

[*March 29, Palm Sunday*] Radio Tokio [*sic*] announced that the relief convoy was sighted and several boats sunk. More propaganda . . . Many of the girls have taken to their beds.

[*March 30*] Many good rumors today: Radio Tokyo announced 27 ships of our 80 ship convoy had been sunk. Perhaps our convoy really is on its way. . . . Hit one Jap Plane. Shouts of cheer. Pathetic, isn't it, to cheer another's tragedy and death?[19]

Some of the nurses found solace in religion. They carried their Bibles to work and on breaks read and re-read their favorite passages. At the chapel at Hospital #2 a group of staff calling itself the Church of All Faiths gathered for services.

No one talked much about their families anymore. Some people wrote letters but now nothing was getting through the blockade. On her twenty-sixth birthday, Leona Gastinger walked down to the creek to cool off while she jotted a note to her mother but she ended up just sitting at water's edge, sobbing instead.

Sometimes the gloom would break. A new joke might make the rounds, or someone would remember a funny song. One evening a pilot returning from a rare supply flight to the southern Philippine Islands delivered a belated Christmas package to Edith Shacklette at Hospital #1. News of the parcel spread quickly, and a crowd gathered to watch Shack tear off the wrapping. What was inside? they asked one another. Cookies, perhaps? Canned peaches? Shack opened the box. On top were layers of tissue paper. Slowly she peeled back the layers. People were on their tiptoes trying to see. And all at once the whispers gave way to a roar of laughter, for there in the bottom of the box was . . . a straw bonnet, an absurd black straw bonnet with a veil. Shack just smiled. She carefully removed the hat from the box, twirled it on her finger, and, with a great show of vanity, set it very carefully upon her head, then the five-foot four-inch blonde in soiled coveralls and heavy army boots vamped around the compound as her comrades howled with delight.

The bonnet reminded the nurses that Easter was only a few weeks away and Imogene "Jeanne" Kennedy of Philadelphia, Mississippi, and Helen Summers of Queens, New York, sat down to write some new lyrics to the "Easter Parade."

> *This year's Easter bonnet*
> *Is an army helmet—darn it!*
> *With olive paint and chin straps*
> *They won't give us the eye*
>
> *With all the dust upon it*
> *We surely hate to don it*
> *But we won't be self-conscious*
> *At the Easter Parade*[20]

ON MONDAY, MARCH 30, the staff at Hospital #1 in Little Baguio were busy caring for their patients when Japanese pilots took direct aim at them and let go their bombs.

The whiz of the falling bombs sounded exactly like the sharp, high-pitched grind of axles and gears made by trucks that climbed the steep, zigzag road on the hill behind the hospital, and so the doctors and nurses showed no alarm. Then the incendiary and high-explosive missiles found their target.

Most of the bombs landed just outside the hospital, spraying the wards with shrapnel and destroying the officers quarters and mess hall, the headquarters tent and the main operating room. Twenty-three people were killed and seventy-eight injured, most of them Filipino workers. American commanders, Colonel Duckworth among them, were convinced the bombings were accidental, a mistake by green Japanese pilots.[21] But the violation of such a neutral site infuriated almost everyone, including General Wainwright:

It was so shocking it made one cry with rage and want to wade in and simply throw fists at the perpetrators. The smooth-voiced Japanese announcer who came on the Manila radio on March

31 to say that the raid was "unintentional" added no balm to the dead and the rewounded.[22]

A week later, however, the bombers returned to the same spot and, unintentional or not, this time their deadly payloads fell directly on the large red cross in the yard.

Nurse Juanita Redmond, a young beauty from Swansea, South Carolina, could barely contain her terror:

This time they scored a direct hit on the wards. A thousand-pound bomb pulverized the bamboo sheds, smashed the tin roofs into flying pieces; iron beds doubled and broke jaggedly like paper matches. Sergeant May had pulled me under a desk, but the desk was blown in the air, he and I with it.

I heard myself gasping. My eyes were being gouged out of their sockets, my whole body was swollen and torn apart by the violent pressure. This is the end, I thought.

Then I fell back to the floor, the desk landing on top of me and bouncing around drunkenly. Sergeant May knocked it away from me, and gasping for breath, bruised and aching, sick from swallowing the smoke of the explosive, I dragged myself to my feet. I heard Freeman, a boy with no legs, calling out: "Where's Miss Redmond? Is Miss Redmond alive?"

Father Cummins said calmly: "Somebody take over. I'm wounded." He had shrapnel in his shoulder.

Only one small section of my ward remained standing. Part of the roof had been blown into the jungle. There were mangled bodies under the ruins; a blood-stained hand stuck up through a pile of scrap; arms and legs had been ripped off and flung among the rubbish. Some of the mangled torsos were almost impossible to identify. One of the few corpsmen who had survived unhurt climbed a tree to bring down a body blown into the top branches. Blankets, mattresses, pajama tops hung in the shattered trees.

We worked wildly to get to the men who might be buried, still alive, under the mass of wreckage, tearing apart the smashed beds to reach the wounded and the dead. . . .

The bombing had stopped, but the air was rent by the awful screams of the new-wounded and the dying. Trees were still crashing in the jungle and when one nearby fell on the remaining segment of tin roof it sounded like shellfire. . . .

I saw Rosemary Hogan being helped from her ward. Blood streamed from her face and her shoulder; she looked ghastly.

"Hogan," I called, "Hogan, is it bad?"

She managed to wave her good arm at me. "Just a little nose bleed," she said cheerfully. . . . "How about you?"

. . . Then Rita Palmer [from Hampton, New Hampshire] was taken from her ward. Her face and arms had been cut and her skirt and G.I. shirt had been blown [open]. . . .[23]

In fact, Rita Palmer had more than a few cuts. "I remember coming to and having long beams of the roof over me and struggling out from under those," she said. "I have no idea how long I was knocked out. I could breathe all right, but one finger of one hand was incapacitated. I didn't even know about the piece [of shrapnel] in my chest for several hours. It didn't penetrate my lung. I had shrapnel in my legs too."

Nearby Cassie, off duty, had taken cover by a tree near the nurses quarters: "A chunk of shrapnel came whistling by and took a hunk out of that tree. [Then she caught sight of Palmer.] I was relieved to see that she was alive, then I noticed her clothes and I thought it was funny to see her running around with her skirt hanging by the buttons."

The ten bombs that fell on Hospital #1 killed seventy-three people instantly and injured 117 others, the three nurses among them.

By now the Japanese had broken through the front lines and were preparing for a final attack. Even though it was clear to everyone—including the War Department—that Wainwright and his emaciated garrisons could not defend themselves against another push, General MacArthur radioed from his offices in Australia, "There must be no thought of surrender."[24]

[*Straub Diary, April 7*] Our line had broken. . . . The 31st had been forced to retreat. How serious the situation is we do not know. Morale is very low tonight.

[*April 8*] Heard a wonderful rumor a few minutes ago. Our convoy with three airplane carriers is 24 hours from here. Almost unbelievable, oh, how wonderful, if true! . . . This serial bombardment is wearing and nerve racking. . . . It is getting dark again and now we will sit under the trees and talk about what tomorrow will bring.[25]

Now the nurses focused on one task—keeping themselves and their patients alive. The women who worked in the admitting wards noticed that in those last desperate days, the wounded came into the hospital wide-eyed with dread.

The women could hear the sound of small-arms fire nearby in the jungle. Meanwhile the enemy had captured Mount Samat in the middle of the peninsula. The Japanese were ready to drive south now, and Hospital #2, with its seven thousand sick, bleeding and mangled patients, was directly in the enemy's path.

Major General Edward King, the senior American officer on Bataan, ordered all allied artillery pieces and ammunition destroyed, lest they fall into enemy hands. Then he sent one of his aides to Corregidor to meet with Wainwright. It was time, he told him, to think about the unthinkable.

Chapter 7

Bataan Falls: The Wounded Are Left in Their Beds

THE WORLD WAR II militarists who ruled Japan had spent decades fashioning the Imperial Japanese Army into a swift, mobile and ruthless force that showed its true face to the world in the late fall and early winter of 1937 as it prepared to attack the city of Nanking. Tokyo's marching orders were simple—take the Chinese city, kill every enemy soldier in it, loot any supplies necessary to sustain the troops during the winter and, by whatever means necessary, prevent the civilian population from mounting an insurgent movement behind Japanese lines.[1]

The battle for the city was over in less than forty-eight hours. Then the real bloodshed began. Japanese troops looted homes, burned villages and rounded up groups of men—a hundred, two hundred, five hundred at a time; old men, young men, boys, it did not matter—and, point-blank, executed them. After that the soldiers of the Rising Sun went house to house, neighborhood by neighborhood, seeking out women and, in an almost methodical way, raped every one of them.

All of this was witnessed by a number of foreign observers: "One poor woman was raped seven times," wrote the American director of the Nanking Refugee Committee. "Another had her five month infant deliberately smothered by the brute to stop its crying while he abused her. Resistance means the bayonet."[2]

Thousands of men, women and children were shot, stabbed, raped, beheaded, disemboweled, mutilated, burned alive, buried alive, hung, castrated and beaten to death. This orgy of blood, this highly organized and officially sanctioned slaughter, became known around the world as the "Rape of Nanking."

Now elements of this same army were poised to savage Bataan, and their reputation for brutality, pitiless lust and torture preceded them.

To the Japanese soldier such savagery was an almost sacred rite, a part of the code of Bushido, the ancient credo of the samurai. In its pure and early form, Bushido called for compassion and generosity toward one's enemy, but the rabid militarists who took over Japan twisted and perverted their history and inculcated in their soldiers a contempt for the defeated and a hate for other races, the white race included. The Japanese soldier obeyed no moral authority other than the emperor and the army. He listened to no inner voice of restraint. When he was ordered to scorch the earth or subdue the civilian population, he fixed his bayonet and took and did what he wanted. If he failed in his duties, he was slapped by his officers or beaten by his sergeants, brutalized so that he might learn brutality's way. He was expected to prove his manhood during battle and after. "Rape in particular, for which the Japanese army was notorious, had much to do with boasts, challenges and competitive virility in a male subculture" that looked on women as chattel.[3]

In 1942, few Americans on Bataan understood the cultural or historic origins of this wantonness, but they knew the facts of 1937, the official reports, the newspaper stories. Nanking had been a shambles, a knacker's yard, gruesome and depraved, and the cries and screams of its men, women and children sounded deep in the American imagination.

ON THE MORNING of April 7, General Wainwright cabled Washington, "The Japanese have thrown fresh reserves into the fight. . . . Heavy losses have been sustained by our forces and by the enemy." He also mentioned the bombings at Hospital #1, concluding, they were "intentional."[4] Late that afternoon an aide to General King, the commander of ground forces on Bataan, made his way to Corregidor to meet with Wainwright.

"General," the aide said, "General King has sent me here to tell you he might have to surrender."[5]

Wainwright, of course, knew King's situation well, even agreed with him, but on his desk lay MacArthur's message—"When the supply situation becomes impossible there must be no thought of surrender. You must attack"—and that is what he ordered King to do.[6]

That evening in another communiqué to Washington, Wainwright reported, "The present Japanese attack is the longest sustained drive of the enemy. . . . Waves of shock troops have attacked almost continuously, without regard to casualties."[7]

The next morning, convinced that King could not hold his ground, Wainwright ordered three battalions of infantry on Bataan—some three thousand men—transferred to the island of Corregidor for what surely was to be his last stand. He also issued orders to the medical corps: the American nurses were to be evacuated as well, immediately.[8]

In a military light, the order transferring the nurses to the relative safety of Malinta Tunnel was simply part of Wainwright's final maneuver; surely the defense of the island would create mass casualties and the nurses would be needed to treat them. But it seems equally clear that Wainwright was reflecting the ethos of his age, the feeling of men that the "fair sex," as the eighteenth-century English journalist Richard Steele first labeled women, was weaker, more vulnerable than men and needed to be protected, preserved, shielded from harm's way. Honor left Wainwright, the old horse soldier, no other course.

For their part, most of the women were appalled by the order and many considered disobeying it. Their code, the Nightingale Pledge, a credo of care, demanded that they stay with their patients. A man's notion of honor was driven by ego, a woman's by an inviolable sense of self built on the sentiment of sacrifice. Real courage required that they think first of their patients, not of themselves. What's more, they did not want to leave their comrades, the doctors and corpsmen who had stood with them under fire; if the men on Bataan were going to surrender and face the enemy, so should the nurses. "We knew what we had to do—take care of these guys," said Cassie. "And we were willing to do anything we had to do, to do it."[9]

Around dusk on April 8 at the battered Hospital #1, Colonel Duckworth summoned Edith "Shack" Shacklette to the riddled shell he called his office.

"The word is that Bataan will surrender tomorrow and we're going to get the nurses over to Corregidor," she remembered him saying. "We don't want to have women around when the Jap soldiers come in. You go and tell everybody to stop what they're doing and take what possessions they can. A bus will be down here in about thirty minutes."[10]

Shack protested at first—she had 1,800 defenseless men in her wards, but the colonel only repeated the order. Leave! he said. Leave, now! So she quickly rounded up her small group of nurses and led them to the bus.

"Of course there was crying," she said. "We hated to leave our patients, hated to leave our group. The bus started off. It was about nine o'clock at night. Just then Colonel Duckworth stopped the bus, made me roll down my window. He handed me the American flag. We had the flag inside on the wall of one of the buildings. He told me when I got over to Corregidor to take it to the commanding officer. . . . I'm always sorry that I gave it away. It was probably just destroyed by the Japanese. I'd give anything to have saved that flag. I cry about it now."[11]

As the nurses at Hospital #1 moved toward their bus, a few of the doctors gathered to say good-bye.

"The nurses scurried into their quarters reappearing almost instantly with a pitiful handful of personal effects," said surgeon Al Weinstein of Atlanta, Georgia. "Farewells were hasty and tearful, kisses sweet and salty."[12]

Some of the women wanted more time "to discuss the details about our patients . . . to leave instructions about those we were worried about," wrote Juanita Redmond. "Some doctors and corpsmen said we'd be back again in a few days—'We'll be seeing you,' they repeated firmly—but nobody believed them. They said it had been good working with us. They said we'd been brave soldiers."[13]

Geneva Jenkins of Sevierville, Tennessee, was asleep when word came for the nurses to flee. "I had gone to bed after laundering my clothes and had stretched them on the line. They said, 'You have to leave,' so I ran off with all my underwear on the line."[14]

Meanwhile, at Hospital #2, Josie Nesbit was ordered to report to Colonel Gillespie. "Tell your American nurses to get down here to my office by twenty hundred hours and only take whatever they can carry in their hands," he said.[15]

The instructions stopped Nesbit cold. "What about my Filipino nurses?" she demanded, almost insubordinate.

"Only the *American* nurses," the colonel said, cutting her short.

Nesbit had made the army her life. She obeyed orders and respected authority, but now, for perhaps the first time in her career, she challenged the chain of command.

"If my Filipino nurses don't go," she said, standing squarely before her superior officer, "I'm . . . not . . . going . . . either." (The Filipinos "called me Mama Josie," she explained later, "and I wasn't going to leave them behind."[16])

Gillespie liked and respected Nesbit, and he called headquarters on

Corregidor and got permission to evacuate all the nurses—Americans, Filipinos and the civilian women working with them.

"Josie was a tiger," said Sally Blaine.[17]

Earlier in the day as the sounds of gunfire grew more pronounced, Anna Williams of Harrisburg, Pennsylvania, climbed the hill behind Hospital #2.

"I wanted to see what was happening because the guns were closer and closer and the smoke was thick," she said. "We were used to having gunfire and things close to us but this you could tell was much nearer. I climbed up the hill to see what was happening and I'll never forget the dejection and the sadness and the awful look on the men as they came along [the road] retreating, covered in bandages and blood and dirt. It was very sad. I knew then that we were going to have to move."[18]

The women left so quickly that one nurse climbed into the trucks with her hair in curlers. Another abandoned a favorite Bible and a copy of Emerson's essays. Leona Gastinger threw her wet laundry and a carton of cigarettes in a pillowcase. Jeanne Kennedy had only enough time to grab her toothbrush, a flashlight and a comb.

Lucy Wilson was assisting in the operating room when the orders reached her.

"By the time we received the word, took off our gloves and gowns in the middle of operations and walked down there, most of the nurses were already gone," she said. "Walking out in the middle of an operation with hundreds lined up under the trees waiting for surgery was devastating to me. This I have to live with for the rest of my life."[19]

The women said nothing to their patients, but lying there in their bamboo beds or on the wet jungle floor, the patients knew. Everyone knew. "Those eyes," said Minnie Breese. "Those eyes just followed us."[20]

Back at the coast the bus carrying the fourteen nurses from Hospital #1 lumbered slowly along the main road toward the docks at Mariveles.

"Civilians banged on the bus pleading to be taken on before the Japanese got them," said Juanita Redmond. "Captain Nelson [a transportation officer driving the women to the dock] would say, 'Take it easy, girls, take it easy. I'm sorry for them too, but we can't take all and it's that or nothing.' "[21]

On board the bus was Preston Taylor, a chaplain from the 31st Infantry who had been transporting patients from the front line to Hospital #1 and now was going to help the nurses reach the docks. In a book after the war, Taylor remembered striking up a conversation with nurse Hattie Brantley from Jefferson, Texas, not too far from his own home in Fort Worth. He'd just come from the front, he told her, and wondered if she knew a nurse named Helen Summers.

"This is your lucky day, Chaplain," said Brantley, then she turned in her seat. "Helen. Hey, Helen. The chaplain wants to see you."

A young, short, dark-eyed woman dressed in army fatigues came forward and Taylor introduced himself.

> *"Helen, I'm Chaplain Preston Taylor and I've just come from the Battle of Mount Sumat, and . . ."*
> *"Yes, Chaplain?"*
> *"And I met this young Lieutenant named Benjamin."*
> *"Yes, Arnold Benjamin. We're going to be married."*
> *"He's dead, Helen."*
> *"Oh, God, no."*
> *"Yesterday, during the battle for Mount Sumat."*
> *She began weeping and coughing. Taylor placed his arm around her and drew her close to him. He told her—*
> *"He wanted to leave you these—"*
> *Reaching into his pocket, he pulled out a gold watch, a key chain, and a college ring.*[22]

When they reached the dock at Mariveles, Taylor and another man "helped carry bags and belongings down to the pier and pitched them to the crewmen" in the launch. As the boat pulled away, the chaplain kept his eyes on Helen Summers. She "managed a faint smile" at first, he said. Then she looked up again "and waved good-bye."[23]

Cassie remembered the docks at Mariveles as a chaos of terror and flight. "Groups of panicked evacuees . . . streamed into the area," she said. The nurses were packed tightly in the small launch. "Some of us sat on our baggage, some on the bottom of the boat, others on the boat's gunwales." On shore the ground rocked each time the allies blew another of their ammunitions dumps, but "we became a little immune to these sounds," Cassie said. Then "suddenly, a deafening explosion . . . echoing and re-echoing against the cliffs surrounding the harbor. It shocked and shook us as we huddled on the floor of the boat. Then came another and still another. . . . We looked back toward Bataan and saw that the three Navy tunnels burrowed into the harbor's hillside were being destroyed lest they fall into the hands of the enemy. We stared . . .

mesmerized. Then . . . looking forward . . . we saw directly in our path the . . . spectacle of the flaming submarine tender *Canopus*. She had been cut loose from her moorings . . . to be scuttled. . . . The explosions of fuel barrels in her magazines was deafening." The launch could not proceed around the exploding vessel so it stopped to wait. "Suddenly the launch rocked and quivered. . . . The helmsman shouted, 'Earthquake!' We could feel the tremors. . . . It was uncanny." Then "the waters calmed" and "we seemed oblivious" after that. "We dreamed dreams and thought thoughts of times, people, places" long gone. Then all at once the launch bumped against the pilings on Corregidor's wharf and "we were . . . jolted back to reality."[24]

MEANWHILE BACK ON Bataan the eighty-eight women from Hospital #2 seemed trapped.

Knots of tired refugees and straggling soldiers clogged the road, and the trucks, buses, jeeps and battered sedans that carried many of the women either broke down or were stuck in traffic. Just then engineers blew up one of the largest ammunitions dumps along the road and for hours nothing on wheels could move around it.

"It was a big mess," said Sally Blaine. "[Some] troops were retreating from the front lines [while others were marching in the opposite direction to face the enemy]. They were worn out and exhausted. Vehicles were breaking down. The noise and the confusion—it was bedlam that night."[25]

Minnie Breese was sick with malaria and dysentery. A doctor had issued her thirty grains of quinine and the drug was making her "deaf as a post" and nauseous.

"I remember vomiting and running behind a bush with dysentery," she said. "I didn't care if I lived or died. I got on the truck and Sallie Durrett took care of me."

The truck broke down and the nurses were forced to the road.

"We couldn't get down to the dock because they were blowing up the ammo dump, so I laid down [next to the road]," Breese said. "Once in a while I'd open my eyes and see the most beautiful fireworks going up through the trees."[26]

Finally, some of the women from Hospital #2 reached the water, but they were so late in arriving, the boat that had been ordered to take them to Corregidor was nowhere in sight. Sally Blaine spotted an officer on the dock and ran after him.

"Hey! You! With the red cross on your arm," she yelled. "Where's the boat that the nurses are supposed to go over on? We're down here to take the boat over to Corregidor."

"Oh," he said. "It came and left."

"Well, what are we going to do?"

"How many are you?" he asked.

"Five."

"Well, I can take you."

The officer loaded his passengers into a small craft with an outboard motor.

"When we went across," Blaine remembered, "the water looked silvery gold. It was calm, early in the morning. I kept looking at the sky and the water and I thought, Well, this may be the last time I see a sunrise.

"We didn't talk," she went on. "This may strike you as funny but during all that time we didn't cry, scream or carry on. You were quiet. You kept your fears to yourself."[27]

Back at the dock another group of nurses arriving late slumped down at the water's edge, exhausted. It was morning by now; the sun was beginning to blaze and the Japanese dive bombers were returning to look for targets on the bay.

The women found a bit of shelter at the water's edge and huddled together, more weary and hungry than afraid. They had not eaten for a very long time and sat on the sand, talking of food.

As women, of course, they attracted some attention and, as it happened, some sailors who stopped to talk with them had a stash of provisions nearby. So there on the derelict beach some of the nurses from Hospital #2 had a kind of last supper on Bataan, an impromptu banquet of corned beef hash, tomato juice, crackers and beans—all left behind by the U.S. Navy. Even the women wracked with dysentery "ate like wolves."[28] They finished off their feast by passing around cans of peaches, spearing the sweet, wet, delicious slabs of fruit with the ends of their toothbrushes.

At length Josie Nesbit arrived. Delayed reaching the docks, she now gathered around her the final group of nurses.[29] The docks were quiet now, not a boat in sight. They'd been abandoned, all right, and now there seemed nothing to do but wait.

A strange kind of quiet descended over the group, a prelude, they felt, to something ominous. They walked to the beach and waited . . . waited quietly for the Japanese to march out of the jungle.

Then someone heard the sound of a motorboat and they rushed to the water. Suddenly, dive bombers appeared overhead, and the boat quickly wheeled about and pulled away.

A few minutes later the threat passed and the skipper tried a second approach, but just then the bombers reappeared, and, for a while, the boat and planes played cat and mouse. At last the pilots seemed to tire of the game and turned away, and the skipper turned back toward shore and cautiously approached the dock.

Crewmen stretched a narrow wooden beam from the hull to the dock, and a few of the nurses, dizzy with malaria, nearly pitched head-long into the bay as they negotiated the tenuous plank. Finally, with everyone on deck, the captain reversed engines and turned toward Corregidor.

Just then the bombers came back.

They blew the dock into a shower of splinters and turned on the boat.

The captain started to zigzag, veering wildly in one direction, then the other, hoping to make himself a more difficult target. Nesbit, convinced they would be hit, told her women to remove their shoes, lead weights in the water. One bomb exploded off the port side, another off starboard, sending up geysers of water that soaked the deck. The skipper kept up his zigzagging, and, with the decks awash, the women began to slip about and grab for one another.

Slightly apart from all this sat Anna Williams, curiously calm, working on her fingertips with a nail file.

"My God, Anna," one of the women said, "what's the matter with you?"

"I said, 'Well, what can we do?' " Williams remembered. "There wasn't anything else to do and I wasn't going to sit there and moan."[30]

A while later the skipper approached the landing dock on Corregidor. "Willy-nilly we piled off that blessed motor launch onto the shaky dock and made for the hillside," Denny Williams, a civilian nurse, said.[31]

A monkey nipped at their heels as they ran for Malinta Tunnel.

Inside, some of the early arrivees were astonished that Nesbit and the latecomers were able to escape. "Oh gee! I thought you were dead," someone told Leona Gastinger.[32]

About one o'clock Nesbit took a roll call. Each of the eighty-eight women who had been in her charge at Hospital #2 answered in a loud, clear voice. Somehow, some way, everyone—including the old and the ill—had escaped to Corregidor.

General Wainwright was delighted to see them. Years later in a memoir, he recalled the happy moment. They were a scruffy lot, he remembered, covered in road dust and grime, weak with fever and chills and still wide-eyed from their getaway across the bay.

> *You may talk all you want of the pioneer women who went across the plains
> of early America and helped found our great nation. . . . But never forget
> the American girls who fought on Bataan and later on Corregidor. . . .
> Theirs had been a life of conveniences and even luxury. But their hearts
> were the same hearts as those of the women of early America. Their names
> must always be hallowed when we speak of American heroes. The memory of
> their coming ashore on Corregidor that early morning of April 9, dirty, di-
> sheveled, some of them wounded from the hospital bombings—and every
> last one of them with her chin up in the air—is a memory that can never
> be erased.*[33]

AFTER ROLL CALL and a meal, the women tumbled onto cots, two to each, and feet to face fell asleep.

Meanwhile, behind them Bataan was falling.

President Roosevelt radioed a message to General Wainwright: "My purpose is to leave to your best judgment any decisions affecting the Bataan garrison. . . . You should be assured of complete freedom of action and of my full confidence in the wisdom of whatever decision you may be forced to make."[34]

From Corregidor Wainwright answered: "I have done all that could be done to hold Bataan, but starved men without air and with adequate field artillery support cannot endure. . . ."[35]

So General King surrendered the peninsula and a terrible silence descended over it. To some of the refugees across the bay on Corregidor, the quiet was more unsettling than the estimated 907 tons of explosives the enemy had dropped on them during the siege.

Now the only messages coming across the water were from flashlights blinking Morse code signals for distress from Bataan's tree lines. Dot-dot-dot . . . dash-dash-dash . . . dot-dot-dot—over and over again.

From Australia General MacArthur announced that he was naming his new headquarters there "Bataan," the better to preserve the memory of the command he had abandoned. Politicians pledged to reconquer the islands soon, and on the Voice of Freedom, a radio announcer read a dramatic tribute: "Bataan has fallen, but the spirit that made it stand—a beacon to all the liberty-loving people of the world—cannot fail."[36]

The surrender made front-page headlines around the world: BATAAN, WORSE BLOW TO AN AMERICAN ARMY, *The New York Times* announced.

Journalists blamed the defeat—the most costly wartime loss in a single battle in American military history—on the overwhelming Japanese army and on hunger, fatigue and disease. Many of the publications at home listed the units that had been captured or were missing in action, but the numbers and the details of the defeat were initially withheld, more for morale than national security. The Japanese, of course, trumpeted their triumph. The Domei News Agency in Tokyo announced that sixty thousand Filipino and American troops had begged for a halt in the hostilities. (Officially, Washington later listed over 78,000 American and Filipino troops as surrendering to the Japanese.)

The number of captives surprised the Imperial Army. General Homma's staff miscalculated not only the number of prisoners—they expected no more than 25,000—but their physical condition as well. Japanese commanders had planned to march their allied captives some nineteen miles to a staging point where trucks and trains would be waiting to take them to prison camps. Now, with more men than they could handle, the Japanese forced the enervated Americans and Filipinos to walk three times that distance, walk under the blazing sun.

The Japanese guards stripped the prisoners of canteens, food, rings, wristwatches, personal papers and anything else they wanted. Then they divided the huge mass of men into groups and herded them on their way.

Somewhere along this walk, an evil reality took hold. The Japanese guards began to shoot anyone who dropped behind or fainted. If an American officer protested the treatment, as many did, they were lashed to trees and beheaded or eviscerated. Other men were bayoneted or beaten with rifle butts, shovels, bamboo canes, golf clubs and fists. Anyone who tried to rest or take a drink was executed or bludgeoned unconscious. The ditches along Bataan's main road soon became filled with headless and emaciated corpses—mile after bloody mile.

The exact figures have been lost to time, but likely some 72,000 men started the trek, and, in the end, only some 54,000 men reached the camps. Thousands more died in their first sixty days of captivity. After the war the allies calculated that less than half of the friendly forces that surrendered on April 9, 1942, lived to see home again.[37] And the long walk from the battlefield that killed so many became a metaphor for wartime depravity—the Bataan Death March.

• • •

AT THE SAME time Homma's victorious troops were herding the Battling Bastards of Bataan into what was soon to become their death march, other Japanese units marched into Hospital #1 and Hospital #2 and captured the 8,800 sick and wounded men the nurses had left behind.

The surrender at Hospital #1 took place at 1:35 P.M. on April 9 when Colonel Duckworth handed over his command to Major General Matsuii, the field commander of the Imperial Japanese Army forces. Matsuii immediately went to the prison ward to check on the wounded Japanese captured by the Americans during the battle. When he discovered how well they had been treated, he seemed pleased and allowed Duckworth and his staff to continue their work.

"We had 1,800 helpless casualties to treat and feed," wrote Dr. Al Weinstein, a surgeon at Hospital #1. "We were [also] afraid that if we were found by isolated bands of Nips trying to escape through the jungle we would be knocked off. Where reason and duty were wedded so harmoniously it was not difficult to make a decision. We stayed."[38]

Six weeks later, the Japanese high command ordered the hospital cleared. The Filipinos were allowed simply to wander home. The American wounded and the American doctors and staff were sent to prison camps.

The surrender at Hospital #2 was less formal. Around 5:00 P.M. on April 9, a group of Japanese infantrymen wandered into the central hospital looking for potable water. A few hours later two Japanese officers and twenty more enlisted men arrived. The officers summoned Colonel Gillespie and told him that all personnel had to remain within the hospital area and that anyone seen outside it would be shot.

The next morning, guards ordered all 5,600 Filipino patients at Hospital #2 set free. Wrapped in blankets and hobbling on crutches, they trudged down the dirt path leading from the hospital to the East Road. When they reached the road they discovered masses of men marching north, guarded by Japanese soldiers. Some of the wounded filtered south, some into the jungle, but many stayed on the road, unknowingly joining the Death March.

The 1,400 American wounded and the 280 officers and enlisted men at Hospital #2 settled back to wait. In the weeks that followed, Japanese troops from time to time would stop by to loot the patients of watches, rings, sunglasses and food, especially fruit juices. Japanese mechanics stripped the generators and appropriated all motor vehicles.

Doctors begged their Japanese captors for more food. Their patients, they said, were suffering. Most men had lost an average of twenty-five pounds. Open wounds were not healing, broken bones not mending. The Japanese, of course, ignored these entreaties. Instead, calculating that the enemy would not fire on its own wounded, they ringed the hospital with twenty-three artillery pieces. "It was obvious that the Japanese intended to use the hospital as a shield against answering fire from American guns (on Corregidor)," the judge advocate general's office wrote in a postwar report.[39]

On April 22, about 3:00 A.M., several stray allied shells from Corregidor fell between Ward 14 and Mess Hall 3, killing five Americans and wounding twelve. A few days later, a large shell fell in Ward 5 but luckily did not explode.

The Japanese guards kept to themselves, then one night some of the Imperial troops reverted to type. Ethyle Mae Taft Mercado, an American from Bicknell, Utah, had been left on Bataan when the other women were evacuated. The wife of a Filipino, Mercado had settled at Mariveles in 1936 and had helped her husband, a local entrepreneur, operate a bar, a laundry and a taxi service. When the fighting broke out her husband sent his twenty-seven-year-old wife and two children to a civilian refugee camp inland. The small family was supposed to be evacuated with the nurses to Corregidor, but by the time Ethyle Mae and her children reached Hospital #2, the women were gone, so the doctors settled the family in a tent and, with everyone else, the Mercados waited to surrender to the Japanese.

Around 8:00 P.M. on April 10, one day after the surrender, an American officer at Hospital #2, recuperating from a bullet wound in his lung, heard a woman screaming in the tent next to him. In the darkness he propped himself up and saw an American medic quickly approach the tent, only to be sharply turned away by a sentry wielding a rifle and bayonet. The cries continued for a while, then stopped. In the morning, Ethyle Mae Mercado stumbled into the officer's tent, bruised and weeping. She'd been raped, she said, at least five times, all through the night. After that the doctors moved her into their quarters to protect her.[40]

A few weeks later the Japanese disbanded Hospital #2 as well. Mrs. Mercado went to a civilian internment camp, the men and doctors to the various wretched prisons that would claim the lives of so many soldiers. In his last official report Colonel Duckworth wrote: "Many of us turned our backs, with mixed emotions, on Hospital No. 2 forever. That this small group in less than 3½ months had built and operated hospital facilities for 16,000 patients is, we believe, a truly remarkable record."[41]

Chapter 8

Corregidor—the Last Stand

ONLY "THE ROCK" was left.

A heavily fortified outpost guarding the entrance to Manila Bay, Corregidor, a drop of land shaped uncannily like a tadpole floating on the water, was defended by heavy mortars, short- and long-range artillery pieces and antiaircraft batteries. With the fall of Bataan there were now some twelve thousand allied personnel on the tiny island—battalions of American and Filipino combat troops, various support units, a large group of dispossessed sailors and roughly a thousand U.S. Marines, along with some Philippine government officials and their families, a handful of American dependents and a few war correspondents.

From the top of its head to the tip of its narrow tail, the tadpole island was some three and a half miles long and, at its widest point on the head, a mile and a half wide. The soldiers who manned the big guns and the Marines who stood vigil along the beach defenses lived in dugouts and burrows and bunkers. Almost everyone else, some ten thousand people, holed up in a complex of well-designed concrete tunnels deep underneath the hard rock of Malinta Hill.

The Malinta Tunnel complex, organized into a series of narrow corridors, or catacombs, called "laterals," was like a small, cramped city with sections for administration, supply, mess, ordinance and a thousand-bed hospital staffed at first by the few dozen nurses originally stationed at Corregidor's post hospital above ground and, later, by the nurses evacuated from Bataan and some civilian volunteers. The gray concrete tunnel complex had been built secretly many years before and had its own power and water supply.

The Japanese knew little about this underground fortress and head-quarters. A main corridor 750 feet long, 25 feet wide, and 15 feet high served as the spine for the laterals. Through this corridor ran a railway line to ferry supplies. Adjacent laterals were used to store food, medicine and ordnance and served as barracks, administrative offices and a hospital.

After the first Japanese bombing on December 29, 1941, most of the seven thousand troops stationed on Corregidor moved into or near the sprawling underground complex.

Army nurses set up the hospital, which soon consisted of a central corridor a hundred yards long and open on one end to the outside, and eight smaller laterals, or wards, that branched off the long corridor and were connected honeycomb fashion by other passages.

The hospital had all the familiar trappings of an infirmary—white enamel bedside tables, iron beds, flush-type latrines, showers, spigots, filing cabinets and refrigerators. In addition to recovery and convalescent wards, the hospital laterals held operating rooms, a dental clinic, laboratories, kitchen and dining areas, a dispensary and sleeping quarters for the nurses.

As in all the laterals throughout the complex, red lights hung from the arched ceilings and flashed warnings of impending attacks, but Malinta Tunnel was so well built, the hospital staff could continue to work during raids, interrupted only by the muffled thuds of bombs and shells landing above.

The Japanese had been bombing the island repeatedly since their December invasion, but, the extensive surface damage notwithstanding, the bombardment had not really hurt the garrison. Now, with Bataan under enemy control, the Japanese moved their big guns south to the peninsula and ordered extra flights of bombers. At times they pounded the Rock so hard it seemed as if they were trying to pulverize it into dust.

Using observation balloons, reconnaissance aircraft and 116 big guns on Bataan, as well as at the Cavite naval base outside Manila, the enemy lobbed so many tons of explosives across the water that some of the nurses who had been in the hospital laterals since the beginning of the war thought that the seventy feet of rock over their heads might collapse on top of them.

In Malinta Tunnel hospital Maude Davison and her deputy, Josie Nesbit, now commanded eighty-five army nurses, twenty-six Filipino nurses, one navy nurse and dozens of civilian women living and working among them. As the bombardment intensified so did the casualties among the beach and artillery crews. Soon single beds became bunk beds, soon bunk beds were welded into triple-deckers.

To the nurses who had been bombed in the open-air hospitals on Bataan, Malinta Tunnel seemed impregnable. For the first time in three months they had a ceiling over their heads, a decent meal every day, no snakes, ants or iguanas in their beds. Their only complaint was a sense of disorientation, for in the tunnel it was impossible to tell night from day. As often as they could the women and their friends gathered outside at the entrance to the main corridor to smoke in the open air, listen to the radio and stare at the stars in the night sky. Sometimes in the crowd of men and women outside the entrance a voice would break into song— "The Yellow Rose of Texas" or "Home on the Range"—and soon a single voice would grow into a sing-along.[1]

In early April, when news spread that a large group of young American women had arrived on the Rock, the hospital complex began to draw a steady stream of visitors.

Maude Davison, a by-the-book officer, reacted in typical fashion: she issued a series of orders designed to enforce strict military protocol. The green coveralls her women wore on Bataan were put away, and the army hired Chinese tailors to sew khaki skirts and military-style blouses. Hairdos once again reflected "off-the-collar" regulations. Some of the women, particularly the younger ones, no doubt bridled under such nickel-and-dime nonsense, but they kept silent. Many in fact found a kind of reassurance and comfort in the old disciplines.

MAUDE CAMPBELL DAVISON, the chief of all army nurses in the Philippines, was fifty-seven years old when the war started, but with the beginning of a dowager hump in her back, she looked older. To regard her, to view her from a distance, was to look upon the image of maternity, compassion, safekeeping and care. She was a small-framed woman who wore her white hair tied back in a bun like a grandmother. The younger nurses even nicknamed her "Ma," but Maude Davison never offered her charges maternal comfort.

"Miss Davison," as she insisted on being called, was a strict disciplinarian who demanded that her nurses follow army regulations, and her rules, to the letter.

A naturalized American citizen, she was born March 27, 1885, in Cannington, Ontario Province, Canada. She began her career as a dietitian working at Baptist College in Manitoba, then she emigrated to the United States and took a job at Epworth Hospital in South Bend, Indiana.[2]

Wanting more, she went west to California and entered Pasadena Hospital Training School for Nurses. Less than a year later, on June 3, 1918, at the age of thirty-three, she joined the Army Nurse Corps.

Her double expertise, nursing and dietetics, made her a valuable officer at a time when the army was assigned the difficult jobs of coordinating casualties of the Great War and helping with refugees abroad and a flu epidemic at home. In the early 1920s she spent thirteen months with the occupation forces in Coblenz, Germany, working with the victims of the famine then sweeping across Russia and Eastern Europe. Back home she returned to school, Columbia University this time, and earned a degree in home economics. At the time less than 10 percent of the women in the United States held college credentials.

Her nurses on Bataan and Corregidor knew none of this. Davison kept her own counsel and usually her own company. The physicians she assisted always admired her; she was "capable," they said—a high compliment in medical circles—a clinician who could adapt to crises and changing circumstances.

She had no family—rather, the army was her family, her life, and she listed its headquarters, Washington, D.C., as her hometown.

The older nurses who knew her said she liked to collect humorous anecdotes but rarely shared these with her women. She also liked her liquor, particularly in the evening after work, often to excess.

The women who crossed her felt the sharp sting of her rebuke. She was blunt and unsparing in her criticism, "mean," said some women, and they intensely disliked her for it.

In some ways she was typical of her generation of leaders—distant and formal, always professional, always demanding complete obedience.

ALTHOUGH SHE DID not show it, Davison must have been impressed with her nurses, particularly the ones who had served on Bataan, for it was clear that three months under fire had honed their skills as no other training could. They were able to dress wounds quickly and efficiently, and they had administered so many anesthetics and painkillers, they now seemed to know the right dosage by heart, by instinct. In a look they could see signs of dehydration and disease. In a voice they could detect the symptoms of distress.

Malinta Tunnel, however, presented them with a new set of disorders. The stale, stagnant air in those damp and close quarters left people with serious respiratory diseases as well as fungus infections and skin boils, nicknamed "Guam blisters."[3] The nurses too developed these blisters, and when they tried to lift patients or climb onto their own bunks, they winced or recoiled in pain. Doctors developed a technique of lancing the welts and painting them with Mercurochrome and salicylic acid.

Twenty-two civilian women also shared the nurses sleeping quarters and mess. The wives of high-level politicians or lucky evacuees most willingly pitched in, carrying food to bed patients, taking temperatures and rolling bandages. A Polish woman with a talent for cooking on the griddle volunteered to make pancakes. Ann Mealor, chief nurse on Corregidor before the war, set down three rules for the interlopers: they were to keep their beds made, their floors tidy and their mouths shut after 9:00 P.M. A few women, society matrons mostly, refused to go along and were shunned. "I could say more [about their] upbringing, selfishness and personal hygiene, but I think that would be unprofessional of me," said Hortense McKay, a senior army nurse.[4]

After two weeks underground the Bataan nurses no longer thought of Malinta Tunnel as a haven, just a different kind of hell.

The incessant bombing was concussive and some of the women developed severe earaches and headaches. Walls and ceilings trembled and shook, medicine bottles toppled out of cabinets, bunk beds bounced across the floor. The concussions increased the air pressure in the narrow laterals and caused the nurses' skirts to wrap tightly around their legs. Each blast shook loose small flakes of concrete and great volumes of dust, and soon there was so much debris passing through the ventilation system, the moist air began to feel viscous and left the patients and staff coughing.

When the generators failed, as they often did, the hospital turned dark, and corpsmen were called upon to hold flashlights for the surgical teams. "If you ever wanted to feel what the darkness of the Egyptian pyramids must have been like," said Hattie Brantley, "you should have been in Malinta Tunnel when the lights went out."[5]

Off duty in their lateral, the nurses read and chatted and wrote in their journals.

[Straub Diary, April 18] All quiet today. No shelling. No bombing. Why?

[April 19] Enemy shelling was heavy for five hours. The atmosphere of the tunnel becomes more depressing as each day passes. Food is fairly good; in fact excellent in comparison to that of Bataan.

[April 21] Four and a half months since I've seen a streetcar, taxi, caleso—that's a Filipino horse-drawn cab—store, movie. We have found the real meaning of being isolated.

[April 25] General Wainwright came through the ward this evening to give Lieutenant Augur, a patient (he was in the coast artillery I think), the Distinguished Service Award.[6]

As time passed and the bombing and artillery attacks increased, the tunnel began to feel like an anthill, a suffocating and oppressive labyrinth of dark, malodorous and crowded passageways. The stale muggy air, the close quarters and the stench of disinfectants, anesthetics and suppurating flesh prompted larger and larger numbers of people to seek a few minutes of fresh air and join the large nightly gathering at the tunnel's main entrance.

On the night of April 26, some two weeks after the surrender of Bataan, a large group of "tunnel rats," as some began to call themselves, stood outside the entrance to the main corridor for their nightly airing. Just as the group settled into conversation and song, the Japanese fired two huge 240mm shells at Corregidor.

One was a dud, the other landed at the tunnel's entrance.

The concussion was so colossal it slammed shut the tunnel's slatted iron entrance gate, and the laterals echoed with screams from the outside. Corpsmen and nurses in nearby laterals sprinted toward the entrance to aid their comrades. When they arrived they had to pry open the iron gate, a grizzly task, for jutting between the slats were body parts and pieces of torn and mangled flesh.

Outside, fourteen men lay dead, seventy wounded.

Cassie stood there open-mouthed at the slaughter. When a severed head rolled around her feet, she started to retch and looked away lest she lose her self-control.

That night nurses and doctors worked nonstop. Even for the Battling Belles of Bataan it was hideous work—tearing away clothing soaked with a bolus of blood and flesh, applying tourniquets to stop the river of red running on the lateral floor, snipping off mangled fingers and toes, watching them drop into a bucket fast filling with amputated flesh.

[Straub Diary, April 26] Last evening . . . many injured, some killed. A most depressing sight. Today people were jittery and not at all anxious to get outside. . . . Awfully hungry tonight. In fact, most of the time. Wonder what butter tastes like. . . . Still on duty in the orthopedic ward. Hospital is filled to capacity. We're using triple-decker beds now.[7]

The daily bombardment was withering. The face of Corregidor, once almost gardenlike, a kind of military resort with flowers and lawns and clubs and pools, an island swept by breezes from the sea—this once lush and pastoral place was now a wasteland, denuded of its natural beauty, reduced to gray rubble and piles of dust, a hot, hardscrabble dot of rock in the crosshairs of a hundred thundering cannons.

Living among the tunnel rats was Leon Ma Guerrero, one of the Philippines' brightest and most talented intellectuals. Guerrero, who worked at the tunnel radio station, kept a diary and made fastidious mental notes about life under siege, and later in a Philippine literary journal, he wrote an essay, "Last Days of Corregidor," that, though embroidered and overdone, seemed to capture both the perverse defiance and dark mood of the tunnel rats.

Reality was a brief cigarette in the dark, a frenzied kiss and embrace beyond the bend of the road, a plateful of beans and a slice of canned pineapple, a throw of the dice, a turn of the card.

Above all reality was a bloody carcass carried on a swaying khaki stretcher along the cavernous gloom of Malinta Tunnel, past the staring crowds suddenly grown hushed . . . into the hospital lateral . . . finally to be laid on the white surgical tables, to squirm and groan and scream and mutter half-remembered prayers and half-forgotten names amid the tinkle of instruments and the rush of water. . . .

Every day it seemed that the line of stretchers grew longer. . . . The narrow hospital corridors were crammed with the wounded, the sick and the dying; convalescents were hurried out to make room for fresh casualties as doctors made their rounds with an increasingly artificial joviality.

Nurses snapped at one another, at the male attendants, at the patients as the intolerable strain continued. An official order commanded all women refugees on the island to lend a hand; and the gossips, the flirts, the Navy wives and the army daughters, except for the old and the invalid, put aside their knitting, their pleasant novels, their compacts, and their cigarette cases to carry soup trays or administer baths and rub-downs with their manicured hands. . . .

Sometimes a nurse and her boyfriend of the evening would melt into a dance under the disapproving eyes of the garrison adjutant. The eyes of the onlookers would grow soft and thoughtful, while other couples would steal out into the perilous night, to lie on the harsh dry grass that was softened by the dew.

Out there a man might indeed forget, gulping down sweetened hospital alcohol, listening to the thin and delicate melody of a Filipino kundiman [a traditional love song], or a muffled laugh—surrendering Mind with all its fears and premonitions to the warm embrace of Flesh.[8]

As the shelling grew more and more ferocious, the psyches of those determined to defend the island grew more and more fragile. A number of soldiers developed "tunnelitis," an unwillingness to leave the laterals for any reason. Some of the nurses, no doubt convinced their end was near, began to get up well before dawn and wander outside in the early morning quiet to see at least one more sunrise, experience at least a few moments of one more day.

On Tuesday, April 28, General Homma held a victory parade in Manila, a ruse to deceive the allies into thinking that he had delayed at least for a while his plan to attack Corregidor.

[*Straub Diary, April 28*] It is surprising that I still have this little would-be diary. Intended to burn it as the Japs were coming into our camp at Bataan, but didn't have time. However I tried to keep from mentioning anything that would be of military value. All in all, this little book has been a companion in my loneliness and sorrow. . . . Every patient in the hospital has been given a gas mask.[9]

The next day at 7:25 A.M. Homma ordered a massive pounding of the Rock, the heaviest artillery and air bombardment of the campaign.

The walls and ceilings of Malinta Tunnel trembled with the concussions and the tunnel instantly filled with dust, choking the patients and staff. Outside, the island was on fire. Even the trees seemed to explode, and when two gasoline dumps were hit the blasts sent smoke thousands of feet into the air. Ambulance drivers risked their lives dodging the explosions and trying to navigate the crater-filled roads to reach the exposed artillery units, where casualties were severe.

The next day the bombardment continued. Clearly the Rock was being "softened up" for an invasion. And it was just as clear that the defenders of Corregidor, now on severely limited rations, short on trained infantry and weapons, without heavy armor, most of all without any hope of resupply, could not repel the well-trained, well-supplied troops that would surely come against them, wave after wave of fighting men determined to raise the Rising Sun on Corregidor's heights and slaughter anyone who got in their way.

In the last week in April, Wainwright was informed that two navy PBY seaplanes were going to attempt to slip through the Japanese blockade, deliver a small load of supplies and take out some passengers— civilian dependents, staff experts and cryptographers requested by MacArthur, and many older officers that Wainwright felt "were in no physical condition to take captivity."[10] The general also decided to include in the group twenty of the Rock's eighty-five army nurses.

No one knows why Wainwright decided to send some of the women out. Was he thinking of them in the same way he thought of his older officers, trying to cull from the group those who for various reasons might not fare well under the Japanese? Or, reflecting the attitudes of his age and perhaps guided by the chivalric code of the warrior, did he mean to get all the women off the Rock—some now, the rest later—lest the flower of American womanhood fall into the hands of the army that had despoiled Nanking?

Early on April 29 Wainwright received word that the planes would arrive that night, and he asked his chief medical officer to give him a list of women to go out. Colonel Cooper met with Maude Davison to decide who would stay and who would be given a chance to escape.[11]

Davison would later tell one of the nurses left behind that she picked the names out of a hat, but everyone quickly saw through this fiction, for many of her choices were obvious. Among the first selected were women in their late forties and early fifties who already were wilting under the physical duress of war—Louise Anschicks, Peg O'Neill, Florence Mac-Donald. Next she selected a few women who were either extremely ill with tropical diseases or who had been seriously wounded during the bombings at Hospital #1—Sally Blaine, Rita Palmer, Rosemary Hogan. Then came the more difficult choices, women, as Ann Mealor later recalled, who were "inclined to be hysterical or anything like that."[12] Josie Nesbit said that Maude Davison was convinced that only the most emotionally stable and physically fit would be able to withstand what was coming.

At 6:00 P.M. twenty army nurses got word to report to the dining lateral at sundown. Davison handed each of them orders that stated they were being "relieved from present assignment and duty and will proceed by first available transportation to Melbourne, Australia, reporting upon arrival to the Commander in Chief, Southwest Pacific Area, G.H.Q., for further disposition."[13] She ordered the women not to discuss their departure with anyone else. There would be no farewells, she said, no good-byes. Each could take one bag, as long as it weighed less than ten pounds. The two PBY's would arrive shortly, and the women should be ready.

The evacuees, of course, ignored the gag order, and the news of their imminent departure soon spread. Few of the women who were to be left behind complained about the evacuation of the old, the sick, the wounded or the emotionally crippled. They "deserved" to go, most said. But also on the evacuation list, they noted, were a half dozen of the most attractive young women in the outfit, and not one of these beauties seemed to fit any of the evacuation criteria. In fact the only thing they had in common were their connections, often romantic, to high-ranking male officers.

"Why them? Why not me? Why anybody?" asked Madeline Ullom, echoing a common ambivalence. "We were torn. On one hand you are certain absolutely [about] your dedication and devotion to the patients, while on the other you wonder just how long you might withstand the trauma of continuing to live under this now impossible situation of constant heavy bombing and shelling. The trauma had to resolve itself in the stark realization that although you, personally, were not selected for the departure list, at least someone you knew [was]. In any event there was little consolation."[14]

Other women were simply angry. When Clara Mae Bickford saw her best friend, Eunice Hatchitt, packing a bag and getting ready to go, she rushed up to her. Hatchitt was young, pretty and attached to an officer on MacArthur's staff.

"Where are you going?" said Bickford, fuming.

Hatchitt just kept packing.

"What are you doing?" Bickford demanded again. "You're leaving! Aren't you?" she yelled.[15]

The two women were close; they had been bunkmates on Bataan and inseparable on Corregidor, even taking their nightly constitutional together outside the tunnel.

Hatchitt couldn't look her friend in the eye. Finally she closed her luggage, reached up and gave her friend a long hug, and quickly departed.

Denny Williams fixed her anger on a pretty woman named Earleen Allen. "Why she was chosen to escape from Corregidor," Williams wrote, "only God knows."[16]

Most of the hard feelings fell on Juanita Redmond, who was beautiful enough to be a movie star.

"As far as I'm concerned," said Cassie, "Redmond was on [that list] because of her connections. Politics works no matter where you are and what the circumstances."[17]

For her part, Redmond "did not know what to think, nor how I felt. I wanted to go, and I didn't want to go. Probably I would never see the other nurses again, and I wanted to stay with them and face whatever was to come; we had faced so much together, I felt like a deserter."[18]

Josie Nesbit, forty-seven years old, was on the list to go, but refused to leave her post. "I want to stay," she told Davison flatly.[19]

Anne Wurts, who had been sick with various ailments for quite some time, was on the list as well, but she too insisted on doing her duty and urged Davison to select someone even sicker to take her place.[20]

As a landing site for the PBY's, Wainwright had chosen a sheltered area in the bay between Corregidor and a tiny island. Minesweepers had cleared the section and placed two lighted buoys in the water. And the Japanese unwittingly cooperated; for some reason they had temporarily lifted their barrage.

The seaplanes set down and taxied to the landing site. Around 11:45 P.M. the evacuees gathered on a dock to board small boats for the short ride out to the bobbing seaplanes. Just before she boarded the boat, Juanita Redmond turned to General Wainwright.

She put her arms around me and kissed me. "Oh thank you general," she cried. We stood there and watched the seaplanes roar and take off and prayed they would not be hit. . . . They sailed right off the water beautifully, pulled out over the side of Cavite beyond the range of the anti-

*aircraft guns and were enveloped in the night. Then we turned and walked
back to our jobs.*[21]

On board the plane the pilots ordered everyone to move forward to
lessen the tail drag during takeoff. Huddled together in the cool, fresh air
that now filled the front of the cabin, some of the fortunate few took a
final look back at their beleaguered island and wept. Others, perhaps lost
in the reverie of their good luck or in the sinking emptiness of regret,
stared straight ahead with hollow eyes. A few sat back and quickly
drifted into sleep.

WAINWRIGHT WAS DESPERATE. He might fight off a first wave, even
a second, but he knew the enemy would keep landing troops, wave after
wave, and once his beach defenses were overrun, once his short-range artillery was silenced, he would be forced back into Malinta Tunnel. All the
Japanese would have to do then was put poison gas in the air ducts or
pull tanks or flamethrowers up to the entrance and throw fire down the
crowded laterals, where thousands of soldiers, many of them wounded,
would be trapped.

The day after the PBY's left, the quartermaster sent the general a list
of shortages—no helmets, no towels, no handkerchiefs, no blankets, no
raincoats, no tarpaulins. Most important, Corregidor would run out of
water and power in thirty days.

Stewed tomatoes and rice appeared regularly on the menu, sometimes augmented with coconut and canned meat presented in a eu-
phemism the cooks called a "casserole."

Water was rationed as well and the women learned to wash their
clothes and take baths in their helmets.

From time to time morale got a boost by seemingly insignificant acts
and gestures. The Voice of Freedom radio programs, broadcast three
times a day from the tunnel radio station, continually encouraged people to persevere. VOF announcers ended every transmission with the
words, "Corregidor still stands!"[22] One day three men braved the bombardment and repaired the halyard on the flagpole above the tunnel, then
raised Old Glory high for everyone to see. General Wainwright tried to
spend part of each day with the troops and made daily visits to the hospital laterals, often walking outside the entrance to smoke and chat with
the nurses. Sometimes the laterals filled with music; a trio consisting of

a harmonica, guitar and a trombone led jam sessions that attracted large crowds. Often the nurses played the part of Red Cross hostesses, taking a turn around the concrete floors with a queue of grateful dance partners. At the main entrance to the tunnel a young Filipino would play old standards on the guitar, songs such as "To You, Sweetheart, Aloha, from the Bottom of My Heart," while onlookers, misty-eyed, softly sang along.[23]

Meanwhile the cannonade continued.

[*Straub Diary, May 1*] Phew! What bombing! Right at the entrance to the tunnel again. Although we were safe, it felt as though rock would tumble around our ears. Not much change in the general situation.

[*May 3*] More intense bombing and shelling. . . . Shell shock cases being admitted now. . . .[24]

AT 7:30 A.M. on May 2 the Japanese began an artillery and air attack that lasted twelve hours. Two officers on Wainwright's staff counted the explosions and estimated that every minute of that period at least twelve five-hundred-pound shells fell on Corregidor. After five hours and some 3,600 rounds, or 1.8 million pounds of explosives, they stopped counting.

On May 3, four days after the PBY aircraft had taken the twenty army nurses and others off the Rock, a submarine, the U.S.S. *Spearfish,* approached the island. The *Spearfish* had been on her fourth war patrol near Luzon when her commander, Lieutenant James Dempsey, received a dispatch from Australia instructing him to proceed to Corregidor to pick up passengers. Although there were four enemy destroyers and one minelayer patrolling near the island, the submarine managed to slip in undetected and surface just outside an allied minefield.[25]

Wainwright picked another group of old or ailing colonels to evacuate, the U.S. Navy sent out six of its officers, a dependent, and Ann Bernatitus, the lone navy nurse to serve with the army nurses on Bataan; then, once more, Colonel Wibb Cooper met with Maude Davison to come up with some names, eleven this time, among them an older nurse, a grief-stricken younger woman unable to work and a nurse whose weight had dropped to seventy pounds.

When Ruby Motley, an army dietitian, heard about the submarine, she went directly to Cooper and boldly asked to be put on the evacuation list. "I knew him quite well," she later recalled. "I said, 'I sure would like to go out on that sub!' I didn't want to go on those PBY planes; they didn't have much of a chance of making it. A sub, I thought, would. He looked at me and said, 'Ruby, you are the only dietitian we have and we can't do without you.' Well . . . I felt like two cents! I never said another word."[26]

As before, Wainwright relied on Cooper and Davison to tell him which women to send to safety, but now he wanted to make one of the choices himself, Gladys "Ann" Mealor.

Mealor had been the chief nurse on Corregidor in the early stages of the war and the general had gotten to know her well. She had worked hard, he felt, and deserved to go home, but Ann Mealor, in her mid-thirties and at the time as sick and weary as any of the women, simply refused.

"I couldn't see how anybody could walk off and leave all those wounded people," she said. "I had enough faith in that old tunnel that I could make it if the japs [*sic*] came in. [After that] I didn't plan on what would happen."[27]

Wainwright later called her decision "one of the most courageous acts of the entire campaign: . . . I consider—and still consider—this a truly great act of heroism. She knew as well as I that she was signing her captivity warrant."[28]

One of the last on the list was Ruth Straub.

[*Straub Diary, May 4*] Last night 13 of us—a navy wife, a navy nurse, and 10 other army nurses besides myself—were called to the surgeon's office and ordered to be ready to leave Corregidor by 7:30 P.M. Wondered how many of the girls were leaving. Wondered if there would be time for General Wainwright to get all the nurses out of the tunnel. Wondered how we would leave.

Again among the women left behind there was anger and ambivalence, though clearly less than before. As their colleagues got ready to leave, some of the women, realizing that this was their last chance to send word home, pressed letters into the hands of those leaving.

[*Straub Diary, May 4, cont'd*] The girls were grand in their wishes for us as we left, although there were tears in the eyes of some, and many wore a look of hopelessness. I was thrilled, but I felt like a heel. What of all those left behind? Would they get away? So many doubts, so many worries . . .[29]

Eleanor Garen gave one of the women a note to her sister.

Dear Lauretta,

Tonight there is a way [to evacuate] some [nurses] so I will send this to you. It is hard to know what to say and how to say it but my mood is not so good. If Jeanne [her best friend Jeanne Kennedy] were going I would feel better but the way things go it makes me bitter. Gastinger is going!

We are living on a bulls-eye and every day is the same. As yet I have no regret over coming here. . . . It is so hot. I know what living on a deserted island is like now. Even though it is crowded and small here I still am lonely. Give my love to the rest of the family.[30]

Wainwright gave his favorite Smith & Wesson revolver to a departing friend with instructions to pass it on to his son. He also sent a complete list of the Americans still alive on Corregidor and a list of recent military promotions.

[*Straub Diary, May 4*] General Wainwright stood at the entrance to the tunnel, shook hands with all of us and gave us his best wishes. Many of the men stood about waving good-by and shouting "Good luck to you!"[31]

At roughly 7:45 P.M. the evacuees, under bombardment, climbed onto a converted yacht for the short ride to the rendezvous point, four miles out to sea southwest of Corregidor. At 9:30 P.M. a large, black shape rose out of the water. From the conning tower a blinking light signaled the yacht's passengers aboard. The evacuees slipped quickly through the hatch belowdecks, the crew loaded baggage and mail, and in less than an hour the U.S.S. *Spearfish* had descended to a depth of two hundred feet and was on its way south to safety.

During the next twenty-four hours Japanese shore batteries fired more than sixteen thousand shells at Corregidor, most at the beach defenses manned by the marines. Sometime before midnight on May 5 under a full moon, lookouts spotted fifteen Japanese landing barges, part of the first wave. Wainwright radioed General Marshall in Washington, telling him a landing was imminent. Then he ordered his men to burn all secret code books and strategic papers.

In their lateral the women waited. Maude Davison and Josie Nesbit huddled together, trying to figure out how they might safeguard their staff. Minutes later an officer approached the lateral and informed the women that the Japanese had landed at Monkey Point, a spot down the beach just northeast of the tunnel. The fighting was fierce, he said. Meanwhile the lookouts had spotted a second wave of enemy barges, this time loaded with artillery pieces and tanks.

The fifty-four army and twenty-six Filipino nurses, along with an army dietitian, an army physical therapist and twenty-one civilian women, passed the hour with their patients.[32]

Throughout the night, men from other laterals came to the hospital laterals and bid the women good-bye.

Chapter 9

A Handful Go Home

NO ONE SURVIVES at war without luck. The evacuees from Corregidor were trying to pull the flower of safety, as Shakespeare called it, from the nettle of despair. A few made it, a few did not.

The two seaplanes that left Corregidor on the night of April 29 rendezvoused at Lake Lanao, on the Philippine island of Mindanao, then hid until sunset, when they tried to take off under the cover of darkness.

A stiff wind had put a heavy chop on the water and the first PBY struggled several times before it became airborne. As it circled in a holding pattern, seaplane number two tried to taxi into position, but the turbulence kept blowing it back to shore, and all at once one of the women aboard heard a crunching sound. A rock beneath the waterline had ripped a hole in number two's fuselage, and the cabin began to fill with water.[1]

In the darkness and wet the passengers disembarked, while a navy boat crew and salvage expert worked on the damaged ship. The colonel who took command of the evacuees from number two said he did not think the PBY could be repaired; therefore, he wanted the group to hide until MacArthur sent a rescue plane or boat. Everyone agreed with the colonel's decision, and together they went inland to seek a hiding place. They made their way to an old hotel a safe distance from the Japanese lines.[2]

By late afternoon the next day the crew of number two had been able to effect repairs and was ready to try again, but the nurses and colonels were nowhere in sight. And now the Japanese were less than twenty miles from the lake—and closing.

The pilots in number two had no choice—they had to take off or lose their ship to the enemy. They waited as long as they dared, then taxied onto the lake, turned the ship's nose into the wind, and gave the engine full throttle.[3]

(The passengers who had been left behind—ten army nurses, three women dependents, a naval officer and an army colonel—tried for almost two weeks to evade the Japanese, wandering from one house or farm to another until, at last, there was no place left to hide. The group surrendered to a unit of the Japanese army about midday on May 11. The men were shipped to military prisons on Luzon. The women worked in a hospital on Mindanao until the early fall, when they were sent to Manila and imprisoned there in a civilian internment camp.)

*P*BY NUMBER ONE set down on the waters of Port Darwin, Australia, around 8:30 A.M., May 1, 1942, an arrival that capped what was then the longest rescue in United States history. To some at Allied headquarters in Australia, the 7,300-mile round-trip flight was nothing short of a miracle.

The ten nurses aboard were bone-weary with fatigue but hardly cowed. Combat emboldens those who survive it, and, according to one officer who claims to have watched the arrival, some of the women still had some fight in them—or at least some leftover anger.

From his quarters near the water, Stuart Shadrick Murray, a naval officer in charge of a submarine division at Port Darwin, watched as PBY number one taxied to the dock.

[The women disembarked] then they locked arms . . . and started down the main street. . . . The Australians . . . got out of their way and would just stand on the sidewalks gawking. The Americans would do the same because these nurses were singing at the top of their voices, and they were pretty loud too, 'Dig a little deeper in your dugout, Dugout Doug' [as MacArthur was called by many of those he'd left on Bataan and Corregidor]. And they knew verses I'd never heard of and none of us had. Apparently they had put it together and it was anything but complimentary. I had the doubtful honor of being told to go out . . . and break it up. . . . I . . . tried to talk with them by walking ahead of them. They were walking at a pretty brisk pace because they were accustomed to marching and I tried to walk backwards first, and almost fell down, then I walked with them and talked over my shoulder and finally I talked them into breaking it up. I might add it

took two or three blocks of walking before I got them to break it up. . . .
They were hardened. There was no question about it.[4]

Hardened? Perhaps Commander Shadrick let his view of women, and of himself, color his memory.

For their part, the evacuees remembered feeling stunned at first, and disoriented. The heavy thuds of bombs were still fresh in their ears, and they stood on the pier, suspended in the moment, trying to situate themselves in a new time and place.

As they began to get their bearings, a few knelt and put their lips to the Australian soil, while others, tears coursing down their cheeks, flung themselves into one another's arms.

Later, during physicals at a local hospital, they stood in front of full-length mirrors, and what they saw shocked them—faces gray and drawn, eyes limpid and hollow, bodies left androgynously flat by months of hard labor and want. (About this time the women learned that PBY number two had arrived empty and that their comrades had been left behind. "We told each other they'd be all right," wrote Juanita Redmond. "You can't [keep] that lot down."[5])

On May 5 the army flew the nurses to headquarters in Melbourne. It was winter in Australia and the women, still in their air corps coveralls, shivered in the cold.

At Port Melbourne Hospital they were issued regulation uniforms, real clothes for the first time in months. "You look almost human again," Eunice Hatchitt told one of her companions.[6] And the army, apparently noticing the same thing, decided it was time to trot them out for the press.

They were good copy, these women who had nursed under the guns in the jungles of Bataan and the tunnels of Corregidor. Their example might inspire other women to take up nursing and military commission. And their story—a tale of courage and escape—might boost the morale of a nation reeling from a series of costly shambles and bitter defeats.

So they took their places at a press conference, sat there politely and respectfully in a room crowded with reporters, answering questions about what they had missed the most—"enormous hamburgers smothered in onions"[7]—and about life under fire.

They did not talk about their guilt, of course. That was a private matter. Alone at night or sleepless in the early morning, the evacuees were haunted—there is no better word for it—by the ghosts of Malinta Tunnel, the ghosts too of the thousands of patients they'd left lying on the jungle floor.

On their second evening in Melbourne, the evacuees got word that Corregidor had surrendered. They thought of their friends, the women they had left behind, and were afraid, but they did not give voice to their fears, did not speak of the unspeakable. Instead they looked for a little light. At least their comrades were no longer under the bombs, they told one another. What's more, the nurse corps had Davison and Nesbit to lead it. Surely they'd get the rest of the group through.

I₂ LATE MAY, wearing new, dark-blue uniforms and garrison caps, eight of the ten evacuees from PBY number one boarded a ship for San Francisco. (Catherine Acorn and Willa Hook had lobbied their superiors to remain in Australia because they wanted "to be near enough to be among the first to go back to Manila."[8]) And on June 11, 1942, after an easy Pacific passing, the still weary but elated evacuees stood at the rail of the ship, looking at what to them must have been a halcyon sight—the Golden Gate Bridge.

"Oh, God!" Eunice Hatchitt said. "I'm home! God bless America."[9]

At Letterman General Hospital on the Presidio army base, doctors treated the women for jungle diseases, chronic fatigue and exaggerated weight loss. They needed to rest, required quiet to restore themselves, and the army tried to shield them, give them that sanctuary, but the interviews they had granted in Australia had been carried in papers at home, and now the relatives of the soldiers captured on Bataan were begging to talk with the nurses, and, ill or not, the women felt they had no choice but to receive them.

The worried, the tormented, the sick-in-the-soul lined up at the public relations office, and hour after hour the women sat listening to their pleas and entreaties.

Had they seen this mother's son? That wife's husband? This sister's brother?

Did they remember a Bobby, a Billy Joe, a Mike or a Phil?

How about the third battalion—did they make it?

Anyone from Opelika, Alabama, come in wounded? See any boys from Murfreesboro, Tennessee?

Some of the relatives wept as they talked; others, unable to speak, just sat there. Now and then someone would faint, shocked into unconsciousness by the awful blow of not knowing anything at all—or hearing the thing they least wanted to hear.

The nurses, of course, knew the terrible truth of the battle—the shortages, the starvation, the wanton sacrifice—but they held back these details. Why add to the weight of the losses, they thought?

When word of these sessions spread, people who could not make the trip west deluged the hospital with mail and telegrams and telephone calls. There were so many inquiries, the Red Cross sent a stenographer to help sort them out. It was a sad business, opening those letters:

"The boy's mother is so ill from worry that I am writing this in her stead."

"He was our only son and . . ."

"My husband and I weren't married very long but . . ."

"We have three children and I don't know what to tell them of their father."[10]

Such heartache was more than some of the nurses could bear. They already carried their own regrets and now some of them felt they were failing these families as well.

"The two hardest periods of my entire life were leaving our sick troops in bed on Bataan and hearing people beg, plead, and cry about their sons when I got home," said Eunice Hatchitt.[11]

Most difficult of all were letters from the loved ones of the women that the evacuees had left behind. Difficult to read, these letters, and difficult to answer.

June 19, 1942

Dear Mrs. Whitwell [Eleanor Garen's sister],

Sorry I have nothing more to report other than a rumor, you know what they're like. But, a Red Cross worker here says five more nurses are in Australia—they're supposed to have escaped *after* Corregidor fell. Now we'll get some good dope even if Eleanor wasn't among those lucky ones. . . .

Sue Gallagher

November 9, 1942

Dear Mrs. Whitwell,

Little Jeanne Kennedy was with [Eleanor] that last time I saw them. They were both well and had not been wounded or ill. I haven't had any word from those over there since I got here in the States in July. . . .

I know that you do want to know what effect the situation there had on Eleanor and I feel sure that I might say that she took it as well as the rest of us and perhaps better than most of us. Her usual high spirits were undaunted and she was as jolly as it was possible for anyone to be. . . .

So far the Y.B.B.'s ["yellow-bellied bastards"] won't give us a prisoner list. . . .

I feel awfully helpless . . . to think that I can do nothing to help get those back here where they belong. . . .

Sincerely,
Leona Gastinger[12]

Dear Mrs. Gates [mother of Marcia Gates],

I can full well realize your anxiety over Marcia. I saw her last in the tunnel at Corregidor. At that time Marcia was looking fine. She seemed quite cheerful and was well throughout the terrible siege. She and I were quite closely associated and I grew to be fond of her. Just a few nights before I left, Marcia and I had quite a long chat together at which time she showed me your picture and discussed you at length. She truly thinks you are the grandest mother ever. She also showed me pictures of her sister.

I appreciate your deep concern and you have my sincere sympathy. Only were it possible that all could have returned. . . . Mrs. Gates, I don't know how we were selected to be among the first to get out. . . . Please try to be brave and hopeful they will all return to us soon.

Sincerely,
Juanita Redmond

August 15, 1942

Dear Mrs. Gates,

Your letter was forwarded to me. . . . I may be wrong but I believe that the girls would appreciate little necessities such as hose, garters, cold cream, bobby pins, little light dresses, slips, panties, brassieres [*sic*], Kotex, candy, soap, wash cloths, towels, nail files, tweezers, bath powder, sanitary belts, stationery, snacks, gum, life-savers, tooth-pastes—oh there are hundreds of light, inexpensive gifts that you could find in a dime store. In our experience, we found that it wasn't luxuries we wanted but the necessities. I believe that money would be worthless. . . .

In the meantime I'll try to find the addresses of some of the parents who have daughters in P.I. and will send the information on to you.

Be good and keep your chin up!

Sincerely,
Ruth Straub[13]

MEANWHILE IN THE South Pacific, another group of evacuees were trying to make their escape.

Like most World War II submarines, the U.S.S. *Spearfish* was a small, crowded vessel, and now, carrying twenty-seven extra souls, passengers from Corregidor—twelve staff officers, a civilian dependent, two enlisted men who had stowed away, a navy nurse and eleven army nurses—there was barely room to turn in place.[14]

As the *Spearfish* slowly and carefully picked its way through the minefields around Corregidor and slipped quietly under the Japanese patrols, the crew warned the passengers to keep still. If the enemy attacked and dropped depth charges, they said, the passengers were to cover their heads with pillows and blankets, and pray.

For many long, hot, malodorous hours, the twelve nurses sat silently and anxiously, waiting for the danger to pass and breathing the stale air. Some thought their rescue ship a shoe box, others imagined it a sardine can.

By the second night, Lieutenant James Dempsey, the ship's captain, had brought the *Spearfish* beyond the blockade and decided to surface.

On deck the passengers got one last look at the Rock, now just a fiery dot on the South China Sea. Standing on deck and staring back at the horizon, they thanked Providence for their deliverance and their luck.

Life at sea in tight quarters "took some getting used to," as one of the women put it.[15] Everything—eating, sleeping and daily ablutions— had to be done in shifts. The crew, of course, got first priority; the *Spearfish,* after all, was a combat vessel, and, passengers or no, it was on patrol in enemy waters.

Eight of the nurses were assigned to four bunks in the aft quarters, and the crew introduced them to the submarine tradition of the "hot bunk," eight hours sleep for the first shift of four, then, sliding between the same sheets, the second shift took their turn.

In the tropical heat the *Spearfish* was a sweatbox and soon the nurses took to wearing men's undershirts and cut-off dungarees. By day the ship ran submerged, but at night it would often surface and fill its compartments with fresh air.

Of all their trials at sea, the women most remembered (most laughed at) their daily struggles with the ship's lavatories, the "heads," as navy called them. The crew was assigned to the aft head, the officers to the head in the torpedo room, and the women to a head near the officers wardroom.

The instructions for using the head were posted on the bulkheads next to each commode, but some of the women felt they needed a degree in mechanical engineering to interpret them.

> *Before using, see that bowl flapper valve "A" is closed, gate valve "C" in discharge pipe is open, valve "D" in water supply is open. Then open valve "E" next to bowl to admit necessary water. Close valves "D" and "E." After using—pull lever "A." Release lever "A." Open valve "G" in air supply line. Rock air valve "F" lever outboard to change measuring tank to 10 pounds above sea pressure. Open valve "B" and rock air valve lever inboard to blow overboard. Close valves "B," "C," and "G."*[16]

If the occupant missed just one step, she was showered with the contents of the bowl, and after a number of these "accidents," the nurses pleaded for help and managed to convince a Filipino mess boy to perform the mechanics of the flush. The women were so grateful for this service, they awarded their official flusher the honorarium "Captain of the Head."[17]

As the ship cruised south toward Australia, the nurses, somewhat rested now, offered the *Spearfish* crew their labor, and they worked in the galley and mess, cooking, washing dishes and helping serve the meals. Their willingness to pitch in made them popular with the crew, and soon their section of the ship seemed to draw a large number of visitors.

Submariners can get a little gamy, but on this passage the men began to show an unusual interest in their appearance and hygiene, changes observed by the crew's resident humorist and poet, a yeoman named McDermott.

WHAT WOMEN CAN DO TO A SUBMARINE CREW
Beyond a doubt you will surely note
If you walk about, a change in the boat.
Swede started drinking coffee
Beast started drinking tea
Pushover keeps buffing as pretty as can be.
Petit Scanlon's smoking cigarettes and washing clothes
And even our dear Yeoman stopped picking his funny nose.
Joey's up and about all the time off watch
Hanging around the mess hall playing the music box.

I'm trying to say in all these verses
We brought aboard a flock of pretty nurses
On that eventful day in May
When we were out Corregidor Way.

The nurses, in the person of Helen Summers, answered with some doggerel of their own:

And now you'll hear our side of the story.
Since we can't take all of the glory
For Swede drinking tea
And the rest of the boys acting funny as can be,
We want you to know we're happy as can be,
Being part of the Navy, though not permanently.
The boat of the deep to us is salvation.
If is wasn't for it we'd be in concentration.[18]

Around the third week in May the *Spearfish* docked at Rottnest Island off Fremantle, Australia, and Ann Bernatitus, the navy nurse, reported to a navy hospital there. The army nurses, meanwhile, boarded a troop train to Melbourne, where army physicians treated their ailments. Then ten of the eleven—Hortense McKay elected to stay in Australia with the Allied forces—boarded the transport U.S.S. *West Point* for the trip home.

The *West Point,* likely taking the safest route home—shipping lanes beyond the enemy's reach—steamed up the western coast of South America, through the Panama Canal, then north to New York.

The War Department had alerted the press to the ship's arrival, and when the *West Point* sailed into New York Harbor on July 2, 1942, its docking was broadcast live by radio across the United States.

In Big Sandy, Texas, some of Lucy Wilson's landsmen heard the broadcast and were so excited they walked a mile outside town to shake hands with her parents and congratulate them on their daughter's safe return.

*T*HE AMERICA THE nurses returned to in the summer of 1942 was a much different country than the America they had left a year or so before. Everywhere, it seemed, there were men in uniform, women too, a shift in gender roles that caught the nurses a bit off guard.

While they had been serving overseas, Congress had authorized the formation of the Women's Army Auxiliary Corps, or WAACS. By the end of the year, the government had won approval for Women Accepted for Volunteer Emergency Service, the navy WAVES, as well as the Marine Corps Women's Reserve and the Coast Guard SPARS. Women, however, were not being trained for combat; instead they were considered replacements for clerical or behind-the-lines workers, freeing up men to fight.

The government especially needed nurses. In the year leading up to the summer of 1942, the ranks of the Army Nurse Corps nearly doubled, from less than 7,000 active-duty nurses to 12,475. During the same period the Navy Nurse Corps grew from 430 women to more than 1,800. The leaders of both corps were given field-grade rank—an important distinction previously denied them—and all military nurses were treated as officers and allowed to wear the various insignias of their grade, although, typically, they were paid significantly less than men of equivalent rank.

With a two-front war, however, the numbers of the army and navy nurse corps were still too low, so the government established the National Council for War Service, an alliance of professional nursing organizations, to coordinate recruiting and meet a goal of 2,500 enlistees a month. Fulfilling that quota required a massive national effort. And to the government, the nurses of Bataan and Corregidor were recruiting posters come to life.

The eighteen "heroes in skirts," fresh from combat and full of stories about life in the field and under fire, were offered as models of sacrifice and devotion to duty, paradigms of American womanhood, at least the kind the War Department wanted. It did not matter that they were still tired and sick. They were needed on the recruiting trail and the warbond hustings.

On July 1, 1942, in the gardens of the National Red Cross Headquarters in Washington, D.C., the government formerly launched its campaign to recruit more nurses. The army nurses who had escaped on the PBY became the first American women decorated for bravery in World War II. Among those attending the large, formal ceremony were James C. Magee, the surgeon general of the United States; John McCloy, assistant secretary of war; Frances Bolton, a congresswoman from Ohio; and the first lady of the United States, Eleanor Roosevelt.

Mrs. Roosevelt had flown in from her apartment in New York especially for the occasion. In the audience were representatives from five Washington-area hospitals, many military and Red Cross nurses, radio broadcasters, newsreel cameramen and scores of newspaper reporters and photographers. The Army Air Force band played rousing music, and the evacuees in their new blue uniforms and overseas caps stood stiffly at attention.

Looking at old, black-and-white glossies of that day, it is easy to read their faces. Clearly the women were weary—the eyes show that. Equally clear is a certain frailty in their expressions, a look, perhaps, of resignation or forbearance or, in some cases, sorrow.

One speaker after another hailed the women's courage. The chairman of the Red Cross compared them with the Minutemen of Lexington and the defenders of the Alamo. Mrs. Roosevelt spoke last. She reminded the audience that her four sons were in uniform and hoped there would be enough nurses on duty at hospitals and aid stations to give them the care they might need. Then she looked at the evacuees and said that the president had been thinking of them: "Your heroism has touched him deeply. To you present today he wishes me to say, 'God bless you for service well done.' To those left behind and held by the enemy, he says, 'Have faith, for the day of liberation will come.' "[19]

Afterward the nurses were invited to tea with the first lady, and when she was introduced to them and shook their hands, she called them "Lieutenant" instead of "Miss," something none of the women ever forgot.[20] She told them how happy she was that they were well, then wished them good luck and Godspeed.

Five days later in a similar but smaller ceremony, the nurses from the *Spearfish* received their medals. The navy honored Ann Bernatitus in its own celebration, giving her a newly created award, the Legion of Merit; she was the only navy nurse in World War II so honored. Her citation in part read:

> *Constantly in the front lines of defense in the Manila-Bataan Area, and on two separate occasions, forced to evacuate to a new position after Japanese bombs had wrecked the Surgical Unit, Nurse Bernatitus courageously withstood the dangers and rigors of tropical combat rendering efficient and devoted service during the tense days of prolonged siege and evacuation.*[21]

In between the ceremonies and appearances, many of the women found their way home, often to unexpected acclaim. About six thousand people turned out at Lockhart High School Stadium in Texas to greet Eunice Hatchitt; the local congressman, Lyndon Baines Johnson, presented her with the keys to the city. In Exeter, Pennsylvania, hundreds of Ann Bernatitus's neighbors gave her a testimonial dinner and a wristwatch. The people of Big Sandy, Texas, held a reception for Lucy Wilson, then went out and bought her a new wardrobe, which she badly needed. Lucy was so grateful, she wore everything handed her, including the size-sixteen dresses that hung like tents on her seventy-pound frame.

After their leaves were over, the women returned to the war-bond and recruiting drives. They made speeches, posed for photographs, gave interviews, christened new ships and accepted honoraria. Few of the nurses, if any, relished this attention. In fact, tired as they were and racked with doubt, they wanted anonymity, not celebrity. But no one protested, no one felt she could say no.

Newspapers and magazines feasted on their story. *The New Yorker, Collier's, The American Magazine* and *Hospitals Magazine* all ran major articles. Ruth Straub's diary was syndicated in newspapers across the country. Two books that turned on the Bataan experience became bestsellers—W. L. White's *They Were Expendable,* which chronicled the exploits of four patrol-torpedo boat officers and one army nurse,[22] and *I Served on Bataan,* Juanita Redmond's first-person account of her time in the jungle and escape from Corregidor.[23]

In all of this the nurses were characterized as selfless, calm, courageous, and certainly to greater or lesser degrees these salutes applied. To be under fire is, of itself, an act worth honoring. And to stand faithfully by their patients with the enemy advancing was, by any measure, a gesture of fidelity and love. But to the evacuees this praise was a burden because it was delivered in a plethora of prose that in many instances was pure fiction or rank, degrading melodrama.

Even *The New York Times Magazine* got carried away, taking the notion of "heroine" to ludicrous extremes.

> *A couple of days before Bataan fell a batch of nurses left the comparative safety of the "hospitals" and slogged forward to do what they could in the front lines. They were rounded up finally, dazed and exhausted, by some officers who tucked them in a jeep and sent them to an embarkation point for Corregidor.*
>
> *A nurse, knowing that one of the officers would never get to the Rock, swiped some vitamin tablets, which were the equivalent of gold, took a jeep, and drove through no-man's land to his gun emplacement to give them to him. Others doled out sedatives to men they felt sure would be wounded. . . .*
>
> *Once when the Japanese were pouring in on all sides just a few miles away, several of the nurses asked the officers to shoot them before they could be taken prisoner.*[24]

Such utter nonsense galled the women. Like anyone who has ever suffered the depravity of war, the nurses wanted to bear witness. And to make a comic myth of such experience was to demean their sacrifice and mock their testimony.

The overwrought prose and preposterous characterizations were in many ways a product of the times. As soon as the first bombs fell on Pearl Harbor and the Philippines, the roles of American women began to change, but common notions about women, the ways the culture cast them, for the most part stayed the same.

Now the "weaker sex" was suddenly being lionized and the result was a confused, if not schizophrenic, portrait of American womanhood: one moment gutsy patriots doing a dirty job, the next vessels of virtue who needed the protection of men—"the nurses asked the officers to shoot them"—women to the very end, as foolish and hysterical as ever.

And nowhere was this confusion, this cultural paradox, more apparent than in Hollywood.

Certainly some of the cinematic excesses committed in the name of nationalism and morale can be accepted, or at least easily understood. The country, after all, was at war, a world war against a fascistic military cabal and a megalomaniac bent on slaughtering anyone in his way.

No medium delivers a message more powerfully than film, and Hollywood was eager to prove its loyalty, utility and service to the cause by producing dramas of women and war that doubled as effective home-front propaganda. Metro-Goldwyn-Mayer's 1943 *Cry Havoc,* an ensemble movie about army women living in underground barracks on Bataan (there were no subterranean quarters, of course), offers a tough-as-nails portrait of the nurses.[25] In 1944 David O. Selznick produced one of the year's top-grossing movies, *Since You Went Away,* a film that focuses on the travails of Anne Hilton, a mother who keeps home and family together while her husband fights overseas. In a central scene, Hilton, played by Claudette Colbert, listens carefully as an elderly lady proudly explains that her granddaughter is one of the nurses stranded on Corregidor, a wartime martyr whose sacrifice leads Hilton to reexamine her selfishness.[26] Donna Reed starred in the 1945 film version of the book *They Were Expendable.* Cast as an army nurse on Corregidor in love with the commander of a PT boat, Reed in one scene was absurdly costumed in military overalls and a string of pearls.[27] Finally there was *So Proudly We Hail,* a Paramount Studios release that stands out from all others in the war-heroine genre because its putative aim was to tell the story of the battle for the Philippines through the eyes of the nurses who served there.[28]

WHEN *SO PROUDLY WE HAIL* went into preproduction, Paramount executives wanted a simple romance. The director and screenwriter, however, were obliged to seek and accept the advice of the domestic branch of the Bureau of Motion Pictures, a division of the Office of War Information that monitored all films about the war. In this case the government rejected the romance formula and demanded that the filmmakers aim instead for some verisimilitude—a realistic depiction of the war in the Pacific, toned down, to be sure, so as not to frighten or demoralize the public.[29]

Throughout the writing and planning of *So Proudly We Hail,* one of the evacuees, Eunice Hatchitt, played a central role. Hatchitt had escaped from Corregidor by PBY. Tall and athletic with a soft Texas accent, she tried to avoid the limelight by staying home, but her convalescence was interrupted by a call from Florence Blanchfield, assistant superintendent of the Army Nurse Corps.

Blanchfield told Hatchitt that the War Department had given Paramount Studios permission to make a movie about the nurses on Bataan, and Mark Sandrich, a director known for his work on musical comedies, and Allan Scott, the project's screenwriter, needed a nurse as a technical consultant. Hatchitt, who believed they were making a "documentary," accepted the assignment.

"I thought it would be the experience of a lifetime, that I could help. I had everything about the Philippines still fresh in my mind," she said.[30]

Why Hatchitt had been culled from the group of evacuees is somewhat of a mystery. She was smart, articulate, attractive and loyal to the nurse corps, a logical candidate for the job, but others, too, likely met Blanchfield's criteria. Whatever the reason, Hatchitt, eager for a change of scene, said good-bye to her family, took a train west, and checked into the Hermoy Apartment Hotel in Los Angeles.

Her initial task was to work with Sandrich, who was in the process of fashioning dialogue from the diaries of some of the nurses. At first Hatchitt liked what she saw. The fictional characters bore some resemblance to the women she had known. She also liked the verisimilitude of the costumes and sets, taken from photographs of Hospital #1 that had appeared in *Life* magazine, right down to the tin roofs and the nurses' air corps coveralls.

But as the film went forward, Eunice Hatchitt began to notice certain inconsistencies in the script and a number of inaccuracies as well. Somewhat naive and certainly untutored in Hollywood's ways, Hatchitt thought the film would be an accurate record of the women's experience, but the producers and the studio, of course, had something else in mind.

SET IN MAY 1942, *So Proudly We Hail* opens on a ship returning home from the Philippines and carrying a group of army nurses who have survived the battles of Bataan and Corregidor. One of the women, Lieutenant "Davey" Davidson (played by Claudette Colbert), sits in a deck chair, apparently in some kind of a stupor. In an attempt to discover the cause of Davey's detachment, a doctor begins to interview her fellow nurses to find out what happened to the group. The women describe their lives in the Bataan jungle—working under the bombs, the long hours, the lack of supplies, the advancing enemy, and so on. Naturally, they find the time to pursue the handsome officers in their midst, and the audience learns that Davey had a romance with Lieutenant John Sommers (George Reeves). As Davey and the other nurses prepare to evacuate Bataan, Sommers is wounded in the leg and Davey assists in the operation, then drags him into a rowboat bound for Corregidor, a woman saving her man from the enemy, a thin reversal that does little to redeem the film's formula characterizations. (Earlier in the movie, for example, the nurses appear trapped by a squad of Japanese infantry until one of them, Olivia Darcey [Veronica Lake], lets down her gorgeous blond hair and walks seductively toward the leering Japanese soldiers, then pulls the pin on a grenade she has secreted in her bosom and blows herself and the enemy to bits.) Meanwhile, Captain "Ma" McGregor (Mary Servoss), the nurses' dauntless leader, is almost masculine in her demeanor as a commanding officer—stalwart, that is, until her son becomes wounded and is carried to the hospital. There, as he is dying, she comes to his side, the weeping, grief-stricken mother. Finally, on Corregidor, Davey marries Lieutenant Sommers, with Ma McGregor's blessing, before he is sent on a secret mission to find some stores of quinine. While he is away Davey is ordered off the Rock to Australia, but she refuses to leave until she knows whether her husband has survived. When she learns he has been declared missing in action, she collapses and falls into a comalike state. The film ends on board the ship steaming for home, with the doctor explaining to Davey's comrades that her stupor is a manifestation of her fear and grief. The doctor then reads aloud one of Sommers's last letters to Davey, a missive that emphasizes the importance of their cause and reassures his wife that one day they again will be together. Davey suddenly regains her senses and with her sister nurses at her side, determines to carry on the fight.

So Proudly We Hail was one of the biggest moneymakers of 1943, in part because the movie was advertised as a "realistic" picture of the fighting on Bataan and Corregidor and an accurate portrayal of women at war. Like every war movie ever made, the film not only reflected reigning cultural views, it reverted to clichés and types. It was storytelling, not history, and as such missed the point.

The women on Bataan and Corregidor simply did what they had to do, no more and no less than the men who fought alongside them. They were not heroes, but their service was considered extraordinary because no one expected them to do what they did. They had not been trained for war as the men had; they were not equipped, in any sense, to take part in battle. It would have been far more accurate to have portrayed them simply as an eclectic assemblage of anonymous citizen-soldiers, ordinary people called upon to perform extraordinary acts.

But life and art are always different, always properly out of sync. And that is why filmmakers wink, or at least look a bit abashed, when they insist that their dramas, their stories, are "realistic." What is more, no one could have told the real story of Bataan—the government likely would not have allowed it—the story of the filth, the hunger, the bungling and the abandonment that took place in the Philippines. To tell the truth would have been to reveal the shameless circumstances that led to the loss of Bataan and Corregidor in the first place, to expose the inadequate supplies, the sloppy military planning and the rank political decisions that led to the Bataan Death March and the capture of 72,000 allied combat troops and seventy-seven American military women.

Still, Eunice Hatchitt, reading the script and looking for "the truth," was upset. When she came to the pages where the character of Olivia Darcey kills herself and her Japanese pursuers with a grenade tucked in her cleavage, Hatchitt popped. The nurses had treated their Japanese prisoners with care and compassion, not the racist rage that drove the Darcey character to avenge her lover in an erotic suicide.

Hatchitt called Blanchfield. She told the colonel that she wanted to be reassigned, but Blanchfield refused and chided the nurse for being so thin-skinned. The director and scriptwriter were allowed some license with the story, Blanchfield said, especially if their movie helped morale and recruitment. Hatchitt argued that, as she saw it, the movie's cardboard characters would disaffect recruits, not attract them. But Blanchfield had heard enough. She ended the conversation by reminding the young nurse that she was under orders. Did she understand? She was to stay at her post and complete the assignment.

Now, with almost every scene, Hatchitt became more and more irritable and provoked. She hated the lovemaking in the foxholes and was embarrassed when the character of the senior nurse begs her commanding officer to evacuate the women off Bataan.

During the filming, two of the movie's stars tried to sit Hatchitt down and soothe her ire. Claudette Colbert and Paulette Goddard often invited the nurse to their homes and asked her to tell them what the war was "really like." The nurse was flattered and a little thrilled to be in such company, but she continued to protest the liberties that both the director and screenwriter were still taking.

So Proudly We Hail opened in June 1943 at the industry's most prestigious venue, Radio City Music Hall in New York. The critics loved it; the audience came in droves, day after day, week after week.

The nurses, however, were embarrassed. They hated the movie—it trivialized their experience, they said, their sacrifice, their ordeal—and they blamed Eunice Hatchitt for everything. She had betrayed them, they said, and it took years, in some cases decades, before they forgave her.[31]

Chapter 10

In Enemy Hands

T HE FIRST WAVE of Japanese came ashore around midnight. By ten the next morning the allies had suffered eight hundred killed and a thousand wounded. The casualties crowded the hospital laterals in Malinta Tunnel. Wainwright, looking at the wounded and the women tending them, seemed ready to act.

> I went over our position in my mind—shaken troops, beach defenses literally pulverized . . . new and uncontested landings . . . But it was the terror that is vested in a tank that was the deciding factor. I thought of the havoc that even one of these could wreak if it nosed into the tunnel, where lay our helpless wounded and their brave nurses.[1]

According to official records and reports, Wainwright "decided" to surrender Corregidor at 10:00 A.M. on the morning of May 6, but clearly the general knew much earlier that he was going to haul down the flag. At some point during the night, he must have told his senior aides and commanders, including those in the medical corps, that he was going to surrender at midmorning, because sometime before dawn, Maude Davison "routed" her nurses out of bed, as one of them put it, to discuss their imminent capture.[2]

Summoned to the hospital mess hall, the fifty-four army nurses looked dazed as they sat down quietly on the long benches and folded their hands on the tables in front of them. Davison looked at the faces— thin, pale, dark circles under their eyes. Now and then in the dank tunnel air, someone would cough. The senior nurse had no book to follow on this one, no official protocol. Her charges had been the first group of military women in combat, and now they were about to become among the first to fall into enemy hands.[3]

Order number one: at all times they were to wear their khaki uniforms and carry their gas masks. Order number two: they were to make sure their Red Cross armbands were always on their sleeve, this in the hope that the Japanese would respect the universal symbol for noncombatants. Finally: they were to stay in the sleeping lateral or, if on duty, in the ward. To wander alone in another lateral would surely invite trouble, she said.

The women looked at their captain, then at one another.

"The bombing had stopped and it was quiet and there was a feeling—well, it's hard to say what the feeling was," said Hattie Brantley. "We were concerned and worried—we had all heard of the Rape of Nanking—but we thought maybe [with the fighting over] things would be for the better."[4]

Hope, of course, is often just a mask.

"I was scared spitless," said Inez McDonald. "The night before surrender I went to sleep in another bed way in the back of our lateral, and I slept with my helmet on my head."[5]

No one was sure what to expect. Would the Japanese shock troops shoot their way into the tunnel? Or would they, as Wainwright feared, point their flamethrowers down the laterals and turn the tunnels into an inferno? Pharmacist's Mate Ernest J. Irwin thought "the Japs would either gas us in the tunnel or march us out and shoot us."[6] One wounded officer handed a nurse his West Point class ring and asked her to make sure the keepsake got home to his wife and daughter.

At 10:00 A.M. the nurses were officially informed that Wainwright planned to go on tunnel radio and in an open broadcast, tell the enemy he was ready to surrender.

When "we heard the surrender broadcast," said Bertha "Charlie" Dworsky, "I don't think there was a dry eye in the place."

An optimist, Dworsky had convinced herself that the enemy would treat the women decently, perhaps even send them home.

"We always felt we were noncombatants, according to the Geneva Convention. If we were captured, we would be put on a Red Cross boat and sent away," she said. "Then the war would be over for us."[7]

The others, less sanguine about their prospects, set about hiding their valuables. One woman slipped her rings onto a safety pin, then secured the pin far down inside her blouse so that no one could see its outline. Another nurse made a huge curl on the top of her head and placed her jewelry inside her hair. A third buried her keepsakes under her pillow.

Angry, almost defiant in the face of the enemy, Eleanor Garen scratched the lens of her camera with a needle, rendering it useless.

"I wasn't defeated," she later told a friend. "I was captured. I didn't surrender—others surrendered me!"[8]

Someone on the operating room staff opened a bottle of liquor. Soon the doctors and nurses were offering toasts to one another and their families back home.

General Wainwright, meanwhile, had dispatched one of his subordinates to meet the Japanese. He was eager to stop the shooting and halt the advance of the enemy tanks. Then he sent a message to the president.

> With broken heart and head bowed in sadness, but not in shame, I report to Your Excellency that today I must arrange terms for the surrender of the fortified islands of Manila Bay. If you agree, Mr. President, please say to the nation that my troops and I have accomplished all that is humanly possible and that we have upheld the best traditions of the United States and its Army. May God bless and preserve you and guide you and the nation in the effort to ultimate victory. With profound regret and with continued pride in my gallant troops I go to meet the Japanese commander. Good-by, Mr. President.[9]

At noon, while a bugler played "Taps," two American officers lowered the Stars and Stripes from the pole outside Malinta Tunnel and in its place raised a white bedsheet. One of the officers cut a small piece of the flag as a memento, then he set the rest of the Red, White and Blue on fire.

Underground the women prepared their remembrance. They ripped a large square of cloth from a rough muslin bedsheet and, at the top, wrote the heading, "Members of the Army Nurse Corps and Civilian Women who were in Malinta Tunnel when Corregidor fell." Underneath in three columns the sixty-nine women signed their names.[10]

"We wanted to leave a record in case we disappeared," said Cassie. "We had no idea what was going to happen to us."[11]

Finally, around 2:00 P.M. Wainwright came face-to-face with his enemy. He met with the Japanese commander of the invasion force and was told that he would be ferried across the bay to Bataan to meet with Homma and arrange (accept unconditionally, the Japanese told him) the terms of the surrender.

As soon as Wainwright left, the Japanese quickly moved to assume control of Malinta Tunnel.

Josie Nesbit gathered the Filipino nurses around her.

"They were frightened—poor little things," she said. "They kept saying, 'Mama Josie! What are we going to do?' I said, 'Never mind. I'll stay with you.' So I stayed with them and the Japs came in. The officer came with his big boots, stomping through there and a sword hanging down through his belt and gun. He stomped through there and the little girls shivered. He went all through the lateral and inspected the place. [Later] they put up the signs: THIS IS THE PROPERTY OF THE IMPERIAL JAPANESE GOVERNMENT."[12]

Elsewhere in the hospital laterals a group of Japanese officers accompanied by a handful of sober-faced American officers ordered the rest of the American women to fall into formation.

The nurses stood mute and edgy. Up and down the line walked the Japanese, looking them over. It was difficult, at first, to read the enemy's face, to separate reputation from reality, reality from fear. Then it became clear that the eyes looking them over were filled with curiosity, not appetite. The sight of women in uniform was so alien to the Japanese that they seemed puzzled, indeed almost confused, by the nurses' presence. For them war was a test of manhood, and women had no business being under arms.

"The Japs had no notion who we were and why we were there," said Jeanne Kennedy.

One of the enemy officers was so curious he bent down and "started feeling" the hem of Kennedy's skirt.

"I was a little apprehensive," she said, "until I realized he just wanted to compare the material of my skirt with the khaki material on his uniform."[13]

A few hours later the Japanese ordered Maude Davison to gather ten of her nurses to pose outside for a series of propaganda photographs. In the group was Madeline Ullom:

"They lined us up out front of the hospital tunnel and they put an armed guard with a gun and a bayonet at each end of us. A Jap officer with excellent English said, 'We are going to take your picture and we're going to send it to MacArthur to show that you are alive and that we are looking after you. Don't be afraid. I know how you Americans feel. I understand you. I'm a graduate of one of your universities.' "[14]

Looking at one of those pictures now, one sees the women in their khaki dresses and Red Cross armbands, white ankle socks and oxford shoes, legs crossed, some staring at the camera, some looking away askance. There is no reading the eyes—the camera was too far away—but three of the women seem to be smiling. Was it really a smile we see or were those mouths draw up in a grimace?

While the Japanese photographer was setting up his equipment, the women had a chance to look around, and what they saw horrified them. There, amid twisted girders and splintered trees, were scores of bloated allied corpses covered by swarms of black and green flies.

Colonel Wibb Cooper, chief medical officer, persuaded the Japanese that the bodies were a health threat, and he was finally given permission to inter them. This grisly work, of course, was performed by American prisoners of war.

The first week after surrender the Japanese herded the seven thousand American and five thousand Filipino soldiers on Corregidor onto a small concrete apron near a destroyed garage.

"The whole area was about one hundred yards on each side," Major S. M. Mellnick told war crimes investigators in postwar testimony. "There was no shelter of any kind and everyone soon put up blanket and shelter-half awnings. The heat was unbearable. For water we had one faucet and one open well. A twelve-hour wait in the water line to get a canteen filled was the usual rule."[15]

For a week they were not fed, then the Japanese gave the thousands of prisoners a little rice with canned tomatoes and sardines.

Every day the men went on work details, cleaning up the island, salvaging supplies for the Japanese, building enemy fortifications and living quarters. On one such detail a Catholic chaplain encountered a sobering aspect of garrison life in the Japanese Imperial Army.

"He was in a detail fixing up a set of quarters topside for the Japanese," said another officer who told the chaplain's story to war crimes investigators. "Arriving at the house with a load of furniture, he found six Filipino girls who had been brought from Manila to Corregidor. They were crying. They had been picked up off the street in Manila and had been taken directly to Corregidor. They had no time to notify their families. They had all been abused by the Jap officers who came to the house. The Chaplain remarked that it was probably the first time in history that a Catholic priest assisted in establishing a house of prostitution."[16]

The nurses, doctors and corpsmen had been ordered to stay at their posts in the hospital laterals and to continue to treat the wounded. Frequently the Japanese paid them a visit, and whenever they approached, the women would stiffen or freeze in place.

"You'd hear [the Japanese] stomping down the corridor with their big shoes and you'd tend to stand at attention and wait for them to go past," said Anna Clark. "It was the uncertainty of not knowing what they were going to do. You just kept doing what you were supposed to do, [but] we couldn't speak with our officers [and] we were allowed outside the tunnel [only] for short periods of time. We weren't allowed to get close to each other."

The Japanese ordered all Americans to pay them obeisance. "We bowed real fast so it wouldn't bother us," Alice Hahn said.

With each of these encounters, the Americans tried to get a sense of their enemy, an idea of what might lie ahead for them.

Sallie Durrett recalled that "a Japanese sign was placed at the lateral where the nurses were sleeping. It said, NURSES OF THE US ARMY. The Jap soldiers would stop to read the sign and then laugh. They thought we were there for other reasons."[17]

Things were quiet for a while, then the looting began.

They took everything—radios, binoculars, jewelry, pens, mechanical pencils, cigarette lighters, silver picture frames. They came by day and they came at night.

"One night," said Eleanor Garen, "I was aroused by someone at my side and realized it was a Jap. He had no business there, but I remained motionless as he took my ring from my finger and removed my most valuable tool, my wristwatch. That watch and I had counted the heartbeats of many men."[18]

Soon one "inspection" seemed to follow on the heels of another.

"A nurse on duty sat up all night long with a bell and the minute a Jap soldier showed his head she rang it," said Ann Mealor. "All the nurses slept in their uniforms. They'd get up and stand at attention until the [Japanese] went through. Sometimes they went through in droves, nearly all night long. You wouldn't get any sleep but you didn't dare lie down."[19]

During the day the Japanese might wander into the operating room or, without warning, appear on a ward. When that happened the women would stand silently next to their desks while the soldiers checked each patient, forcing many from bed to join the thousands of men herded together outside in prisoner-of-war pens. In a short time the only American men left in the hospital were those so sick or wounded they simply could not move, about four hundred of them.

The Japanese colonel in charge of the Japanese army medical department seemed to get on well with Colonel Wibb Cooper, and for a while relations between the Americans and their Japanese counterparts were tolerable. Each day, the colonel or an assistant met with Japanese doctors to present their patient and hospital reports. When an enemy soldier needed surgery, an American doctor assisted a Japanese surgeon, with an army or civilian nurse administering the anesthesia.

After a while the nurses began to grow accustomed to the presence of their enemy. One midnight in late May, Cassie was sitting at a desk on ward duty, finishing some paperwork, when a Japanese soldier approached and gestured that he wanted to sit down.

"Help yourself," she said.

As the soldier settled himself in a chair next to her desk, he reached for an old copy of *Cosmopolitan* magazine. Flipping through the magazine he came across an advertisement that showed a woman sitting with two small children, and he became excited, pointing at the picture and poking Cassie on the arm.

"Yes, yes," said Cassie, trying to ignore him. "She's a good-looking woman, so are the kids." Then she returned to her paperwork.

The guard looked a little disappointed, then he brightened for a moment, as if he had remembered something, reached inside his tunic, and retrieved a snapshot of a Japanese woman and two small children. He was smiling now, and, using gestures, he began to tell Cassie the story of his life.

> Twice he said, "boom, boom, boom," and pointed to himself and to his family. I figured he was telling he had survived two campaigns and that he hoped to see his family again. Next, he took a pencil and paper and drew an outline of Japan, Hawaii, and the United States. He sketched a boat with smoke curls carrying his family to Hawaii. Then he drew a second boat going to San Francisco. Finally, he drew a train with smoke and made "choo-choo" sounds to Chicago. Then he smiled and looked at me.
>
> Up to that moment I felt pretty well put upon because of what had happened to me. But this is my enemy? His fears, hopes, and family are not basically different than mine. The only difference was his slanted eyes and yellow skin. In a way, we were both victims of our own government situations. That poor sucker was also out in the field.[20]

But such rapprochement was rare. When the Japanese thought an American or Filipino was being "disrespectful," they beat him or, in some cases, lined him up in front of a firing squad. In the hospital if a corpsman or doctor tried to intervene when a guard pulled a patient out of bed for a work detail, the doctor was knocked to the ground. A nurse was cuffed by a guard just for talking with a doctor. Another woman, slow to follow a guard's orders, got a stinging slap with the flat side of his bayonet.[21] Then came an incident involving a woman named Mary Brown Menzie.[22]

Although Mrs. Menzie was listed as an army nurse, she was, in fact, new to the group. Soon after the war began, her fiancé, an officer on MacArthur's staff, managed to insinuate his betrothed, a registered nurse, in the nurse corps, the better to position her for possible evacuation. Once on Corregidor, the couple married. After surrender the colonel was forced to join the herds of POW's penned up topside under the blazing sun. His wife, meanwhile, remained on duty with the nurses, but slept in a secluded area of a lateral that she and her husband had sectioned off for themselves with a bedsheet. Now, for company, she invited another nurse to join her.

At 2:30 A.M. on May 9 Mary Brown Menzie felt someone shaking her awake from a deep sleep. She opened her eyes slowly, and as she began to focus she saw a man's shaved head. The man was a Japanese and, save for the towel around his waist, he was naked.

Just then Menzie caught sight of the knife.

The man looked hard at her and made a gesture—if she cried out he would pull the blade across her neck and slit her throat.

She tried to slip past him out of bed, but he pushed her back down, pointed his knife at her eyes and began to mount her.

She threw her right forearm across her eyes to protect her face, and in the struggle the man cut her wrist. The wound seemed momentarily to unnerve him. In the confusion that followed Menzie broke free, and with her roommate in tow, ran screaming into the nurses lateral.

The next day Maude Davison reported the incident to Colonel Cooper, who relayed it to the Japanese, who in turn "investigated" and concluded that the assailant was most definitely an American or Filipino.

After that Mrs. Menzie and her roommate moved their belongings into the relative safety of the nurses' lateral. (The Japanese guards were so amused by the incident and the "investigation," they took to walking by the nurses quarters in their G-strings, laughing.)

As the weeks passed, the American rations began to dwindle.

"The Japs found this cracked wheat that had been sent there maybe a year or two before; it was full of weevils," Ann Mealor remembered.

"They'd cook that for breakfast. You'd look down and those weevils would be floating on top. You dipped them off and went ahead with your breakfast."[23]

Soon the women began to forage for food. One nurse discovered a large hole in a wall near their sleeping quarters leading to a crawl space that opened into another lateral filled with canned goods the allies had stashed before the island fell. Night after night the nurses would tap this little stockpile. They waited for the guards to pass, then two or three of them would climb through the hole, while others acted as lookouts. A while later the foragers would return with as many cans of tomatoes and sacks of flour as they could hide in their foot lockers. This gambit, however, was not without its risks. One evening Josie Nesbit's foray was cut short when the lookouts yelled to her that the guards were unexpectedly returning. Nesbit was in such a rush to get back to her bunk before they discovered her gone, she laid open her scalp on the low ceiling as she scrambled out of the crawl space.

About this time, the nurses took on a second nemesis. Several weeks before the Japanese landed, a family of monkeys moved into a stand of trees near the tunnel entrance and a day or so later began to wander into the hospital laterals. The day before surrender the women spotted a large male squatting next to a bed, eating a patient's food. When the monkey was done he turned to the man in the bed and started to groom him, picking fleas off his head. In the days that followed, the wounded soldiers took a liking to the creature, nicknamed him Tojo, and spent hours trying to impersonate him. The nurses joked that sometimes it was hard to tell who was monkey and who was man.

For their part, however, the women hated Tojo. He took their soap and their yarn. One nurse found him at her washstand brushing his teeth with her toothbrush. Another discovered him crawling out from under a bunk with one of her shoes. A while later he took to tearing the bunks apart and smearing mud on the clean white sheets. If the women went after him and confronted him in a passageway, he was apt to growl and snap at them. Sometimes he actually chased them through the wards.

One afternoon as Cassie sat sewing at her bunk, Tojo climbed up next to her, put her scissors in his mouth, and jumped onto the next bed. Just then Cassie's bunkmate, Phyllis Arnold, appeared. When she saw the mess the monkey was making of her gear, she got very angry, grabbed a sheet and threw it over the animal like a net. The monkey fought hard to free himself, but Josie Nesbit rushed over to help and together the women captured him.

They wrapped the furious ape in a sheet, and he tried to kick, rip and scream his way free, but they prevailed and dragged the enraged bundle to a nearby room used as a prison cell, tossed it inside, and firmly shut the door.

A guard who had seen them come into the corridor now wandered over to check on the fuss. Curious but cautious, he slowly opened the door to the cell.

The sheet was rolling around the floor and the guard lowered his rifle and poked at it with his bayonet. Tojo, in no mood to be tickled, suddenly broke free, rose up on his hind legs and turned on the man. The guard did what any good soldier would do: he took aim and fired.

The monkey fell dead, the guard returned to his post and the women sat back to enjoy the sweet irony of one of their enemies eliminating another.[24]

Colonel Cooper, meanwhile, had convinced the Japanese medical commander to let him move the hospital topside into the shell of a building that used to be Fort Mills Hospital.

"On June 25th, the movement out of the tunnel into the marvelous atmosphere of the renovated old hospital was completed," the colonel said in his report. "A holiday atmosphere prevailed all over the place. We all had an 'it's good to be alive' air about us. We had secured a radio. We were sending out parties throughout the Island for green stuff to eat. . . . The Japanese Commandant . . . had given positive instructions that no Japanese soldier or any visitors from off the Island would be allowed to enter my hospital without his personal permission. He visited the hospital . . . presented the staff with a large iced cake of which he was very proud, some small cakes and some beer."[25]

To the nurses, leaving the tunnel and moving into the bombed-out shell of a building topside was like moving into the garden of Eden.

"The gardenia trees were in full bloom and, oh my, it was such a thrill to get out of those stinky hot tunnels and miserable mess into the open air," said Anna Williams. "The roof was off and it was just a shell but it was still good to be in the air and to be alive outside. I've always loved flowers. I got a corpsman and we went out and cut the gardenias and put them in wash basins and put the basins all around the patients."[26]

The nurses settled the sick and wounded into the new quarters, stretched gauze over the beds to protect them from mosquitoes and tried to get them something to eat. The blue sky, the open space and the sea air brightened everyone.

A week later, on July 2, the chief Japanese medical officer informed Colonel Cooper that the sick and wounded were being transferred to Manila. The patients, and all male medical personnel, would be loaded on a freighter, the *Lima Maru*, at four o'clock that afternoon. The nurses were to remain with the colonel in the hospital overnight, then in the morning walk down to the harbor and board the ship.

It appeared that everyone—nurses, doctors and patients—were simply being relocated to a hospital on Luzon near Manila. The next morning at the dock, the women were put on small boats and ferried out to the freighter. There was no gangway or hull ramp, so they had to climb a long rope ladder to the deck.

"I did pretty well climbing," said Madeline Ullom, who had contracted dengue fever two days earlier. But "I had a temperature of a hundred and four" and when "I got about three rungs from the top, everything started swimming around. I knew the bay was full of sharks and if I fell in the water that was the end of it. So I climbed the last rungs and got up. Many of the girls were sick with malaria and dengue. When we got to the top of the ship, many of them laid down just about where they landed."[27]

As the freighter lifted anchor and pulled away from Corregidor for the three-hour trip to Manila, an English-speaking officer approached the group.

"A nice Jap gave us tea and rice cakes," said Ullom. "We thought as long as he did that maybe he'd tell us something. 'Where are we going and what are you going to do with us?' [someone asked]. He said they were taking us to a school outside Manila where there were medicine cabinets full of stuff. Beds were there. First they were going to unload the patients from the boat and take them to the hospital. We thought that was all right."[28]

By midafternoon, the *Lima Maru* was approaching the city docks. The harbor, once an almost pristine place, was now a filthy cove littered with the steel hulks of partially submerged ships. Manila, once the Pearl of the Orient, seemed derelict and lifeless.

The men were unloaded first. Those too ill or wounded to walk were put on trucks. The others, including the doctors and corpsmen, were ordered to line up in ranks behind the trucks. As the vehicles and men started to move slowly up the street, Cassie, Eleanor Garen, Josie Nesbit and the other women waved, then began to queue up to follow, but the guards held them back and marshalled the women into three flatbed trucks. As the trucks moved off, the women suddenly realized they were headed away from the line of men, not toward it.[29] Again they were being taken from their patients and separated from their comrades, the doctors and corpsmen. For most of the women it was the worst moment of the war. A few began to cry. Others sat quietly, too filled with woe to speak. Madeline Ullom innocently thought that the Japanese drivers had simply made a mistake and headed in the wrong direction.

"I told them they were taking the wrong road," she said. "They didn't say anything. I told them again. I said, 'This is not the way to Paranque. That road up there, that next road up there!' They tapped me on the back with a bayonet. I decided I'd better keep still."[30]

An hour later a high masonry wall surrounding what appeared to be a large compound came into view. The trucks slowed down a bit, then turned sharply and passed between open iron gates—the gates to Santo Tomas Internment Camp.

Chapter 11

Santo Tomas

*L*ONG BEFORE THE Imperial Japanese Army landed on the shores of Leyte Gulf to begin its invasion of the Philippines, the War Ministry in Tokyo assembled a team of military planners to write a script for its conquest of the islands. The planners picked out targets for bombing, and landing sites for the troop barges. They calculated the routes for their infantry attacks and set target dates to capture the major cities.

Part of the plan, of course, involved the administration of the capital, Manila, once it had fallen into Japanese hands. In the years before the war, Japanese spies and Fifth Columnists in Manila fed information back to the planners in Tokyo, and by the time General Homma's victorious troops crossed Manila's Pasig River, the Japanese had mapped out every major building in the city and knew exactly what they wanted to do with them.

Among the institutions marked for occupation was a Dominican academy, Santo Tomas University. Founded in 1611 by Spanish Dominican priests and named after Saint Thomas Aquinas, Santo Tomas shut its doors in early December during the first week of bombings. Before that, it was the intellectual home of some six thousand students and three hundred faculty. The college sat on a sixty-acre rectangle of land north of the port area in a busy section of the city. The Dominican priests had carefully enclosed their large campus with a twelve-foot concrete-and-stone wall. Midway down Espana Boulevard the wall was interrupted by a run of iron fence, and in the middle of the run were two huge iron gates that opened onto the spacious grounds.

The high masonry walls and iron fence were originally intended to create a quiet compound for the contemplative Dominican fathers and their students. Now this bulwark allowed the Japanese to jerry-rig Santo Tomas into a prison.

In January a Japanese officer and a platoon of soldiers took possession of the abandoned campus and began to receive prisoners—foreign civilians working and living in Manila, or "enemy nationals," as the Japanese called them—Americans, Britons, Australians, Canadians, Dutch, Poles, Norwegians and French. By July, Santo Tomas University had been converted to Santo Tomas Internment Camp, or STIC, as it was called derisively by the some 3,800 men, women and children who came to be imprisoned there.[1]

B EHIND ITS IRON fence and high walls, now topped with barbed wire, STIC was a kind of teeming international village. Here were accountants, bankers, engineers, farmers, housewives, insurance agents, mechanics, miners, merchants, seamen, secretaries, stenographers, saleswomen, salesmen and teachers. Here too were aircraft workers, architects, a bakery instructor, six bartenders, three cosmeticians, nine dancers, dentists and doctors, one decorator, one dressmaker, one florist, three golf pros, five governesses, one hairdresser, a dozen or so journalists, one lady's maid, one laundress, a meteorologist, many missionaries, one model, enough musicians for a small band, one polo player, four plumbers, two restaurant owners and a few cooks, one saw filer, one statistician, several social workers, stevedores, two surveyors, one tennis pro, one X-ray technician, six tobacconists, one veterinarian, six welders and two wrestlers.

Roughly a quarter of the 3,800 internees were children under the age of eighteen and roughly another quarter were over sixty, most of these, men. Among those in the middle, ages eighteen to fifty-nine, roughly two fifths were women, half of whom were married.

All these people were forced to coexist on a walled rectangle of land roughly ten city blocks long and eight blocks wide. From the air the sprawling compound—"concentration camp," some said—looked like a small town with buildings of various sizes, tree-lined streets and walkways, plazas, greens, open lots, maintenance and repair shops, equipment sheds and athletic fields.

In the middle of this campus-turned-wartime-town was "Main Building," a huge edifice three stories high and more than a block and a half long built of pale limestone, sandstone, concrete and stucco. Atop the third story and directly over the front entrance was a square two-story tower, and atop the tower was a cupola capped with a large white cross. The effect of these stacked architectural apogees was that the symbol of God was set so high it could be seen for miles.

Main Building was actually an immense quadrangle built around two interior courtyards. At ground level was the front entrance. Directly overhead was a canopy, and two stories above that, between identical flanking cornices, was an enormous clock with black hands and a white face. Leading up to the front entrance was a large concrete apron or open plaza. The front facade, formed by two identical wings spreading out from the front entrance, was at least a thousand feet end to end. This long, white expanse of stucco and windows was interrupted by a series of recesses, bays and pilasters that gave the illusion of several facades, or smaller fronts, stacked together. The great length and unusual height of Main Building, along with its ornate architectural decorations and designs—a combination of Moorish shapes and angles and classic Greek capitals, dados and cornices—made the building seem at once palatial and official, a place fit for the business of education and religion, the erudite and the divine. Clearly it was a structure that was meant to make the individual seem small in the face of some larger scheme, some grand set of purposes.[2]

Located as it was in the epicenter of the campus, Main Building, with its giant clock and towering crucifix, stood solidly as a source of power and authority. For the internees it was also a compass point, the place against which all other places on the sixty-acre campus were measured.

Main Building served as the central dormitory for the internees. Men and women were housed in separate quarters—ten, fifteen, twenty or more packed into classrooms converted into large, common boudoirs and barracks. To the right of Main was the Education Building, a dormitory just for men. To the left, not far from one of the stone walls, was the gymnasium, where some seven hundred elderly men were made to sleep. Behind Main was the Annex, sleeping quarters for women with young children. And to the left of that, just inside the east wall, the Dominican fathers had their own area—a compound within a compound—sectioned off with barbed wire.

Unlike the military war prisons in the islands, especially the cruel, pestilential hellholes of Bilibid and Cabanatuan, the grounds of Santo Tomas at first seemed spacious. Four avenues radiating from Main Building divided the campus into quadrants, enough space for the internees to build a "Theater Under the Stars," their grand name for an outdoor stage for evening musicals and entertainment, and across from the main plaza on an expanse of grass, a baseball diamond, a basketball court and, beyond that, a field for football, soccer and field hockey.

But all that acreage and all those amenities were really an illusion, for inside the buildings life was lived belly to back. In each dormitory, the internees were allotted only the space occupied by their metal beds or bamboo cots, not one inch more. To relieve the oppression of such tight quarters, the prisoners soon took to building small outdoor sheds, or "shanties," as they liked to call them. At night the internees were confined to their dormitories but the Japanese allowed them to spend their days in their shanties. Made of scraps of lumber, woven palm mats, tin, blankets and bamboo, the rough-hewn pieds-à-terre were the internees sanctuaries.

The shanties were built in clusters on the open lawns and gently sloping grounds among the acacias and cyprus, and in time the clusters began to look like subdivisions and took on names: Glamourville, Foggy Bottom, Garden Court, Southwest Territory, Out Yonder and Jungletown. Sometimes the "citizens" of these small towns elected unofficial mayors and chiefs of police. They surrounded their little shacks with flower beds or climbing vines or privacy hedges, then carved out grids or footpaths and named them Fifth Avenue, Hollywood Boulevard, MacArthur Drive, Papaya Lane, Camote Road. In time the shanty owners became the camp elite, the people who seemed to have the most control over their tightly circumscribed lives.

*T*HE MILITARY PRISONS in the islands came under the rule of the Imperial Japanese Army. To a Japanese soldier, surrender and capture were dishonorable acts, and the Japanese guards treated allied military prisoners with contempt and abject brutality, beating, torturing and murdering them. The civilian internment camps, however, such as the one at Santo Tomas, were, during the early years of the war, governed by the Department of External Affairs, part of the Japanese occupation authority, and the bureaucrats whose business it was to cage up thousands of foreign nationals looked on those in their charge with simple indifference and neglect.

The commandant of Santo Tomas was a civilian, R. Tsurumi. When the camp opened in January 1942, he ordered the first group of internees to set up their own administration to manage the camp's day-to-day affairs. He also told them they would have to use their own funds to supplement the subsistence, or maintenance, allotment provided by the Department of External Affairs. And so the first men and women to enter Santo Tomas in early January formed two management boards, the Executive and advisory committees. These policy and oversight councils, composed of British and American businessmen, managed every aspect of camp life and enforced camp rules. By the summer of 1942, with the population of the camp now in the thousands, the internee government had set up sixteen subcommittees to regulate their diurnal exigencies and affairs: food, housing, medical services, education, sanitation, recreation and discipline and so on.

The Japanese gave the Executive Committee a financial allotment that amounted to thirty-five cents per person per day to run the camp. This pittance was applied to the purchase of all food, utilities, medical supplies, construction and maintenance and sanitation materials—in short, all the myriad and manifold expenses of maintaining a sixty-acre campus-turned-town and the feeding, housing, clothing and keeping alive of a population that would come to number 3,800 men, women and children.

In many ways the disparate talents and skills of the group helped the internees to survive. Some were good at building a government, others at rebuilding a generator. Plumbers repaired broken pipes while shoemakers resoled shredded sandals. A number of people joined labor gangs to clean the buildings and grounds or work in the camp kitchen. Teachers worked in camp school with the children or organized extension classes for the adults. In the late winter of 1942, the eleven navy nurses captured in Manila when the army retreated to Bataan were sent to Santo Tomas and assigned to the camp hospital working under Laura Cobb, who was later named hospital superintendent.

Work made the time pass more quickly, so it was not hard for the Executive Committee to marshal volunteers or enforce a rule that every able-bodied internee had to work at least two hours a day. A gang of fifty men were detailed to dig up an old landfill in the northeast corner of the campus and convert some seven and a half acres into a camp vegetable garden. At first the labor of digging out old cans and bottles, tilling the soil under the tropical sun and carrying water in five-gallon cans across hundreds of yards of ground was hard on these bankers and bureaucrats, but, in their parlance, it paid off. In time they were able to harvest and send to the camp kitchen thousands of pounds of eggplant, okra, corn and *talinum* (a green leafy vegetable).

Some people came into the camp with money, a lot of it, others with only the clothes they had on their backs. The Finance and Supply Sub-committee worked hard to make sure everyone—rich or poor, society matron or street prostitute—had the basics: a subsistence diet, minimal clothing, essential medical care. Anything else, anything extra, the internees had to provide themselves.

The Japanese allowed Filipino fruit and vegetable vendors into the camp, and internee entrepreneurs were given permission to purvey clothes, housewares, ice cream, candy and coconut milk. In time there was an internee-run coffee shop and a Filipino laundry. To mitigate profiteering, the Executive Committee set up an official camp store that sold secondhand clothing and a camp canteen that offered soap, sugar, flour, vinegar and canned goods, all at cost plus 10 percent.

Thus Santo Tomas was, in some ways, a porous prison, with official merchants, marketeers and mongers coming and going throughout the day. And adding to this flow of goods and services was a daily contingent of unofficial suppliers as well, Filipinos mostly, the relatives, friends or former employees of many of those behind Santo Tomas's walls.

Every morning these good samaritans would queue up at the Package Shed, a tiny wooden hut near the nipa-palm buildings occupied by the camp guards at the iron front gates. There the samaritans would deliver to their imprisoned friends and relatives bundles of food, clothes, household items, money, and chairs, tables and building materials for the shanties. Japanese guards checked each parcel for weapons, liquor, notes and other contraband, but they were not as vigilant with bundles leaving the camp, and often the samaritans walked away carrying bundles of dirty laundry with messages tucked inside—a love letter, perhaps, to a husband or fiancé suffering the dreadful deprivations and torture of Japanese military prison, or a secret intelligence report to the underground resistance movement in Manila or the guerrillas fighting in the mountains and the hills.

In time the package line became a kind of town square, a gathering spot. The guards had orders to prevent any contact between the samaritans and the internees—packages were dropped off and labeled for later distribution—but each day hundreds of internees collected inside the main gate to catch a glimpse of their kin, couriers, deliverymen and package carriers, and soon there developed dozens of private codes and secret languages between those behind the iron fence and those who approached it.

Most spoke to one another in a kind of prison-camp pantomime, swaying in a particular way or hopping on one foot or the other. Others scratched themselves in a certain way or at certain spots. Many worked out complex signals with head and hand movements. Standing back from the crowd and watching all this, it sometimes appeared that the crowd inside at the front gates was afflicted with a series of nervous disorders. No one, of course, could begin to imagine what the Japanese made of this daily show.

Porous as it was, however, STIC was still a prison, and one day in February the Japanese decided to underscore that point. Three restless internees—Englishmen Thomas Fletcher and Henry Weeks and Australian Blakely Laycock—had gone over the wall at night and had been recaptured. Back at camp they were hauled into a room next to the Japanese commandant's office and beaten so severely their cries and screams echoed for hours in the warm afternoon air.

The next day the Executive Committee posted a notice, obviously edited by the Japanese, saying that the men had been severely punished and were being transferred to another camp. Two days later the internees of Santo Tomas learned that the men had been court-martialed and condemned to death, and the following afternoon the head of the Executive Committee, an American businessman named Earl Carroll, and two room monitors from the dormitory where the escapees had lived were driven to a Chinese cemetery. There they saw Fletcher, Weeks and Laycock standing in a ravine by a freshly dug grave. The Japanese wanted to send a message to the internees, and Carroll and the room monitors were meant to deliver it. What happened next comes from an account Carroll gave to A.V.H. Hartendorp, the secret camp historian.

> *The men were led to the edge of the grave . . . and now made to sit side by side on the mound of earth thrown up, their feet dangling in the hole. . . . Three of the soldiers . . . drew their pistols . . . and, standing on the other side of the grave, facing the blindfolded men, fired at their hearts. Fletcher slumped against Laycock, the man in the middle, and both fell forward into the hole. Weeks remained seated and was shot once more before he toppled. Carroll heard the men groaning as the soldiers stepped to the edge of the grave to look in. The one detailed to end the life of Weeks fired a third shot. Then all three soldiers fired their pistols into the grave. The groans still continued, and Laycock and Weeks were given still another bullet each. The Commandant shook his head, saying to Carroll . . . that it was too bad his men had not been equipped with rifles. Groans still sounded from the grave, the soldiers returned, one of them laughing, and fired another volley of three shots. . . . Some Filipino cemetery workers now approached to fill*

the grave. They were ordered back until the soldiers themselves had first
thrown in some earth, the groans, even then, having not entirely subsided.[3]

B Y THE SUMMER of 1942 the society of the camp and its routine had
been well established.

Food and medicine aside, the biggest problem in STIC was boredom,
the dunning routine of staying alive. Work was the best antidote, and
right behind that was the satisfaction of learning something new. The
Education Subcommittee created an elementary and high school, with a
faculty of twenty-three and a student body of almost six hundred. Meanwhile the college professors interned at STIC offered courses for their fellow internees in Spanish, French, Tagalog, Japanese, Latin, art, music
appreciation, typing, shorthand, mathematics, business theory and English as a second language. The Recreation Subcommittee offered golf
and calisthenics lessons and organized leagues in baseball, basketball,
volleyball and soccer. The Religious Subcommittee set up services and
Scripture classes and crafted "The Ten Commandments of STIC," a be-
havioral code that stressed honesty, cooperation and decency.[4] The Entertainment Subcommittee marshalled the professional musicians and
entertainers in camp. David Harvey MacTurk, an impresario known to
everyone as Dave Harvey, produced vaudeville shows, sing-alongs and
plays. His first revue included a sword swallower, a tap dancer and an
accordion solo. Harvey was a natural impresario and his stand-up routines on camp life drew large audiences, sometimes as many as two thousand people. At one show he shocked the audience when he walked to
the center of the stage and in a low but firm voice began to carefully recite the words to "The Star-Spangled Banner." Slowly the members of
the audience rose to their feet as they listened. The Japanese did nothing,
apparently believing that Harvey's little monotone was just some idle pa-
tois between jokes.

Like all small cities, STIC had its miscreants. The Committee on
Order had to deal with the handful of adult ne'er-do-wells who refused
to work and instead spent their hours drinking smuggled liquor or home
brew. Then there were the thieves. In a place of pervasive want, everything had some value to someone and the camp Fagins stole everything
from a Longine watch to a simple spoon.

The Committee on Order also dealt with people who regularly broke
curfew, and among the regulars were those inamoratas and inamoratos
caught in flagrante delicto. The Japanese, reserved by nature and prud-

ish in society, had forbidden public displays of affection. They even forced husbands and wives to sleep apart in segregated dormitories. (At one point the commandant proposed putting up a large tent in a corner of the campus so married couples could couple during the day in common coitus, but the internees rejected this nonsense.) If a woman became pregnant, the Japanese jailed the responsible husband or boyfriend and confined the woman in a special hospital outside the camp. Thus the men and women of Santo Tomas were forced to pursue their passion surreptitiously, so they met, at first, in the shadows and quiet corners of Main Building or, later, during the day, in their shanties. A number of women exchanged sex for money, food, clothing, whatever they needed to survive, but no one really censored such behavior. Some social mores fall away on survival's steep slope.

Overall the morale of the captives, given their material losses and deprivations, was remarkably high, and this spirit was sustained, in part, by the daily broadcasts of the camp radio station. For two hours every morning the Japanese allowed internee disc jockeys to play music and make announcements over a system of loudspeakers. The music was primarily old standards and big-band tunes—for reasons no one could explain, the Japanese forbid them to play jazz—records that the disc jockeys had collected from their fellow prisoners. Secretly this same crew built a shortwave radio and monitored foreign stations to collect the news. They could not, of course, relay this information directly over the loudspeaker; the Japanese fanatically censored everything in camp. So the deejays devised a kind of code, playing records that suggested the course of the war and the Allied advances and victories. For instance, when the tune "There Will Always Be an England" came on the air, it was easy to guess that Great Britain had weathered yet another Nazi blitz.

J ULY 2 ARRIVED sunny and hot. A light breeze blew dust from the athletic fields toward Main Building. By late afternoon the air had grown still and the intense tropical heat had turned the campus into an oven. On most days like this, most of the internees would have retreated to the shade or their shanties. But the Japanese had told the Executive Committee to prepare for a new group of Americans, a very special group, and on this particular summer afternoon, a large crowd of internees, numbering in the hundreds, had gathered to wait near the main gate and on the concrete apron in front of Main Building.

Just before four o'clock, three flatbed trucks turned down Espana Boulevard, then passed between the iron front gates and past the guards in their nipa huts. As the trucks made their way slowly up the esplanade to the plaza, dozens of people along the way pointed to the vehicles and began to count the occupants. Aboard the trucks were sixty-nine women, among them the fifty-four army nurses from Bataan and Corregidor—thin, tired and anxious about their fate.

The nurses managed to smile a bit and wave to the crowd now surrounding them, now yelling and waving, pushing fruit in their faces, mangoes and papayas and bananas, and with each offering, each gift, came a question, a plea, really, for news, any word at all of the men on the Death March, the men captured on Corregidor, husbands and fathers and brothers from whom, of whom, there had been no word, no sign, no nothing.

"No talking!" yelled a stone-faced sentry as he shut the iron gates.[5]

The trucks veered around the crowds, coming to a stop on the concrete apron in front of the Main Building.

Cassie, Eleanor Garen and the others slowly climbed down to the ground. Inside Main Building another crowd of men and women, desperate for news of their loved ones in uniform, had lined the hallway and stairs and as the nurses passed by, anxious voices yelled out the names of soldiers or units or battlefields.

The guards yelled for silence.

The women were whisked down the hall and into a small room where guards registered them and searched their belongings. They were hot and tired and thirsty and the process of the guards pawing through their possessions and grilling them seemed agonizingly slow. As the afternoon wore on, a number of women asked to use a lavatory, and the guards gave them permission, one at a time, to leave the room.

Outside in the corridor the internees, eager to get a look at the new arrivals, had formed a gauntlet, and as each nurse emerged from the room and made her way down the hall to the lavatory, hushed colloquies took place. The internees wanted information about the troops; the nurses, meanwhile, were anxious for news of the war.

In quick murmurs and asides, the crowd in the hallway gave the women great news . . . Allied victories at Midway and in the Coral Sea and Jimmy Doolittle's daring daylight bombing of Tokyo. The tide was beginning to turn, they whispered, and these tidings, the first for the nurses in months, made the Battling Belles weep.

As the afternoon passed, camp cooks sent in a lunch of noodle and vegetable stew and hot chocolate and pineapple. The women suffering from malaria and dengue fever were especially dry and thirsty and feasted on the fresh fruit, so sweet, so cool and full of juice.

Meanwhile the guards continued to pull apart the women's bags and bundles. A soldier rummaging through Peggy Greenwalt's gear came upon a large brightly colored piece of silk and, curious, he pulled it from her bag. Greenwalt tried to fight off her panic, for in his hand the guard was holding an American battle flag, the unit colors of the Twelfth Regimental Quartermaster Corps. The day Corregidor fell, the leader of the quartermasters, Colonel Frank Kriwanck, gave his flag to Greenwalt and made her promise to smuggle it home for him. Now Greenwalt and the others stood frozen with fear. Would the flag anger their captors and bring brutal reprisals? The guard held the pennant up, as if to study it. Clearly he was perplexed, especially by the insignia, a bald eagle with arrows in its claws, set on a field of red and gold. Then, Greenwalt got a bolt from the blue. She rushed forward, took the flag from the guard's hands, draped it over her shoulders as if it were a shawl and, with a bit of posturing and a little strut in her step, acted as if she were showing the guards the latest in women's fashion. The impromptu performance amused her captors, and, as it turned out, preserved a battle flag so dear to so many men.[6]

The Executive Committee had made room for the nurses in Main Building, but typically the Japanese had plans of their own. As soon as the registration was finished, guards hustled the women back into the trucks and drove them across the campus and through a side exit to a building directly across the street from the main compound—the convent of Santa Catalina. Here, the women were told, they would live under lock and key until further notice. The enemy intended to isolate them from the other internees, even the nuns in the convent. They would be allowed outside for exercise two hours a day, would get their meals delivered from the camp kitchen and would have absolutely no contact with anyone, save their guards. In effect the Japanese were holding the group incommunicado.

Across the street in the main camp, news spread quickly of this special confinement. Although the Japanese often acted capriciously, making decisions one day and, for no apparent reason, reversing themselves the next, no one in camp could quite figure out why they wanted to wall off the nurses. Some said the enemy was wary of the women because they were military, but others pointed to the presence of the navy nurses, and they'd been in camp since March.

"The [real] story was they wanted us to forget the atrocities and the horrible treatment [of the male prisoners]," said Hattie Brantley. And, of course, not "to talk to the civilians about it."[7]

Whatever the case, the women were weary and racked with fever, and they slumped down onto their narrow cots of woven palm fibers on the second floor of the convent and tried to sleep. An offshore breeze made its way inland, and through the open windows came the scent of hibiscus from the garden below.

Their first week in camp the women worked on healing themselves. A score were suffering from malaria, dysentery, arthritis, hepatitis, stomach cramps, leg ulcers and dengue fever. A physician from the main camp hospital, accompanied by Laura Cobb, visited the convent often that week. For the most part the women slept, rising only for meals or mandatory roll calls. After seven days of treatment and convalescence, most began to mend and move about.

Although they had been a military unit—the Army Nurse Corps in the Philippines—they had rarely spent so much time together. Working different shifts at different hospitals and clinics, they had been closer to their patients and the doctors than to one another. Even on Bataan and later in Malinta Tunnel, they'd had little chance to bond or coalesce. In effect the nurses were a corps in name only. Now, without the distraction of their work and the divided loyalties the practice of medicine imposes, the Angels of Bataan and Corregidor were suddenly women unto themselves, a band of sisters, as it were, whose mission was simply to survive.

So they fell back on what they knew, the customs and routines of women. They organized their two rooms on the second floor of the convent into an army barracks—palm cots placed just so, personal items stowed neatly away, everything uniform and in its place. The strong ones scoured the floors of their quarters, got down on their hands and knees with hard brushes and harsh soap. Those still ailing sewed and washed and did the ironing. A couple of women got yarn from the main camp and wove socks and underpants for those who needed them.

They shared books—Archibald Cronin's *The Keys of the Kingdom,* Henry Bellamann's *King's Row* and John Buchan's *The Man Who Was Greenmantle*—played card games too, bridge mostly, and talked. They talked with one another like they had never talked before, and as the days passed, they began to know one another too. Old friendships were renewed and new ones inaugurated. In the evening they often sat together at their second-story windows and watched the sun set, the great golden disc slipping from a flame-white sky into the Oriental night.

After dark they held sing-alongs and talent shows. Blanche Kimball from Topeka, Kansas, had a flair for telling fortunes with playing cards and soon had her friends engrossed in reading the future. Everyone, it seemed, wanted Blanche to turn over the eight of hearts, the card that signaled what many missed and most longed for—a love affair.

In late July a woman named Ida Hube, an old friend of Josie Nesbit and Maude Davison, came into the women's lives. Hube, a German-born citizen of Switzerland, had joined the American military as a nurse, serving in the corps in the Philippines until 1910, when she married a wealthy German importer and moved to Europe. She returned to the Philippines in 1939 after her husband died, took up residence in the posh Manila Hotel and lavishly entertained her former army friends, Davison and Nesbit among them. When the Japanese occupied Manila and began classifying citizens of foreign birth, Hube was identified as a German national and since the Japanese considered the Germans their allies, she was free to move about Manila as she pleased. And what pleased her at the moment was helping her old friends.

One July morning Hube's large black limousine stopped at the convent door and out she stepped, a vision of Victorian elegance—the big hat, the white gloves, the lace parasol.

After some negotiating the Japanese allowed Maude Davison and Josie Nesbit a few moments alone with their friend outside the gate. The three talked quietly, the nurses detailing their months under fire. Ida Hube was alarmed at the condition of the two thin and haggard figures, and as the guards hustled her back into her car, she promised to return. A few days later her limousine reappeared, this time loaded with gifts: sweet cakes, canned milk, Ovaltine, nuts and candy, fresh fruits and vegetables, bread and sugar, sewing kits and clothes. And there was one thing more, a small token to make the nurses feel like women again. Each of the sixty-nine women imprisoned in the convent received a pocketbook. (During the long months of captivity that were to follow, twice a week two Filipinos in Mrs. Hube's employ would arrive at the package line pushing carts stuffed with bundles for the nurses—bundles of food, sanitary napkins, needles, thread, yarn and money. Atop this bounty, the good woman always placed a bouquet of flowers. Sometimes she would follow her largess in her limousine. The younger nurses loved her panache and delighted in watching her alight from her big black car in her broad-brimmed hat, then pop open her black parasol and with her carefully gloved hands check the contents of the carts to make sure everything was there. In the middle of a war at a prison-camp gate, Ida

Hube seemed a somewhat comic figure, an absurd apparition, but the younger nurses stifled their laughter for she was their deliverer, the woman Josie Nesbit called the Angels' "Guardian Angel."[8]

The convent began to seem smaller, the days longer, the nights without end. The nurses tired of playing cards and reading books and watching the scintillating sunsets.

"I want to get back to work," Josie Nesbit told one of her colleagues. "I don't know how you feel, but I'm getting bored with nothing to do all day."[9]

Just then, as it turned out, Dr. Thomas Fletcher, the camp medical director, and Earl Carroll, chairman of the Executive Committee, convinced Commandant Tsurumi that the metallurgy building was too small to continue to serve as a hospital and that the best place to put the sick and injured was Santa Catalina convent. They also convinced the Japanese that the new hospital could not be adequately staffed by the navy and civilian nurses alone, so the army nurses were ordered released from their confinement and told they would soon be working in the hospital, with Maude Davison as its superintendent.

Their move into the main prison camp took place on a hot, sunny day the third week in August. (Ida Hube sent along six roasted pigs to celebrate their release from isolation.) After the nurses were settled, Davison and Nesbit made out work schedules, deciding who would work each shift and on each ward.

At first some of the younger nurses balked at their new duties. They wanted no part of caring for civilians or living under civilian rules; they were military officers, they argued, and if they could not work for their own kind, they did not want to serve anyone. The dissidents riled Maude Davison, who called the nurses together and reminded them that they were still officers in the United States Army, that their country was at war and that, like it or not, they would follow their orders. A few days later another group of young nurses, hoping for more freedom and bitter about being under the thumb of a woman they considered an antique and a martinet, directly challenged Davison's authority. They were civilians now, they argued, and not subject to her control, but the captain was resolute. One way or the other, she told them, she was determined to keep the group intact. And, in the end, her iron will prevailed.

"Because of Miss Davison's domineering manner and antagonistic attitude whenever approached on the subject, the nurses submitted to her control rather than confront her with requests for shorter hours of duty or changes in assignment," Josie Nesbit recalled.[10]

Nesbit was equally determined to keep the Angels together. Her worry, however, went beyond the good order and discipline inherent in the chain of command. She wanted to preserve the group's sense of self—women loyal to women, women committed to women.

Clearly she was thinking of their survival, of the strength that comes from being part of a group and sharing the respect and good reputation the group enjoys. In other words, what really worried Josie Nesbit was men.

Save for the generosity of Ida Hube, the nurses were broke. As government employees they had no cash, no money to buy the food they needed to supplement the subsistence diet provided by the Japanese. Nesbit and a few of the older women were worried that the younger nurses might sell themselves, like a number of hungry or destitute women in camp, to men wealthy enough to pay for their pleasure.

Nesbit knew, of course, that she could not decree celibacy or dictate morality. So she gathered the older nurses around her and they tried to instill a sense of esprit de corps in the younger women. They spoke at length about their duty to their country and to themselves. They had volunteered for this assignment, Nesbit reminded them. Yes, they had expected a paradise, not the wasteland of war, but that was the way things had turned out. Now their job was to survive and get themselves home, all of them, together, and the only way to accomplish this was to help one another. Everything they did reflected on the group, and the group was their only salvation. If they maintained their pride and identity as army nurses, keeping alive the nurse corps' traditions of dedication to the sick and camaraderie among women, then they might make it, survive without the shame that survival so often brings.

"Whatever else could happen, first and foremost, we would conduct ourselves as Members of the United States Army Nurse Corps," she wrote years later. "This was paramount and absolutely inviolate! We reasoned that if we hoped to remain integrated emotionally, our first and primary duty was to carry on in our most professional capacity—that of nurses."[11]

So it was the work that would save them, their sense of themselves as professionals, the knowledge that they were part of something larger and more enduring than any one of them alone, and that something was the group.

The group finally became solvent when a few of the more trustworthy businessmen in camp realized that the women, with their back pay accruing safely in government accounts, were a good risk and advanced them interest-free loans.[12] With a little money in their pockets, the nurses could now buy duck eggs, caraboa milk, papaya and bananas. A few indulged themselves with a haircut at the internee-run beauty parlor. Others pooled their money and bought shanties from internee contractors, furnishing these day shacks with a few pieces of furniture, some old dishes and cooking utensils, and a makeshift stove.

On September 9 the Japanese, consolidating their civilian prisoners in the southern islands, brought to Santo Tomas a group of foreign nationals captured on Davao and Mindanao. In this lot were the evacuees from Corregidor who had been stranded on Lake Lanao by seaplane number two—three civilian women and ten more army nurses, two of whom had been wounded on Bataan and badly needed treatment.

Now all but two of the military nurses captured during the first six months of war were in Santo Tomas. (Ruby Bradley and Beatrice Chambers, who had been stationed at army Camp John Hay in Baguio, two hundred miles north of Manila in upper Luzon, were being held in an internment camp on that base along with 466 other foreign nationals taken into custody in northern Luzon Province.)

As the weeks passed at Santo Tomas, the sixty-four army nurses and eleven navy nurses quickly came to see that for all its apparent amenities—the food stalls, the entertainment, the daytime shanties—STIC was still a prison, a place of the keepers and the kept. It was also clear now that any hope for a quick victory had been an illusion. The war was going to last a long time, weeks giving way to months, months adding up to years. And soon the sixty-acre campus would feel as small and confining as a postage stamp.

Chapter 12

STIC, the First Year, 1942

*I*N OBVIOUS WAYS the work of war is easy, "kill or be killed." Survival, however, is another matter, much more difficult, for it requires an endurance, a cunning and a strength of will that fighting does not.

*A*FTER THE MOVE from the convent to the main camp, Cassie was on edge. In the convent she had not felt the reality of "prison." Now, thrown in with thousands of others behind a concrete wall topped with barbed wire, she realized for the first time that she was a captive, shackled by the circumstances of war.

"The lack of freedom, you know?" she said. "The first time in your life you were not free—it was a terrible moment."[1]

So she resolved to keep busy.

"I was not," she said, "going to moan in my beer."

She filled up her day with projects and reading and exercises, "anything," she said, to "keep my sanity."

Every day she put in four hours at the camp hospital. It was wearing duty, filled with repetitive and tedious tasks, but Cassie was happy to have the work. She gave her patients a sponge bath, fed them rice gruel from the hospital kitchen, administered the morning's medications. Some of her charges suffered from "tropical itch," a skin disease common to foreigners, and she spent hours dressing their sores. Working with the sick gave her a kind of perspective and comfort. Whenever she felt a surge of self-pity—and in those first few months in the main camp she was often seized with a fit of melancholy—whenever she wondered why, at the age of twenty-five, fate had taken her freedom and thrown her in "elbow to elbow" with a throng of strangers, she consoled herself with the notion that at least she was healthy, free of the diseases and emotional illness that kept the hospital wards at Santo Tomas so full.

Soon she had a routine. Up early she washed her long, dark hair in a cold shower, then tied it back with a ribbon off her face and neck. After work she would sometimes repair to her cot in Room 38 of Main Building and read or knit underwear and socks. She often worked a patch of garden, one of many tiny plots of ground that the Executive Committee leased to internees who wanted to grow their own vegetables—*talinum,* corn and *camotes* (a type of sweet potato). The patch was no bigger than a parking space, but she loved the labor of tending it. The sun felt good on her back, the earth thick and cool in her hands. When she closed her eyes and shut out the noisy, malodorous camp, she could almost imagine herself back in Massachusetts in the fields on her hands and knees next to her father and brothers, weeding and hoeing the dark soil behind their house, that wood-frame building where she was born and where her life would always be waiting.

She saw herself as "a down-to-earth, no-frills girl" who cared little about hairstyles and makeup, a plain woman, much like her close friend Eleanor Garen. "Country gals," they called themselves, young women with memories of hard work and want, convinced that the country in them, the lesson they had learned at home, would help get them through. They understood each other, supported each other too, often catching the same work shift in the hospital. Afterward, walking together in Father's Garden, a quiet spot where Dominican priests had once passed the time, they would trade stories of home—Elkhart, Indiana, where Eleanor lived, and Bridgewater, Massachusetts, the place most on Cassie's mind.

Once she was settled, Cassie signed up for classes at the camp adult school—Spanish with Peter Richards, who taught her possessive pronouns and the sequence of tenses, or on Thursday evenings music appreciation with Father Visser, who taught her the Catholic view of art. "Harmony and melody," he said, "develop a high appreciation to what is out of tune with moral truth." Under the circumstances, it seemed a concept the class could easily embrace.[2]

At night Cassie returned to her room to chat with her bunkmates: Rita Palmer, Edith Corns, Letha McHale, Alice "Swish" Zwicker, Clara "Bickie" Bickford, Earlyn "Blackie" Black, Rosemary "Red" Hogan.

She enjoyed the good talk and easy society of those evenings. When she was in trouble, however, and needed good advice or a steady hand, she usually turned to Josie Nesbit.

"Josie always made me feel she was my friend, my bulwark, the person I went to if I had work or personal problems," she said

Cassie worried about Josie. The war had been hard on the forty-eight-year-old senior nurse, and the months of combat seemed to have left the lean, five-foot-eight-inch woman looking ever more angular. At times, Cassie thought Josie looked downright gaunt.

Often that first year and a half, Cassie was able to lose herself in play. The Japanese had imprisoned two American golf pros from Manila's posh courses and they came into camp with their golf bags slung on their shoulders. One of them joined the faculty of the adult school and gave regular lessons to eight students.

"What he'd have us do was stand in a row with clubs and try to perfect our grip, our stance," Cassie said. "Once in a while he would let us take a swing at a real golf ball, but if we had a bad hook the ball went over the wall. Then we had a terrible time trying to get the Japs to go out into the streets and look for the ball. [Since] balls were at a premium, we hit on an idea. We crocheted little casings out of string, little round casings, stuffed them as hard as we could with cotton, and then drew the string together. We ended up with a little ball—what we would know today as a whiffle ball. So there we would stand, this class, swinging away."

Her real passion, however, was baseball. Well schooled by her brothers, Cassie could scoop up grounders, shag line drives and make throws across the width of the infield to first base. She organized a team of nurses to play in the women's league.[3] Cassie played shortstop, Eleanor Garen was the catcher, Bickie Bickford pitched and Adele Foreman covered second base.

Their toughest competition came from a team of girl teenagers fielded by the Bureau of Education. Young, fast and strong, the girls dominated the league and were led by a fourteen-year-old "orphan" named Terry Myers. A spirited, dark-haired girl, Terry bore such a striking resemblance to Cassie that it set people talking.[4]

Before the war the Myerses, who were Americans, owned a large and successful trucking, storage and stevedore business along Manila's bustling waterfront. The family—Terry, her mother, father and two brothers—lived the comfortable life of American colonials: private schools, servants, a big house with a wraparound porch. At regular intervals their mother, Frances Myers, took the children home to the

United States to experience what she called "the American way of life." On one such trip in the spring of 1941, she went to California with Wally, the youngest; Terry and Ken, the oldest, were supposed to join them during the Christmas holiday. When the Japanese attacked two weeks before Christmas, Terry, Ken and their father were stranded like the other foreign nationals in the Philippines. Her father decided to join the guerrillas and sent the children to live with their grandparents in sub-urban Manila. In mid-January 1942 the four were interned at Santo Tomas, but a day or so later, in an effort to free up space in camp, the Japanese let a number of the elderly, Terry's grandparents among them, return to their homes, leaving the Myers children alone behind the walls, the first Santo Tomas "war orphans."

Terry thrived in prison. Without the tether of a parent, she was free to do as she pleased. Like most teenagers she was constantly hungry and spent most of her time scheming for food. She worked as a serving girl on the camp chow line, slipping a few extra ladles of stew into her own portion. Then she trotted over to the commandant's office to work with those detailed to clean the stores of rice; for this labor she would wear a pair of overalls with deep pockets, which she turned into storage silos for the portions she daily purloined. When she learned that the hospital kitchen had the best food in camp, she convinced Maude Davison to make her a nurse's aide and took her meals with the Angels.

To Terry camp life "was like a holiday." She told herself, "We'll only be in camp a short time before the Americans arrive. Why not run a lit-tle wild?" And that is exactly what the tomboy did.

When the army nurses rolled into Santo Tomas that hot day in Au-gust 1942, one of Terry's friends was in the crowd that greeted them. The girl watched as the women disembarked and noticed that one of them looked just like Terry.

"Hey, guess what?" she said, seeking her friend out. "The Japs just brought your sister into camp!"

Cassie met her double at the camp hospital and liked her right from the start.

"I got attracted to Terry's personality, her athletic ability and the wonderful way that she was taking the experience," she said.

The feeling, according to Terry, was mutual, and soon the look-alikes were friends, Cassie and "Little Cassie," as everyone called them.

Little Cassie became part of Big Cassie's circle of friends. She worked in the hospital and ate her meals with the group. During the long, hot af-ternoons, she would sit with some of them under a banyan tree and play cards or just shoot the breeze. The women liked to talk about food and fashion, music and dance, and the teenager, wide-eyed, loved to listen, especially when the talk turned to men and romance. Toward the end of the afternoon they would form an ad hoc chorus, divide up the voices and sing the standards of the day.

> *"Chattanooga Choo-Choo,*
> *You're gonna take me back home.*
> *Chattan-ooga . . . Chattanoo-Ga! . . .*
> *All aboard."*[5]

Terry was also a talented mimic, and her send-ups left the nurses in stitches. The teenager called their captain "Old Maude Davison" and parodied her grumpy ways. She nicknamed Ann Mealor "Cobweb Annie" and "Miss Clean" because Mealor was always scolding the young volunteers who scrubbed the hospital operating room. Terry had them down pat, but the teenager was smart enough to know when to stop. She understood that the nurses were "tight-knit," like a big family. "They were very protective of each other," she said. "And any member could call someone else an SOB or lazy, but don't let an outsider do it." So she watched her tongue, sharing her most private thoughts only with her "big sister," waiting for the moments when they were alone, strolling shoulder to shoulder in the shadow of the outer wall.

In time Cassie's prison life took on a pattern. She had her work, her friends, her growing friendship with Terry. And it was just about then, just as she was getting accustomed to the camp and its routines, that she decided to work for the underground.

Weekly, through the package line, word would filter into camp about the treatment of the twenty thousand American soldiers, sailors and marines who had been captured during the fall of Bataan and Corregidor. Those who had survived the Death March had been taken to prison camps in northern Luzon, and there, between April and July, some two thousand POW's died of malaria, beriberi, dengue fever, gross malnutrition, dysentery and the incessant assaults of their keepers. Many were flogged so severely, the guards literally beat the flesh off them. Many were worked so hard, they simply dropped dead.

Finding a sufficient number of able-bodied men among the prisoners to bury the dead was not the least of the problems with which the camp authorities were confronted. It was not unusual to have several of the burial

*detail drop dead from exhaustion and overwork in the midst of their duties,
and be thrown into the common grave which they were digging for their
dead comrades. Not infrequently men who had collapsed from exhaustion
were even buried before they were actually dead.*[6]

The internees at Santo Tomas were outraged by this ruthless cruelty,
and many of them, particularly the army and navy nurses—comrades of
the men the Japanese were slowly and savagely exterminating—were determined to help. Most of the military doctors from Bataan and Corregidor, along with their corpsmen and medics, had been sent to Bilibid
Prison in Manila, another pestilential hellhole. When the nurses discovered that their colleagues were imprisoned nearby, many began to work
for the Philippine resistance movement, which was smuggling food,
clothing, medicine, money and information into the military prisons.

Early in 1943 Cassie had a relapse of malaria and the camp doctors,
worried about her liver, sent her to Philippine General Hospital for tests.
(The Japanese commandant regularly allowed STIC's doctors and nurses
to transfer their sickest patients out of camp to better equipped facilities
in the city for surgery and complicated treatment.)

Leading the underground smuggling operation were a group of
Roman Catholic priests, and just as she was about to leave STIC for
Philippine General Hospital, one of them approached Cassie. The father
came right to the point. Would she be willing to serve as a conduit for
money and messages? She promptly said yes, and during her first days in
Philippine General, Cassie tried to find sympathetic Filipinos to act as
couriers to carry messages to the prisoners in Bilibid and Fort Santiago.

"I would try to engage anybody who would talk to me while I lay in
bed," Cassie remembered. "I could speak enough Spanish and a little bit
of Tagalog so I figured the Filipinos were apt to [work with] me."

Straightaway she made several contacts and became part of the underground. The priests from STIC visited her often and passed her
money, which she hid under her bedclothes. Then, when the time was
right, she would pass the cash to her contacts, in this way funneling
thousands of pesos to her imprisoned male comrades.

"I worried a little about the risk," she said. "But you had to trust
these people if you were going to be a conduit and help some GI out in
some awful hellhole."

When she got back to camp, she, along with other nurses, kept at it,
smuggling notes and money in hollowed-out fruits or stuffed inside medical supplies that were sent to the prisons.[7]

In addition to all of this—her work, her sports, her smuggling and her circle of friends—she took up writing. In a creative writing workshop at the adult school, she sat through lectures on "effective sentence structure" and "rhetorical questions" and "matters of emphasis," then sat down to execute a series of essays, some formal, such as a disquisition on the pleasures of reading, and some personal, such as her ironic account of the first days of the war.

> *When War in the Pacific broke out, it came to me not as a superlative tragedy, but as an interruption of the most exasperating kind to my personal plans. The reason for this egotistical view of one of history's great disasters was that few young women could have been less forewarned and conscious of the War's imminence than I was; but in particular, no one could have been more ignorant of the meaning of war-time Army Hospital Service. I had arrived in Manila six weeks before the War prepared for a two-year tour of duty which would be filled to the brim with the excitement of the tropics.*
>
> *[After the first attack] as I sat there with my hand raised [to volunteer for duty at Fort Stotsenberg], I found it hard to believe that not far away men had been slain ruthlessly, and their poor disfigured bodies heaped together and crowded, in ghastly indiscrimination, into quickly provided common graves, as though they were nameless vermin. What did the immediate future hold in store for me? How would the War ultimately affect me?[8]*

THE DIVERSIONS ASIDE, prison was still prison, with all its discomforts and deprivations.

When the army nurses moved to the main camp, they were housed at first in a small structure behind Main Building—sixty-four women squeezed into four small rooms; each woman had a space about six feet long by forty inches wide, an area the size of the average front door. The women slept head to toe (for privacy), dressed standing (side by side), waited to use the one available toilet (with dysentery such waiting seemed an eternity), and took turns brushing their teeth at the only sink.

"The close proximity to so many people—even in the army you had more privacy," said Alice Hahn. "There wasn't any room to read a book at night or do any of the other little things people like to do."[9]

On duty they ate in the hospital kitchen, but most of the time they were caught up in the one activity that consumed all internees—standing in line.

At breakfast they queued up to get their meal tickets verified, then queued up again to get a ladle full of mush and a weak cup of coffee or tea or some other anemic simulacrum. After breakfast they lined up at tin troughs to do their laundry. (The nurses adopted the camp custom of soaking their clothes in buckets overnight to loosen the dirt, which saved soap and cut down on scrubbing and waiting time.) They strung a clothesline near their quarters and assigned one of their number to sit guard over the drying garments, lest one of the camp's chronic looters make off with their clothes. In the afternoon they queued up again to buy supplies. Then came dinner and more waiting as the men on the serving line slowly ladled out vegetable soup or vegetable stew. Finally came bedtime and the last lines of the day, these to brush one's teeth or use the toilet.

"How can I best describe my three years at STIC?" said Sallie Durrett, "waiting, waiting in a long line for a meager meal two times a day, waiting in line to go to the bathroom or take a shower, waiting in the hot sun for three hours for a half a cup of salt, waiting in line to wash my clothes in the tin trough, waiting for some word from home."[10]

The interminable lines, the incessant crowds and the dunning monotony of the long hot days affected everyone differently.

Hattie Brantley concentrated on "keeping body and soul" together: "By the time you filled your day with four hours of duty and washed your clothes, dried them and did a few things for yourself—read a book—the day was gone. They passed with amazing rapidity. And every day we said, 'Help is on the way; it'll be here tomorrow.' We lived on faith and hope and trust and good prayers from home."[11]

Anna Williams took classes in public speaking and joined a chorus: "I did different things to keep my mind busy. I didn't get upset. I wouldn't let myself worry ahead on things."[12]

Bertha Dworsky held on to hope—"If you gave up hope, you would have just folded up and died"—and a good book. She liked all-consuming novels, such as *Gone with the Wind,* but soon noticed that fiction had its own discomforts. "Every time you'd start reading, the people in the book were always eating or drinking or doing something that made you always think of food."[13]

And food was often all they thought about. Their subsistence diet left them continuously hungry and in many cases weak. "We could only work three or four hours a day on the amount of food we were getting," said Rose Rieper.[14]

Each meal revolved around one of three main dishes: *lugao,* a watery rice concoction; *moogow,* a vegetable ragout that only occasionally had a few slivers of caraboa in it; and finally, in Anna Williams's words, a "weevily cornmeal,"[15] which, according to Frances Nash, "tasted like wallpaper paste."[16]

If they had money the women would queue up to buy a duck egg or a little caraboa milk, a papaya, perhaps, or a banana. "I traded the cigarettes I got for cans of milk," said Ann Mealor.[17]

They also struggled to keep themselves clothed. On duty the nurses worked in their khaki blouses and skirts—a uniform without insignia. Off duty they wore whatever they could scrounge. "We made underwear out of worn outer clothing," said Eunice Young. "I wore wooden shoes for three years to save my one pair of leather shoes for the day of liberation. I thought it would take only a few weeks or months at the most."[18] When their clothing developed holes or tears, they covered them with embroidery floss, sometimes stitching monograms or meal-ticket numbers and even scenes from camp over the holes. When their pajamas and housecoats began to wear out, they made new ones out of bedspreads and curtains and towels.

At night they slept on *bejucos,* rough-hewn cots of woven fibers or reeds or sometimes wooden slats. These natural materials allowed for good ventilation in a tropical climate, but they also invited bedbugs. "Every morning you poked through the weaving of your bed looking for them but they didn't come out until nightfall," said Cassie.[19] The women tried pouring hot water or kerosene on their cots, but nothing worked. "If you've ever been bitten by [bedbugs], it's pretty awful," said Earlyn Black. They "were our biggest enemy."[20]

Mostly the women tried to keep busy, to distract themselves from the heat and the crowds, the vermin and the deprivation. "The people who went down the fastest were those who didn't have anything to do," said Ruby Motley. "If you had work to do, you were so much better; you didn't have time to think—that's what ruins you."[21]

Eunice Young and a friend decided to volunteer for the night shift at the hospital. No lines for them, no crowds. In the morning, at the end of their shift, they ate in the hospital mess hall, then went to bed in a small but quiet dormitory set aside just for the night staff. "At night we'd wake up, eat the evening meal and go back on duty. That way we didn't have to fret about what was going on in the camp—what the Japs had been up to that day, who had been taken out and brought back, all the petty things that can go on in prison camp. The secret to being a survivor is to keep busy."[22]

The other internees worked too, of course, and the camp rule that everyone had to spend at least two hours a day laboring for the commonweal produced some interesting, if incongruous, scenes—society matrons up to their elbows in rice and cornmeal looking for worms and weevils . . . bank presidents scrubbing urinals and toilets . . . business executives wielding picks and shovels in sanitation trenches or reclaiming landfill for a garden. Most accepted their new station with equanimity, but several, those to whom the status life was everything, seemed to lose, along with their identity, the will to live. They walked around camp looking pale, dirty and disheveled. A few even refused to get out of bed and after a short time appeared at the hospital with intestinal maladies, heart problems and other complaints characteristic of chronic depression, anxiety and emotional distress.

Imprisonment, in fact, took its toll on everyone. Jammed together on queues and in quarters much too small to accommodate them, the internees lost their psychological space and thus their individuality. In the shower, for example, people washed in groups, circling under a spray head. "You stood there in front of everybody," said Gwendolyn Henshaw. "You had no privacy, so you just kind of close your eyes, and pretty soon you just kind of keep closing down and closing down because you can't stand that stuff."[23]

To Sally Blaine, the shower circle, with eight or so women rotating under a sprinkle of water, seemed like a kind of human merry-go-round, and when she lost her inhibitions and began to study the figures on this impromptu carousel, she noticed that one of them, a determined smoker, had found a way to have her morning cigarette while she washed herself. (As the woman stepped under the water, she would stick out her lower lip and tilt the cigarette straight up, out of the way, a neat maneuver that allowed her to lather, wash, rinse and rotate under the sprinkle of water without missing a puff.)

The "shower smoker" became one of many running jokes among the nurses. And as their collective sense of humor returned, so did their collective sense of mischief. The Japanese had ordered the internees to bow to the guards, and when the nurses entered Santo Tomas they were given lessons in the proper obeisance. Now the women decided to have some fun.

"Usually when a group of internees passed a guard, they all bowed together and he bowed once in response," said Eunice Young. "Well, we hit on the idea of having thirty nurses pass the guard at spaced intervals. Just as the guard finished one bow, another nurse would come along and bow; two dozen bows in as many minutes and the guard usually took a walk. After that when the guards saw the nurses coming, they'd turn their backs so they didn't have to bow to us."[24]

As the months passed, many of the women, ignoring Josie Nesbit's admonitions about men, began to wander about camp and mix with the other internees. "We were at an age where we pretty soon formed alliances with men," said Alice Hahn. "We had friendships pretty much the same way we would in normal life, the normal boy-girl relationships, what you would expect. I met my husband in prison camp. He was a Pan American operations officer who had worked at Cavite Naval Yard."[25]

Still, in close company or on their own, the Angels of Bataan and Corregidor struggled like everyone else in camp to get through the dislocation of another prison camp day.

"We lived in the past, completely in the past," said Inez McDonald. "We told things that we did as a child. We'd talk and talk and tell the same stuff until finally someone would say, 'Oh, shut up! You already told that six times.'

"You couldn't look forward to anything," she went on. "We'd tell ourselves, Oh [our troops will] be here by my birthday; they'll be here by Christmas; they'll be here by my next birthday. Then Christmas would come, then Easter, then Thanksgiving. But I never felt they wouldn't come. I never felt that I wasn't going home."[26]

Chapter 13

Los Banos, 1943

O<small>N</small> T<small>HANKSGIVING</small> D<small>AY</small> in 1942 the Americans in STIC decided to create something of a traditional holiday feast. The Finance Committee had approved the purchase of turkeys, and camp cooks roasted the birds until they were a golden brown and gave everyone a little bit of meat. After the meal, hundreds sat around the athletic field near the main gate and cheered as the East and West football teams, made up of young men from across the camp, met in the first Talinum Bowl.[1] Some of the nurses in the crowd wore red hibiscus in their hair as a kind of substitute for lipstick.

As Christmas 1942 approached, the women were busy scrounging and making gifts. One nurse sewed images of shanties and tropical flora on small pieces of linen—Santo Tomas cocktail napkins, she called them. Another, a whittler, roamed the campus for scrap wood to carve into crosses. Still others scrounged for toy blocks and clothespins and used them to fashion necklaces. Eleanor Garen cooked up jam from native limes. A few women got together to make rag dolls for the little girls in camp. When everything was done they gathered to label each gift with tags cut from old Christmas cards.

Commandant Tsurumi had no interest in promoting Christmas spirit, however, and, as his captives prepared for the holiday, he announced a paper shortage and suspended publication of the internee newspapers, first the *Internews,* which was later called the *STIC Gazette,* a bulletin of new regulations and changes in the camp government along with a calendar of social and sporting events, then he suspended the *In-*

ternitis, a literary magazine that sold for thirty centavos and carried mostly short fiction and cartoons. (The last issue featured a rendering of Santa Claus on a Philippine donkey, muttering to himself, "I'll have a tough time making it this year.")[2]

The South African Red Cross sent in several truckloads of packages stamped PRISONER PARCEL. Shared by the internees, each package held cans of bacon, meat spread, margarine, condensed milk, tomatoes, marmalade, cheese pudding, soda, crackers, tea, sugar, a chocolate cake and a piece of soap.

Just before Christmas, a Filipino courier secretly delivered to the nurses a special gift from three army engineers who had gotten to know the women on Corregidor. The Japanese had been holding the men on the Rock to help them repair Malinta Tunnel. During this labor the engineers had come across small amounts of cash that desperate soldiers had stashed in the walls, and when their captors weren't looking, the engineers secretly collected the booty, stuffed it into an envelope and arranged to have it smuggled into STIC. "It won't do us any good here," they wrote in a note to the nurses. "Maybe it will make your Christmas merrier."[3]

On Christmas Day the army nurses set up a long table behind their quarters. At each place they set a handwritten name card. The entrée was canned meat. During the meal Josie Nesbit reminded her colleagues that prisoners or no, they were better off this Christmas than last—when the Japanese were dropping bombs on them.

On New Year's Eve, lights-out came at 10:30 P.M. At midnight the nurses who had not yet drifted off heard a lone siren wail in the warm night, then from beyond the wall and across the barbed wire came the sound of a few, desultory firecrackers.

A week or so later the army nurses were told that the Executive Committee was moving them into Main Building and planned to turn their present quarters into a children's hospital. Some of the women balked at the move. They were settled in, they said, and sent a letter to the Committee protesting the relocation and outlining their grievances. A few days later they were surprised, if not slightly embarrassed, when they realized that their new quarters were a step up from the old. Their four rooms on the second floor of the Main Building overlooked the plaza, and outside in the hall they were able to set up their own private dining area, an arrangement that allowed them to eat together and share their food. But the privacy and the extra few inches they gained in their new quarters came with a price: they now had to share a bathroom with three hundred other women. Cotton curtains around the four toilets allowed them a few moments of solitude, but there was usually a long, long wait to use one of the five washbasins or, in groups of eight, to pass under one of the four dribbling shower heads.

Meanwhile the camp census was beginning to grow. In January 1943 Santo Tomas Internment Camp was "home" to 3,263 men, women and children.[4] By May 1 there were nearly 4,200 people in STIC and, fearing epidemics, riots and worse, the Japanese decided to set up a new internment camp at a relatively remote site not far from the town of Los Banos, roughly 42 miles, or 68 kilometers, southeast of Manila on the shores of Laguna de Bay. The commandant told the Executive Committee that he wanted a group of eight hundred male volunteers to establish the new camp and settle there. If the committee could not supply the names, the Japanese would come up with their own list.

In effect the mandate for such labor pulled from STIC the eight hundred most able-bodied men in camp, young men who had the skill and strength to set up a water and sanitation system, a kitchen, a hospital and general housing—in short, to build from scratch a new prison. While most of the younger, unattached men looked forward to a change of scenery, many others, husbands and boyfriends of the women in STIC, did not.

Among those on the list was Dr. Charles Leach, a physician from the Rockefeller Foundation who, in early December 1941, was on his way to Chungking, China. The outbreak of war stranded Leach in Manila and he was taken into custody when the Japanese entered the city. In early January he and a handful of civilian nurses set up a camp hospital; then, when the navy nurses arrived in March, he invited them to work with him, and soon the civilian doctor and the eleven women in blue became close. In July when the fifty-four army nurses arrived in camp, the Bluejackets worried they would lose their military identity. They were "Navy" and they had no intention of letting the army reign over them. (No doubt there was some lingering resentment from the first days of the war when, in the minds of the navy women, the Army Nurse Corps had fled to Bataan, abandoning the small navy contingent to the enemy.) Still they managed to get along with the army, even work together in the camp clinics, but when the navy women heard that Leach, their advocate and ally, was leaving for Los Banos, they again felt abandoned.

That night as Laura Cobb lay on her cot, her friend, Mary Rose "Red" Harrington, knelt beside her and whispered through the mosquito netting.

"Laura," she said, "why don't you volunteer us to go up country with Leach and the men?"[5]

Cobb knew that her young redheaded friend had a point, and the two began to list the pros and cons of leaving Santo Tomas for the wilds of Los Banos. They liked the idea of a fresh start and of a smaller camp. They especially liked working with Leach. Most of all they wanted their own hospital again, wanted to do things the "navy way." A few hours later Laura Cobb went downstairs to the offices of the Executive Committee and offered her navy unit for the new camp.

The next morning Red Harrington got up early, waiting for word that the Executive Committee had reached a decision. She badly wanted to go, to get out from under Davison and the army and away from the overcrowding. She waited and waited, but the morning passed without word. Perhaps something had happened, she thought. The Japanese were always reversing themselves. When the afternoon arrived, Harrington reported for ward duty. Around four o'clock, navy nurse Goldia O'Haver came through the door.

"You're relieved of duty, Red," she said, smiling broadly, as if something was up. "We're moving in the morning. Go pack your stuff."[6]

When this word reached the army nurses, Maude Davison found herself with a crisis. Several of her younger charges had fallen in love with men who were being transferred to Los Banos, and now the women wanted to accompany their paramours to the new camp. As always, Davison was unswayable and flatly refused the requests. No matter what the cost, she told Josie Nesbit, she was going to keep her corps together.

In truth Maude Davison's authority was empty, her power an illusion. Though no one ever tested or vetted her official position, the nurses at that point, by law, likely held the status of civilians; they were in a civilian internment camp, not a military prison, submitting to civilian rules and living under civilian oversight. Davison could insist on good order and military discipline all she liked; the young nurses were free, relatively speaking, to do as they pleased. And yet . . .

In the end they followed orders. They submitted to their captain because they had been raised and trained to respect authority, even when that authority no longer applied to them. What's more, they were nurses, members of the community of healers, and honest healers always put the interests of their patients ahead of themselves. There were hundreds of sick internees in the hospital at Santo Tomas and barely enough nurses to treat them. Finally and above all, they were comrades, bound by a fidelity and love born of sacrifice and suffering. They had been bombed together, escaped together, captured together. Now the Angels would wait together too, wait for deliverance.

On moving day, Friday, May 14, 1943, the entire camp awoke before dawn. The internees who were being transferred to Los Banos filled the plaza in front of Main Building with their luggage, pots and pans, folding chairs and large woven bags filled with clothing and linen. The Japanese guards, of course, poked through everything. After breakfast, the eight hundred men who were being transferred lined up for a roll call. The new Japanese commandant, A. Kodaki, wished everyone in the group good luck and good health, then twelve army trucks appeared and the internees loaded their gear and climbed aboard as the crowd on the plaza shouted and cheered and waved good-bye. Here and there in the throng, a number of young women stood sobbing.

The navy nurses climbed aboard the last truck. Helen Grant, a Scottish nurse, and Mrs. Basilia Torres Steward, a Filipino nurse married to an American, joined them. The driver started the engine and all at once over the camp loudspeakers came the melody of "Anchors Away." As their truck turned down the esplande toward the iron front gates, the women looked back at the crowd, tears streaming down their faces.

By the time the truck carrying the navy nurses reached the Tutban railway station, the male internees had already been loaded into boxcars for the journey north. Japanese soldiers ordered the women to break into groups of two or three and join the men in the cars, then they slammed the metal doors shut, and the train pulled away from the station.

The temperature inside those sealed steel containers rose steadily and quickly, and soon the cars began to stink of sweat and the leftover stench of cattle. Guards cracked the doors a bit for some fresh air, but whenever the train slowed they shut them tight again, sealing the prisoners inside. The noise, odor and heat were so overpowering that the men and women could do little more than sip from their water bottles and shut their eyes against the discomfort. Soon everyone was soaked in sweat and struggling for breath. For seven hours the prisoners were locked inside those metal boxes. Edwina Todd figured she lost almost ten pounds along the way.

At last they reached the town of Los Banos and were allowed to disembark. After a day in a cattle car, the hot and humid air felt as refreshing as a cool breeze off Manila Bay. A convoy of trucks arrived and took the internees to their new home, the campus of the University of the Philippines College of Agriculture and Forestry, a rural facility at the base of Mount Makiling, about a mile from Los Banos, on a twenty-five-acre plateau of tropical rain forest, roughly two thousand feet above sea level.[7]

A double ring of barbed wire surrounded the facility, which consisted of several medium-sized buildings, a gymnasium and scattered bungalows and cottages. The men moved into the various buildings, the women into the infirmary. (Later, when the camp population would swell to more than two thousand, the Japanese brought in Filipino labor gangs to construct long leaky barracks with nipa roofs, woven walls and dirt floors.)

In the weeks that followed the internees set about building their new home, a kind of prison village. They nominated an executive committee, assembled a water and sanitation system, planted a large vegetable garden along the camp perimeter. Soon the fertile soil of Luzon gave them plenty of vegetables to add to their daily allotment of rice. Once again the navy nurses and Dr. Leach set up a hospital, this time turning a foul infirmary—a portable boiler the previous staff had used to sterilize instruments had been left with the remnants of cooked food in it—into a twenty-five-bed facility on the edge of the plateau. When they needed equipment, they turned to the handymen in camp, who fashioned emesis basins and bedpans from corrugated roofing and old tin cans.[8]

Laura Cobb liked the new camp and was glad she had listened to Red Harrington. She was in charge again, head nurse—head mistress, really, for she saw her job as much more than just supervising nurses. In Manila before the war she often seemed as much house mother as head nurse. Perhaps at forty-five she thought she had to mother her young charges, and she often inserted herself in their lives, attending their cocktail parties, suggesting things for them to ship home, advising them on the latest fashions.[9]

Cobb, a career officer, had been in charge of the twelve-member nursing staff at the U.S. Naval Hospital in Canacao, at the south end of Manila Bay. She had joined the navy in 1918 after a short stint as a schoolteacher in Atchinson, Kansas. A quiet, slender woman with dark hair and wire-rimmed glasses, she was known for her good manners, her stylish clothes and her supreme self-confidence. She had done two tours in the Philippines and had held enough important posts Stateside, and received enough commendations along the way to establish her authority. She was as firm as Davison, but much more courteous, more engaged. The navy, more than the army, was known for its social rituals—dinners, dances and banquets—and Laura Mae Cobb, with her hazel eyes, tailored clothes and "ladylike ways," as her nurses described her, negotiated navy society with style and grace. Even toward the end of the war when malnutrition turned her hair gray and left her five-foot-seven-inch frame looking like a spindle, she still managed to keep her faded–blue denim field uniform neat, still insisted on presenting herself as well as she was able.

In the early days at Los Banos, however, she worried only about doing her job. Almost everything the hospital needed had to be scrounged, built, jerry-rigged or invented. Dr. Leach, for example, had warned that in the steamy environment of Los Banos, tuberculosis would be epidemic, so as a precaution, the nurses developed a cough syrup of onion juice and sugar that managed to check the hacking, expectorating coughs that began to appear in many of the prisoners. Encouraged by their luck, they also tried other "natural treatments" too—a tea from guava leaves for bacillary dysentery and an elixir from mango leaves for high blood pressure and diabetes. (The guavas worked but the mango elixir, recommended by local "healers," turned out to be so much snake oil.) The adhesive tape supplied by the Japanese was useless—it adhered to nothing—but internees who had been pharmaceutical representatives before the war tapped sap from a rubber tree inside the wire and mixed the sap with oil to form a sticky paste. When a patient needed a dressing, the women simply reached into a large jar of homemade paste with a bamboo spatula, spread a line of the goop on either side of the wound, and placed a piece of gauze or cloth on top. And there was more—drinking glasses fashioned from the beer and Coca-Cola bottles left behind by the students, straws cut from indigenous reeds and mosquito netting woven from a porous material found in banana fiber.

Every evening before curfew, that first group of internees at Los Banos would gather in groups. Some would sit in a coffeehouse shanty for a watery brew of local herbs, others on the playing field to watch the sunset, listen to music, stage skits or hold sing-alongs. One night some lyricist manqué surprised the thirteen nurses in camp with a new version of "The Sweetheart of Sigma Chi."

> *Let's give a cheer*
> *For our navy gals,*
> *Who can't be beat for style.*
> *The bumps and jars*
> *of the old box cars,*
> *They took them with a smile.*
> *They volunteered for a real tough job*

With a cheerful look in their eyes.
While the road is long,
Let us tell them in song,
They're the pals of us eight hundred guys.[10]

The pals, as it turned out, needed help. Thirteen nurses could not possibly take care of so many patients, so Laura Cobb asked Red Harrington and Dorothy Still to train a few of the men as hospital orderlies. Red started sizing up every man who came in for treatment, looking for anyone who would be willing, and able, to help with bed baths, enemas, examinations and everyday care.

One afternoon she noticed a bright-faced young man sitting in the waiting area. His ankle was wrapped in a cloth and he needed to see a doctor. He had "nice features," this internee. In fact, the closer she looked, the more she noticed how handsome he was. Who is that good-looking kid in the torn pants? she asked herself.[11]

At twenty-eight Mary Rose Harrington had no trouble meeting men. In Manila before the bombs she had been squired to dances and tennis matches by some of the most attractive physicians and officers on base. Now she was staring at the camp garbage collector, one Thomas Page Nelson, before the war an employee of the Department of the Treasury.

While Dr. Leach treated Nelson's ankle, Red Harrington tried to size him up. His camp job, he said, was an easy one. Not much garbage in a place where everyone was scrounging for food.

In that case, Red replied, "How about coming to the hospital and working with us?"

Page, as he was called, took a long look at the woman in front of him—the gorgeous hair, the dazzling blue eyes, the alabaster skin and Cupid's-bow lips. Work with her? Sure, he said. When did she want him to start?

That summer Page and three other men took training from the nurses. They learned how to scrub for procedures, handle linen, bathe patients and select the correct instruments for the various examinations and medical procedures performed by Dr. Leach and his nurses. Page seemed to like the work—or the company. Most of the time he teamed with Red and soon they were spending their evenings together as well. They liked to sit at a table in the bamboo coffeehouse, a "very elegant shanty," as Red described it, talking away from the watchful eyes of the Japanese guards.

One Sunday afternoon, about three months after they had first set eyes on each other, Page approached his lover, dug deep into a pocket of his pants and pulled out a sapphire ring. He was dirty and he was tired, he told her, but he loved her very much; he very much wanted to marry her.

Red smiled. She kissed him, then whispered yes.

The next day Page Nelson took his bamboo folding chair to a carpenter friend and had it converted into a love seat. In the evenings the couple would carry their little bench to the camp playing field, where they would sit with the others, watching the stars, telling jokes about the guards or listening to records, especially Red's favorite, "I Got Spurs that Jingle, Jangle, Jingle." What else would a girl from Elk Point, South Dakota, really like?[12]

What both wanted most of all was what prisons never provide, privacy. They built a shanty of their own behind the hospital on top of the camp septic tank. And when their friends teased them about its malodorous location, their riposte was to brag that they had the only shanty in camp with a cement floor. They ate their meals together there, and when no one was looking they stole a kiss or an embrace. They never talked of marriage, though, of a full life together with a house in Virginia where Page lived, a home with children and a future. They had no future, they said, only time, uncertain time, and for the moment, at least, each other.

*T*HE EXODUS TO Los Banos created a momentary lull at Santo Tomas, and that moment of stillness seemed to slow passage of time, or at least remind everyone that liberation was far from at hand.

The army nurses had been in camp for more than a year now. Most, in fact, had passed a birthday there.

[ELEANOR GAREN NOTEBOOK, PAGE 6] Yesterday [3-8-43] was my birthday—Twas only a year (sometimes it seems a century and then again only yesterday) that I went on night duty in Bataan. . . . Yesterday was a far cry from that scene. . . . We decided to go visiting to the shack [the nurses shanty] or, as we phrase it, "to the country for the day." So I stood in one line for bread and another for meat. By noon we had gathered up all our parafinalia [*sic*]. . . . It was a nice afternoon with the girls dropping in with presents for me. Charles gave me a pair of pliers. I had to work or rather do duty at 3 P.M. but didn't get there until 4 P.M. then after 9 P.M. Helen [Cassie] Whit and Adele had a birthday cake for me. So all in all I had a lovely day. Yet how much happier I was in the jungle working hard than here loafing.[13]

Eleanor Garen was a contemplative and interior woman, smart and shy, a ravening reader and sometimes writer, with a broad smile and self-effacing laugh that masked an abiding loneliness and an ego hobbled by self-doubt.

She enjoyed the sorority of women and had a small circle of confidants, women who liked to play marathon games of gin rummy, mah-jongg, cribbage and bridge. As they played they smoked thin cigarettes rolled from the crinkled, indigo paper that came wrapped around the cotton bandages used in the hospital, and they would joke that when they got home, they were going to make a fortune selling "blue cigarettes." To these friends, this clique that went to classes together and played baseball together too, Eleanor seemed so gregarious, so "happy-go-lucky,"[14] but she was also a private, often solitary woman. Most nights she would sit on her *bejucos* in the Main Building, scribbling her thoughts in a blue-lined composition book.

[GAREN NOTEBOOK, PAGE 1] Preface: Every writing of any length has some sort of an introduction. Being an average individual I of course will follow suit. There comes a time, very frequently under the present status quo, when the necessity of unburdening one's load becomes essential. Hence, the need for this note book. It will be a patch work book full of scraps of this and that with no unity or even coherent sequence. As long as it relieves the overflow and fills its primary function, it will be a good safety valve. It is not a diary.[15]

Indeed it was not, but it was no psychogram either, no raw log of her dreams and fears, reveries and desperation—at least not in the conventional sense. She did, in fact, "unburden" herself, relieve the "overflow" of worries, but she did this obliquely through some of the most gifted mediums that have ever tried to give voice to the psyche and the soul.

She had apparently acquired an old anthology of poetry and prose, and night after night she would scan the pages for lines of verse or prose that expressed her mood, her state of mind, then copy them in her notebook.

Early in her journal, for example, she turned to Socrates to express the one idea that likely preoccupied most of the sentient internees. ". . .

No one knows whether death, which they in their fear apprehend to be the greatest evil, may not be the greatest good."[16]

Later she called on Blake to help her break down the prison camp walls.

> *To see a world in a grain of sand*
> *And a heaven in a wild flower,*
> *Hold infinity in the palm of your hand*
> *And eternity in an hour.*[17]

And in Stephen Crane she likely saw her own sense of isolation.

> *A man said to the universe:*
> *"Sir, I exist!"*
> *"However," replied the universe,*
> *"The fact has not created in me*
> *A sense of obligation."*[18]

She loved children and spent a great deal of time with them. The boys could always count on her for a game of catch, and the girls knew she would take part in their imaginary trips and tea parties and push them on the swings. Some afternoons, she would sit for hours and read them fairy tales.

Some of her melancholy no doubt came from pain. Although her friends never knew it, she had been suffering for six months with the swollen ankles, nausea and blurred vision that comes from avitaminitis, a condition brought on by malnutrition. A camp doctor gave her a shot of thiamine, vitamin B-1, but the shot did not help, so he ordered more injections and told her to eat as much meat as she could scrounge. Clearly, he said, she was developing beriberi, a very dangerous and often fatal disease. Just as she began to mend, she came down with chronic osteoarthritis and her joints became inflamed and started to deteriorate. The doctor prescribed fifteen grains of aspirin a day and told her to take things easy for a while, stay in her room and read.

> *Let me lie in bed and rest:*
> *Ten thousand times I've done my best*
> *And all's to do again.*
>
> A. E. HOUSMAN[19]

...

THREE DAYS AFTER the navy nurses and eight hundred men left for Los Banos, some eight hundred new internees rolled through the gates of Santo Tomas, among them 325 men over the age of fifty and seventy-seven women and their children, 198 of them, all under the age of five.

Many of the older men were veterans of the Spanish-American War, Americans who elected to stay in the Philippines in 1898 when the war was over. Now these elderly veterans suffered from arthritis, heart disease and other conditions that required intensive nursing care. The large number of new children also taxed the hospital staff, for the youngsters were frequently breaking their bones in rowdy games or contracting fevers and diarrhea from playing in the dirt.

The hospital grew—it had more operating rooms now, new wards, outpatient clinics, a laboratory, a pharmacy and a kitchen. The average daily census was climbing, around one hundred in late 1942. The camp mortality rate, meanwhile, had reached 19.2 deaths per one thousand internees by the end of 1943, up from 13.2 deaths earlier that year.[20]

During the monsoons of late summer and early fall, people were forced indoors. The longer the torrent, the dirtier and more foul-smelling their quarters became. The corridors in Main Building were cluttered with tables and baby carriages and racks of wet clothes. The adults, who were bored, and the children, who were restless, began to get on one another's nerves. Babies cried, youngsters shrieked, old men shouted their complaints. The nurses, meanwhile, tried to crochet or read, play cards or nap, but it was impossible, and they eagerly waited to begin their four-hour shifts at the hospital. At work, at least, it was quiet.

In early September 1943, the internees got news that a repatriation ship, the Teia Maru, was headed toward Manila, and soon the camp was wondering aloud who might be freed. Some argued that surely the old and sick should go, while others made a case for mothers and their children. The army and navy women knew it was unlikely that they would be repatriated; they were military, after all. What's more, they were badly needed in camp. The Executive Committee met with the commandant and soon had a list of 127 people who would be shipped home on the Teia Maru. Most were transients stranded in Manila at the outbreak of the war—missionaries, doctors from the Rockefeller Foundation on their way to Far East assignments, newspapermen, businessmen and families traveling from Shanghai and Hong Kong. One name saddened the navy nurses—Dr. Charles Leach, the head doctor at Los Banos.[21]

The lucky group left in late September, and although their leaving had no apparent effect on camp life, it came to serve as a sober benchmark, for just after that, the conditions in both camps worsened.

By late fall 1943 the internees often went days without meat. Camp cooks started serving "chili sine carne" and succotash and vegetable stew. Meanwhile the price of bananas, yams, squash and beans soared. There was news from the underground of food riots in Manila and other cities. People began to guard closely their stores of canned goods, hiding them from the hungry burglars who stalked the camp looking for something to stop the ache in their stomachs.

The nurses pooled their money and bought fruits and vegetables to share. For protein they baked peanut loaves and poured boiled peanuts and peanut sauce over rice. Still they were hungry and soon found their energy flagging. After six or seven hours a day working in the ward and standing in lines, they were exhausted.

In mid-November a typhoon with sixty-mile-an-hour winds dumped twenty-seven inches of rain on Manila in three days. The water and wind destroyed shanties and most of the gardens.

As Christmas 1943 approached, the nurses were beginning to feel the dunning effect of twenty months' captivity. They again made Christmas gifts, dolls and stuffed animals, for the camp children, but Eleanor and Cassie noticed that the women did so with less enthusiasm and vigor than the year before. Even their homemade Christmas cards reflected the sober mood.

It is never Merry Christmas
When you're feeling sad and blue
And the one you care the most for
Forgets to think of you.
But when hopes and dreams are fading
And your fondest joys depart
You can still have Merry Christmas
If it's Christmas in your heart.[22]

Still they had at least one thing to celebrate—the arrival of Ruby Bradley. Bradley and another army nurse, Beatrice Chambers, had been trapped in Camp John Holmes far north in Baguio when the shooting started. For months Maude Davison had been trying to arrange their transfer to STIC. Chambers, in a decision she would later regret, decided to stay behind, but Bradley jumped at the chance to be with her comrades again. She arrived at STIC that September carrying a mattress and half a bar of soap. She looked thin and drawn, but she was tonic to her friends.[23]

On Christmas Day, the navy women at Los Banos enjoyed a quiet meal among their fellow internees. Meanwhile at Santo Tomas, the army nurses decided to observe the holiday together. Ida Hube had sent in special gifts and packages of food. After religious services the nurses sat down at long tables they had set up on the lawn beside the hospital. It was a warm, clear day and their disposition and outlook were better than they had been in weeks. They officially welcomed Ruby Bradley to their midst, then set to eating. In her journal Josie Nesbit wrote, "cheerfulness prevailed."[24]

On New Year's Eve, Manila was quiet. No whistles, no horns, no bells. Few of the women looked forward to the new year. Realists, most of them, perhaps they sensed the emptiness, the slow and inexorable ruin, 1944 was going to bring.

Chapter 14

Eating Weeds Fried in Cold Cream, 1944

URING THE FIRST week of 1944, control of Santo Tomas and the other civilian prison camps passed from the Japanese Bureau of External Affairs to the War Prisoners Department of the Imperial Japanese Army.

The army's reputation for cruelty was well known, and a short time later when the new camp commandant, Colonel S. Onozaki, arrived on the campus of Santo Tomas, now a worn and shabby place, no one was surprised when "he told the Internee Committee that" he planned to "isolate the camp from any contact with the outside, and that as a result of this new policy, the internees could expect more arduous regulations than in the past."[1]

First the army shut down the package line, the internees' one link to the outside world. No longer would the bundles of extra food, clothing, housewares or provisions be allowed into camp. Gone too was Ida Hube's black limousine and the cart full of bounty for the nurses that always followed her.

Then the commandant announced that instead of giving the Executive Committee an allowance for provisions, the army would supply the camp with food. He promised fish, cereal, vegetables, sugar, salt, cooking oil or fat and tea when it was available. Implicit in the statement was an assurance that there would be enough to go around. He was lying, of course.

When the first shipment fell short, the internees used what money they had left to buy extra staples from the few officially sanctioned vendors and bodegas still allowed to operate inside the walls. Soon, however, the stocks at these little stalls ran low. The 1,400 loaves of cassava bread STIC usually received each day dropped to 1,000 and then to 500. Milk deliveries dropped from 130 to 95 gallons a day. All that was left in the official canteens were items like vinegar and spices. As a consequence, the lines at the mess hall grew much longer, and it seemed to many internees that the Japanese wanted them hungry, perhaps to control them, perhaps to starve them to death.

Each month brought new restrictions. The commandant abolished the Executive Committee, and for the first time the guards began to patrol the campus with fixed bayonets. The army assembled a crew of male prisoners to clear a ten-foot-wide "security zone" next to the walls, a measure that forced the dismantling of many shanties. More soldiers arrived, roll calls doubled, one at 8:00 A.M., another just before dusk. The internee radio station was censored; "broadcasts" now consisted of a few songs and essential announcements. All electrical appliances were confiscated.

No one, of course, knew why, exactly, the Imperial Army had assumed control of the civilian prison camps, but clearly the war was going badly for the Japanese. The Allies had won important battles in New Guinea, New Britain and the Gilbert and Solomon Islands, and the internees at Santo Tomas reckoned that the army was tightening its grip on the occupied territories with new waves of repression.

"The first two years were day before night compared to 1944," said Frances Nash, thirty-four years old, of Washington, Georgia. "The Japs began to really clamp down. Practice blackouts were started and we were restricted to an area a couple of blocks, instead of having the run of the sixty acres. From seven P.M. until six A.M. we were locked in our rooms. All contact with the outside world was cut off."[2]

In many ways the camp hospital was a mirror of the growing misery at Santo Tomas. First the Japanese expelled the handful of Filipino physicians and nurses who had been helping out on the wards. Then they stopped the practice of channeling the severely and chronically ill to hospitals elsewhere in the city; now no matter how serious or complicated the medical problem or operation, it had to be dealt with at the camp's understaffed and ill-supplied dispensary. To offset some of the load, the doctors and nurses decided to reorganize the camp's clinics and dispensaries. They turned part of the gymnasium into a geriatric service for men and in another building opened a special eighty-bed isolation hospital for those with contagious diseases. They also opened a twenty-four-hour clinic and small emergency room in Main Building. (The clinic quickly became so overwhelmed with complainants, the nurses working there set out simple medications, such as aspirins and laxatives, in small bowls and told people to treat themselves.)[3] Finally, when all else failed and the main hospital reached capacity, doctors simply started discharging patients, sending some of the sick out to fend for themselves.

In the camp at large, each week brought more harassment—inspections, unannounced searches and capricious cancellations.[4] The Japanese closed the rodent control center, the soap shop, the textile department and the library. Many of the men in camp were pressed into labor gangs to build guard sheds and sentry boxes and to string barbed wire. Late one night the guards rousted everyone from bed, looking for a hidden radio. After more than two hours combing the campus they gave up. (The radio, the camp's only connection to the outside world, was maintained by a camp electrician, who had bolted it inside a five-gallon can and arranged to have it moved from room to room, building to building.)

Next the Japanese ordered the internees to elect room monitors, people who would take a twice-daily roll call, divide the bread-and-egg ration and record the problems in the room. The army nurses picked Edith Shacklette, a popular thirty-six-year-old senior nurse, to represent rooms 38, 39, 40 and 41 in Main Building. "Shack," as the five-foot-four-inch blond Kentuckian was called, had been a head nurse on Bataan and made a lot of friends when she refused to surrender her sense of humor and perspective to the exigencies of war.[5] She went about the business of being room monitor with the same evenhanded thoroughness and attention to detail she had shown in combat.

> [Shacklette Monitor's Diary, 3-2-44] . . . Bread issue cut in half tomorrow. Rec'd our first individual pkgs from home.[6]

> [3-7-44] . . . No talking in halls after 11 P.M. Checking nurses teeth tomorrow.

> [3-9-44] . . . Persons throwing garbage on floor will be punished. No more toilet paper at present.

> [3-18-44] . . . Noise in hall . . . at nite—children running and playing must be stopped. Promptness at all roll calls is demanded.

Still, all of this, the harassment by the Japanese and the tension that comes from forcing some four thousand people to live belly to back, paled in the face of the advancing hunger.

In March the bread issue and sugar ration were cut in half. In June, the peanut supply was reduced. Fish and vegetables supplied by the Imperial Army were, more often than not, spoiled or rotten when they arrived. The internee leaders, who still had access to what was left of the camp funds, decided to buy bananas and a few pigs, but the purchase amounted to only a few mouthfuls per person. Breakfast now was usually cornmeal mush, a cup of coconut milk and a banana (every other day the camp cooks added a tiny bit of sugar to the mush); lunch was corn soup, a little rice and ginger tea; supper consisted of cooked rice, boiled corn and white radishes (two or three times a week they'd add a few shards of fish to this gruel).

Then, as spring moved into summer, rations were cut again. The adults in camp went from a diet of 1,490 calories a day to 1,180 calories, less than half what the average person requires to maintain minimum health. The bananas were gone and rice became a periodic, rather than regular, staple. As a substitute camp cooks turned to *camote,* a fibrous sweet potato, but this simulacrum played havoc on the weakened intestines of the internees.

Now the main kitchen and hospital kitchen served only two meals a day. It was not unusual to see children scrounging through garbage cans by the Japanese army mess hall for scraps of food. (In her testimony for the American War Crimes Office, Hattie Brantley told investigators: "At frequent intervals during 1944 . . . I witnessed the slaughter of cattle by the internees for consumption by the Japanese; no part of this meat was allowed to the internees but occasionally the internees were given the bones of the cattle. . . . I had frequent occasion to witness the Japanese sentries eating meals that had been brought to their posts and these meals during this entire period included a sufficiency of fresh eggs and citrus fruits and an abundance of rice; part of this rice was frequently thrown away.")[7]

At the camp mess hall, people waiting on line for something to eat fainted from hunger. A survey conducted by the internees showed that on the average the men in camp had lost 31.4 pounds, the women 17.7 pounds. (Many individuals lost as many as fifty pounds. Eleanor Garen and Red Harrington, for example, lost some forty pounds each. Cassie, who weighed 145 pounds before the war, now was approaching 100.)

The malnutrition led to a variety of ailments: neuritic pain (inflammation of the nerves), parasthesias (numbness in the hands and feet), ocular pain (sharp ache in the eyeballs and blurred sight or double vision), pellagra (raised red spots on the skin that eventually become dry and scaly, and bleed), ariboflavinosis (sores on the lips and a red and swollen tongue) and anemia (reduced red blood cells causing extreme fatigue and weakness). The lack of proteins and vitamins led to small epidemics of measles, whooping cough, bacillary dysentery, and left almost everyone else dizzy with headaches.

Josie Nesbit, a veteran clinician normally self-possessed in the presence of suffering, was unnerved by the changes she saw taking place in her nurses.

"Their eyes gradually sank deeper into hollowed cheekbones," she noted. "Their gait slowed down more and more as their strength grew less. Even their shoulders drooped noticeably."[8]

The ache of hunger left their tempers short and their moods incendiary. Sally Blaine, twenty-nine years old, from Bible Grove, Missouri, a pretty and petite woman with curly brown hair, had a run-in with a bunkmate.

"Every night she'd come ask me after the lights were out, 'Sally, are you hungry? Wouldn't a steak taste good? Would you like to have some chocolate pie?' And I'd say, 'Oh, be quiet! Please don't talk about it.' But she always wanted to talk to me about food and I would dream of chocolate cake," Sally said. "I didn't really care that much about chocolate cake except if I had sweet milk to drink with it. I'd dream of chocolate cake and in the dream I'd start to drink my milk and it would be buttermilk when it got to my mouth. I didn't like buttermilk and the bad taste would awaken me."[9]

At Los Banos the internees were starving as well, and Red Harrington and Page Nelson began to quarrel. "We were both practically chewing on each other," said Harrington. "We got awfully snappish toward the end. I wasn't sure what was going to happen."[10]

The Santo Tomas Ladies Baseball League canceled its season; the nurses and other women on the teams did not have enough energy to lift a bat.

The internees inundated the camp commandant with letters of protest, letters that told him they were starving to death. The commandant considered the matter, then told his prisoners that their profound loss of weight was likely due to "prolonged internment, separation from families, and lack of regular communication."[11] The Imperial Army, he went on, could not be expected to satisfy the dietary predilections and native tastes of its European and American captives. And why should it? In prisoner-of-war camps in the States, American jailers did not try to find Japanese food for his countrymen. The world was at war, the commandant reminded the internees, and they should be more patient and less disagreeable. Their health was fine, he said, but if they wanted more food, perhaps they should consider making handicrafts to sell to the Filipinos or maybe they might try breeding fish in the campus swimming pool.

In the face of such absurdity and prevarication the internees tried to husband their strength and fight their despair. Cassie, twenty-seven years old and in her prime, was so enervated by malnutrition she navigated through the day like a crippled octogenarian:

> We lived on the second floor of Main Building. We had a stairway to the second floor and the stairs were on two levels. You went up, say, six steps, then there was a landing, then you had another eight steps to go. Well, it got to the point where you had all you can do to make the first set of stairs when you discover that you have to sit down and take a breather before you take on the next set of stairs. They had to make benches and put them there on the landing [so people could rest]. The writing was on the wall.[12]

On June 7 a rumor spread that the Allies had invaded France, and when the internees' secret radio confirmed the news, the camp disc jockey followed his morning announcements on the loudspeaker with the song, "Over There."

Throughout the day the camp buzzed with speculation. Maybe now, people said, maybe finally, American forces would return and rescue them. The gamblers in camp laid odds they'd be home by Christmas. One of the nurses fashioned a foot-high doll from rags, dressed it in a khaki uniform and hat and named it the Any-Day-Now Doll.[13] Other nurses formed "The Day Club," their motto—"If not today than surely tomorrow."[14]

The Japanese reacted to the Allied advances with another round of repression. No more impromptu meetings or social events; in other words no gatherings at all without official permission. At the same time, lightbulbs and matches were rationed.

The harassment, of course, only made the hunger worse, and the hungrier they became, the more they turned their backs on the conventions of society, the rules that give daily life its rectitude. Food began to disappear regularly from the camp kitchens, the fish-cleaning areas and the vendors' stands. The common want was undermining the common good.

...

*T*HE SUMMER WAS hot, the days heavy with boredom, fatigue and worry. The camp waited for rescue but rescue was nowhere in sight. In the sky above Manila, Japanese Zeros buzzed one another in mock dogfights. Inside the walls the sentries and guards prepared fighting positions and practiced combat drills.

As fall approached there was still no sign of a fleet or an invasion force. Then on September 21 the waiting turned to wonder.

The camp had just settled into its morning routine. Cooks were trying to figure out how to stretch the camp's rations for dinner, the nurses were at work in STIC's hospitals and clinics and many people were trying to summon enough strength to weed their garden patches and coax their vegetables to grow. The morning sky was noisy again with the buzz of aircraft, and the gardeners working their little patches looked up and cursed the racket coming from above the clouds. Then, all of a sudden, the planes broke through the thick cover, and those on the ground were startled by the markings on their wings—white stars and blue circles, the insignia of American aircraft!

The allied raid clearly surprised the Japanese and the city erupted with the sound of antiaircraft fire. Inside STIC the guards hustled the internees into their quarters and posted armed sentries at the entrances. A crowd gathered in the lobby of Main Building.

"They're here," people cried, tears welling up in their eyes. "Thank God, they're here."[15]

Some of the men swore that two of the aircraft had dipped their wings over the camp, a salute or perhaps a signal, they said.

At the hospital the nurses hugged and kissed one another. A few even tried to dance a little jig.

The raid lasted two hours, and from beyond the walls the internees could see smoke rising in the direction of Manila's waterfront. At 3:00 P.M. a second wave of planes appeared overhead, and the internees celebrated all over again. Camp cooks marked the occasion with a double serving of rice and vegetable-meat gravy for dinner. Tomorrow, some people told themselves, tomorrow they would be eating hamburgers.

The commandant ordered a 6:00 P.M. curfew and the internees spent the evening watching the western sky light up with the orange glow of a hundred fires. After the evening announcements the camp disc jockey played three songs: "Pennies from Heaven," "I Cover the Waterfront" and "It Looks Like Rain in Cherry Blossom Lane." In her diary Edith Shacklette wrote, "Glorious."[16]

Every day thereafter air-raid sirens sounded across the city. The bombings clearly were a prelude to an invasion, but it was anyone's guess when the invaders would arrive, where they would land or how long it would take to liberate the camps. The Japanese had a huge force in the islands and they were dug in and well fortified. Perhaps the allies planned to first rout them from the southern islands of Mindanao, Cebú, Negros and Samar before attacking the largest land mass, Luzon, where the heart of the Imperial Army, some 275,000 troops, was waiting. And it was on Luzon, of course, where the Japanese had collected most of their civilian and military prisoners. Surely, some said, they would come to Luzon first and liberate the camps—Bilibid, Cabanatuan, Los Banos, Santo Tomas.

During a lull in bombing, the Japanese army put another two hundred soldiers in Santo Tomas. The new troops immediately began bayonet practice on the plaza and close-order drill on the playing fields. They turned the cupola on Main Building into an observation post, a good point from which to direct artillery against an advancing enemy. It did not take long, of course, for the internees to figure out that these measures would make Santo Tomas a target for allied bombers and cannons. And they sent a letter to the commandant accusing him of using them as human shields. The commandant's reply was brief:

> The Government of the United States has not been officially informed that the Santo Tomas University was to be used as an internment camp. Therefore, officially it has no protective status. However everything possible will be done to protect the internees of the camp to the fullest extent.[17]

So they were on their own. The internees set up air-raid drills, dug bombing trenches, set aside blankets to cover the windows, put fire buckets in every room, established a first aid station in the library.

On the morning of October 15, American bombers returned, and the War Prisoners Department of the Japanese Imperial Army reacted to the new round of raids by again cutting the supply of food.

The result was a diet of less than 1,000 calories a day, with only 24 grams of protein, 202 grams of carbohydrates and 12 grams of fat per person.[18] Navy nurse Dorothy Still had almost no body fat and so little

control over her abdominal muscles, she was sure she could feel her intestines and stomach bounce with each step.

That fall the International YMCA sent two hundred ducks to STIC,
and some of the internees dreamed of a duck dinner, but the birds yielded
so little meat, cooks ended up serving a dollop of ground duck over a
scoop of rice. On the camp bulletin board the kitchen crew wrote: "Two
hundred ducks, 293 lbs gross, 190 lbs net; the ducks were starving
too."[19]

Some people started eating weeds—flowers and roots. (Dorothy Still
took a chance on another species, an indigestible green with sharp edges
that cut her rectal sphincter muscles and made her bleed.) Most people
simply waited on line for peelings from the kitchen. (A few of the nurses
grew a little *talinum* and okra, then fried their meager harvest in the cold
cream that came in Red Cross kits.)

A number of internees were convinced that the Japanese were trying
to kill them, literally starve them to death, but more likely than not the
enemy's policy, if it had one, was simply indifference—the Japanese did
not care whether their captives lived or died. The Americans and other
foreign nationals were an afterthought, an annoyance for an army of occupation that would soon be an army under attack.

Still, weapon or no, malnutrition was killing people. Like a bullet or
a bomb, it had become an instrument of war, slower than conventional
weapons, to be sure, but just as lethal. And the nurses, who had witnessed the awful inventory of battle on Bataan and Corregidor, now cat-
aloged casualties of another kind.

In September the camp hospital recorded seventy-five cases of
beriberi (a disease caused by a lack of thiamine), twelve cases of pellagra
(niacin deficiency) and four cases of scurvy (a condition attributed to in-
sufficient vitamin C).

Beriberi took two forms: wet, the most common, and dry. Patients
with dry beriberi developed raised and bleeding red spots on their skin
and complained of painful hands and feet, and as their nerve endings lost
the ability to transmit impulses to their muscles, they would suddenly
lose control of their extremities. Their feet became so tender they walked
very slowly and very carefully across campus, navigating between the
pebbles and cracks as if they were negotiating a road filled with hot
coals.

Wet beriberi was worse, a disease that made the extremities swell—
swell so much, so grotesquely, the skin stretched tight and took on a

frightening luster. Usually hands and feet and arms and legs became so distended, the patient could not move. The wards filled with these bloated bodies, these moaning unfortunates, and the nurses tried to comfort them by placing pillows and blankets under their swollen limbs, but beyond this, and a transfusion of plasma or a shot of thiamine, both in short supply, there was little anyone could do. More often than not the patients would begin an inexorable slide toward death. First came intense pain, then a period of profound indifference to reality, then a coma and, finally and mercifully the end. Without protein the heart simply could not do its work.

Until October 1944 the hospital was recording an average of two deaths a month. That climbed to seven and threatened to go much higher.[20] The elderly went first; malnutrition exacerbated their chronic ailments and ravaged their aging hearts. Then came the death of fifty-year-old Reynolds North, apparently of love. He was thought to have given so much of his portion to his children he starved himself to death, and his passing sent shivers through the other parents in camp who often went hungry so their little ones would live.

In the hospital the dying were screened off with sheets. Most people passed quietly, though some nights the moaning and death rattles from behind the hanging white linen filled the ward with a chorus of woe.

As the deaths mounted, disposing of the bodies became a problem. Until the summer of 1944 the dead were transported out of camp by a hearse, but a severe fuel shortage put an end to these trips, and the funeral parlor that interred the bodies from STIC began to send a pony and pull cart to retrieve the remains, often many days after the fact.

"Due to climatic conditions [the bodies] would decay very quickly and large rats would attempt to eat them until finally some of the other prisoners would cover the bodies with old boxes or whatever could be found that was suitable," said Madeline Ullom in testimony for the War Crimes Office. The bodies were transported in wooden caskets, "old filthy boxes that had not been cleaned since the last trip, and usually were much too short, and as a result would have a terribly demoralizing effect on other prisoners due to the fact that under the existing circumstances they figured that they would no doubt be the next to go."[21]

Marie Adams, a Red Cross director in camp, arranged these spectral pickups and deliveries: "The *funeraria* sent in a native *corromata* with a feeble little pony. Sometimes we would send three bodies out at once and they would have to be tied onto the little cart to avoid sliding off. In several instances, the end of the boxes had to be cut off to allow the longer

Western bodies to be placed therein and the boxes would be taken through the streets with the feet sticking out of the end of the box. In December 1944 the pony died and from then on the *funeraria* had to send in a little hand cart . . . with two small Filipino boys to drag it."[22]

The American bombings of Manila through the early fall helped maintain morale in camp. People seemed particularly cheered when the explosions took place before the air-raid sirens sounded; the Japs had been caught off guard, they said, just like all those dead American boys at Pearl Harbor.

Mostly, however, the men and women of Santo Tomas just waited. When, they wondered, were the Americans going to land? Finally, on October 20, 1944, at Leyte Gulf, far south from the capital, a large force of American troops came ashore to liberate the Philippines. When word came over the hidden radio, the camp rejoiced. Many of the internees believed they would be home in time for turkey and all the trimmings, but a few no doubt understood that this was only a preliminary battle. Each of the islands would have to be taken, and there was still no indication that the allies had moved onto Luzon, the island where the main enemy force was waiting.

The Japanese in STIC reacted to the news with more inspections, more searches, more confiscations. Armed guards stormed into the hospital and ordered the nurses to open the locked cabinets where they kept medications, then the guards went through the wards, ransacking everything along the way. After a two-hour search they confiscated two typewriters and robbed the patients of their money.

This game of cat and mouse made the nurses angry, and their anger no doubt helped sustain them. They were determined, they said, to outlast their captors, so determined they began to celebrate a change in their physiology that, under normal circumstances, would frighten and trouble most women—they stopped menstruating.

In early 1943 a camp physician surveyed 1,042 women in STIC and found 125 had stopped menstruating. He concluded that their anxiety and fear had caused a nerve and hormone imbalance, and he called these cases "war amenorrhea."[23] The doctor tested the urine of two amenorrheic women and found they had normal levels of pituitary hormone but no ovarian hormone. Once the women adjusted to camp life, most seemed to return to their normal cycle. Now, in late 1944, starving and afraid, many women across the camp again had stopped menstruating.

Menstruation is a woman's biological signature, the body renewing and preparing itself to conceive life, to perform a function only women can perform. Nothing is more unique to women, more naturally and inarguably feminine. "Now you're a woman," mothers would tell their daughters, after the girls' first flow. But starving in Santo Tomas, the women of the Army Nurse Corps cared little for metaphors or symbols of sexual identity. With their bodies wasting away and their lives literally hanging in a dangerous biochemical balance, they did not want to lose one ounce of blood or body fluid and they desperately hoped their flow would dry up.

"I used to pray my period would stop," Cassie said, "especially when I'd hear, Well, so-and-so missed her period again this month. I'd think, When the hell am I gonna stop this stupid business?"[24]

When one of their number would develop amenorrhea, the nurses would hold a small party to celebrate, and if a woman was unlucky and got her period, there was always someone to console her.

"I can't afford this heavy flow," Red Harrington told Laura Cobb. "Why is this happening to me?"[25]

THANKSGIVING DINNER WAS a ladleful of rice with a cup of vegetable stew and a spoonful of green *camote* tops. Twelve people died in November. At that point the internees were living—enduring—on an average of 960 calories a day. The camp commandant complained that the children in STIC were pestering his army cooks with their begging. He warned parents to keep them away from the army's kitchen. Another fuel shortage temporarily shut down the main camp kitchen and the internees could not boil water to cook rice.

Some people responded to their privations with humor. One of the camp cooks, for example, posted the following recipe:

Santo Tomas Emergency Biscuits
  2 cups rice flour
  1 teaspoon salt
  2 teaspoons shortening
  1 teaspoon soda
  1 tablespoon vinegar
  Water to mix

Make a stiff batter. Roll batter on board. Dust with rice flour. Cut into biscuits with top of corned beef tin. Place in greased pan and bake in hot oven till well browned. (Serve only when you have absolutely nothing else in the house—J.E.M.)[26]

In fact, Santo Tomas was seized by recipe mania, a kind of psychosis of imagination in which people tried to satisfy their cravings by copying recipes from cookbooks and magazines. Often they would gather to argue about their favorite dishes and discuss in great detail everything from the ingredients to the place settings. "A strange kind of madness swept the camp," wrote Frances Nash.[27]

The most popular recipes were those rich in fat and calories. "Patients [in the hospital and clinics] would sit there with swollen feet from beriberi and scurvy and trade recipes," said Anna Williams. "We wrote up whole recipe books, but it was only a banquet of words."[28]

Edith Shacklette, ever the clinician, consulted with dietitian Vivian Weissblatt to make sure her fantasy lunch was nutritionally well balanced.

Avocado and grapefruit salad—tart French dressing
Cheese sticks—Melba toast (mustard with cheese)
Chicken a la king in paddy shells (make shells or use toast baskets)
Asparagus or peas
Ice cream with fruit sauce
Coffee[29]

Sally Blaine found a recipe in a novel. "I was reading *How Green Was My Valley* and the boy described a stew—I think he called it—that his mother made. It [had] potatoes and peas and carrots and a little bit of beef or lamb—yes, it was lamb, I think—and it sounded so delicious that I read the recipe over and over again as I read the book. Six months after I got back to the States, I got the book out of the library and turned to that recipe to read it—and it didn't sound good at all."

One day Sally stopped by a friend's shanty after her shift at the hospital. "He gave me a cup of coffee and he had some bourbon and sugar. That just perked me up like nobody's business. You'd be surprised what a tablespoonful of bourbon and a teaspoon of sugar would give you."[30]

On another occasion Gwendolyn Henshaw was making ward rounds when a doctor pulled her aside. "He said to me, 'Would you like a little meat?' I hadn't had any in a long time. I said, 'Sure, what do you have?' 'Oh some meat,' he said. 'I'll give you some.' So he gave me a little bit in a dish and the next day, making ward rounds again, he said to me, 'Well how'd you like that meat?' I said, 'Well, it was pretty tasty. It tasted like young pig.' He said, 'Well that was cat.' He'd caught the last stray cat running around camp and cooked it up. We ate everything. The pigeons all disappeared and God knows what else."[31]

Minnie Breese wondered, "Who was going to make it first? The [army], the marines or the vultures?"[32] Someone answered they hoped it was the vultures—at least they could try to eat the birds.

A woman in the bunk next to navy nurse Peg Nash told her that she did not want to be buried in prison camp. Please, the woman said, get me home, at any cost. Nash, swollen with beriberi, turned to the woman and smiled. "We can't bury you here," she said. "You don't have any nice clothes to put on."[33]

Their humor, however, always gave way to the truth: starvation is a slow assault on the body, an inexorable attack. Every day brings with it some small loss of function, and with each loss, each violation, the victim seems smaller, somehow less human than the day before.

"I'd wake up in the morning and when I'd stand up I'd start urinating [on myself]," said Sally Blaine. "It was absolutely so embarrassing, it was terrible. Some of the girls really flooded themselves in front of other people. Josie went to the camp central committee and she told them we've got to have more meat for these girls."[34] (Nesbit convinced the committee that if her nurses could not work, the ill and dying would really suffer and she managed to get them an extra ounce or two of meat a week, enough to quell most of the incontinence.)

Even the youngest and strongest of the internees began to fail. More than half the camp had swollen hands and feet. Their body chemistry was so askew from malnutrition, they were always dizzy with headaches or had toothaches, bleeding gums and sore tongues. More and more they complained of pain in their viscera, and the nurses and doctors began to notice a large number of cases of inguinal hernias and intestinal obstructions. With weak abdominal muscles and little fat to support and protect their vital organs, the slightest exertion could cause serious internal injury. Other patients developed intestinal obstructions from severe constipation and came to the hospital writhing in pain and vomiting. Across campus everyone seemed to walk at a snail's pace, so anemic they had to pause frequently for breath or rest. To the nurses the camp took on a geriatric look.

At one point many of the sick turned into thieves and began to plunder the camp's supply of plasma (blood serum is rich in protein, and protein prevents the leakage of fluid from the bloodstream into surrounding tissue—the cause of swelling and pain in wet beriberi).

"If a man had plasma ordered for him in the clinic, he didn't dare lose his grip on the bottle," said Sally Blaine. "He carried it in his arms to whatever clinic or doctor was going to give it to him. If he dared to put it down, someone was likely to steal it. That's the truth."[35]

The fighting in late 1944 made it impossible for the International Red Cross to ship its annual holiday packages of meat and food to Santo Tomas, and with severe food shortages in the islands, all the agency could manage at Christmas were a few sacks of rice and beans, and some vegetables and salt. In fact the food shortages were so severe, and the need so desperate, that the black market almost priced itself out of business. A kilogram of sugar cost $105. A pound of margarine was $90, a pack of thirty cigarettes $18. The wealthy internees offered Japanese guards jewelry for food: one platinum-band diamond ring—one and a quarter karats, originally purchased for $575—bought five kilos of sugar and five packages of tobacco.[36]

Christmas approached with funereal gloom. The Japanese refused to allow any gifts into the camps, the Americans had not bombed the city in three weeks and everyone at every prison was hungry all the time. Their daily diet now contained only twenty grams of protein, two hundred grams of carbohydrates and five grams of fat.

A few days after the Allied bombing raids resumed, the Japanese, for no apparent reason, arrested four of the internee leaders and led them away. Everyone wondered who would disappear next. Were the Japanese planning to execute all of them, a few at a time?[37]

On Christmas morning the internees awoke to a cryptic present. During the night American planes had dropped leaflets on Manila.

The Commander-in-Chief, the officers, and the men of the American Forces of Liberation in the Pacific wish their gallant allies, the people of the Philippines, all the blessings of Christmas, and the realization of their fervent hopes for the New Year, Christmas 1944.[38]

Many took the leaflet as a sign that their liberation was at hand, but nothing happened. No word of ships sighted offshore or planeloads of paratroopers filling the sky.

One day slowly and painfully gave way to the next. Allied bombers continued to attack the city and its suburbs while inside the walls at

Santo Tomas, the internees grew weaker, their faces wan and gray, their eyes empty.

The nurses told one another they looked, and felt, like old women: hollow cheeks, wrinkled skin, thin hair, legs as thin as pipe stems. When they stood in front of a mirror, they said, they saw the faces of their grandmothers. A camp survey showed that, on the average, male internees had lost fifty-one pounds during their internment, women thirty-two.[39] Five-foot-six-inch Eleanor Garen was down to 118 pounds, a good portion of that the fluid in her grossly distended limbs.

"My legs were ten times swollen, just like walking with the trunks of a tree," she said. "When I woke up in the morning, I had to watch myself because from my elbows down I didn't have any feeling in my hands or arms—my legs either. I'd just sit there or drop."[40]

The entries in Eleanor's notebook, her selections from her anthology of poetry and prose, were fewer now, but much more pointed.

The quality of mercy is not strained;
It droppeth as the gentle rain from heav'n
Upon the place beneath. It is twice blest;
It blesses him that gives, and him that takes.
    SHAKESPEARE

Human life is such a little thing,
The passing of a moment,
That is all.
    HELENE MARTHA BALL[41]

Sometimes Eleanor and her best friend, Jeanne Kennedy, would slowly make their way to Eleanor's garden patch and pull the green tops off her potato plants, fold them into cylinders and imagine they were eating ice cream cones; this bizarre behavior turned their lips, tongues and teeth green.

At this point Eleanor had a chronic nasal drip and cough, pleurisy and a tender abdomen. She tried hard not to think of home or her mother, Lulu, lest she become homesick or seized with pangs of self-pity. She hated feeling sorry for herself. When she had the strength for it, she tried to keep busy gardening or sitting with the children, drinking imaginary cups of imaginary tea. Sometimes she would backslide and lose control of herself, especially when it came to Maude Davison. "Had night duty twice within this month. The old lady is hepped on a few (a certain few) for it," she wrote bitterly.

Then she would catch herself and regain her balance. "Dear Garen, This is to yourself. Remember life is not a bed of roses."[42]

By mid-January the camp diet was down to seven hundred calories a day per person. The menu for Saturday, January 13, 1945, was: breakfast, one ladle watery mush, one cup hot water; lunch, one ladle soybean soup; dinner, *camote*-bean-rice stew.[43] A doctor at the hospital ate his laboratory guinea pig. Another man climbed to the roof of Main Building, baited mouse traps with coconut flakes, and managed to catch a few sparrows; he meticulously split the little birds into portions and shared them with two friends.

Frances Nash, a tall, slender, outspoken Southerner, tried to chronicle the mass dissipation: "I saw my friends faces with the skin drawn tightly across the bones, eyes unnaturally bright and deeply circled. . . . I worked in the clinic and people would come up to me crying and begging and asking what to do about getting more food. People were dazed. . . . On my way to some task I would find myself standing absolutely still, staring into space. I had trouble remembering the days and the dates. There were times when my mind could not recall a time when I had lived as anything but a prisoner. It was easier to remember my childhood than the year before the war. I thought of the boys and girls I had gone to school with, the games we had played, the toys I received at Christmastime. . . . There was nothing beautiful in our lives except the sunsets and the moonlight. I would sit at the window for hours, dreaming of home."[44]

The Japanese, meanwhile, maintained the fiction that the "detainees" were being well treated. A Japanese doctor named Nogi, the medical officer in charge of the prison camps in the islands, called together the physicians at Santo Tomas and demanded they remove the words "starvation" and "malnutrition" from all internee death certificates. Theodore Stevenson, the camp's chief physician, refused and resigned his position. The next day an armed guard marched the good and honest doctor off to jail.[45] By the end of January, three, sometimes four people a day starved to death.

There was little difference now between the health of the nurses and the health of their patients, perhaps that due only to the few grams of protein or milligrams of thiamine the nurses were receiving. Several women, in fact, looked just as jaundiced as the people they were treating. And the work was hard. It took all the women's energy just to change a simple dressing or administer a standard treatment. Any exertion exhausted them, and before moving on to the next patient they would have to sit and rest their painfully swollen legs.

But every day they reported for work. They worked because they were nurses and the sick called them to duty. It was good work, honorable work, especially here among the dying, where they were needed most, and especially now, when their own existence hung in the balance. In a way the work sustained them, for it gave them something most of the others in camp did not have—a mission, a reason to get up in the morning and struggle through the hunger, want and sorrow of another day.

The camp was now surviving on one meal every twenty-four hours, usually a cup of vegetable gruel, and the results were always predictable.

Death roster for January 23, 1945: Roy M. Huggins—malnutrition, arteriosclerotic heart disease; Fred H. Moran—beriberi, pellagra; Henry S. Peabody—malnutrition, enteritis.[46]

No one, save a loved one, cried or mourned these diurnal passings.

"When you get to the point where you begin to wonder if you're going to be around or not," said Dorothy Still, "it begins not to matter."[47]

By February 1, each day had become a death watch. Three, four, sometimes five people a day succumbed to malnutrition. Maude Davison developed an intestinal obstruction and was hospitalized. Marie Adams, the American Red Cross field director, fell ill with beriberi; the hospital was overflowing so she was taken back to Main Building and put to bed there.

Surveying all this, Frances Nash wrote, "By this time we had stood more than I had ever thought the human body and mind could endure."[48]

Chapter 15

And the Gates Came Crashing Down

O N JANUARY 9, 1945, troops of the American Sixth Army, part of the large invasion force assembled to take the main island of Luzon and at last liberate the Philippines, established a solid beachhead at Lingayen Gulf, a spot on Luzon's west coast roughly a hundred miles north of Manila and the campus of Santo Tomas.

Some 275,000 Japanese troops in defensive positions up and down the huge island were dug in and ready to meet the invaders. The Americans advanced south and east; the going was slow at first, the fighting often bloody, but General MacArthur, eager to retake Manila, pushed his commanders to pick up the pace.

Three weeks after the initial landing, some 150 army rangers from the 1st Cavalry Division, accompanied by a larger force of Filipino guerrillas, staged a daring raid through Japanese lines near the town of San Jose, some fifty miles southeast of the beachhead, and freed five hundred survivors of the Bataan Death March, held there in a small prison camp.

The raid intrigued MacArthur, especially the tactic of the quick punch through enemy territory.

"Go to Manila," he told the commander of the 1st Calvary Division, Major General Vernon D. Mudge. "Go around the Nips, bounce off the Nips, but go to Manila. Free the internees and Santo Tomas."[1]

A bold and imaginative officer, Mudge formed two "Flying Columns," small units of roughly seven hundred men supported by tanks, howitzers and trucks. The quick, light columns were ordered to "cut right through the enemy," as one officer put it, and "get into Manila before he knows what's happening."[2]

Down Route 5 went the Flying Columns, while overhead marine corps dive bombers, scouting and clearing the way, protected the columns with bombs and cannon fire.

Forty-eight hours later, on the evening of Saturday, February 3, the Flying Columns fought their way into the suburb of Grace Park, then crossed the Manila city limits.

Guerrillas met the cavalrymen and guided them through the empty city streets, past nests of snipers, down Espana Boulevard and up to the large, iron gates of Santo Tomas University.

ALL THROUGH THE dark, early morning of February 3 the emaciated men, women and children of Santo Tomas had listened to the sounds of shelling and explosions across the city. The fighting seemed especially intense to the north, where they could see fires burning in the direction of Grace Park.[3]

Eleanor Garen "had a funny feeling that night."[4] The Japanese soldiers on guard duty outside the wall were singing, like men having one last moment together. More ominously, earlier in the day soldiers had placed large barrels under the central staircase in Main Building.

Dynamite? whispered a few panicked internees.

Rose Rieper snuck a look at the barrels and saw something else, some "stuff," as she put it, "soaked with kerosene." She and some of the other nurses were convinced the commandant meant to "blow STIC up."[5]

At first light a group of the internees working in their gardens spotted two reconnaissance aircraft flying over Grace Park.[6] The camp waited for something to happen, but morning, then the afternoon, passed without incident.

Just after the late-day gruel, more planes returned, this time marine corps dive bombers, eight of them. The formation buzzed over the camp and one of the pilots tossed a small object from the cockpit, a pair of aviator's goggles with a note attached.

"Roll out the barrel," it said. "Santa Claus is coming. . . ."[7]

Sometime after dusk the nurses could hear the sound of gunfire to the north in the direction of San Francisco del Monte.

"The Japs ordered everyone to stay in the building," said Dorothy Scholl. "The guards were very nervous and excited and irritable and quarrelsome with each other."[8]

Then without warning, the power went out, leaving the camp in darkness. Dorothy Scholl saw flares go up just outside the walls, then she heard the sound of machine-gun fire.

Minnie Breese heard the shooting too . . . and remembered the barrels with the kerosene-soaked wicks sitting under the stairways.

They're going to burn us, she thought.[9]

Bertha Dworsky was in a shanty with a friend. "We heard [more] gunfire. [The Japanese] ordered us back to our rooms and told us to stay there. We saw some searchlights at the entrance of the gate. We could smell gasoline and we thought that the Japanese were going to . . . destroy us all."[10]

But the fumes were not coming from under the stairs. Instead the smell seemed to emanate from just beyond the wall by the front gate. Then the nurses heard rumbling, heavy mechanical rumbling, very loud and very near.

The Japanese began to shout nervously. The rifle and machine-gun fire sounded very close now, just on the other side of the wall.

All at once there was a loud clap and shudder, like the sound of iron toppling to the ground.

"Tanks were crashing through the gates," said Bertha Dworsky. "I happened to be in the front building with a room above the front entrance. Tanks rolled up to the front door."[11]

But whose tanks? For a moment, for a long moment, no one was sure. The lead vehicle came to a stop in front of Main Building and two shadowy figures in some sort of uniform appeared in front of it. One of the figures seemed to be looking up at the windows. The figure just stood there for a moment, waiting in the darkness. Then he stepped forward and said something so unmistakably American, the crowds huddled in Main Building knew their deliverance was at hand.

"Hello, folks!" he said.[12]

Screaming and shouting, tears rolling down their enervated faces, the crowd now burst onto the plaza, encircling the tanks and soldiers from the American 44th Tank Battalion. Many of the internees dropped to their knees in the darkness and put their hands together and prayed. Others, overcome with emotion, or just frail from famine, fainted or fell insensate in the dirt.

Then, from somewhere in the back of the throng encircling the tanks, a lone voice started to sing.

"God . . . bless A-mer-i-ca . . ."

And the crowd, swarming in the searchlights, instantly joined in.

> *". . . Land that I love.*
> *Stand beside her,*
> *And guide her,*
> *Through the night*
> *With a light*
> *From above."*[13]

Some reached up and gently touched the small American flags painted on the steel shell of the vehicles or just stood there staring at the nicknames inscribed on the barrels—BATTLIN BASIC, GEORGIA PEACH, KLANKIN KOFFIN.[14] Almost everyone wanted to touch their liberators, these soldiers who had fought their way through a hundred miles of enemy territory to free the starving camp, touch them to make sure they were real.

"The men in the tanks looked like giants to us because we were all so emaciated and thin," Bertha Dworsky said.[15] Someone standing next to Rose Rieper asked one of the soldiers, "My land, how come you fellows are so big?"[16]

Accompanying the column of liberators was Carl Mydans of *Life* magazine, a well-known American photographer who had covered the battles of Bataan and Corregidor and had been interned in Santo Tomas as well. Mydans, repatriated in 1943 with other American correspondents, was determined to be among those first through the gates when the camp was liberated, and he dispatched the following note to his editors:

> *I was picked up bodily, full camera pack, canteen belt and all, and carried on the hands of the internees over their heads—nor could anyone hear me or them—except one loud din of endless voices all shouting and crying. The whole drama of entering the gate and the reception of the internees and the excitement that lasted in the camp all night, when almost no one went to bed, I was unable to photograph. I had no bulbs and it was in blackout.*[17]

Everybody "was laughing and crying, hanging out the windows, shouting and screaming and waving," said Dorothy Scholl. "It was a wild scene of joy and happiness."[18]

Cassie couldn't stop staring at her liberators. "Those troops that night were like from another planet. They were so young, healthy-

Liberation

*U.S. Army artillery firing from STIC, February 1945. Main
Building in background. "The fortified campus of Santo Tomas
became a natural target, and the enemy started to lob shells into
the crowded compound."*

U.S. SIGNAL CORPS

Liberated army nurses leaving Santo Tomas Internment Camp, February 12, 1945. "At 10:20 A.M., under a blazing sun and clear sky, the sixty-six army nurses climbed into two open trucks. Hundreds of internees and American troops surrounded the vehicles." U.S. SIGNAL CORPS

"They shouted adieu and bon voyage and good cheer. . . . Slowly the vehicles began to roll down the esplanade . . . the women . . . passed through the front gates to freedom." U.S. SIGNAL CORPS

Leyte Island, Philippines, February 19, 1945. The nurses "stood smartly in formation . . . as Brigadier General Denit announced [they] were being promoted. . . . Then . . . he handed them battle ribbons." U.S. SIGNAL CORPS

Leyte Island, Philippines, February 1945. Navy nurses listening as Admiral Kinkaid invites them to dinner. Dottie Still is sitting on a chair. She said, "I was so tired, I couldn't stand up anymore. We went to his Quonset hut to eat steak, which I couldn't swallow. So Red [Harrington] ate them both."

U.S. SIGNAL CORPS

February 1945. Army nurses arriving at Hickam Field, Hawaii. Maude Davison is third from the left, front row. "A band played 'The Star-Spangled Banner' and . . . some of the nurses, overwhelmed . . . knelt down on the tarmac and kissed the ground." U.S. SIGNAL CORPS

Red Harrington, Captain Camerer and Laura Cobb, Hawaii. The women are wearing army uniforms given to them on Leyte. People mistook them for army nurses. "The reception was so low-key the navy women sardonically began to call themselves the 'Silent Angels.'"

BUREAU OF MEDICINE AND SURGERY ARCHIVES

Post Exchange, Hawaii. Cassie trying on lipstick. "The army issued each woman 150 dollars advance pay, of the thousands owed them.... They bought [lipstick], pens, wristwatches, jewelry, purses, shoes."

U.S. SIGNAL CORPS

Hawaii. Left to right: Rita Palmer, Alice Zwicker and Mildred Dalton eating ice cream. "They were celebrities now, and the press recorded their every word, dogged their every step."

LETTERMAN GENERAL HOSPITAL PHOTOGRAPHIC LABORATORY

Home

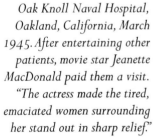

Oak Knoll Naval Hospital, Oakland, California, March 1945. After entertaining other patients, movie star Jeanette MacDonald paid them a visit. "The actress made the tired, emaciated women surrounding her stand out in sharp relief."

San Diego, California. After leaving the Oak Knoll Naval Hospital, Red Harrington "went home on a ninety-day leave to be with her widowed mother."

Left to right: Cassie, Rose Cassiani (sister), Madeline Cassiani (sister-in-law), and her children Ann and Peter.

HELEN CASSIANI NESTOR

Rita Palmer (left), who was wounded on Bataan, and Cassie in front of liberation photos in an exhibition, Army Nurses in War, displayed at the American Nurses Association annual convention in New York City, spring 1945.

RECRUITING PUBLICITY BUREAU, U.S. ARMY, GOVERNORS ISLAND, N.Y.

Eleanor Garen as Queen for a Day, October 1945. "Eleanor was a bit embarrassed by the whole thing."

BERT PERRY, PICTURE SURVEYS, INC.

"Beautiful models paraded in front of her wearing the clothes she'd won."

BERT PERRY, PICTURE SURVEYS, INC.

Eleanor and her mother, Lulu, South Bend, Indiana, 1945. When Lulu first saw her daughter she said, "Eleanor, Eleanor, you are here at last."

ELEANOR GAREN

An "Angel of Bataan and Corregidor and a young captain had fallen in love. On November 3, 1945, in Bridgewater, Massachusetts, Cassie and Ed [Nestor] were married. The wedding party included two of her comrades, Phyllis Arnold [left] and Rita Palmer [right]."

HELEN CASSIANI NESTOR

Dorothy Scholl Armold with her children in the 1950s. Clockwise from left: Edward, Harold Jr., Dorothy, Carolyn and Norman. Her son Harold Jr. said, "I was proud that she had received the Bronze Star, but I didn't think of her as a hero."

DOROTHY SCHOLL ARMOLD

Ruby Bradley in the 1950s after she returned from Korea. "The most decorated woman in American military history." U.S. ARMY

Eunice Hatchitt in 1992 at a fiftieth anniversary commemoration of World War II. EUNICE H. TYLER

The Later Years

Sally Blaine in 1945. "I was sure there weren't going to be any more horrible things in our lives."

SALLY BLAINE MILLETT

A group of Angels at the dedication of the Nurses Memorial on Mount Sumat, Bataan, April 1980. "Sixteen of the nurses . . . returned to the Philippines on a special tour. . . . [They] retraced their wartime steps, visiting the battlefields, the prison camps, the old bases." SALLY BLAINE MILLETT

Washington, D.C., April 1983. Their first official reunion since the war. Back row (left to right): Army nurses I. McDonald, E. Black, S. Blaine, J. Kennedy. Front row (left to right): Navy nurses R. Harrington, P. Nash, D. Still, and army nurse E. Young. VETERANS ADMINISTRATION, DOROTHY STARBUCK

Eleanor Garen, Indiana, 1990. "Sometimes my memory is clear as a bell. Other times I can't even remember you."

SUSAN SACHARSKI

Red Harrington Nelson, Virginia, 1980s. "Everything is nice and peaceful around here."

DR. JAN HERMAN, U.S. NAVY MEDICINE

Cassie, Pennsylvania, 1990. "Her favorite spot in the stone farmhouse . . . a large wooden rocker. . . . She reads her paper there."

ELIZABETH NORMAN

Cassie with Terry (Little Cassie) Myers Johnson, Pennsylvania, 1994, during their last visit before Terry's death in 1995. "I can't believe she's gone."

ELIZABETH NORMAN

Dorothy Scholl Armold (left) with Helen Gardner Rozmus during a tour of the Pentagon, 1992. "Dorothy . . . had suffered a stroke . . . but . . . whenever she caught anyone looking at her, she would . . . flash them a smile and wink." ELIZABETH NORMAN

Red Harrington Nelson (left) with Ruby Bradley, 1992. "The last stop on their tour was the Nurses Section . . . a gently sloping graveyard of small gray markers . . . [here] were buried nurses who had served in every fight since the Spanish-American War." ELIZABETH NORMAN

While a soldier played "Taps," the Angels stood around the Spirit of Nursing monument and spontaneously saluted their friends who are buried there. Left to right: D. Still, P. Nash, R. Bradley, R. Harrington, M. Ullom, S. Blaine, P. Greenwalt, Cassie. "It's so final," one of them whispered.

Elizabeth Norman

Cassie paused at the grave of her friend Rosemary Hogan. "The two had worked in tandem . . . on Bataan . . . and in Santo Tomas they were bunk-mates. Rosemary died in 1966 before the two got a chance to see each other again. Now on a level patch of ground, Cassie found her, stone 21 422."

ELIZABETH NORMAN

looking, pink cheeks filled out, you know, all of them. I felt as high as a kite."[19]

Eleanor Garen was exhilarated as well, but could not stay on her feet. "I got so tired that I said, 'The heck with this,' and I went up to my room. Soon a [soldier] woke me up and said, 'You're not supposed to be up here.' And I said, 'I'm going to sleep. I don't care what happens!' "[20]

MEANWHILE, ACROSS THE plaza at the Education Building, the Americans ran into trouble. The Flying Column had come through the front gate so quickly, the Japanese had no chance to flee, and now, trapped inside the walls, some seventy officers and men were holed up in the Education Building and holding some two hundred internees hostage, men, mostly, and a handful of women and children who had been visiting them when the Americans attacked the front gate.

The Japanese were demanding safe passage out of camp and through the American lines, so they could join their own forces. The hostages, meanwhile, were yelling to be released.

"Let us out!" they hollered from the second-floor windows of the Education Building. "The Japs won't let us out. They're holding us in here!"[21]

The Japanese commandant ordered five of his officers to negotiate with the American commanders, who were waiting in front of Main Building. The Japanese officers emerged slowly from the Education Building and moved warily through a large crowd of internees that had gathered on the plaza. The crowd grudgingly parted to let the enemy through; the internees were angry from three years of calculated neglect and lethal indifference. And now they were outraged at the taking of hostages.

"Kill them!" someone shouted, as the Japanese officers passed, and several others picked up the cry.[22]

When the Japanese reached Main Building, American soldiers encircled them and ordered them to hand over their weapons and swords and raise their hands. To the Japanese, of course, such submission was humiliating and dishonorable, and one of the group, a lieutenant named Akibo, was slow to comply. Well known to the internees as the officer in charge of roll calls and ritual kowtowings, Akibo was one of the most hated men in camp. Now he seemed hesitant to surrender. He lowered his hands and started to reach for a small pouch slung on his shoulder, the little sack where most Japanese carried their suicide grenades.

As Akibo's hand reached his pouch, [a tank commander grabbed a rifle and shot him]. . . . Groaning and writhing on the ground, he was seized by the legs and dragged to the Main Building clinic, internees kicking and spitting at him, one or two men even slashing him with knives and some women burning him with cigarettes. . . . As he was lifted onto a table, his hand grenade rolled out onto the floor and was carried out in a soldier's helmet. He was then taken to a woman's room next to the clinic and put on a bed, but when the owner of the bed came in, she rolled him off it by lifting the sheet, saying that she did not want the pig in her bed. He died about eleven o'clock.[23]

The Americans sent word to the sixty-five Japanese left in the Education Building to surrender immediately. When the enemy refused, the Americans opened fire.

After a two-minute fusillade, the Americans repeated their demand. This time, the Japanese began shooting. In the firefight that followed, one American soldier was killed and three others wounded. Some of the hostages on the upper floors were also wounded. Finally the shooting stopped and, by early morning, the two sides settled down to a standoff.

The standoff, however, blocked the way to the camp hospital, which was on the far side of the Education Building, so the Americans set up a temporary operating room and emergency ward on the first floor of Main. The Flying Columns had a number of wounded, and with other units pushing into the city, more casualties were coming into camp all the time.

Though weak and faint from hunger, the nurses rushed to their work, caring for the wounded.

"Oh God, I was happy!" said Sally Blaine. "We put the wounded men in a first-floor dormitory room, about seventeen, eighteen of them. Around three-thirty that morning, I went into the room to look at these soldiers and the first guy in bed was a great big sergeant. I looked at him and I touched him on the shoulder and I said, 'You have no idea how good you look to me.' He reached up and touched me on the cheek and he said, 'You have no idea how good *you* look to *me*.'"[24]

The women worked through the night, helping the army doctors and medics who had come into camp with the relief column. As they moved from bed to bed, changing dressings and giving medications, the women drew on what they had learned in the jungles of Bataan and the laterals of Malinta Tunnel. They remembered their business, all right, but their long period of isolation had left them out of touch with the advances in medicine developed across four years of war, and when an army doctor asked Rita Palmer to fetch some "penicillin," she had no idea what the man was talking about.[25]

In fact, everything seemed to have changed, even simple things, like the way people talked. Denny Williams couldn't figure out why a soldier was referring to himself as a "GI."

"GI's?" she said. "What outfit are they?"

"Government Issue." The soldier laughed. "That's what they call ordinary soldiers now."

"I'm an army nurse," Williams shot back, "and soldiers are never ordinary to me."[26]

Rose Rieper noticed that each GI carried his own provisions, a kind of packaged food she had never seen before, "K-rations," the men called them.

"Can I have those rations?" Rieper asked.

"Ma'am, if you'll eat that," said the soldier, "you *must* be hungry."[27]

The next morning more troops and equipment arrived. It was the first morning in three years that the internees did not have to line up for roll call and bow to their keepers. MacArthur, seizing on the success of the Flying Columns, decided to step up his timetable and began a full-scale offensive to take the capital. Meanwhile, inside Santo Tomas the commander of the Flying Columns continued to talk with the Japanese holed up in the Education Building.

Many of the internees, exhausted from the excitement, tried to sleep, but the city began to echo with the sound of gunfire and the rumble of tanks, and besides, there was just too much to talk about, and eat— chocolate, bread and butter, coffee, real coffee!

Then "we were told we could send a message home to our families," said Sallie Durrett. "We had been so intimidated by the Japs for so long, I asked the sergeant in charge, 'How many words can we put on this message?' And he said, 'Hell, lady, you're an American. Put as many words as you want.' "[28]

Early the following morning the Japanese in the Education Building were allowed to join their forces, and they marched out of the camp, carrying their wounded and dead on litters. Afterward the internees held a brief flag-raising ceremony on the balcony over the front entrance of Main Building. It was an impromptu event—the loudspeakers were broken—but somehow the word spread and soon crowds of internees and soldiers had gathered to watch. As two men pulled the Stars and Stripes up the pole, the crowd again broke into song. Carl Mydans recorded the event with his camera, and in notes accompanying his negatives he wrote:

> There are some shots of the Internees waving and singing . . . as the Flag
> went up for the first time over the main building entrance. There was much
> emotion shown here and more weeping by both the Internees and some of
> the hard bitten soldiers than at any other time since the moment of liberation.[29]

The weeping, however, was bittersweet. During the deliverance of the camp seven more internees had died of starvation or heart disease brought on by malnutrition. Six GI's also had given their lives liberating Santo Tomas. Their coffins, fashioned from supply crates, rested on the east patio. On the lids a few women had carefully positioned bouquets of flowers.

Santo Tomas had become a kind of staging area and artillery position and central dispensary rolled into one. The army sent in more doctors, medics and nurses. Word arrived that many of the other prison camps had also been freed, and some of the military POW's began to show up at Santo Tomas with information about the husbands and boyfriends of many of the women in camp.

At midmorning on Wednesday, February 7, General Douglas MacArthur came through the front gates. Military police ushered the supreme commander and his retinue through the crowd and up a staircase in Main Building to the rooms on the second floor where the army nurses, the women he had abandoned on Corregidor, were waiting to greet him. No doubt some were bitter—thousands of veterans of MacArthur's command had suffered horribly at the hands of their captors and many held the general responsible for their travail—but in that first blush of freedom, old antipathies faded. "Dugout Doug," as many had called him, had kept his promise; he had returned, and now Edith Shacklette, standing there in her bathrobe, "nude as a Jay-bird otherwise," on an impulse "up and kissed" the general on the cheek.[30]

*T*HE BATTLE FOR the city was now being waged with bloody results. The Japanese were entrenched south of the Pasig River, and the fortified campus of Santo Tomas became a natural target for their big guns. Just after MacArthur departed, the enemy started to lob shells into the crowded compound. Some of the incoming rounds exploded in the Dominicans' garden and among the remaining shanties. Later Main Building, crowded at the time with internees, took a direct hit.

"We had a lot of casualties," said Anna Williams.[31] Ten internees, including two teenagers, were killed and a score of others injured. The new round of bloodletting and death muted the euphoria of the moment.

"Having so many casualties come in during the liberation," said Jeanne Kennedy, "well, that put us back down for a little while."[32]

Among the dead was Dr. Walter Foley, a minister who often helped out at the hospital. His wife, Mary Foley, another favorite of the nurses, was badly mauled by shrapnel. When this news reached the nurses, Sally Blaine rushed to Mrs. Foley's side.

"I went up to her room, went up to speak with her," Blaine said. "I was going to ask her if I could do anything for her. I looked at her and saw she lost her arm [severed by a shell fragment at the right shoulder]. I really lost my composure there and I couldn't speak. She said, 'Sally, you know me? I'm Mrs. Foley'—I always called her 'Mrs. Foley.' I said, 'Of course, I know you.' And she said, 'Where's Frances Helen [her teenage daughter]?' I said, 'She's over here.' So Frances Helen went up to her mother and [Mrs. Foley] said, 'How is Daddy?' I knew Mr. Foley had died [but, obviously, his wife did not]. This little girl, who weighed about 90 pounds, said, 'Mother, Daddy is all right. Don't you worry about Daddy one minute. He's all right now.' Then the girl turned around and came back to me. I said, 'Frances Helen, do you really know about your father?' She said, 'Yes, I know—I know he's dead, but I didn't want Mother to know it yet.' She was fourteen, fifteen, at the most. Oh God!"[33]

All night the artillery boomed, and the nurses sat on their windowsills in Main Building and watched Manila burn. Many thought back to Bataan, of course, the sound of the big guns, the fires in the night. In the days that followed they worked six-hour shifts, surgeries, mostly, some three hundred of them. Off duty they tried to sleep and eat—oh, how they ate!

"To-nite! Colonel Hall brought the operating room force 4 big cherry pies," Edith Shacklette wrote in her diary. "We ate it with cream on top. Then I had my big slug of bourbon. If my stomach stands this I guess I'm o.k."[34]

On February 9 more help arrived—one hundred army nurses from the States. The women of Santo Tomas, gaunt and haggard, stood wide-eyed and open-mouthed as their colleagues, flush with good health, climbed down from open trucks. Standing next to the Angels, the replacements seemed so wholesome, so sturdy, so full of life. Their skin was pink, not the pasty gray of prison camp, and their hair was soft and rich with color and curls. The Battling Belles told one another they looked like grandmothers, women weathered by the exigencies of time and unhappy circumstance.

Now, of course, with replacements on the job, the Angels were free to think about their future. Sally Blaine, worrying about what might be ahead, wandered off by herself, unable to sort out her emotions. An army major happened to spot her walking alone and, noticing the look of sorrow on her face, he approached and put his arm around her shoulders.

"Aren't you one of our girls?" he asked.

"Yes," she said. "I am."

"Well, wouldn't you like to go home?"

It had been so long since she had allowed herself to think of Bible Grove, Missouri, and her mother's Sunday dinners, the question rattled her prison-camp reserve. And for the first time in years, Sally Blaine broke down and cried.[35]

The next day word spread that the nurses would be the first group to leave Santo Tomas, and they quickly began to tie up loose ends. Cassie, Rita Palmer and Swish Zwicker sought out Little Cassie and said good-bye. She was seventeen now, self-reliant and strong.

Cassie said, "You take care of yourself, kid." Then the nurse felt a lump in her throat and tears began to well up in her eyes.[36]

Others stole off quietly for one last embrace with their lovers, and one woman, Bertha "Charlie" Dworsky, gave in to an impulse and decided to get married. That night at 7:00 P.M., with a half hour's notice to her friends, "Charlie," as everyone called her, became the wife of internee John Henderson, and every nurse in camp not on duty attended the ceremony in the university museum chapel.[37]

For many of the women the wedding was the fulfillment of a common dream, the dream of a husband and a home, the desideratum of a "normal" life. But it signaled a kind of loss as well, the disbandment of their unit, the last assembly of the Battling Belles of Bataan. Never again would they take their identity—their strength, spirit and character— from the group. They would never need one another in the same way, never require the kind of trust, loyalty and self-sacrifice that so ennobled them, that made them seem bigger and somehow more significant. They had survived and in surviving they had given the best of themselves.

From now on, only memory, and perhaps a longing for what they had lost, would bring them together.

ON FEBRUARY 12, classrooms 38, 39, 40 and 41 on the second floor of Main Building were noisy with packing and good-byes. The packing went quickly—a few cotton dresses, some shorts, worn khaki blouses and skirts, a cup, a spoon, a little unfinished needlework, that's all. Throw it in a bag, take a long last look at the *bejuco* and the bedbugs. Peggy Greenwalt carefully folded the 12th Regimental Quartermaster flag that Colonel Frank Kriwanck had given her the day Corregidor fell. She was going to keep her promise now and carry it home.[38]

At 10:20 A.M., under a blazing sun and clear sky, the sixty-six army nurses, along with civilian nurse Denny Williams, dietitians Ruby Motley and Vivian Weisblatt, physiotherapist Brunetta Kuehlthau and Red Cross field director Marie Adams climbed into two open trucks at the front of Main Building. Three of the women helped sixty-year-old Maude Davison, now extremely weak from an intestinal obstruction, settle down on the wooden seat next to them.

Hundreds of internees and American troops surrounded the vehicles. They shouted adieu and bon voyage and good cheer. Dressed in fresh khaki blouses, skirts and overseas caps, the women at least looked crisp and clean, military. The drivers started the engines and the crowd parted to make a path. Slowly the vehicles began to roll down the esplanade. Some of the women looked back at Main Building, at its clock and cupola and large white cross, then the trucks picked up speed and before the women could turn forward again, they had passed through the front gates to freedom.

THE FIGHTING CONTINUED across hundreds of miles of battlefield on Luzon, and the enemy gave ground slowly, particularly in the southeast at Los Banos, where some 2,100 internees, eleven navy nurses among them, were still starving at the hands of their captors.

Red Harrington, Laura Cobb and their fellow prisoners at Los Banos were living on five hundred grams of unhusked rice a day, nothing else. When a desperate few tried to sneak out for food, the camp's executive officer, Lieutenant Sadaki Konishi, issued a warning that such miscreants would be shot, but the hungry sometimes know no fear, or are driven to discount it. Pat Hill, an employee of Marsman Mining Company, slipped under the wire one night and was returning with some pigs when guards shot him in the back and chest. Later George Louis, a manager with Pan American Airways, was wounded in the shoulder while creeping along the fence line. Some of the internees rushed to his side to help him, but Konishi and the guards pushed them back. For two hours Louis lay bleeding to death, then, perhaps impatient, Konishi handed a guard his pistol and the guard put a bullet in George Louis's head.

It is likely that the allies had intended to liberate Los Banos along with the other camps—American commanders knew the prisoners were starving—but intelligence agents estimated the Imperial Army had at least six thousand troops in the province, too many to overcome with a full-scale assault. The answer, they concluded, was a raid, a foray into the camp to swoop up the captives and spirit them to safety.

MacArthur turned to Major General Joseph Swing, commander of the 11th Airborne Division, to plan the raid. Swing's strategy was simple but tricky: an infantry battalion would stage a diversionary assault, a ruse, on a nearby bridgehead while army paratroopers and local guerrillas overwhelmed the camp garrison, then amphibious tractors would move into position to carry the internees away. Los Banos was 42 miles from Manila and twenty miles behind enemy lines, near the shores of Laguna de Bay; the allies had to strike quickly with a small force, grab the internees and get out before the enemy had a chance to close in behind them.[39] Success depended on timing, and surprise. Swing guessed that the best time to attack was in the morning, around seven o'clock, when the Japanese were doing their daily exercises.

On the night of February 22, some three weeks after the liberation of Santo Tomas, an American army reconnaissance platoon crossed Laguna de Bay in canoes and rendezvoused with guerrilla units near Los Banos. Along the shore of the bay fifty-four amphibious vehicles maneuvered into position. A reinforced infantry battalion was poised at a spot along Highway 1. And at Nichols Field in Manila, nine C-47 aircraft carrying a company of paratroopers lifted off the runway and headed for Los Banos. Just before seven in the morning the allies made their first move.

Amphibious tractors set up a road block to prevent Japanese reinforcements from reaching the camp, and the infantry battalion staged its diversion.

At the time Red Harrington and two other nurses were finishing up the night shift at the camp hospital. The Japanese guards had just started their daily calisthenics. The hospital was quiet; Red was preparing dressings, old rags washed out and hung up to dry, when she heard a drone above. She looked skyward and, startled, saw a large white parachute with a dark object attached, drifting down about a hundred yards on the other side of the barbed wire.

Gosh, she thought, they're dropping supplies and they're missing us.[40]

When she looked more closely, the object began to move. Then came the pop of gunfire and the crack of small explosions.

"Oh, God," said another nurse, "please don't let our boys get shot!"[41]

The internees scurried for cover or dropped to their stomachs in the dirt. Quickly the paratroopers overwhelmed a pillbox outside the fence and killed its occupants. Meanwhile on the other side of the camp, Filipino guerrillas and army reconnaissance rangers rushed the front gate with grenades and bazookas, surprising the Japanese troops in the middle of their calisthenics. Some of the enemy broke in the direction of the internees' barracks, but the raiders took aim and gunned them down. In less than fifteen minutes, the raiding party had killed more than tenscore of the enemy and had put the rest to rout.

There was little time to celebrate; the Japanese were sure to launch a counterattack. So when the amtracs arrived, the soldiers loaded the old, the sick, the women with children and the casualties from the raid—two GI's dead, three wounded—into the vehicles and away they went. Everyone else was ordered to follow on foot, roughly a mile and a half to the bay. As the column headed for the water, a rear guard put the camp to the torch.

"I looked around and the whole place was on fire," said Peg Nash. "I didn't even care. We all felt the same way."[42]

The column moved quickly toward the water's edge. Across the bay was the town of Mamatid, safely in allied hands. All the Americans had to do was reach it.

The nurses rode the amtracs, tending the sick and wounded. Peg Nash and Edwina Todd each cradled a newborn infant in their arms; they had taken the babies from the nursery when the shooting started and now were helping the mothers who were too weak to tend them.

"When we got to the beach, the Japanese started to fire," said Nash. "Stray bullets were going in every direction. I covered the baby with a great big hat and I lay down on the sand over her. Later I ran across the beach with her and got into another amtrac."[43]

Four hours later the entire party had crossed the bay to safety, and 2,136 internees and eleven navy nurses were in Mamatid, eating real food and thanking their liberators for their lives.

THE TWIN-ENGINE C-47's carrying the army nurses of Santo Tomas out of Manila circled over the city before it headed south to Leyte. Edith Shacklette, looking out a window at the battle-damaged city, spotted the sixty-acre campus where she and the others had spent three years as captives.

"Freedom is ours," she wrote in her notebook.[44]

Sitting there, reflecting for a moment, the women said they felt lucky, and with good cause. Not one of them had been killed in battle. What was more, no one had starved to death, this in a prison camp where the death rate at the end was seven times that of civilian life. Finally, more than half their comrades in the Army Medical Department, some 750 physicians and enlisted men who had served with them on Bataan and Corregidor—these men were dead.[45]

As their plane island-hopped south the women tried not to think about their losses and were careful not to celebrate their luck, at least not out loud. At one airfield a crewman sprayed the cabin with DDT; he was sorry, he said, but the nurses might be carrying contagious bacteria. As the white mist filled the cabin someone joked she could hear the bedbugs dropping on the deck. At another stop they had doughnuts—"Manna from Heaven," said Anna Williams—and coffee.[46] At a third they sipped their first cold Coca-Colas in three years.

All along the way everyone seemed so friendly. Many of the nurses had not yet shaken off the dark psychology of survival and the lachrymose mood of the camp, and the bonhomie at first bewildered them.

"It's astounding how everyone laughs all the time and is so good humored and carefree," Shack wrote.[47]

In every port and at every airfield they saw long lines of ships and planes and huge stacks of supplies and equipment, and they were astounded. Much of the technology was new to the women, Rip Van Winkles in khaki who sat gawking at what the missing years had wrought. The massive stores of material also made them remember the long spring of 1942, staring out at Manila Bay for the relief convoy that never came.

When they finally arrived at the 126th Army General Hospital on Leyte, many of the seventy-one women were still seriously ill and needed immediate treatment and rest. Maude Davison was in the worst shape; sixty years old, she was reeling from her intestinal obstruction and the aftereffects of starvation. Louise Anschicks and Myra Burris were recovering from prison camp surgeries. Frances Nash limped badly from beriberi and probably had an infected lower leg. Sally Blaine had malarial fever, chills and dehydration. Seven other women were so ill they were immediately admitted to a medical ward.

As for the rest, they were overwhelmed by the moment, by "real beds" with genuine inner-spring mattresses and clean, white sheets and steak dinners with all the trimmings, including peas, pineapple and tomato juice. (Afterward some of the women, laughing, said they hadn't eaten meat in so long their jaws ached from all the chewing.) In a letter home, Shack wrote, "All this and heaven too. . . . I can't write more—so tired—so happy."[48]

So the group rested at the hospital for a week, catching up on the present and trying to recover from the past. They wanted to look like women again, like the women they used to be, attractive and well turned out. The staff nurses at the 126th, eager to be of service to their professional kin, stopped by with a lode of cosmetics.

"I feel like an old Model T taken in and rejuvenated—have heavy colored finger and toe nail polish, new lipstick to match and lovely cream," Shack wrote.[49]

Phyllis Arnold, Rita Palmer and Cassie borrowed bathing suits and headed for the beach, but when they got there and disrobed, "we began to realize how horrible we looked," Palmer said.[50]

The army issued them new uniforms, white seersucker for the summer and dark wool for the winter.

"We had never worn a uniform like this before nor had even seen one," said one of the women. "We strutted and primped, bemoaning our loss of weight. . . . We hadn't realized that there was still a very strong spark of female vanity in us [after] all those years of wearing the same shirts and skirts . . . during our internment."[51]

Doctors put the group through lab tests and physicals, making careful notes on their condition and the consequences of three years' captivity. The physician examining Eleanor Garen found that her hemoglobin, red blood cells and white blood cells were normal. Her chest X ray was clear and there were no ova or parasites in her system. Her pulse and blood pressure were good and she had twenty-twenty vision in both eyes. But she had an enlarged liver, a tender abdomen, bouts of dysentery, some bad teeth and was underweight by more than ten pounds. "Progress good," the doctor wrote on her chart. "Feels well except tired."[52]

And then the press arrived. Dozens of newspaper reporters and photographers, magazine writers and newsreel cameramen descended on the 126th and tried to turn a tale of duty, loyalty, professionalism and endurance into a heroic myth.

"One of the greatest ordeals American women ever have undergone," declared the *San Francisco News*.[53] Lee G. Miller, a correspondent for the Scripps-Howard newspaper syndicate, wrote from Leyte, "The cumulative effect of a dozen interviews was a realization that the American female can be just a touch more than wonderful. . . . Why, they looked fresher and more like girls back home than the WACS and Red Cross workers around here. . . . The Japs weren't putting out much of anything, aside from rice and an evil smelling sort of fish, although to give the devil his due they didn't molest the nurses."[54]

After a few days of this hyperbole or, in some cases, hysteria, the army finally had the good sense to move forty-nine of the women, those most ambulatory, to the 1st Convalescent Hospital, a secluded facility set up on one of Leyte's beaches. There, grateful to be out of the public eye, Shack and the others settled down to rest:

> To-nite we are in a tropical paradise! . . . It's the tropics movie land asks for. The loveliest beach stretching for miles. About 50 yards in front of our tents are breakers that would surpass Waikii [sic] . . . a harbor stretching for miles full of ships. . . . In the midst of pineapple palm groves, a clean cot, a full stomach, and that luscious sound that only waves washing against the sand can make—and that we never expected to hear again![55]

So they sunbathed and swam in the surf. For the first time since 1941 they ate cookies and ice cream. At night in a private showing, they watched Fred Astaire take Ginger Rogers in his arms and dance across the screen.

Their only "work" was to sit for interviews with attorneys from the adjutant general's office, which was collecting statements and testimony for war crimes trials. The women were eager to cooperate, and they spent hours providing thousands of details for the court.

"They just about know every eye tooth I have left," Shack wrote.[56]

Later there were beer parties and jeep rides and dinners with generals on tables covered with white linen and silver.

Toward the end of the week, they donned their new Class A olive-green uniforms—flown in from Australia especially for them—and stood smartly in formation in two ranks under the palms as Brigadier General Guy Denit, chief surgeon in the Southwest Pacific, announced that the women were being promoted one grade in rank. Then as each stepped forward he handed them battle ribbons won by those who served in the Pacific theater—and the Bronze Star for valor.[57]

Then on February 19, fifty-four of the women, and a few members of the press, boarded two C-54 aircraft and took off for the first leg of their long flight home. The others would soon follow on a hospital plane and link up with their comrades in Hawaii.

Their "homecoming flight," as the military labeled it, touched down initially in Siapan, where the women had their first hamburgers, then they flew to tiny Kwajalein Island, where they were met by an old colleague, Juanita Redmond, who was assigned to escort the group home. Redmond had been evacuated from Corregidor on a PBY seaplane in 1942 and now here she was, standing on the runway, waiting to greet the women she had left behind. Some of the older nurses told "Red" they were happy to see her. "You look wonderful," they said. Some of the others, however, perhaps too tired, too bitter for such gallantry, greeted her with silence or a sideways glance.[58]

After refueling at Johnson Island, the C-54's continued to Hickam Field, Hawaii, where a band played "The Star-Spangled Banner" and where some of the nurses, overwhelmed by the feeling of the motherland beneath their feet, knelt down on the tarmac and kissed the ground.

During a layover in Hawaii, the women were given permanents, facials and manicures.

"We had tub baths," said Bertha Dworsky. "And somebody found silk stockings for us."[59]

The army issued each woman $150 advance pay, of the thousands owed them, then drove the newly minted first lieutenants to the post exchange where they bought pens, wristwatches, cigarette lighters, jewelry, perfume, purses and shoes.

Finally, forty-eight hours later, they took off for Hamilton Field, San Francisco. At last they were really headed Stateside, Mainland U.S.A., home.

[FEBRUARY 16, 1945, WASHINGTON D.C., 12:07 P.M.]

AM PLEASED TO INFORM YOU THAT OFFICIAL REPORT JUST RECEIVED STATES YOUR DAUGHTER SECOND LIEUTENANT ELEANOR M GAREN LAST REPORTED TO HAVE BEEN RESCUED BY OUR FORCES NOW ENJOYING A

BRIEF REST AND WILL BE RETURNED TO THE UNITED STATES BY FIRST
AVAILABLE AIR TRANSPORTATION FURTHER DETAILS WILL BE FORWARDED
PROMPTLY WHEN RECEIVE.

THE ADJUTANT GENERAL[60]

The South Bend *Tribune* had called her with the news several days
before and now a reporter had arrived at 3001 Roger Street to listen to
Lulu Garen talk about her daughter's homecoming.

"How long do you think it will take her to fly from Manila to San
Francisco?" she asked her interviewer. "I think I'll plan to leave for the
coast as soon as I know she is on her way. She can rest there with relatives and we'll come home together when she is strong enough to make
the trip.

"Do you think I could get a train reservation?" she went on. "I know
things are pretty crowded now but maybe they'd let a mother travel to
meet her daughter after all these long years of hoping."[61]

Chapter 16

"Home. We're Really Home."

THE WORLD WAS still at war in February 1945, as four propeller-driven Skymasters carrying the nurses of Bataan and Corregidor made their way east across the Pacific to San Francisco and home. The war was going well, America and its allies were winning, but a lot of fighting and loss lay ahead. Before the final victory, thousands more soldiers, sailors and marines would be added to the rolls of the dead and the lists of the wounded.

Without public support, the government could not have asked for such sacrifice, and it kept its public relations machine, its propaganda effort, rolling right along with the convoys of men and materiel. The Angels of Bataan and Corregidor, with their unusual and dramatic story, were a public relations coup, and the government went to great lengths to exploit their homecoming.

Certainly most of the military planners who helped to stage the elaborate ceremony marking the women's return were sincere in their desire to honor the nurses' sacrifice, but it is equally clear that the government was keen to turn these "heroines" into recruiting icons, well-coiffed, smartly uniformed symbols of American womanhood serving their country and supporting the war.

For almost two weeks that winter, a committee of high-ranking planners from two army commands sat in daily conference, generating dozens of letters and directives and circulars on every detail of the reception. The four C-54's carrying the nurses from Hawaii to Hamilton Field would taxi to a prearranged spot on the runway apron and form a kind of half square, in effect the backdrop and wings of a stage. Two officers would board each plane and escort the nurses down the stairway to the tarmac and into a neat formation. Then there would follow addresses by the assistant surgeon general of the United States, the mayor of San Francisco and a representative of the city's chamber of commerce. A band would play and flags would fly and a mob of reporters and photographers and newsreel cameramen would record the event for the world to see.

Sometime after noon on Saturday, February 24, 1945, the C-54's carrying the Angels of Bataan and Corregidor were beginning their initial approach to Hamilton Field. For the women on board it had been a long journey—thirty-seven hours' flying time across some 7,500 miles of Pacific Ocean. On the final thirteen-hour leg from Hawaii, most had slept, but now, sensing the end of their travels, they began to stir. "As one plane neared the California coast, the excitement mounted," wrote a pool reporter on the flight.

> One blond girl burst into the cabin from the pilot's compartment and cried: "I see California!"
>
> Almost all the nurses spontaneously began singing: California here I come . . .
>
> When the plane's wheels touched the runway, a great simultaneous sigh went through the place and the nurses said:
>
> "Home. We're really home."
>
> And one of them added, "I never expected to see it again."[1]

Their uniforms were too large and they were tired and nervous ("every girl wore a tremulous, red-lipped smile" was how the Associated Press described their demeanor[2]) but they were glad to be home—oh, how they were glad to be home! And as they emerged into the bright California sun, a band played Sousa marches, and the crowd of 1,500 that had gathered to watch them started to applaud and cheer.

> In this group awaiting the nurses were Generals, Colonels, high-ranking civilians, including Mayor Lapham of San Francisco. Not one dry eye could be seen. Tears were streaming down cheeks of even the toughest old Army men.[3]

Army public relations officers and their factotums tried to hustle the arrivees into position to begin the welcoming ceremony, but as soon as the women looked at the crowd, a gathering that included many of their mothers, fathers, brothers, sisters, lovers and close friends, they broke ranks and rushed forward, a stampede of sentiment, grabbing hold of their kin and swinging them round and round in a whorl of kisses and embraces and utter delight.

The keynote speech was delivered by Brigadier General Raymond W. Bliss, assistant surgeon general of the army.

"Your self-sacrifice has demonstrated that the high standards of the nursing profession are something real, and the Army Nurse Corps glories in the picture you present to our fellow Americans," the general said. "Your courage is an inspiration to the women of our country and in history you will take your place with the pioneer women who have helped establish the ideals on which we live. . . . You have fought the good fight. We are grateful to the Almighty for your safe return and we stand humble in your presence."[4]

In later years, when the army no longer needed them and refused to decorate their leaders or even recognize them as a group, many of these modern-day pioneers would remember the general's words with a certain contempt and bitterness. But now, on a bright California day, they were just happy to be home, and they made ready to proceed immediately to Letterman General Army Hospital at the Presidio where they were to spend several days in further medical exams and debriefings.

> *A long convoy was drawn up at the ramps and after excited reunions . . .*
> *[the nurses] climbed into army trucks to be taken to Letterman . . .*
>   *"We're really back in the army now, girls," one of them said as they*
> *boarded their convoy.*[5]

Like Alices in Wonderland they gaped at the passing scene: the green hills along San Francisco Bay, the new automobiles on the road, the thriving city—their prison-camp daydreams played out under a brilliant blue sky.

At Letterman they were assigned to Ward A-2, by army standards luxurious accommodations, with flower-filled vases and radios and boxes of candy and Kleenex next to each bed. Beauticians came in to give them cuts and perms, then quartermasters and tailors arrived with three hundred uniforms and pairs of shoes flown in especially for the women.

For the first two days they rested and visited with family and friends, underwent physicals and more tests, had dinner with big shots, like the actor Joe E. Brown, who had lost a son in the Pacific theater. Then on the third day, the army held an official ceremony on the hospital grounds.

The dais was filled with army brass, a priest and a rabbi. The podium was set on a patio with the hospital as a backdrop, and sitting at the windows in their maroon bathrobes, looking down from the upper floors, were hundreds of wounded soldiers. The two nurses who had won the Purple Heart came up to the podium to officially receive their medals,[6] then each of the women was handed a white envelope with her name and serial number typed neatly on the front. Inside was the following letter:

THE WHITE HOUSE

WASHINGTON

TO MEMBERS OF THE ARMY NURSE CORPS BEING REPATRIATED

FROM THE PHILIPPINES ON 23 FEBRUARY 1945:

It gives me special pleasure to welcome you back to your native shores, and to express, on behalf of the people of the United States, the joy we feel at your deliverance from the hands of the enemy. It is a source of profound satisfaction that our efforts to accomplish your return have been successful.

You have served valiantly in foreign lands and have suffered greatly. As your Commander in Chief, I take pride in your past accomplishments and express the thanks of a grateful Nation for your services in combat and your steadfastness while a prisoner of war.

May God grant each of you happiness and an early return to health.

Franklin D. Roosevelt[7]

They were celebrities now, and the press recorded their every word, dogged their every step.

When Doris Kehoe, Brunetta Kuehlthau and Helen Hennessey set out for a day of shopping and sight-seeing, Jane Eshleman Conat of the *California Call Bulletin* grabbed a photographer and went along.

With girlish giggles and unabashed enthusiasm, three of the returned Army nurses today made their first off-post reconnaissance tour—to San Francisco's downtown shopping district.

Lieutenant Helen Hennessey, 31 years old, pert blonde who has been away from her Leavenworth Kan. home four years, gasped as she made a frontal attack on a cosmetic counter.

"Flower mist," she sighed as she fondled the labels she has dreamed about in the dank, sweating jungles of the tropics.

A supply of bath powder and toilet water came across the counter. . . .

Nurse Helen's unbelieving eyes found their range of a hat counter in a Grant Avenue shop.

"Oh," she squealed, "those hats."

They looked fondly and sadly, for the hats that warm women's hearts and their husband's sarcasm are not for the girls in uniform. They just aren't GI.

They noticed that "almost everyone wears earrings now . . ."

So the tour progressed—past flower stands, where Helen wanted to buy violets but didn't because they weren't "regulation."[8]

The press, and to some extent the government as well, seemed bent on feminizing the nurses. Like the Japanese, wartime America, 1940s America, had trouble thinking of the women as anything but "women"—somewhat vain, sometimes frivolous, always vulnerable. If they said anything to challenge this stereotype, anything insightful, shrewd or sagacious, it simply went unreported.

"If we didn't tell the papers what they wanted to hear, they didn't listen," said Phyllis Arnold. On Bataan, for example, the nurses had cared for enemy wounded and had learned a valuable lesson of war: suffering knows no uniform. "As soon as we tried to point out anything where, because of war, it could happen to both sides, we were considered poor copy," Arnold said. "I've been reading over reports of things I was supposed to have said and it's not true."[9]

Even the normally sober *New York Times* got swept up in the moment. In an editorial celebrating the nurses' return, the paper called them "one of the beautiful legends of the Pacific War."

Still, the *Times* seemed much closer to the mark than most when it also said:

No one has suggested that the sixty-eight . . . were unique among members of the Army Nurse Corps. It was the tragic experience, bringing out high qualities of heroism and unselfishness, that was exceptional. The recognition they have received is more than a recognition of them as individuals. It is a tribute to the spirit of their Corps, to feminine tenderness joined with skill and courage.[10]

That winter, the government gave the press another big story from the war in the Philippines. Censors released captured pictures taken by Japanese photographers during the Bataan Death March. The details of that lethal sixty-five-mile trek had been known for some time, but not widely publicized. America, after all, had been defeated in the Philippines in 1942, and at the time the government was worried about morale and the national mood. Now, however, three years later and with the war going well, the grim photographs were released to the press, and America awoke to front pages filled with images that were both gruesome and shocking—American captives with spectral eyes, American corpses laid out like cordwood. The stark black-and-white photos seemed to make the country, tired from four years of fighting, angry all over again.

Either by coincidence or design, some of the survivors of the Death March were shipped to Letterman General Hospital a week or so after the nurses arrived there. Several, in fact, had been patients in the jungle hospitals of Bataan.

"Smitty!" cried nurse Frankie Lewey when she saw one of her former patients. "Let me look at you! Fine angel I was leaving you there on Bataan in a body cast!"[11]

Swish Zwicker took a picture of the reunion and sent a copy to young Terry Myers in Manila.

"Look at these men," she wrote. "They made their own peg legs. This is what we left behind us. So you wonder why we were so bitter and disgusted with . . . Santo Tomas."[12]

Slowly as the days passed the women began to reorient themselves, but they had been out of circulation, out of the culture, for so long, they could not shake their sense of dislocation. "This all seemed like the movies," Madeline Ullom said. "People moving about dressed in pretty clothes. They weren't acting. They were living."[13]

There was a lot to learn: how to eat with a knife and fork again, how to negotiate a busy street, how to buy things that were rationed. By early March they were ready and the military began to clear them for travel home. Their orders called for a sixty-day leave, then a stretch of several weeks additional rest and recuperation at one of the army's "redistribution stations," convalescent facilities located in resort areas such as Asheville, North Carolina; Tampa, Florida; and Santa Barbara, California. After that, they were told, they had their choice of duty; they could work wherever they wanted.

So home they went, home to Georgia, New Mexico, Illinois, Texas, Missouri, Ohio, Colorado, Indiana, Massachusetts, Michigan, Pennsylvania, Connecticut, Wisconsin and Tennessee. When they landed, little girls came rushing up to them with bouquets of flowers and the local police gave them motorcycle escorts. Boy Scouts and Girl Scouts and old men in American Legion campaign caps stood in the town square and waited to greet them. Bands played, and politicians made speeches and showered them with tributes and gifts: keys to the city, railroad passes, sets of silverware and tea wear, new watches, new nursing pins, free meals wherever they went.

> At 1:28 A.M. yesterday [Frances Nash and Mildred Dalton] came back [to Washington, Georgia], far more than three years older, wiser in ways unfamiliar to many, and veterans of both mistreatment and kindness.
>
> Lt. Nash, tall and spare, ran down the portable steps of the big airliner at Chandler Field to the arms of her mother and father, Mr. and Mrs. James Nash, who live on a small northeast Georgia farm. . . .
>
> Mr. Nash murmured, "Fran, it's been a long time."
>
> [Several days later at home] she wore a soft red flannel robe and she lounged lazily in an easy chair, idly smoking and talking in a quiet husky voice. Her eyes were red and her face showed the effect of beriberi. . . .
>
> She was home at last, within the safe walls of her father's pretty, green-roofed bungalow . . . surrounded by adoring members of her family. . . .
>
> It was no wonder she rubbed her eyes every now and then in a dazed way, and admitted: "I'm numb, really, just numb. I guess it will take a little time to sink in.". . . Said her father, "This is the greatest day of our lives."[14]

Minnie Breese and Rose Rieper decided to travel together to St. Louis.

> Underweight and tired, but smiling happily, the two "angels of Bataan and Corregidor" arrived at Lambert—St. Louis Municipal Airport from the west coast at about 2 A.M. to be met by rejoicing relatives. It was raining as they stepped from the big silver plane. . . .
>
> "My little girl," Mrs. Amelia Breese whispered as she pressed her heroine daughter tightly to her. "Thank God! Oh, thank God."[15]

Inez McDonald made her way back to Tupelo, Mississippi.

> This excited little city of 9,000 offered the town today to its "Angel of Bataan"—and slim, blonde Lt. Inez McDonald chose a hair wave.
>
> The keys to the city—23 of them, opening the doors of the town's leading business establishments—were turned over to the Army nurse who has returned home after nearly three years in a Japanese prison camp in Manila.

"I think everything from curling irons to railroads is included,"said Mayor J. P. Nanney during ceremonies honoring the farm girl from nearby Plantersville.

"I can use the curling irons,"smiled Lt. McDonald. "My hair got pretty straight during those years in prison camp. I'd like a hair-do."[16]

The "girls" were playing a role, of course, putting on a good show, the show the folks back home expected. Most of the women knew better than to discuss their abject despair, their death dreams and the lingering effects of starvation and malnutrition, effects that would one day perhaps cripple them or shorten their lives. That was the ugly side of sacrifice, the cost of all their tenderness, skill and courage. And only Eleanor Garen made the mistake of baring her psyche, exposing her wounded soul.

"Some people told me I was exaggerating things, that conditions could never be that bad," she said. "Others told me to simply forget what happened. I knew I was not exaggerating and I have not to this day been able to forget any of it."[17]

So most simply put themselves on parade and allowed themselves to be the heroes people wanted. They did their duty and made speeches and public appearances, gave interviews and accepted awards. Soon the limelight became disabling. By the time Bertha "Charlie" Dworsky got home to San Antonio, she was "a nervous wreck."

"Everybody wanted to talk with you. And everybody wanted you to make a speech," she said. "You were trying to catch up on what life was all about, you were suffering from malnutrition, you were insecure in public, and suddenly you were thrown into chaos and confusion. Everywhere people wanted to ask questions: 'How did the Japs treat you?' 'What were your experiences?' Well, they wouldn't understand if you tried to tell them. All I wanted was peace and quiet. I just wanted to go back to a normal life."[18]

How did the Japs treat them? The question was really an evasion, a backhanded way of asking what many people wanted to know but did not have the temerity to put into words: Had they been "violated?" Had the rapists of Nanking dragged them into a dark corner of Malinta Tunnel or caught them at night on the floor of a Santo Tomas shanty and defiled them?

Rosemary Hogan was so disgusted with the question, so provoked by all the innuendo and insinuations—prurience often posing as a concern for national honor—she sat down and wrote a candid answer:

As the folks back home in Chattanooga, Oklahoma, got the story, the Japs had chopped off my arms, cut out my tongue and left me pregnant. Just to vary the theme, someone said my legs had been amputated. . . .

After all the terrible, and terribly true, stories about Jap atrocities against soldiers and civilians, I suppose it was just too much for the people in the States to believe that any of us—the sixty-eight nurses from Bataan—could have escaped the same beastly treatment.

Take the infantryman who had been celebrating the capture of Santo Tomas on beer.

This soldier strolled casually into our little hospital, stopped, and stared in amazement to find Army nurses there.

"Well, tell me," he said, "how did the Japs treat you?"

"It could have been worse," I said.

"Didn't they do anything to you?"

"Sure. They locked us up in this place."

"Damn it," he insisted, "I mean, did they rape you?". . .

I never heard the ghastly rumors about myself until I had been home a week. Then a girl friend said:

"I guess you've heard all the frightful things that have been said about you?"

I had not, but it seemed that an officer from Fort Sill, Oklahoma, where I had been stationed before the war, called this girl and asked her, "Did you hear what happened to Rosemary?" That was when I was supposed to have lost my arms and tongue. "I know it's true," he said, "because I checked it."

Someone else said I was seen coming home on a bus. I had a cape around me—to cover my mutilation and shame. . . . I learned that this same nurse-on-a-bus story went all around the country. . . . A reporter, checking with the War Department, said the maimed nurse was reported to have been seen on a bus in Texas.

I am getting a little tired of this tongue-wagging.[19]

W HEN ELEANOR GAREN returned to South Bend, Indiana, WSBT radio was at the airport to broadcast the event live to its listeners, and the South Bend *Tribune* assigned two reporters and a photographer to record the arrival and tributes that followed.

South Bend's "first lady" came home Saturday after a 9,000-mile trip from the horrors of a Japanese prison camp in Manila to the mother who has been waiting here through all those agonizing months. . . .

The big TWA plane bearing her on the last leg of the journey home glided out of the gray western sky, circled St. Joseph county airport, landed and taxied to a halt. The door opened, and there stood the girl for whom all South Bend has only admiration and respect.

Lieut. Eleanor Garen, army nurse, heroine of Corregidor, stepped from the airline shortly before 3 P.M., neat and trim in her new army uniform, but thinner by many pounds. . . . She stepped alone from the big silver ship and directly into the waiting arms of her mother, Mrs. Lulu Garen, who had been counting the minutes since hearing that Miss Garen was on her way home.

. . . Miss Garen's first words were, "Oh Mother, it's good to be home." But Mrs. Garen could find only the words, "Eleanor, Eleanor, you are here at last."[20]

Lulu Garen wore a white gardenia for the occasion, a gift from a few of the men at a local Bendix plant who regularly ate at her restaurant. Eleanor's three brothers—Reese, Paul and Dana—were there. The temperature was below freezing and the wind was up, and as Eleanor, dressed only in her uniform, began to shiver, one of her brothers slipped off his topcoat and placed it across her shoulders.

Eleanor didn't shed a tear and neither did her mother, but the reunion was touching and few others in the little knot of relatives and friends were dry-eyed. The brothers, in particular, made no attempt to hide their tears and clutched their sister in tight embrace.[21]

A Red Cross volunteer acted as a chauffeur and drove the family home to 3001 Roger Street and a living room filled with bouquets— "like walking into a flower garden," the paper said—and beaming relatives.

In the days that followed Eleanor sat for interviews that led to a series of three articles in the *Tribune*. She said things like "Why are people making a fuss over me?" or, "I've heard they call us 'the Angels of Bataan.' The only angels of Bataan are the angels in Bataan, those wonderful boys who fought and died there. The angels of Bataan are still there."[22]

Then when the interview was over and the reporters and relatives retired, Eleanor Garen isolated herself and refused to leave the house.

"I was not used to all this freedom," she said. "I had a hard time going out.

"I felt lost."[23]

RED HARRINGTON AND the ten other navy nurses from Los Banos arrived in San Francisco in mid-March. By that point the press was weary of the story, so there were no banner headlines to greet them, only a small article in the *San Francisco Chronicle*.[24] The reception was so low-key the navy women sardonically began to call themselves "the Silent Angels."[25]

Still their professional kin remembered. At Oak Knoll Naval Hospital in Oakland, California, they were treated like military royalty. (Three of the women needed immediate care: one's knees kept buckling from dry beriberi, another suffered from a heart ailment and could barely walk and a third had difficulty breathing.) The hospital staff gave each nurse an orchid, and a cosmetics company supplied them with a box of makeup. Later movie star Jeanette MacDonald paid them a visit and joined eight of them in a group photo. Standing there fresh as an April day in her black, lace-topped gown and holding a bunch of long-stemmed red roses, the actress made the tired, emaciated women surrounding her stand out in sharp relief.

A week or so later, Red Harrington went home on a ninety-day leave to San Diego to be with her widowed mother. She also learned that a ship from the Pacific carrying some Los Banos internees was soon to dock in San Francisco, and she wondered if Page Nelson was among the passengers. Early on a Sunday morning in April she made her way down to the city pier to wait for the liner to arrive:

> "I got to the dock and there was the ship coming in. Then I saw quite a few guys I knew standing along the rail, guys from the Treasury Department who had been in camp. They were yelling, 'Hi, ya, Red! Hi, ya!' It was thrilling. There were eight hundred men on that ship, but I did not see anything of Page. Well, guess what? He was over on the other side of the ship, standing there, looking at a tugboat.
>
> "The Treasury Department had rooms for their employees at the Plaza Hotel so that's where we stayed. Next day we went into town and tried to find Page a white shirt, which was in really short supply. One of the clerks looked at him and said, 'Say, did

you come in on that ship yesterday?' He said, 'Yes.' So she reached under the counter and said, 'How many shirts do you want?'

"We went back to San Diego so Page could meet my mother, then we visited a local church to find out about getting married. The Father said, 'Well, by law we have a four-day waiting period in California and I could marry you on Friday night.'

"We went down the street and had a beer. Page said, 'You know what day that is?' I said, 'Yeah, that's Friday the thirteenth.' And so we married on Friday, the thirteenth of April. He went to Washington the next day and I followed him soon afterward."[26]

CASSIE CAME HOME and found sorrow waiting.

She had sensed something was wrong a few days after she landed in San Francisco. One of the city's newspapers had set up free long-distance telephone service for the nurses at Letterman Hospital, and Cassie eagerly queued up to call:

"Well, everybody was calling so you had to wait your turn. When my turn came, I called home and my sister [Rose] answered and, of course, it was great. I wanted to speak to Ma because she'd been sick [with heart disease]. Rose said, 'She's upstairs,' and not able to come downstairs. When I called home the second time my brother [Charles] answered and he gave me pretty much the same story and I accepted that too. The third day comes along and I called again and they tried to put me off again, saying that she was not able to come downstairs. After that call, I went back to my room and got to thinking, 'This is crazy. There's something going on.' Even if my mother was nothing but skin and bones she would have insisted to be carried downstairs to talk to me on the phone.

"I talked to Maude Davison. I said, 'I'd like to check out of here as soon as possible because I want to get home as soon as possible.' Well, she tried to say that we would all be arranged transportation . . . blah, blah, blah . . . and I said, 'No, I'm going to get home on my own.'

"The next morning at breakfast, General Bliss was sitting at the head of the table and I overheard him say that he was going back to Washington the next morning. I don't know what possessed me, but, just out of the blue, I said, 'How are you getting back, General?' He said, 'Well I have my own plane, of course.' And I said, 'Would you like to have some passengers?' And he looked at me kind of funny. I said, 'I live on the East Coast and I have reason to believe that I need to get home as quickly as possible.' And he said, 'By all means. You're welcome to fly with me. If you can round up other nurses that are ready from the East Coast that are free to go, I can take six of you.'

"We got into Denver overnight and the next morning flew to Washington. I checked into Walter Reed for the night and tried to make some calls to get myself on a civilian flight to Boston. Later I'm walking down the hall from my assigned room and coming towards me is this nurse I had been stationed with at Camp Edwards in the early days. When she realized who I was, she ran up and put her arms around me. 'Oh, Cassie,' she said, 'I'm so sorry to hear about your mother!'

"That's how I found out my mother was dead."[27]

It seems that Maude Davison had known all along. Cassie's family had called the chief nurse just after the women landed at Letterman. They told Davison they thought it was best to keep Cassie in the dark until she got home.

"That really set me off," Cassie said. "How dare they think I could not handle the information! I was very miffed and I let my family know in no uncertain terms."

In Washington she found a seat on an American Airlines flight for Boston. Waiting at Logan Airport was her family and a dozen reporters. She smiled, of course—by now most of the women had learned how to put on a public face—smiled past all that was on her mind, all that was pulling at her.

"Hey," she said, looking at the gang of reporters and photographers, "what's all the excitement about? Are all these people hanging around to see me? . . . I haven't done anything special."[28]

A few days later, Bridgewater turned out to honor her. First was a parade down the main street—she sat waving from the backseat of a convertible owned by Leo Nourse, one of the town's selectman—then at Maan Auditorium, the whole town toasted her. On stage behind her sat Mrs. Sample, her first-grade teacher; Maurice Walsh, her high school civics teacher; Father Grimes, her parish priest; and Margaret Dieter, the superintendent of her nursing school. Cassie in her new tailored uniform stood on the apron of the stage, smiling and full of gratitude for her neighbors and friends. It was good to be home, she told herself, as she listened to one testimonial after another, good to be with all the people she knew and held close. She thought too of her mother, naturally. Cassie's imprisonment had been hard on the small, frail woman. Over and over Mrs. Cassiani had told her children that she lived for the day her daughter would be free, the happy day a telegram would arrive telling her that her Helen was on the way home. And she almost made it. Sarah Cassiani's heart stopped beating just three days before American tanks broke down the gates of Santo Tomas Internment Camp.

A few days after her parade and fete, Cassie had a dream, a recurring fata morgana of homecoming and loss:

> It was always exactly the same; the dream would start with me on a ship with many people. I can't tell you whether these people were fellow prisoners or anything like that, but I'm on a ship coming home from somewhere. [Then] I find myself at the head of my street, High Street, where I was brought up. I'm walking down the sidewalk, midday, and nobody comes out to meet me, all these people I've known all my life. I see them looking, pulling the curtains apart, peeping to see who this is coming down the streets. A couple of them were working outdoors; Agnes Frawley was sweeping her front steps; she looked up and saw me coming down the street and she went in the house. My mother was sitting out on the side lawn and my niece and nephew were playing around. When they finally realized somebody was coming down the street, the kids looked up and they immediately ran to my mother's lap and began clutching her. As I got closer and closer there was not a sign of recognition from the two kids, or my mother. And then the dream stops right there, just a few feet from her. Isn't that strange?[29]

Chapter 17

Aftermath

MAUDE DAVISON WAS the Angels' first casualty.

Had her health improved she might have achieved high rank and office in the postwar nurse corps. Under her command, the nurses had held together as a unit, fulfilling their duty to their country and their ancient obligation to the injured and sick. Even in prison during the nurses' dangerous decline, Davison had insisted on good order and discipline, and in doing so gave her women a way to live, a structure to survive. It was not discipline for discipline's sake, rather a prescription for endurance and courage. Stick to the job, she had told them, and they might just make it home. She may not have been genial or empathetic, but she was a leader, the captain who had brought her unit through, and that kind of an officer usually won favor with the high command.

But Maude was too sick to assume another post, and on January 31, 1946, some ten months after her liberation, she retired from active military service and gave up the office she had served so faithfully and, by most lights, so well.[1]

With no family to enfold her, she turned to an old friend. As a young dietitian in a Baptist hospital in turn-of-the-century Manitoba, Canada, she had befriended the family of a Baptist minister, the Reverend Charles Jackson. Not long thereafter, the Jacksons emigrated to the United States, and, following their lead, Maude moved south as well. The reverend landed a parish in Pasadena, California, while Davison ended up in the Midwest as a dietitian at Epworth Hospital in South Bend, Indiana. Soon she decided to add a nursing certificate to her portfolio and moved west to Pasadena, where her good friends the Jacksons had settled, and enrolled in the Pasadena Hospital Training School for Nurses. She rented a room in the Jacksons' house and once again shared in their comity and good cheer.

Now, many decades later, retired and with no hometown to welcome her or kin to give her a bed, she returned to Pasadena and the family that had once befriended her.

The reverend was alone now. His wife had died more than a year before the war and his two grown sons had lives and families of their own. The retired nurse and the widowed reverend became friends all over again. Soon their friendship evolved into companionship, and in 1947, seventy-five-year-old Charles Jackson and sixty-one-year-old Maude Davison were married.

The wedding was a private affair. Maude did not invite her old comrades, the women she had served with through four difficult years of war. Still, word of the wedding spread, and some of the Angels wondered what kind of a man would marry a woman they remembered as remote, taciturn and unyielding.

Robert Jackson, the reverend's son, said his father was a lonely man. He married Maude because he knew the nurse "would take care of him."[2]

"Davy," as the Jacksons called her, turned out to be as formal and distant in married life as she had been in uniform. She ran the reverend's household with a firm hand, deciding who could visit and who was not allowed in the house. In time the reverend's friends began to drift away, and the couple, for the most part, kept to themselves, reading, listening to the radio or watching their black-and-white TV. In the evening Davy would ignore the reverend's Baptist proscriptions and pour herself the good, stiff cocktail she so enjoyed.

The reverend's two sons "felt bad" that their father had lost so many cronies, but they clearly saw how fond he was of his second wife, so they held their tongues and kept up their visits.

"I tried to get close to Davy but she was a stickler army nurse," said Robert Jackson, who settled nearby with his own family. "There was no friction between us but we were not close."

Maude was still sick, quite sick, in fact, and Robert urged her repeatedly to register for veteran's benefits, but she turned these entreaties aside, even when it was obvious she might soon need care in a hospital.

"The army has taken care of me nearly all my life," Maude snapped, "and they'll take care of me when I need them."[3]

In the early summer of 1956 Maude suffered a massive cerebrovascular accident—in common parlance, a leviathan stroke that left her in a deep coma.[4] At first the local veterans hospital refused to admit the former prisoner of war, the woman who had stood under the bombs on Bataan, refused because she had not done their paperwork. The Jacksons finally petitioned the regional office of the Veterans Administration and the VA at Long Beach at last gave her a bed.

Every morning Charles Jackson sat beside his comatose wife, holding her hand and giving her the succor he had once thought she would give to him. At first, Maude, unyielding as always, kept breathing. Then, a few days later, the years of starvation and travail finally took her. On June 11, 1956, at the age of seventy-one, Maude Campbell Davison Jackson, Major, U.S. Army Nurse Corps, Retired, became the first of the Battling Belles to fall.

Typically her comrades learned of her death only after she had been interred. Many said they would have welcomed the chance to say goodbye and offer a last gesture of respect to their chief, their dedicated commander.[5]

Charles Jackson, traveling alone with the remains, returned the body to their native Canada and buried his wife in a coffin draped with a large American flag. To this day no one, neither her stepson, Robert, nor any of her comrades who survive, know where to find her headstone.

*M*AJOR DAVISON HAD always impressed her superiors, so much so that right after the war, her physician comrades at arms petitioned the army to award Maude the high honors they believed she deserved.

The case went to the U.S. Army Awards and Decorations Board.[6] Initiating the appeal, Colonel Wibb Cooper, the Corregidor surgeon who had commanded the wartime medical units in the Philippines, recommended his one-time chief nurse for a Distinguished Service Medal, the army's third highest decoration.[7] Cooper argued that her extraordinary leadership, from the fall of Manila in December 1941 through the surrender on Corregidor in June 1942 to the nurses' liberation in February 1945, demonstrated without argument the remarkable effect of Maude's command.

> *It is my feeling that no group of American nurses have ever been subjected to a more difficult or hazardous situation than during the Philippine campaign and the influence of Major Davison's leadership was a large contributing factor toward the outstanding, dignified and courageous*

performance of this small group of nurses. . . . As chief nurse . . . responsible for all nursing activities . . . she displayed exceptional leadership and judgment . . . and by her cheerful and energetic manner of carrying on her duties under the most unusual and trying conditions, she was an inspiration not only to the members of her own corps, but to all others with whom she came in contact.[8]

Maude had other supporters as well, among them Brigadier General LeGrande A. Diller, an aide-de-camp to MacArthur, who reminded the decorations board that

these nurses had never been under fire before and yet acquitted themselves in the highest traditions of the military service. . . . With meager equipment, extremely short of help, and under the most trying circumstances, every nurse without exception conducted herself in a manner which solicited the highest praise. To a large degree this sterling conduct which has now become a tradition is attributable to the outstanding characteristics of Major Maude C. Davison. She organized, planned, and controlled the nurses with vision, a keen understanding of the desperate military situation, sincere consideration for the welfare of the nurses under her command, and above all the extreme physical needs of the battle patients. She was always calm in the face of anger, extremely heroic and seemingly tireless. I have heard many of the nurses say that when they felt they could not go on any longer, the sight or the thought of Major Davison gave them the added inspiration to carry on.[9]

And, as if that and other encomiums were not enough, Douglas MacArthur himself weighed in:

Major Davison, in her capacity as Chief Nurse, Philippine Department, and subsequently Chief Nurse, United States Army in the Philippines, was the leader and symbol of the entire nursing corps which so distinguished itself throughout the Philippines Campaign. Her performance was outstanding and an example to all. The standards set by her and through her corps, established a precedent not only within the gallant forces of Bataan, but for the entire nursing corps in our Army in all theaters.[10]

Her medal seemed assured, but in the growing file about the case was a curious and, as it turned out, injurious paragraph from a most unlikely source.

*In my opinion the position of Chief Nurse, although very important, is not
one of great responsibility within the meaning of the qualification of the
Distinguished Service Medal. I recommend the award of the Legion of
Merit to Major Maude C. Davison.[11]*

The Legion of Merit was a lesser laurel, more of a commendation for
a job well done than a medal for valor and sacrifice. In short that paragraph
was a slap in the face . . . and it came from the real hero of Bataan and Corregidor, General Jonathan M. Wainwright, the battle leader who had
stood by his troops to the end, and was captured and beaten by his enemy.

That Wainwright, of all people, would raise a technical point—ques-
tioning the scope of Davison's responsibility and the size and importance
of her command—is almost inconceivable. Here was the same man who,
as Bataan was falling, told the country, "You may talk all you want of
the pioneer women who went across the plains of early America and
helped found our great nation. . . . But never forget the American girls
who fought on Bataan and later on Corregidor."[12]

Perhaps as a soldier of the old school, a stickler for regulations,
Skinny Wainwright did everything by the book, even if that meant denying honor to someone he had publicly praised and admired. It is also possible that his own brutal imprisonment left him bitter, and when he
weighed his trials against those of the women, he concluded that their
service and sacrifice were of a lesser order. Who can say? The effect of
his paragraph, however, was devastating. The Awards and Decorations
Board, in the person of a major general named H. R. Bull, concluded that

*The position [of] Chief Nurse of a field command is not considered a posi-
tion of great responsibility in the Distinguished Service Medal sense. The
position normally is lacking in duty requiring the exercise of independent
initiative and responsibility. The Legion of Merit, therefore, is considered
the appropriate medal.[13]*

Then, responding to an appeal made to the Secretary of War, Bull
added the final slur.

*Although the circumstances of Major Davison's services for which the Dis-
tinguished Service Medal recommendation is made are most exceptional
and no doubt call for independent decisions and actions not normally required of a person in her assignment, it still does not appear that this case
comes within the basic policy governing the award of the Distinguished*

Service Medal. . . . In determining the degree of responsibility in this case it is apparent that a large share must have been carried by doctors and commanders. . . .[14]

Sexism or intraservice enmity? Were military men, for example, incapable of thinking of military women in the same light as themselves? Were they so fixed in 1940s gender roles that they could not acknowledge what others seemed to see? Perhaps. It is also possible that the members of the army decorations board had never seen heavy combat, and like many an "armchair commando" were convinced that the boys in the field were telling war stories, exaggerating things. Finally the case might have turned on simple malice: a large number of army generals and field-grade officers in Washington did not like Douglas MacArthur, and they might have been using Davison to take another slap at him.

Whatever the case, Laura Cobb, the other chief nurse in the Philippines, received the same treatment from her service, the navy.

Cobb too wanted to stay in uniform but, like Davison, had been enervated by war. During a stint at the naval hospital on Treasure Island, near San Francisco, her first postwar assignment, Cobb realized she no longer had the stamina for the work; even simple administrative chores exhausted her.

She had lost more than thirty-five pounds at Los Banos and still suffered the lingering effects of severe beriberi. She pushed herself at first; she was only fifty, after all, a lieutenant commander and well positioned for a distinguished career, but she was just too weak and too tired to carry forward. On June 1, 1947, after twenty-six years of service to her country, Laura Cobb packed her things and put in her papers.

She settled in Los Angeles at first, and from time to time would have dinner with Red Harrington Nelson, who often stopped by on her way to San Diego to visit her mother. Then in 1964, after the sudden death of a sister, Cobb moved back to her hometown, Wichita, Kansas, where she lived quietly for many years, pursuing her books and hobbies. When she finally became enfeebled, she turned over her legal and financial affairs to one of her nieces and was admitted to a nursing home. In 1982, at the age of eighty-six, Laura Mae Cobb died quietly in bed.

Like Davison, Cobb had colleagues who greatly admired her, and in 1946 one of them, former Fleet Surgeon Captain K. E. Lowman, began a campaign to win the chief navy nurse the recognition he believed she deserved.

Lowman tried to persuade his superiors to award Cobb a Legion of Merit for "her brilliant leadership and steadfast devotion to duty."[15] His request was quickly denied and, again, like Davison, Cobb was given a lesser medal, the Bronze Star.

Then Dr. Dana Nance, the civilian medical director at Los Banos Prison Camp, wrote to the navy high command, recommending a special-unit commendation for Cobb and the ten other navy nurses at Los Banos.

"They gave unstintingly of their time and professional skill beyond the call of duty for the alleviation of the suffering of the fellow civilian internees in Japanese internment camps," he said.[16] But this appeal failed as well, and, like the women themselves, the case simply faded away.

As for all the others, the seventy-five women who had survived the shooting, the bombardments, the prison camps, the famine and disease, they were left in a kind of limbo.

The postwar planners who were busy at work in the summer of 1945 apparently overlooked the nurses. As the nation prepared to welcome home millions of men and women in uniform, no one really stopped to consider in any systematic way the special circumstances of the Angels of Bataan and Corregidor and Santo Tomas. No one, in short, seemed to know how to deal with them.

Physicians and psychologists working with former prisoners of war focused exclusively on the health of men, not women. The boys, they said, needed "lots of tender loving care."[17] The girls, meanwhile, were never mentioned.

Their wartime illnesses—tuberculosis, fungus infections, intestinal disorders, severe dental problems, just to name a few—often became chronic and, in many cases, disabling.

For many months Anna Williams stayed at Letterman General with severe hepatitis. Verna Henson suffered from the same disease and her liver became so swollen that the medical staff treating her worried about a fatal hepatic rupture. Gwen Henshaw began a decade-long struggle with amoebic dysentery; she finally needed a hemorrhoidectomy to ease her symptoms. Sallie Durrett had dysentery too and was convinced it had permanently damaged her intestinal tract. Earlyn "Blackie" Black was often doubled over with cramps and digestive distress; after ten years of this, a doctor finally realized she'd been carrying a hookworm since prison camp. Sally Blaine's joints and limbs ached all her life from malaria and dengue fever. Edith Shacklette always wondered whether her hearing loss came from the concussions she suffered under the bombs in Malinta Tunnel. Peg Nash had pulmonary tuberculosis; the condition was so severe navy doctors retired her eight days short of ten years service; eventually she was "cured," but the disease left her so weak she could never again work in a hospital. Gwen Henshaw's tuberculosis went undiagnosed for a year—her physicians had dismissed her complaints as "unremarkable"—and by then the disease had spread to both lungs and forced her into bed for eighteen months. Alice "Swish" Zwicker was diagnosed with tuberculosis and doctors had to remove one of her lungs. And almost every one of the seventy-seven Angels had dental and gum problems from three years of prison-camp food, diets dangerously low in calcium and vitamin D. Gwen Henshaw and Millie Manning lost all their teeth, while many of the others suffered from damaged roots, bleeding gums and chronic gingivitis.

The older nurses seemed to have suffered the most. Mina Aasen was fifty-six when she was liberated from STIC. She had been a member of the Army Nurse Corps since July 1918 and, after liberation, planned to work as an administrator at Letterman General Hospital for a few years until she could qualify for her thirty-year pension. A few weeks into the job, Aasen began to sense something seriously wrong with her. She started to forget details and work schedules, and after only four hours of light paperwork, she would become so tired she had to go home and rest. With her memory unreliable and her stamina rapidly fading, her superiors started to wonder whether she could do her job, and they ordered her to appear before the hospital's Disposition Board for an evaluation. On January 16, 1946, the board reported its findings.

This officer was prisoner of war of the Japanese from 6 May 1942 to 3 Feb. 1945. During this 33 month period she lost 40 pounds in weight. . . . In November 1944 she developed ankle edema, marked weakness, periods of confusion and disorientation, easy fatigability, loss of memory, irritability, emotional instability, inability to concentrate and exhaustion. Following liberation and treatment with vitamins, she regained weight but memory had not improved. . . . In November 1945, because a routine stool examination showed endamoeda hystolytion [a parasitic amoeba that causes dysentery and liver abscess], she was hospitalized and treated. However even under hospital management, the fatigue, exhaustion and memory loss, retardation of mental processes, and forgetfulness had continued. Board . . . made a diagnosis of neurasthenia [chronic fatigue and lassitude] manifested by marked general retardation in all mental processes, abnormal fatigability, depression of vital forces, loss of appetite, some malnutrition. All secondary to prolonged excessive expenditure of energy to having been a prisoner of war.[18]

Ten months later, after twenty-eight years in uniform, Mina Aasen retired as a captain. When cataracts, arthritis and memory problems began to affect her ability to live alone, she moved from San Francisco to Minot, North Dakota, where she had grown up, and into a retirement home. In April 1974, at the age of eighty-four, Mina Aasen died in her sleep.

She had told her friends that she wanted a military funeral at her gravesite, but April 6 was a bitterly cold and snowy day in Minot, so the services were performed in the sanctuary of Zion Lutheran Church. As she had requested, someone sang the hymn "Beautiful Savior, King of Creation," then the members of Post 573, Veterans of Foreign Wars, carefully removed the flag from her coffin and folded it into a neat triangle, just as military custom prescribed.[19]

IN WAYS THAT perhaps only old campaigners would understand, the Angels' debased physiology was less disabling than the deep and unsettling melancholy that soon began to take hold of them.

There was no escaping the faces of the dead—dead comrades, friends, lovers and, especially, the patients, all those men they had left behind. Many of the women felt they should have stayed longer in the jungle and begged to be imprisoned with the sickest of the sick, the worst of the wounded.

Psychiatrists seemed to assume that the nurses' training and experience had somehow left them immune to the psychological ravages of combat and imprisonment. In a study of women in the military, one researcher postulated that the nurses' emotional problems would be "less complex in many ways"[20] than those of other veterans. Their self-awareness, their understanding of the human psyche, their involvement with hundreds of patients, along with the protected environment and discipline of a hospital—all gave them the skills and mechanisms they needed to cope with their troubles. In other words, their status as clinicians and the hard work and long service in the cause of human suffering had left them less vulnerable than the average soldier. Their profession has somehow rendered them insensate.

In fact, the opposite was true: they felt too much.

[Eleanor Garen Notebook, February 23, 1946] Much has happened in the interim. Tonight I am alone. The first time in a long time. It is terrible to be so. Once upon a time I longed to be by myself but the war taught me comradeship—so I am afraid of being alone. To belong to no one gives one a lost feeling. Perhaps the war is not to blame but the advancing years are making their mark upon me. I have come to the conclusion that I am destined to be a barren solitary woman. . . . I have often wondered why I survived. Surely I am [not] necessary to anyone. There are so many who died that are needed by their family. Tomorrow will be a year since my return to United States. Why? What purpose have I in life. It is as ashes in my mouth, so futile, so useless to myself as well as to other[s]. It is not a question of adjustment, but of me being me.[21]

Chapter 18

Across the Years

So they slipped back into the mainstream. Some married and had children while others sought careers, several in the service. (Ruby Bradley, for example, rose to colonel and, along the way, ended up at war again.) Overall, however, there was no pattern to their lives, no common thread leading to a common judgment, some unequivocal conclusion, the final lesson of women at war.

The most that can be said of the Angels as a group is that, like the rest of postwar America, they chased the American dream, "not a dream of motor cars and high wages merely," but a dream "of values," of "a richer and fuller life."[1]

LIKE MANY OF her comrades, SALLY BLAINE came home to trouble.[2] In August 1945 she learned her mother was dying and rushed back to Bible Grove, Missouri, just in time to say good-bye.

A while later at the Army Redistribution Center in Miami, Florida, Sally met "Zip" Millett, an army officer who had been captured by the Germans and imprisoned in Europe. Zip was twelve years her senior, but with so much in common, Sally instantly took to him.

"He was a real nice man, nicer to me than ninety-nine percent of the men I'd ever seen," she said.

In May 1947 Zip and Sally were married. Sally left the service, and the couple moved to Fort Bragg, North Carolina. "I was sure," she said, that "there weren't going to be any more horrible things in our lives."

She still ached from malaria and dengue fever and started having nightmares: "I must have been having horrible dreams—I don't remember them—I just know I soaked my nightgown." It was good to have someone like Zip at her side, someone who had also suffered the deprivations of prison. Most nights he would gently wake her and calm her.

Eighteen months after they married, their first son, Van, was born, then came their second child, Bill. Perhaps remembering the children of Santo Tomas, Sally turned their house into a palladium: "My husband used to say, 'My God, if the children weren't sick, you'd make them sick, the way you watch over them.' "

Nine years into their marriage, Zip Millett was diagnosed with leukemia, and he died shortly thereafter. "I never cried—I couldn't—there was no time to cry," Sally said. "I had two little boys and I was afraid that if I started weeping, someone would step in and make all my decisions, and I didn't want anybody to do that."

She moved her family to California, established a home and raised her sons to be self-reliant. In the early 1970s an acquaintance put Sally, then in her mid-fifties, in touch with a man she'd known in Santo Tomas, Dick McGrath. After a brief courtship, Sally and Dick were married. Soon, however, Sally was convinced she had made a mistake.

In good times Dick was fine, but "when things got rough," Sally said, "he went to pieces. He couldn't hack it. He just couldn't relate well to people outside [of prison camp]."

Dick wanted Sally to take care of him, but "I had lived for seventeen years with my boys without a husband and I was tired of babying people," Sally said. And in 1977 the two divorced—"dissolved is a nicer word for what happened," Sally insisted.

In later years Sally settled in San Antonio, Texas, near some of her old comrades. Her back pain worsened and her joints ached so bad she had to wear braces to walk, but the supports did not slow her down. She simply bought bigger clothes to shroud her scaffolding.

"There is still stiffness and pain in my legs," she said in 1993, "but Van told me two days ago, 'Mother, you look fantastic.' So I'll settle for that."

BERTHA "CHARLIE" DWORSKY was the first of the Angels to marry. Two days after the American tanks broke down the front gates at Santo Tomas, Charlie and her prison-camp boyfriend, John Henderson, were wed in the university chapel. Home a year later, she resigned her commission and, for a long time, stayed away from nursing as well.

"I never wanted to see the inside of a hospital again," she said. "I just sort of tried to meld into civilian life and be a homemaker and a mother [to her son, John]. I lived in the state of Washington for eighteen years. You just wanted to block everything out you possibly could and not even tell people where you had been or what you had been through. Eventually people would find out, but it wasn't until later.

"After we moved to California, my husband lost his job and I decided, maybe, I should work full-time. I applied to the Veterans Administration hospital in Palo Alto. They were so short of nurses, they were glad to see me. I worked on a geriatric ward with psychiatric patients. After my husband was able to find work again, I quit. The work was just too strenuous."[3]

In 1975, after thirty years of marriage, Charlie and John divorced. She never talked about her marital troubles, and her former comrades did not press her for details.

In February 1992 Bertha Dworsky Henderson died of cancer.

*E*UNICE HATCHITT, one of the lucky group evacuated off Corregidor in June 1942 and, later, the nurse sent to Hollywood to serve as the technical adviser on the film *So Proudly We Hail,* went right back to the fighting, this time in Europe.

She was named chief nurse of the 53rd Army Field Hospital in the European theater of war, and on July 16, 1944, not long after D day, she landed with her unit in Normandy, France, then followed General George S. Patton's Third Army into occupied Europe and the German heartland.

The surgeons who served with her were astonished by her skill. Her experience in the jungles of Bataan had left her one of the most experienced battlefield nurses in the army.

She was on duty in Europe in the early winter of 1945 when she read of the release of her comrades from Santo Tomas. "When I saw that in the papers, I cried, Oh, how I cried. People came up to me and asked, 'What's going on?' And I said, 'I've just had the most wonderful news.' "[4]

Not long afterward, the assistant chief of the Army Nurse Corps, a major named Danielson, was touring the European battlefields and made a point of seeking out the former Angel of Bataan.

"Eunice," she said, "after two and a half years in combat, don't you think you've had enough? [Wouldn't you like] to get started home?"

"Yes!" said Hatchitt. "Bless you."

During the war Eunice Hatchitt married a man she'd met in Manila, Lieutenant Charles Tyler, a West Point graduate and ordnance officer. (Tyler had been ordered home in October 1941, two months before the Japanese attacked.) For two decades the Tylers made the military their life, then in 1966 Charles Tyler retired. He and Eunice looked forward to traveling and relaxing and spending long weekends with their son, Charles III, and their daughter, Patricia. Five years later, however, Charles Tyler suffered a massive heart attack and died.

Afterward Eunice moved to San Antonio to be near some of her old comrades. In 1998 at the age of eighty-six, she was regularly playing eighteen holes of golf, practicing yoga and signing up for sessions of ballroom dancing. And if anyone asked, the answer was "Yes!" she could still get into her uniform.

D{ortothy} Scholl also married a boyfriend from the war, Harold Armold, a survivor of the Bataan Death March.

> An engagement which began in Manila shortly before the defense of Bataan and Corregidor, ended in marriage in the Episcopal church in Evergreen [Colorado] last Thursday for Capt. Harold A. Armold and First Lieut. Dorothy Scholl, after four years of waiting, worry and fear.
>
> On the night Captain Armold was taken prisoner at Bataan, Lieutenant Scholl, an army nurse, was evacuated to Corregidor. Neither knew what became of the other and thru three and a half years of imprisonment each feared the other was dead. When they met again recently at Fitzsimmons General Hospital, where both were convalescing, their marriage planning was resumed. . . .
>
> "We were the fortunate ones, you know," Captain Armold commented. "Not many came thru."[5]

Dorothy and Harold had four children: Harold Jr., Carolyn, Norman and Edward. Harold Armold was a career military officer, while Dorothy stayed at home.

"She cooked the meals and took care of everything," Carolyn, their daughter, said.

But Dorothy was feeling restless, and early in 1970 she told her family she was thinking of going to work again, back to nursing.

"You're a mother," Carolyn protested. "You can't work."

And that seemed to be the end of that. But a year later, Harold was diagnosed with cancer of the esophagus, and when he died shortly there-after, Dorothy took a refresher course in surgical nursing and went to work at a local hospital.

She nursed for almost a decade, then retired. In 1980 she signed up for a special trip to the Philippines arranged by American veterans who had fought there during the war. And perhaps because of her health, or the memories she knew the trip might evoke, she asked Carolyn to ac-company her.

Growing up, the Armold children had heard little of their parents' military service. Dorothy and Harold rarely raised the subject, and the children knew not to prompt them. Once, for reasons she never ex-plained, Dorothy dug into a drawer and brought out her medals to show to her son, Harold Jr.

"I thought it was unusual for a woman to have a war medal," he said. "I was proud that she had received the Bronze Star, but I didn't think of her as a hero."[6]

Now, as Carolyn watched her mother and a few of the other Angels slowly navigate the old laterals of Malinta Tunnel on Corregidor and talk of what had happened there and in the jungles of Bataan, she began to look with new eyes on the woman she had thought of as only a house-wife.

"I took Mother out of the traditional role and began to see her as a pretty remarkable lady," Carolyn said.

In 1991 Dorothy Scholl Armold had a stroke that left her with some weakness on her left side and forced her to walk with a cane. She lives with Carolyn and Carolyn's husband, Rick Torrence, in central Okla-homa.

*I*N JANUARY 1964, after twenty-eight years of service, MADELINE ULLOM, fifty-three years old, retired from the Army Nurse Corps and moved to Arizona to live in the sun.

She kept busy in retirement, working as a member of various veter-ans groups, including the American Defenders of Bataan and Corregidor (ADBC), and speaking out on veterans' issues.

On January 26, 1982, she testified before the U.S. Senate Veterans Affairs Committee, then investigating the sometimes scandalous neglect and indifference at the hospitals and treatment centers run by the Veter-ans Administration.

Her testimony, which included a dramatic summary of the nurses' time on Bataan and in Santo Tomas, marked the first major public appearance by an Angel since the end of World War II.

Not until later did I apply to the Veterans Administration for compensation and I was granted 30% disability for arthritis I contracted during my stay in prison camp.

I have great reluctance now to apply for further disability because I am acutely aware that such application results only in a hassle.

. . . I know dozens of my former nurse companions who have made application and have met with nothing but opposition.

If I have a gripe to air it would be that not only I but many of my former Nurse-Prisoners-of-War went through the throes of a living hell above and beyond what is normally required of nurses. . . . Sherman's observation that "War is Hell" was a mild description of what we faced in combat as well as in the prison camps and still be denied if we apply for what we deem to be just compensation.

. . . I know of no other group in our history who are more entitled to total compensation yet fail to receive their just dues. . . .

I cannot understand why those who survived the Bataan Death March and subsequent imprisonment under the Japanese have to go through life feeling rejected by the very government they served.

I wonder if I can state to you . . . that of our original sixty-eight army nurses, twenty-six have died since our release.

I do not, and I repeat, I do not believe all of their deaths were attributable to old age, although some Veterans Administration individuals would have us believe so.

I am convinced their deaths were premature and directly related to their stay in a Japanese prison camp.[7]

Denny Williams came home to the news that her husband, Bill, had been killed in 1945 when Allied bombers unknowingly sank a Japanese ship ferrying American prisoners of war to the Japanese mainland.

"I was happily married and madly in love," Williams recalled. "I loved the Philippines and always said I'd live there the rest of my life. What a turmoil Bill's death threw me into. I lost my home, my husband and my health was not so good. I did not know what the future held for me.

"Every time I'd see the back of a big man in uniform I'd think, 'That's Bill! They made a mistake.' Of course, they didn't."

So Denny turned to the sanctuary of the army.

"The army was security for me," she said. "I knew people and I wanted to be with my own kind."[8]

She spent over a decade serving as a nurse-anesthetist at various hospitals Stateside and overseas. In the early 1960s she retired as a lieutenant colonel. She too lived quietly in San Antonio, Texas, until her death in 1997.

TERRY "LITTLE CASSIE" MYERS, the teenager "adopted" by some of the Angels, moved to the United States after the war and for a number of years roamed the country: "I was a little wild for a while. I'd spent so much time in prison camp that I had to do some of the crazy things adolescents do—only I was a bit older. I ran around, traveled, did my own thing."[9]

She married an air force officer, had two sons and two daughters, divorced, and worked at various jobs. In 1967 she became chairperson of the National Convention of American Ex-POWS, and this experience gave her a taste for public life. In the early 1970s she settled in Las Vegas, Nevada, became involved in Republican politics, including two presidential campaigns, and served as a delegate to the Republican National Convention. Along the way she also started a public affairs and market research company.

In her spare time she helped organize several reunions of Santo Tomas internees: "Most of us try to remember the good times we had in camp and erase the bad times. If you thought of the sad things all the time, you'd be a mental case."

As for her "big sister" and namesake, Cassie, Terry went to see her right after the war, then a number of years passed without contact between the two. Finally in 1994 she traveled to Pennsylvania to spend a week with her friend.

They talked, went to lunch and argued politics. Less than a year later, at the age of sixty-nine, Terry Myers Johnson died from scleroderma, a fatal disease that attacks the internal organs.

"What a shock!" Cassie said. "I can hardly believe it, such a vital woman. Knowing Terry, she would never tell me she was sick. When I saw her last summer, she said she'd had no problems since liberation, but I can't help but wonder if she knew she was dying and made the trip to see me to say good-bye in her own way."[10]

...

Josie Nesbit, Maude Davison's second in command and, by most lights, the Angels' real shepherd and good counsel, came home and married Bill Davis, a man she had met in prison camp.

Though she rarely let on, Josie's life with Bill was often filled with his troubles. In 1964, fifteen years after they were married, Bill's employer, a scientific research firm, retired him on a disability. "It all dates back to him being a prisoner of the Japs," Josie told an army interviewer in 1983 collecting the women's stories for the government.

"He still has horrible dreams that they're after him" and believes that they're "still going to get him," she said. "He won't go out of the house."

Despite her husband's recurring emotional problems, Josie remained loyal to Bill, managing their life together and telling anyone who would listen, "I depend on him because he remembers things and I don't. He is my helper and protector."[11]

Strong and self-possessed, Josie spent her dotage on the move. Well into her nineties she continued to drive her own car on errands and to activities at church. And she was still the Angels' cynosure, their mother confessor, steady hand and conscience. Every year she remembered to send "my girls," as she insisted on calling them, birthday cards and Christmas greetings. And the women counted on these regular missives to remind them of what they once were.

In March 1992 many of the surviving Angels gathered in Washington, D.C., to celebrate the fiftieth anniversary of their capture, but Josie, then ninety-eight years old, was too enfeebled to make the trip.

"My heart and spirits and love are always young," she said in a note she sent in her stead. "They are big enough to embrace all of you."[12]

Josie Nesbit Davis died on August 16, 1993, four months before her ninety-ninth birthday, from respiratory failure brought on by a stroke. By her own arrangement, her ashes were scattered in the Pacific Ocean somewhere off the California coast near San Francisco.

Ruby Bradley was on duty at the camp hospital on the morning of December 8, 1941, when the Japanese bombed Camp John Hay in northern Luzon. A short time later she surrendered and was interned at Baguio, then, in 1943, she was transferred south to Santo Tomas. There she quickly earned a reputation as one of the most durable and reliable women in camp—also one of the most patriotic, a bit of a jingo, perhaps, but one with an abiding sense of humor: "I used to tell everyone to roll with the punches, so to speak. When faced with worms, say, 'Aha! Protein! Just what my country and I need at this moment. This I will eat for the good of my country.' "[13]

She was also something of a philosopher as well, though she let no one see it: "I sometimes used to wonder—when an individual returns to the world of free people, will he be able to forget everything he has experienced, will he be embittered, broken and disillusioned, or will he have enough strength to find purpose and meaning in life again."[14]

Her source of meaning was the army. After liberation, Ruby spent a few weeks with her family in Spencer, West Virginia, then reported to her first postwar duty assignment—Fort Myers, Virginia. There, circumstance cast her in a classic military conundrum—the old salt under the thumb of a young and insecure tenderfoot.

Bradley was a thirty-seven-year-old first lieutenant; her supervisor was a twenty-five-year-old major. The major had no public profile and little experience; Bradley was a decorated war hero with eleven years in uniform. The young major's first move was to billet the former prisoner of war in a tiny, claustrophobic attic above the main nurses quarters. Then she prohibited Bradley, one of the most experienced nurses in the army, from dispensing medicines; imprisonment, the major claimed, had left the old salt too "unreliable" to handle medications. Finally the young supervisor assigned the veteran lieutenant the most onerous of hours, a day-night split shift. Bradley took about two minutes of this, then put in for a transfer.

In October 1945, she was promoted to captain and a year later became chief nurse at McGuire General Hospital in Richmond, Virginia. After that the army sponsored her at the University of California at Los Angeles, where she earned a baccalaureate in nursing administration.

Smart and tough, Bradley often drew on the lessons she had learned under fire and during her captivity. One day at Fort Eustis, Virginia, for example, she was assigned to supervise a ward of paraplegics, men damaged in combat, always a difficult group for nurses to manage. Ruby walked onto the ward just as aides were handing out breakfast.

"Good morning," she said cheerily, surveying the rows of beds and the faces of the men.

Maybe he was just trying to test the new nurse or perhaps his loss had finally brought him to a boil—whatever the case, one of the young paralyzed soldiers took his tray of food and hurled it to the floor.

"Good morning? What's so damn good about it?" he said, seething.

Ruby reeled to face the young man. "You listen to me," she said, looking down at him. "Where I came from, anyone would have been glad to get a bit of this food. In prison we got up hungry and went to bed hungry; we stayed that way. You're getting better care here than I could give my patients in the war. Most of them are gone. There isn't anyone in this hospital who wouldn't work to the bone to take care of you. But I've never heard one of you say 'Thank you' or 'I'm glad for my life.' You've got a future ahead of you. Many don't. You can do a lot for yourself. The time to start is now!"

In July 1950, Bradley was ordered to report to Fort Bragg, North Carolina, to take over as chief nurse of the 171st Evacuation Hospital, a unit headed for a "police action" in a cold and dusty place called Korea.

Ruby was off to war again. From August till December, the evacuation hospital shifted its position along the front lines, treating wave after wave of casualties. "It got to the point," Ruby remembered, "where I didn't want to see another drop of blood."

From Taegu the hospital moved to Pyongyang, then up to Kongyang, and just as the unit was settling in, the Chinese formally entered the fighting. Hundreds of thousands of "Chi-com" (Chinese Communist) troops joined by North Korean regulars came sweeping across the 38th Parallel— and the 171st Evacuation Hospital was right in the enemy's path.

Quickly aircraft and ambulances started to evacuate patients and staff. Bradley sent her subordinates out with the first round of evacuees and stayed to supervise the withdrawal of the rest. "Some of the girls who came back [to help] said they could hear the North Koreans going by. We were really that near [the fighting]. We were right up there [and by this time] we didn't know how to get out."

Headquarters, meanwhile, suddenly remembered Ruby had once been a prisoner of war. "Now, I didn't know this till later on," she said, "but they said [to whomever was in charge], 'You get her out of this. We can't have that happen to her again. Get her out as fast as you can.' " As her evacuation plane taxied down the runway, Bradley could hear the sound of sniper fire just outside the aircraft door.

In 1951 she was named chief nurse for the Eighth Army, supervising the work of some five hundred army nurses at various hospitals and aid stations across Korea. Along the way she was promoted to lieutenant colonel, and in June 1953, with the Korean truce talks under way at Panmunjom, she was handed orders for home. The commander of the Eighth Army, General Maxwell Taylor, decided to give her a big send-off. He had been so impressed with her three years of combat service in

Korea, he ordered a full-dress military review and parade for her departure, the first time a woman in the American military had been so honored.

Bradley again returned home a hero, and the government and many
other organizations showered her with rows of medals and honors.
Ralph Edwards, a television personality who wore his patriotism on his
sleeve, made her a guest on his popular program, *This Is Your Life*.[15] Afterward the National Broadcasting Company established a scholarship
in Ruby's name at her alma mater, Philadelphia General Hospital.

On March 4, 1958, Ruby Bradley became one of three women in the
army of the United States to be awarded the permanent rank of colonel,
an extraordinary achievement for any woman.[16] In the years that followed she won more medals and more honors, and finally, in 1963,
Colonel Ruby Grace Bradley, fifty-five years old, retired from active service, the most decorated woman in American military history.[17]

She hung her uniform in a closet and immediately went back to
work, this time quietly and inconspicuously as a supervisor for a private-
duty nursing service in Roane County, West Virginia, where she had pur-
chased a small ranch. She stayed on the job for another seventeen years,
then, finally, she decided to stop. Periodically after that, the army and
various veteran organizations would call on her to speak at their dinners
and banquets and official ceremonies.

These days she stays close to home. Cataracts keep her from driving
at night and long-distance flights leave her exhausted. When strangers
ask to drop by for a talk, she hangs an American flag out front to mark
the house for them. She is always well turned out for these sessions—hair
brushed, lipstick neatly in place, medals set out on a side table in case
anyone asks. She likes to joke with her interviewers—"Please don't say I
served in the Civil War"—and when she is asked to sum up her professional life, forty-five years in the service of the sick and injured, she sits
back and smiles.

"That's easy," she says. "I want to be remembered as just . . . an
army nurse."[18]

AT FIRST MARRIED life left RED HARRINGTON cold.

She and Page Nelson had settled in Washington, D.C., near his work
at the Department of the Treasury and his family in Virginia, and Page,
busy boning up on all the laws and regulations that had changed during
the war, no longer doted on Red the way he had at Los Banos.

"He always had his nose in papers, which irritated me," she said. "We were kind of chewing on each other."[19]

Red decided to take up nursing again. She'd had her fill of blood and guts and, looking for something less sanguine, she took a job in a clinic at the Federal Map Service, handing out pills for headaches and colds. After a few months of this, husband and wife found their balance and settled down to domestic life, weekends picnicking in Virginia parks and on Saturday nights dancing at nightclubs in the capital.

In 1946 Red became pregnant and, like many of the Angels, immediately began to wonder whether the malnutrition she had suffered during the war would affect her fetus. She was so worried about her protein deficiency she stuffed herself with steaks and cheeses and drank gallons of milk. In fact she took in so much protein she became edematous and her arms and legs swelled with excess fluids. Her doctor finally corrected the imbalance, and she gave birth to a healthy son.

Three more children followed, and in 1948 Red and Page bought a large, comfortable farmhouse in suburban Virginia. They rarely talked about the war; occasionally they might recall something humorous, some little burlesque or absurdity of prison camp life, but for the most part their days at Los Banos were behind them—at least in conversation.

In truth the experience had shaped them in deep and abiding ways. The Nelsons encouraged their children to bring friends home for dinner, and these visitors soon learned the family's one inviolable rule: they could eat as little or as much as they liked, but no one—*no one!*—was allowed to leave anything on the plate.

Many years later, when her children had families of their own and the Nelson grandchildren came for a visit, the rule still held. "You know what, Grandma?" one of the little ones once said. "I never knew anybody that could get a plate as clean as you do."

Page eventually retired, and Red spent a good deal of her free time working for the Red Cross, scheduling blood drives and the like. For a while she took care of Page's ninety-three-year-old mother.

The Nelsons are still in the same house, and when a visitor approaches on a warm fall afternoon, Red, now eighty-five years old, sometimes waits on the open front porch.

Visitor: "How is everything going, Mrs. Nelson?"

Answer: "Well"—she glances about as if she should check—"Everything is fairly nice and peaceful around here."

• • •

AFTER ALL THE parties and speeches and homecoming hoopla were over, ELEANOR GAREN took out her checkbook and sat down to pay off an old prison-camp debt. She easily could have forgotten the obligation; the internee businessman who'd lent her the money, Carroll C. Grinnell, an executive for General Electric in Manila, had been murdered by the Japanese just before Santo Tomas was liberated. But Eleanor was no deadbeat. Grinnell's two-hundred-dollar food loan had helped save her life, and repaying him—or in this case, his company—was a matter of honor. So she made out the check, slipped it into an envelope and sent it off to New York. A few weeks later when the treasurer of General Electric mailed her a note of thanks, she felt relieved. Now there was nothing from the war left hanging over her—nothing, that is, save the weight of her memories.

Her first postwar duty station in 1945 was on Ward D-9 at Birmingham General Army Hospital in Van Nuys, California. Most of her patients were wounded veterans, and it was easy for Eleanor, a combat nurse, to strike a rapport with them. Soon she became one of the most popular nurses on the ward, and in October 1945 some of her patients decided to show their gratitude by, literally, putting her on a pedestal.

The Mutual Broadcasting System had just launched a new radio show on Sunday afternoons called "Queen for a Day," a program to celebrate women and, in doing so, provide an advertising venue for women's products. The producers apparently decided to give one of their Sunday shows a nursing motif, the "Florence Nightingale Queen for a Day," and they invited the patients at Birmingham General to vote for their favorite nurse.[20] The boys on D-9, of course, knew exactly the nurse they wanted, and they must have lobbied the other wards to go along because before she could say no, thank you, Eleanor Garen found herself in a makeshift studio in the hospital's auditorium, sitting on a "throne," a huge, gilded chair with clawed feet and lion's head arms, a fake diamond tiara on her head and a red velvet robe with white fur trim draped over her shoulders.

Jack Bailey, host of the program, extolled Eleanor's work and achievements, then a line of beautiful models paraded in front of her wearing the clothes she'd won, including a $4,000 chinchilla coat. Eleanor was a bit embarrassed by the whole thing; the long months of speeches and rallies and awards that had followed her homecoming had left her feeling a bit used and somewhat cynical. "It was all just propaganda," she said, "but I went along with it."[21]

In some ways the propaganda was pointless, for in the fall of 1945 the armed forces were beginning to demobilize, and the Army Nurse Corps was forced to consolidate its ranks. This downsizing reduced both positions and promotions, particularly the number of supervisory and management slots available at military hospitals.

Eleanor was sure that her war experience would expedite her captaincy, but her superiors at Birmingham General refused to promote her. What had she done? she wondered. Had she made a mistake? Or did someone resent all the publicity she'd been getting? Without a promotion, she thought, she might be forced to leave the service.

The months that followed left her restless and edgy. She turned to friends and relatives with political connections and asked for help, but there was little anyone could do.[22] In the meantime some of those close to her were urging her to prepare herself to leave the service. By the spring of 1946 she'd reached a breaking point and was so depressed she had to see a psychiatrist.

The promotion, of course, was not the principal source of Eleanor's trouble. Her disquiet really came from the war. She simply could not reconcile the sacrifice she'd made—the suffering that had earned her the sobriquet of hero—with the indifference and anonymity she was experiencing in everyday life:

"During the last year of the war you'd go out the front gate at the hospital to catch a bus and everybody'd stop and pick you up, just strangers giving you a ride. But after the war was over, nobody would stop."

She wanted recognition, her just rewards, and yet she wanted her privacy too, no more hoopla, no more saccharine celebrations. And this conflict, this ambivalence, crippled her.

"I wanted to get away from it, all that kind of bologna," she said. "People kept saying, 'You have to forget about it,' and that's what I tried to do—forget about it. But I wasn't able to and when I tried to talk about it, a few people said, 'Oh, you're bragging,' stuff like that. I said, 'No, I'm not bragging, I was there. That's three years out of my life. Why can't I talk about it?' Even other nurses weren't willing to listen. Nobody was."

Then came word that the army had given her a permanent commission, and in February 1948 she was assigned to the 97th General Hospital in Frankfurt, Germany.

Europe was just the tonic she needed. She toured the museums of Paris, picked tulips in the Dutch countryside, ate bratwurst in the beer halls of Munich. Two years later she was stationed in Hawaii, back in the tropics again. She returned to college too, studying philosophy and psychology at the University of Hawaii. Then in 1959, at the age of fifty, Eleanor Garen finally decided she'd had enough of the army and retired with the rank of major. Her last duty station had been El Paso, Texas, and with her monthly benefits of $393.75 and some savings, she bought a little house there with a garden in back.

She was happy in El Paso, traveling and doing volunteer work, most of all reading. Then without warning her old troubles returned. A niece recognized that Eleanor was suffering from depression and helped her find an analyst.

"I tried to forget the war for so long, but I got so discouraged and everything and so depressed," Eleanor said. "I finally admitted to feeling guilty that so many men on Bataan were killed because the army didn't want American women falling in Japanese hands. I was thinking those boys died there so miserably and they lived so terribly. It was really awful."

In time her melancholy passed and she stayed in El Paso until 1985 when, at seventy-six, her failing health forced her to give up her house and return to South Bend, Indiana, and a small apartment in Saint Paul's Retirement Home. She filled her little rooms with her books and some native art from the Philippines. She seemed content there, telling her old friends and Santo Tomas comrades:

> I am doing the "ages of dinosaur" because I passed my 80th birthday. It is hard for me to get around, and oh! to remember. Sometimes my memory is clear as a bell and I can laugh over the fun and funny things we did together. Other times, I can't even remember you when I run across your names. It just seems to come and go. So you see, I really do miss the keen memory I always had. At the present time, I am on oxygen. What a task! Little prongs in my nose, and of course, the tube that is so long. With it I go from room to room. I use a walker in the apartment but have a wheelchair for longer distance which they have fixed with an oxygen tank. The dining room is on this floor where I take my meals. Getting to sit at the table is a real treat. . . . My life is quiet. . . . The best thing to wish for is good health.[23]

Now and then a few of the men from a local veterans group would drop by to talk, and Eleanor would spend hours arguing with them about the battles in the Pacific, War Department policies and the strategy of the Japanese. "The way I looked at it," she said, "I wasn't defeated, I was captured. I didn't surrender; the army surrendered me."

Then around Christmas 1992, her mind began to falter. She started to forget faces and names, and the nursing staff at the home reported that Eleanor seemed to be living in the past. She would talk about "buckets of blood" and "tunnels," submarines and gas masks. Her family and the staff at the home worried that she had lost her mind, but three weeks later she returned to the present, unaware of what had happened.

"Glad I do not remember too much," she wrote a friend. "What I hear, the flashbacks were really bad. Guess I did give them a bad time."[24]

In November 1993, she developed an upper respiratory infection, which strained her aged heart and lungs. Her niece wanted to send her to a hospital for treatment, but Eleanor, for reasons she never made clear, refused, and on November 26 at the age of eighty-four, Eleanor Garen died in bed.

She had told her friends and relatives that if someone wanted to assign her an epitaph, it should be something simple, something like "I just took care of the men."

AFTER HER LEAVE, HELEN "CASSIE" CASSIANI made her way to the Army Redistribution Center in Santa Barbara, California, to rest and recuperate with other veterans recently returned from combat. In the mornings she would listen to reorientation and career lectures; in the afternoons she would play golf, tool around town or sit by the sea. She was also spending a lot of time with a fellow New Englander, an artillery officer who had served in North Africa, Sicily and France, Edward Nestor.

Nestor was smart, handsome and easygoing, and soon he and Cassie were inseparable. By the end of their leave, the Angel of Bataan and Corregidor and the young captain had fallen in love.

On November 3, 1945, in Bridgewater, Massachusetts, Cassie and Ed were married. The wedding party included two of her comrades, Phyllis Arnold and Rita Palmer, and some "surprise" guests from Santo Tomas as well. An army chaplain and three missionary priests who had been in prison with Cassie had learned about the wedding and, with the help of the priest performing the ceremony, had secreted themselves behind the altar. Just as the priest began to perform the Nuptial Mass, the three walked out on the chancel and seated themselves, their presence a gift to a nurse they greatly admired.

In the years that followed the Nestors began to build a life together. Ed earned a degree from Harvard Business School and went to work for various companies, while Cassie stayed home to start a family.

Month after month they tried to conceive, and month after month they failed. Cassie, naturally, wondered if the privations of prison camp had left her barren, but instead of consulting a doctor, she and Ed decided they would visit an adoption agency.

"We were getting to be old, thirty-two years or something like that," Cassie said. "We thought, 'The heck with this, let's adopt.' And soon they were the parents of a baby boy they named Mark.[25]

After Mark, they adopted Peter, and the family seemed to be thriving. Then Ed received a letter that, in Cassie's words, made the family's heart drop.

America was at war in Korea and the war was going badly. The government needed more men. And Ed Nestor had in his hand an official letter calling him back into uniform.

The news cut Cassie to the quick. She knew the risks of combat; she'd seen the slaughter. She also worried that once Ed was gone, the courts might see her as a single parent, void the adoption and take Peter away.

As it turned out, the judge in the case understood the circumstances, and as Ed prepared to report for duty, the judge waived the customary one-year waiting period for adoption and Peter legally became their son. Ed went to Europe instead of Korea, and eighteen months later he was mustered out of uniform. Soon the Nestors were preparing to bring home their third child, Sarah.

In the years that followed, Ed made a number of profitable investments and was able to retire early. The family settled into an elegant nineteenth-century stone farmhouse on two bucolic acres in Pennsylvania near Valley Forge.

There Cassie became the epitome of postwar womanhood—the happy homemaker, worrying about her children's colds and eating habits, squiring them to Little League games and soapbox derbies, cooking, cleaning, making cookies and cakes for PTA bake sales.

In 1980, with her children grown and gone, Cassie felt her days were empty and, at the age of sixty-three, she decided to take up nursing again. She registered for a refresher course at a local hospital, relearning the sounds of the heart and the rhythms of the body. But medicine and nursing had changed; it was no longer the hands-on profession Cassie had grown to love, a job that required instinct and judgment, a fine touch and an adroit ear:

"I walked into an intensive care unit and I was shocked. Machines ran everything, even the intravenous fluid lines. The nurses seemed like paper pushers. Well, this was not for me. No! I would be a fish out of water. I wanted contact with patients."

With her recertification in hand she began to look for a job. At first she thought of a nursing home—they always needed more staff—but the prospect of such work depressed her. Then she spotted a classified ad asking for a private-duty nurse to care for a Vietnam veteran in the last stages of multiple sclerosis. She thought, That's just about my speed at this stage of the game, and she started work the next week.

The patient's name was Charlie. He was completely paralyzed and in need of a lot of care. Cassie fed him and bathed him, administered his treatments and changed his sheets. In their quiet moments she would sit next to Charlie, hold his hand and talk with him. When he lost the ability to speak and had to take food through a tube, she would gently stroke his arm and tell him about her day. Five years later "sweet Charlie finally died," and when Cassie went home and sat down and thought about all that had passed between them, she could not help but remember the boys on Bataan. "I felt I had really done something pretty good again," she said.

Cassie and Ed are still in their stone farmhouse. In recent years Cassie has suffered a mild stroke and developed a cardiac arrythmia. She cannot seem to summon the energy that animated her middle age and kept her on the move in later years, but she still sews and recently was making curtains for Sarah's new house. She also insists on working in the garden and cleverly positions chairs at various spots in the yard so she can rest when she begins to wear down.

Her favorite spot in the stone farmhouse is near a doorway between the kitchen, with its large fireplace, and the living room. Here she has placed a large wooden rocker and in front of it a coffee table. She reads her newspaper there and sometimes in the afternoon jots notes to her many correspondents:

Dear Beth [1/21/97]

Hope you're getting over the holidays and are back to the normal grind. . . .

Well, I've reached the big 80! this month. Had no idea I'd ever reach this age! And in reasonable good health and spirits.

Ed is doing O.K. However, any exertion while out of doors in this cold and wind becomes very distressing to him. He sends his very best wishes for the New Year. As do I.

Be good to yourself.

Love, *Cassie*[26]

Afterword

O<small>F THE NINETY-NINE</small> army and navy nurses who went to war on December 8, 1941, some sixteen were still alive in 1998. Among the living and the dead, I know Cassie best, or as well as any student of history can know her subject. Perhaps it is more accurate to say I felt most comfortable with Cassie, woman with woman, and in that concert have come to care for her.

A bit of this comes from our proximity; I live in New Jersey less than a two hours' ride from Cassie's home in eastern Pennsylvania, so across eight years of researching and writing the Angels' history, I've seen her often, more often than the other twenty women I was able to encounter and interview. Also, in oblique ways she reminds me of my mother, Dorothy Riley Dempsey.

Though my mother and Cassie have never met, Dorothy often asks after my friend. They are of the same era, and during the war Dorothy enlisted in the women's division of the United States Coast Guard, the SPARS. Her wartime service was more of an escapade than anything else—she trained in Palm Beach and served in Boston as part of a special unit of musicians and singers entertaining the troops—but she is fiercely proud of her days in the SPARS. To borrow a line from Stephen Crane, she mingled in one of the great affairs of the earth and she never forgot it.

She never forgot the Angels either. She was still in the SPARS when they came home in 1945, wartime celebrities and the idols of almost every woman in uniform. My mother was in awe of their fame and celebrated the triumph of their utterly stunning survival. Almost from the day I began my research, she insisted I tell her everything I uncovered, every detail of the women's lives. A few years ago when my mother became part of a national effort to memorialize the contributions of American women in uniform[1] and made the rounds speaking to local civic groups, she would call me first, hoping for the latest detail or anecdote. "Anything new on the nurses?" she would say.

I made a point of telling each of the Angels about my mother and how my sisters and I grew up with their war. Somewhere in our crowded house in Lyndhurst, New Jersey, there was always a picture of Dorothy in uniform, and sometimes, for a Halloween party or perhaps a play, she would let one of her five daughters slip into it. I remember I was impressed by the weight, the heavy blue wool; I also recall feeling that I had put on a piece of time. Perhaps in some dim, inchoate way, my long search for the nurses of Bataan and Corregidor, my interest in the role women have played in the profession of arms, began the day I first wore my mother's history.

THE HANDFUL OF Angels who survive are old and ailing, and it is unlikely they will all gather again as they did for many years at various conventions, symposiums and reunions. The largest of these took place in 1983, when the Veterans Administration honored them as a group and thirty-one of the women attended. They gathered again in 1992 when a business group brought some of the survivors of Santo Tomas to Washington, D.C., to honor American military women who had been prisoners of war, and I was invited to observe the occasion.

Thirteen of the Angels made their way to the capital that cold and wet March weekend. They arrived in sackcloth. "Charlie" Dworsky Henderson, who had helped plan the fete and had so much looked forward to the company of her old comrades, died less than a month before, and her passing served only to underscore the sobering reality of loss that regularly leaves its mark on this group.

Many of those who could not make the trip sent messages.

To the POW nurses of the Philippine[s]—As time goes by I appreciate you all more and more. May we meet in eternity. God bless you.

Mary Jo Oberst
Owensboro, Kentucky

Just tell the group I love each one. I'm living in the Lutheran Home, have a nice apartment. . . . This past June I was 81, have three lovely daughters that are married. Count my blessing every day as I feel there is an angel on my shoulder.

> Ethel Thor Nelson
> Tacoma, Washington[2]

The centerpiece of the weekend was a gala banquet held Friday night at the officers club at Bolling Air Force Base. Several hundred people attended—military officers, government officials, business and civic leaders, men who had fought on Bataan and Corregidor, a contingent of reporters, and, according to many in the room, the largest number of women generals and women admirals ever gathered under one roof.

The room was ablaze in red, white and blue—bunting, flowers, garlands and confetti. Even the cheesecake had small American flags stuck on top. A military band dressed in World War II–era uniforms filled the hall with the sentimental melodies of Duke Ellington and Glenn Miller.

The Angels, of course, stole the show, or to put it more precisely, they were regarded with such veneration that they sat there quietly, like human shrines. People approached them slowly, almost devoutly, to ask for autographs and pictures. Sometimes someone would start to reach out to touch one of them, then think better of such sacrilege and quickly pull back.

Madeline Ullom, unabashed as ever, helped restore some balance and perspective to the evening; her frock was a black evening dress, her footwear white tennis shoes.

Chaplain Eileen O'Hickey delivered the invocation, referring to the Angels as "daughters of courage." For the keynote address the organizing committee drafted a Vietnam-era navy pilot, Giles Norrington, who had been shot down and imprisoned by the enemy for five years.

> *The women we honor tonight . . . were thrust by circumstance into a situation not of their own choosing. . . . No three words ring with such somber resonance as these three: prisoner of war, P.O.W.—dear God, how miserable the existence. . . . I am honored to have served in circumstances similar to yours . . . dear sisters. . . . You are, after all, vital proof of Susan B. Anthony's birthday observation: "Failure is impossible."[3]*

Then everyone stood and filled the hall with song. They sang loudly and with a fervor I had never before heard: "God . . . bless . . . America . . . " And as I watched Cassie and Red and some of the others, I wondered whether, in that moment, they were back in Santo Tomas, standing in front of Main Building in an ebullient crowd, singing their song of deliverance.

At dinner I sat next to Helen Gardner Rozmus, who now lives in Florida. Swept up in the affair and eager to interview as many of the women as I could, I only picked at my filet mignon. Helen, like the others, cleaned her plate. "What?" she said, looking at my leavings. "Aren't you hungry?"

The next day two chartered buses carried the women, their military escorts and the rest of the party on a tour of the capital's landmarks. It was cold, gray and wet that Thursday, and as we pulled up to our first stop, Helen looked out the window and shivered. "I don't feel like getting off the bus, but I don't want people to think that I'm decrepit, so I'm going," she said.

Dorothy Scholl Armold had suffered a stroke and needed help navigating in her walker. She was having trouble speaking as well, but I noticed that whenever she caught anyone looking at her, she would show her pluck by flashing them a smile and wink in reply.

A couple of the women seemed easily disoriented and the others were careful to look out for them. "Where do I go next?" Ruby Bradley asked a couple of times. Sally Blaine Millett said, "So what if she's confused. She's with us."

They may have been wizened, gray and hobbled, but they were still the "girls."

"Com'on, girls, let's go!"

"Look at that, girls!"

"Hey, girls, do you remember . . . ?"

Jeanne Kennedy Schmidt looked around the bus, taking in all the faces, then turned to me and, with a kind of quiet pleasure, said, "I know these women like the back of my hand."

Hattie Brantley, for years the group's official spokeswoman, was, as usual, complaining about the press. "Why can't they get it right," she kept saying to her comrades. And, as if to underscore her point, one of the women was trying to give one of the reporters a lesson in Philippine geography. "No, no, no," she was saying. "It's Li-may, *L-i-m-a-y*, not Lammie."

When the bus stopped and the women alighted at the various sites, they often stood arm in arm or shoulder to shoulder. And if someone became bewildered and wandered off, someone else would go after her.

"Come on with me," she would say. "We were wondering what happened to you."

The last stop on their tour was the nurses' section of Arlington National Cemetery, a gently sloping graveyard of small gray markers. Above the graves on a hill was a statue of a woman in a cape and cap, the "Spirit of Nursing" monument. In this section were buried nurses who had served in every fight since the Spanish-American War.

It was drizzling; the trees were still bare and the grass had brown spots and ruts. The women placed a wreath of red, white and blue carnations at the base of the monument, an army bugler played "Taps," then, without a word, the thirteen women put their hands to their foreheads and offered their dead comrades a last salute.

They turned and started back down the hill to inspect the graves. "It's so final," one of them whispered as she surveyed the long rows of light gray stones.

Cassie set out by herself to search for the grave of Rosemary Hogan. The two had worked in tandem at Hospital #1 on Bataan, and at Santo Tomas they were bunkmates. Rosemary died in 1966 before the two got a chance to see each other again. Now on a level patch of ground, Cassie found her, stone 21 422.

She stood there for a moment, staring at the small marker, her hand trembling a bit as she put a finger to her lips. She reached down and placed a bouquet of flowers on the wet grass, then stood erect again and fished for a tissue to wipe her cheek.

Epilogue

W<small>E ARE NOT</small> likely to see another group of women like Cassie, Josie, Sallie and the others, not in the American military. Neither the modern army nor the modern navy has an all-female nursing unit. What is more, we cannot apply the lessons of the past to the current debate about the place of women in the military. The question is not whether women can do the job, but whether they should want to. On this I offer no opinion other than to say I have lived with the consequences of war and combat for the twenty-six years I have been married. The man who shares my bed is marked by the memory of his year on the battlefield, and not a day goes by without its dark shadow crossing his face.

Although I have used the epithets of "hero" and "angel" throughout, I have tried not to aggrandize my subjects—they were, from first to last, nurses. To call a woman a nurse, however, is to give her more than a moniker. In an ironic way, the ethos of a nurse is like that of a soldier. Research has shown that soldiers fight not for their country or for a cause, but out of love for their comrades. They care deeply about the men in the mud beside them, and they are willing to risk all and endure anything to prove it.

This same ethic—call it an ethic for the other person—is instilled in every nurse. From their student days forward, nurses are told that they have an almost sacred obligation to those in their charge—"The patient always comes first"—and, thus, caring for the sick and injured becomes a kind of prepossessing sentiment, like comradeship. Even now, decades later, the Angels feel it. During my interviews, it was not their own fears or suffering that most haunted them, it was the memory of a certain evening on Bataan in April 1942 when they received word that the peninsula was about to fall to the enemy and they were ordered to leave their patients, just leave them there on bamboo beds in the middle of the jungle in the path of the advancing enemy, thousands of wounded and bleeding and feverish men, unarmed and utterly helpless. Some of the nurses thought of refusing that order. They wanted to stay because that is what a comrade does, that is what a nurse does. But they were soldiers too, and soldiers obey orders. So they left—and for the rest of their lives they have regretted it. Fifty years later, I watched them weep inconsolably in the telling. That kind of loyalty and sense of sacrifice and duty stands out in sharp relief in our era.

Nursing is also an intimate profession, much more so than the profession of medicine. Surgeons and physicians perform their tasks then depart. It is the nurse who remains at the bedside, changing the bloody dressing, washing the injured body, listening carefully to every beat of the heart. It is one thing, of course, to do all this in the safety of a State-side hospital; it is quite another to do it in the middle of a jungle, starving and afraid and wracked with malarial tremors.

So we will not call them heroes or angels, but what they were, what they are—women, made remarkable by history and ennobled by suffering and love.

We can learn many lessons from such women. First, that loyalty, sacrifice, obedience and discipline are genderless. Honor may have begun as a male code but the sense of selflessness it requires is much more characteristic of women. The abiding camaraderie that sustained the nurses under fire and in prison should have surprised no one. Maude Davison and Josie Nesbit had an easy time holding their small band together because that is what the women wanted. They prized their affiliation, their sorority, their womanhood because, as women, they were more naturally comrades than men. I do not mean to suggest that women cannot act independently or that among us there are no individualists. History has long since put that canard to rest. Instead, I think that men feel compelled to prove themselves in isolation, while women feel compelled to prove themselves in accord. The voice of a woman is the voice of connection,[1] and this inclination to keep close, to define oneself through affinity, kept the women going.

But I stray. I started out to tell a story and promised to let the details of that story speak for themselves. So, one last time, let me go back.

...

*I*N 1980 SIXTEEN of the nurses, members of the large veterans group The American Defenders of Bataan and Corregidor, returned to the Philippines on a special tour. The men and women retraced their wartime steps, visiting the battlefields, the prison camps, the old bases. One morning the group was driven to the top of Mount Samat on Bataan to dedicate several memorials. One of these monuments, a stone with a brass plaque, had been erected by the men of the Death March to honor the nurses.[2] Its inscription, in part, can easily stand as history's final word:

> *In honor of the valiant American military women who gave so much of themselves in the early days of World War II. . . . They lived on a starvation diet, shared the bombing, strafing, sniping, sickness and disease while working endless hours of heartbreaking duty. . . . They truly earned the name "The Angels of Bataan and Corregidor."*

Acknowledgments

I AM GRATEFUL TO many people who graciously shared their expertise, insights and experiences.

Most of all, I am indebted to the twenty Angels who told me their stories: army nurses Earlyn Black Harding, Sally Blaine Millett, Ruby Bradley, Hattie Brantley, Helen Cassiani Nestor, Dorothea Daley Engel, Bertha Dworsky Henderson, Helen Gardner Rozmus, Eleanor Garen, Peggy Greenwalt Walcher, Eunice Hatchitt Tyler, Verna Henson Hively, Jeanne Kennedy Schmidt, Dorothy Scholl Armold, Madeline Ullom, Lucy Wilson Jopling; navy nurses Dorothy Still Danner, Peg Nash and Mary Rose Harrington Nelson; and civilian nurse Denny Williams, who returned to the Army Nurse Corps after the war.

I also thank relatives of the Angels who cooperated with my requests for interviews and gave me permission to use published and unpublished material: Mina Aasen's niece, Gladys Bruhn; Maude Davison's stepson, Robert Jackson; Eleanor Garen's niece and nephew, Doris Sante and Dennis Kennedy; Dorothy Scholl Armold's children, Carolyn Torrence and Harold Armold. And especially Mr. Edward Nestor, a World War II veteran of the European theater, who offered his opinions and recollections about his life with "Cassie."

The candor and generosity of two people who knew the Angels well, Samuel B. Moody, a Bataan Death March survivor, and Terry "Little Cassie" Myers Johnson, provided different and important perspectives on the group.

Archivist Susan Sacharski and nurse Sharon Eifried spent hours interviewing several Angels and locating archival material. They were of enormous assistance during the years I was shaping this project.

I also came to rely on a network of active-duty and retired military nurses: World War II veterans Dr. Jeanne Quint Benoliel and Signe Cooper; Army Nurse Corps historians Major Nona Bice-Stevens, Major C. J. Moore, Colonel Mary Sarnecky, Lieutenant Colonel Iris West, Brigadier General Connie Slewitzke USA (retired), and Rear Admiral Fran Shea Buckley USN (retired) helped me understand the American military culture and locate crucial information about the Angels, some of which had been lost for almost fifty years.

Historians across the country not only gave me full access to material in their collections but also shared their particular expertise. Among these are: Alan Aimone, United States Military Academy Special Collections Division, West Point, New York; Paul Grey, National Personnel Records Center, St. Louis, Missouri; Harry Noyes III, U.S. Army Health Services Command, Fort Sam Houston, Texas; curators Thomas McMasters and Ronald Burkett, U.S. Army Medical Department Museum at Fort Sam Houston, Texas; Paula Ussery, Admiral Nimitz Museum, Fredericksburg, Texas; and Brigadier General Wilma Vaught USAF (retired) and her staff at the Women in Military Service to America headquarters in Virginia.

I also wish to thank those at the following archives: the National Archives in Suitland, Maryland; Philippine Archive Collection in Washington; the Bureau of Medicine and Surgery of the United States Navy; and the Center for Military History in Washington, D.C. These collections contained four valuable resources—the Army Nurse Corps archives at the Center for Military History held Josie Nesbit's personnel rosters and her 1945 unpublished report listing names, dates and descriptions of Manila, Bataan, Corregidor, Santo Tomas Internment Camp (STIC); the Army Nurse Corps Oral History interviews, conducted from 1983 to 1984 with thirty-one of the army and navy POW's, provided details from those nurses who had died or were too frail to meet with me; the National Archives in Suitland, Maryland, had boxes of classified testimony that the nurses had given to judge advocate officers in 1945 for use in war crimes trials (these interviews offered details of specific prisoner-of-war incidents after surrender); the Philippine Archive Collection at the National Archives in Washington, D.C., held Bataan hospital rosters, diaries, unit records and memorabilia, which furnished the senior medical commanders perspectives on the war.

I received photographs through the goodwill of individuals from the

American Red Cross, Washington, D.C.; the U.S. Naval Hospital, Oakland, California; the Minot *Daily News,* Minot, North Dakota; and the Scott and White School of Nursing Archives in Temple, Texas.

Other scholars and experts assisted me in filling in crucial gaps in the Angels' story. Mr. Richard Arnold from the Rutgers University Foundation helped me locate Terry "Little Cassie" Myers Johnson; Elizabeth Ann Watkins and other librarians from Dana Library on the Newark campus of Rutgers University uncovered many books and articles; Dr. Davis Joel Steinberg, president of Long Island University, shared his expertise of Filipino activities during the war; architect Andrew Attinson, AIA, helped in the description of the buildings at Santo Tomas University; former Veterans Administration officials Dorothy Starbuck, Charles Lucas and Edward Rose candidly recalled the events of the 1983 POW reunion; and Alice Booher, Southeast Business and Professional Women (SE/BPW), kindly invited me to the 1992 POW celebration in Washington, D.C., which gave me an opportunity to observe the Angels as a group.

My mother, Dorothy Riley Dempsey, was a source of information and cultural references from the war years. After a half century, her memory remains sharp, especially about the music of that era. My dear, late father, John J. Dempsey, spoke often about his time in combat as a young lieutenant in a tank destroyer unit of the 2nd Armored Division in Europe. He taught me a great deal about the long-term impact of war on veterans.

I thank Esther Newberg for her tenacity and forbearance, and Bob Loomis for his craftsmanship and steady guidance.

A POET, TEACHER and friend, Jean Armstrong lent her skill, helping me to pare down and reorganize the manuscript. I deeply appreciate her generosity, patience, skill and good humor.

I collaborated on this book with my husband, the writer Michael Norman. He spent six months every day helping to reshape the manuscript and polish the prose. We have been married for more than twenty-five years. After so long working and living together, it is hard to know where my sentences end and his begin.

A WORD ON the title: I was against using the word "Angels" there. Men—not women—apply that appellation to nurses and most of us find it denigrating, insulting and just plain silly. Men use it to remind women to sacrifice, to work long hours for low pay and not complain. It is meant to idealize women, to push them to be perfect, because that is the kind of woman, the kind of nurse, men want.

I'm no angel, and neither were the gritty women of Bataan. They were human beings, as brave and as fearful as their male comrades, but after much thought, and a little prompting from literary friends, I came to see the word "angel" as the only metaphor that married the conflicting ideas of bravery and compassion, heroism and care.

The nurses of Bataan and Corregidor were in every sense "at war," side by side with men. The difference was that they carried a battle dressing instead of a gun. They fought, and fought fiercely, to preserve life as everyone around them was bent on taking it. In that light "Angels" seemed just right.

Finally, for the record, the title is meant to echo two lines from Shakespeare's *Henry V:* "We few, we happy few, we band of brothers. / For he who sheds his blood with me shall be my brother."

MONTCLAIR, NEW JERSEY
1998

Appendix I: Chronology of Military Nurses in the Philippine Islands, 1940–1945

March 1941	War maneuvers and air-raid drills begin.
Summer 1941	Douglas MacArthur assumes command of U.S. forces in the Far East. More troops and nurses arrive from Stateside. Military dependents and unnecessary civilians leave for the States.
July 1941	Miss Maude Davison promoted to captain, replaces Miss E. Valine Messner as Chief Nurse USA in the Philippines.
November 1941	Last army transport leaves Manila for the United States. Eighty-seven army nurses on duty, double the number from one year earlier. Twelve navy nurses at Canacao Naval Hospital, outside Manila.
December 7–8, 1941	Pearl Harbor, Hawaii, bombed. Guam, Wake Island and Midway attacked. In the Philippines, Camp John Hay in Baguio and Clark Field at Fort Stotsenberg bombed. Five army nurses from Sternberg Hospital in Manila go to Stotsenberg Hospital to help. President Roosevelt declares war.
December 10, 1941	Canacao Naval Hospital in Cavite shelled.
December 11, 1941	Canacao Naval Hospital evacuated. Twelve navy nurses move to Sternberg Hospital in Manila. They are assigned by the army to various makeshift medical facilities.
December 13, 1941	Fort McKinley, seven miles from Manila, evacuated. Twenty army nurses move to Sternberg Hospital and are reassigned around the city.
December 22, 1941	Two hundred miles from Manila, Camp John Hay evacuated. Two ANC leave this post with other medical personnel and attempt to walk to Bataan to join the allied forces there. Major portion of General Homma's army lands at Lingayen Gulf, north of Manila.
December 24, 1941	At 11:00 A.M. Stotsenberg Hospital near Clark Field ordered evacuated. Twenty nurses arrive at Sternberg Hospital at 4:00 P.M. ANC begins to evacuate Sternberg. Twenty-five American (twenty-four ANC, one NNC) and twenty-five Filipino nurses ordered to Bataan via trucks. General MacArthur leaves Manila for Corregidor. MacArthur declares Manila an open city.

December 25–26, 1941	ANC ordered to be ready to evacuate all personnel still in Manila. Twenty ANC leave the city by ship; nineteen go to Bataan to begin to set up Hospital #2, one to Bataan Hospital #1 at Limay, Bataan. Seven other ANC arrive on another boat at Limay.
December 25–28, 1941	Ten ANC, one physiotherapist, evacuate from Sternberg Hospital, arrive at Corregidor. Twelve ANC and one dietitian remain behind in Manila.
December 28, 1941	Two ANC, Ruby Bradley and Beatrice Chambers, return to Baguio and surrender. They are interned at Camp John Hay, now a POW camp. The physicians and other medical personnel remain in the mountains and continue their attempt to get to Bataan.
December 29, 1941	Twelve ANC and one dietitian evacuated from Sternberg Hospital to Corregidor. Corregidor is bombed for the first time. Military personnel begin to move underground into Malinta Tunnel.
December 31, 1941	Last ANC, Floramund Fellmuth, leaves Manila on a provisional hospital ship, eventually arrives in Australia. The last army military personnel leave Sternberg Hospital. Eleven navy nurses with other naval medical personnel at Saint Scholastica Girls School in Manila. First patients, two surgical, one medical, admitted to Hospital #2 on Bataan.
January 1, 1942	Four wards functioning at Hospital #2, Bataan. Josie Nesbit arrives from Corregidor to become chief nurse at #2.
January 2, 1942	Japanese enter Manila. Eleven navy nurses surrender. They are held at Saint Scholastica Girls School with patients and other medical personnel.
January 9, 1942	Seven wards functioning at Bataan Hospital #2.
January 16, 1942	One hundred eighty-two major operations performed at Hospital #1, located at Limay, Bataan.
January 23, 1942	Medical personnel travel into the Bataan jungle to a spot nicknamed Little Baguio and begin to set up a new site for Hospital #1.
January 25, 1942	Eighteen nurses leave Limay about 9:00 A.M. Hospital #1 relocated to Little Baguio to avoid enemy bombings.
February 6, 1942	Forty-eight ANC and twenty-three Filipino nurses working at #2 with seventeen wards functioning. Japanese reinforcements land on Luzon.

February 10, 1942	Edith Shacklette named chief nurse at Hospital #1. She replaces temporary head nurse, Rosemary Hogan.
February 20, 1942	Nurses hold first of two dances at Hospital #1. Lull in the Bataan fighting.
March 1, 1942	Quinine on Bataan exhausted.
March 8, 1942	Eleven navy nurses taken to Santo Tomas Internment Camp, Manila.
March 11, 1942	General MacArthur leaves Corregidor for Australia. General Wainwright in command of Bataan and Corregidor forces.
March 30, 1942	Bataan Hospital #1 bombed at 10:17 A.M. Patient and male personnel casualties. Final Japanese assault on Bataan begins.
April 3, 1942	Captain Maude Davison visits Bataan from her HQ on Corregidor. More nurses ordered from Corregidor to Bataan to help with increasing casualties.
April 5, 1942	Easter. Japanese increase attacks on Bataan.
April 6, 1942	Only fifteen of the original twenty-four nurses remain on Corregidor. The other ANC have been sent to Bataan.
April 7, 1942	Bataan Hospital #1 bombed shortly after 10:00 A.M. One ward demolished. Two ANC, Rosemary Hogan and Rita Palmer, wounded.
April 8–9, 1942	All seventy-two ANC and one NNC ordered from Bataan to Corregidor. Twenty-six Filipino nurses, one dietitian, one physiotherapist, one Red Cross field director and five civilian women accompany them. Hospital #1 group leaves the Mariveles dock about 11:30 P.M. and arrive about 3:00 A.M. at Corregidor. Hospital #2 group caught behind exploding ordnance. Reach Mariveles around sunrise.
April 9, 1942	Allies on Bataan surrender to the Japanese at 6:00 A.M. Last boat with Hospital #2 nurses leaves Bataan about 8:00 A.M. All American and Filipino women safely on Corregidor by 1:00 P.M.
April 29, 1942	Two PBY planes leave Corregidor with twenty army nurses and other passengers. At a refueling stop on Mindanao, one PBY hits a rock on takeoff and is unable to fly. Ten ANC stranded. The other PBY plane arrives safely in Australia.

May 1, 1942	Continuous bombing and shelling of Corregidor. Nurses remain on duty in Malinta Tunnel Hospital.
May 3, 1942	Eleven army and one navy nurse leave Corregidor on a submarine. Safely arrive in Fremantle, Australia.
May 6, 1942	General Wainwright surrenders to the Japanese. Fifty-four ANC among the American forces on Corregidor. Japanese order the nurses to remain inside Malinta Tunnel.
May 10, 1942	Ten nurses stranded on Mindanao surrender.
June 25, 1942	Fifty-four army nurses, staff and patients ordered out of Malinta Tunnel. Arrive at ruined Middleside Hospital on Corregidor about 9:00 A.M. after a two-and-a-half-mile hike.
July 2, 1942	Fifty-four ANC removed from Corregidor about 5:00 A.M. by boat. Arrive Manila 11:00 A.M. Transported by truck to Santo Tomas Internment Camp (STIC) in Manila. Taken to Santa Catalina Convent, outside the main camp grounds.
August 25, 1942	Fifty-four army nurses move into main internment camp (STIC).
September 9, 1942	Ten army nurses stranded on Mindanao arrive in Manila; sixty-four army nurses now at STIC. Army nurse Maude Davison in charge of Santa Catalina prison hospital. Eleven navy nurses work under her command.
December 25, 1942	First POW Christmas. Sixty-four army nurses share presents and special meal outside Santa Catalina Hospital.
May 14, 1943	Eleven navy nurses move to the newly established internment camp at Los Banos and set up a hospital to care for other POW's. Navy nurse Laura Cobb in charge of Los Banos hospital nursing staff.
Summer 1943	Army nurse Ruby Bradley arrives at STIC from John Hay Internment Camp in Baguio. The other army nurse, Beatrice Chambers, elects to remain at John Hay.
September 26, 1943	One hundred twenty-seven civilians from STIC and Los Banos leave on a repatriation ship. No military nurses among them. Sixty-five ANC in STIC, eleven NNC at Los Banos.
December 25, 1943	Second POW Christmas. Food less plentiful. Nurses share Red Cross relief supplies.
January 1944	Japanese War Prisoners Division takes over all Philippine POW camps from civilian command. Issues series of restrictive orders.

February 1, 1944	Army nurse Josie Nesbit notes signs of weight loss and malnutrition in the nurses.
March 1944	Mail from USA arrives. Nurses allowed to send home censored twenty-five-word postcards.
September 21, 1944	Death rate from malnutrition in STIC and Los Banos increasing. American pilots bomb Manila for the first time.
October 20, 1944	Allied troops land on southern Philippine island of Leyte. General MacArthur arrives on Leyte.
December 25, 1944	Third POW Christmas. Scarce food. No gifts allowed into camps. No holiday parties.
January 2, 1945	Allies land on Luzon, Philippines.
February 3, 1945	1st Cavalry liberates STIC. All sixty-five ANC in STIC alive after almost three years as POW's.
February 5, 1945	Army nurse Mabel Robinson arrives with nearly one hundred ANC. Relieve STIC army nurses from duty. Army nurse Beatrice Chambers from Baguio reunited with other former POW army nurses.
February 12–19, 1945	Sixty-six ANC, two dietitians, one physiotherapist, one Red Cross field director and civilian nurses flown to Leyte. Medical tests done; nurses given uniforms, promoted one grade and presented with medals.
February 19–23, 1945	ANC island-hopping across the Pacific.
February 22, 1945	11th Airborne Division liberates Los Banos Internment Camp. Eleven navy nurses freed.
February 23, 1945	Sixty-six ANC arrive in San Francisco. Reunited with friends and families. Taken to Letterman Hospital for evaluation.
March 10, 1945	Eleven navy nurses arrive in San Francisco. Taken to Oak Knoll Hospital for evaluation.
March 1945	Sixty-six ANC and eleven NNC released from hospitals. Travel to their hometowns.
May 8, 1945	Germany surrenders.
July 5, 1945	General MacArthur announces fighting in the Philippine Islands is over. Complete allied victory.
August 6, 1945	Atomic bomb dropped on Hiroshima.
August 15, 1945	Japan surrenders.

Appendix II:

THE NURSES AND THEIR HOMETOWNS

Navy Nurse Corps Prisoners of War

1. Chief Nurse Laura Mae Cobb, Wichita, Kansas
2. Mary F. Chapman, Chicago, Illinois
3. Bertha R. Evans, Portland, Oregon
4. Helen C. Gorzelanski, Omaha, Nebraska
5. Mary Rose Harrington, Elk Point, South Dakota
6. Margaret "Peg" A. Nash, Wilkes-Barre, Pennsylvania
7. Goldia "Goldie" A. O'Haver, Hayfield, Minnesota
8. Eldene E. Paige, Lomita, California
9. Susie J. Pitcher, Des Moines, Iowa
10. Dorothy Still, Long Beach, California
11. Edwina Todd, Pomona, California

Civilian Nurses Imprisoned with the Navy Nurses

1. Helen G. Grant, Scottish nurse
2. Basilia Torres Steward, wife of an American

Navy Nurse Corps Evacuee from the Philippine Islands

1. Ann Bernatitus, Exeter, Pennsylvania

Army Nurse Corps Prisoners of War

1. Maude Campbell Davison, Washington, D.C.
2. Josephine May "Josie" Nesbit, Parlin, Colorado
3. Mina A. Aasen, Minot, North Dakota
4. Louise M. Anschicks, Mendota, Illinois
5. Phyllis J. Arnold, Minneapolis, Minnesota
6. Agnes D. Barre, Orange, Texas
7. Clara Mae "Bickie" Bickford, Tivoli, Texas
8. Earlyn "Blackie" Black, Groesbeck, Texas
9. Ethel "Sally" L. Blaine, Bible Grove, Missouri
10. Ruby G. Bradley, Spencer, West Virginia
11. Hattie R. Brantley, Jefferson, Texas
12. Minnie L. Breese, Arlington Heights, Illinois

13.   Myra V. Burris, San Antonio, Texas

14.   Helen "Cassie" Cassiani, Bridgewater, Massachusetts

15.   Beatrice E. Chambers, Manila, Philippine Islands

16.   Edith M. Corns, Cleveland, Ohio

17.   Mildred "Millie" Dalton, Jefferson, Georgia

18.   Kathyrn L. Dollason, Augusta, Georgia

19.   Sallie P. Durrett, Louisville, Kentucky

20.   Bertha "Charlie" Dworsky, Halletsville, Texas

21.   Dorcas E. Easterling, Abbot, Texas

22.   Magdalena Eckman, Pine Grove, California

23.   Eula R. Fails, Houston, Texas

24.   Adele F. Foreman, Masten, Pennsylvania

25.   Earleen Allen, Chicago, Illinois

26.   Helen L. Gardner, Aberdeen, Ohio

27.   Eleanor Mae Garen, South Bend, Indiana

28.   Marcia L. Gates, Janesville, Wisconsin

29.   Beulah M. "Peggy" Greenwalt, Seattle, Washington

30.   Alice J. Hahn, Chicago, Illinois

31.   Helen M. Hennessey, Leavenworth, Kansas

32.   Gwendolyn L. Henshaw, Los Angeles, California

33.   Verna V. Henson, Trinity, Texas

34.   Rosemary Hogan, Chattanooga, Oklahoma

35.   Geneva Jenkins, Sevierville, Tennessee

36.   Doris A. Kehoe, Pacific Grove, California

37.   Imogene "Jeanne" Kennedy, Philadelphia, Mississippi

38.   Blanche Kimball, Topeka, Kansas

39.   Eleanor O. Lee, Lonaconing, Maryland

40.   Frankie T. Lewey, Dalhart, Texas

41.   Dorothy L. Ludlow, Little Rock, Arkansas

42.   Inez V. McDonald, Tupelo, Mississippi

43.   Letha McHale, Haverhill, Massachusetts

44.   Winifred P. Madden, Montello, Wisconsin

45.   Gladys Ann Mealor, Gorgas, Alabama

46.   Mary Brown Menzie, New Orleans, Louisiana

47.   Adolpha M. Meyer, St. Louis, Missouri

48.   Clara L. Mueller, Philadelphia, Pennsylvania

49.   Frances Louise Nash, Washington, Georgia

50.   Mary J. Oberst, Owensboro, Kentucky

51.   Eleanor "Peg" O'Neill, Providence, Rhode Island

52.   Rita G. Palmer, Hampton, New Hampshire

53. Beulah M. Putnam, Worthington, Ohio
54. Mary J. Reppak, Shelton, Connecticut
55. Rose F. Rieper, St. Louis, Missouri
56. Dorothy Scholl, Independence, Missouri
57. Edith E. "Shack" Shacklette, Brandenberg, Kentucky
58. Ruth M. Stoltz, Dayton, Ohio
59. Ethel M. Thor, Tacoma, Washington
60. Madeline M. Ullom, O'Neill, Nebraska
61. Evelyn B. Whitlow, Leasburg, North Carolina
62. Anna E. Williams, Harrisburg, Pennsylvania
63. Edith M. Wimberly, Campti, Louisiana
64. Anne B. Wurts, Leominster, Massachusetts
65. Eunice F. Young, Arkport, New York
66. Alice M. "Swish" Zwicker, Brownville, Maine

Other Women Imprisoned with the Army Nurses

1. Marie Adams, field director for the American Red Cross
2. Brunetta Kuehlthau, army physical therapist
3. Ruby Motley, army dietitian
4. Vivian Weisblatt, civilian dietitian
5. Maude "Denny" Denson Williams, nurse-anesthetist. Member of the Army Nurse Corps before and after the war.
6. Marie Atkinson
7. Betty Bradford
8. Betty Brian
9. Illa Mae Chalek
10. Marie Gould
11. Rita Johnson
12. Catherine Nau
13. Fontaine Porter
14. Mildred Roth
15. Ana Wingate
16. Marie Wolf

Army Nurse Corps Evacuees from Corregidor (1942)

1. Catherine M. Acorn
2. Dorothea M. Daley, Hamilton, Missouri
3. Floramund A. Fellmuth, Chicago, Illinois (left Manila in December 1941 by ship)

4. Leona Gastinger, Alabama
5. Susan Downing Gallagher
6. Nancy J. Gillahan
7. Grace D. Hallman, Georgia
8. Eunice C. Hatchitt, Prairie Lea, Texas
9. Willa Hook, Renfrow, Oklahoma
10. Ressa Jenkins, Sevierville, Tennessee
11. Harriet G. Lee, Boston, Massachusetts
12. Mary G. Lohr, Greensburg, Pennsylvania
13. Florence MacDonald, Brockton, Massachusetts
14. Hortense McKay, Amherst, Minnesota
15. Mary L. Moultrie, Georgia
16. Mollie A. Peterson, Arkansas
17. Juanita Redmond, Swansea, South Carolina
18. Mabel V. Stevens, Nebraska
19. Ruth W. Straub, Milwaukee, Wisconsin
20. Helen Summers, Queens, New York
21. Beth A. Veley, San Jose, California
22. Lucy Wilson, Big Sandy, Texas

Bibliography

Adams, J. T. *The Epic of America.* Boston, Massachusetts: Little, Brown and Company, 1931.

Allied Naval Forces Based Western Australia. USS Spearfish Special Mission. Serial SA-115. 3 June 1942. Operational Archives, Naval Historical Center, Washington, D.C.

American military women prisoners of war. *The Congressional Record-Senate, 138*(54), S5341–42, April 10, 1942.

American Nurses' Association Convention reports. *The American Journal of Nursing, 42*(7), 754–55, 1942.

"Angels of Bataan saved—work on!" *San Francisco News,* 1, Feb. 5, 1945.

"Army, Navy leave city." *The Manila Bulletin,* 1, Dec. 27, 1941.

"Army nurses from the Philippines now in Australia." *American Journal of Nursing, 42*(7), 820, 1942.

Ashton, P. *Bataan Diary.* Santa Barbara, California: P. Ashton, 1984.

Aynes, E. A. *From Nightingale to Eagle.* New York: Prentice Hall, 1973.

Bailey, M. "Raid at Los Banos." *Military Review,* 51–66, 1983.

Baker, M. J. *Images of Women in Films: The War Years 1941–1945.* Ann Arbor, Michigan: UMI Research Press, 1980.

Baldwin, H. "Bataan's eleventh hour." *The New York Times,* 1, April 8, 1942.

———. "Bataan's epic of valor." *The New York Times,* 5, April 10, 1942.

Barker, A. J. *Prisoners of War.* New York: Universe Books, 1974.

Barton, M. "Outline history of the Navy Nurse Corps," unpublished paper from the Bureau of Medicine and Surgery, United States Navy, Washington, D.C., 1989.

Basinger, J. "So proudly we hail." *American Film, 10,* 64, 1985.

"Bataan nurses are honored during busy week at Letterman." Letterman General Hospital, *The Fog Horn, 4*(29), 1, March 3, 1945.

"Bataan speaking." *Newsweek, 19,* 21, April 20, 1942.

"Bataan worst blow to an American Army." Associated Press release, April 9, 1941.

"Battered Bataan." *Newsweek, 19,* 17, March 2, 1942.

Beck, J. J. *MacArthur and Wainwright: Sacrifice of the Philippines.* Albuquerque: University of New Mexico Press, 1974.

Belote, J. H., and Belote, W. M. *Corregidor: The Saga of a Fortress.* New York: Harper & Row, 1967.

Biography of Stuart Shadrick Murray, Admiral, USN, Retired. September 18, 1956. Operational Archives, Naval Historical Center, Washington, D.C.

"Bloody Bataan." *Newsweek, 19,* 21–22, Feb. 9, 1942.

Booher, A. "A song is sung for American heroines: POWs from 1984 to 1992." *The Stars and Stripes—The National Tribune,* 5; 8, April 27, 1992.

Bowman, J. B. "Nurse Corps: History of nursing in the navy." *United States Naval Medical Bulletin,* 26 (1), 123–31, 1928.

Brown, D. M. *Setting a Course: American Women in the 1920s.* Boston: Twayne Publishers, 1987.

Brown, M. "The joys of meeting pays the pangs of absence." *Trained Nurse and Hospital Review,* 114, 411, 1945.

Bruhn, G. E. *Memories of Mina.* Minot, North Dakota: Gladys E. Bruhn, 1982.

Bulosan, C. "Bataan." *The Saturday Review,* 26, 20, March 20, 1943.

Bumgarner, J. *Parade of the Dead: A U.S. Army Physician's Memoir of Imprisonment by the Japanese, 1942–1945.* Jefferson, North Carolina: McFarland & Company, 1995.

Bureau of Medicine and Surgery United States Navy, NavMed 939. *White Task Force.* Washington, D.C.: U.S. Government Printing Office, 1945.

Calip, J., and Guerrero, J. "Liberation of Los Banos internees." In Liberation Day Anniversary Souvenir. Published by the Officer Corps of the Laguna Chapter Hunter Veterans Legion, 1947. Limited circulation.

Campbell, D'Ann. *Women at War with America: Private Lives in a Patriotic Era.* Cambridge, Massachusetts: Harvard University Press, 1984.

Captain Ann Bernatitus, Nurse Corps, United States Navy, Retired, August 8, 1968. Navy Office of Information. Operational Archives, Naval Historical Center, Washington D.C.

Cates, T. R. *The Drainpipe Diary.* New York: Vantage Press, 1957.

Chapman, J., and Chapman, E. *Escape to the Hills.* Lancaster, Pennsylvania: The Jacques Cattell Press, 1946.

Clarke, A. R. "The invasion of Luzon." *The Army Nurse,* 2 (8), 9–10, 1945.

———. "Thirty-seven months as prisoners of war." *American Journal of Nursing,* 45(5), 342–45, 1945.

Comeau, Genevieve K. *A Concise Biography of Major Maude C. Davison, ANC.* Historical Unit USAMEDS, Walter Reed Army Medical Center, Washington, D.C., 1961.

Concerning the Army Nurse Corps. Alma T. Skoog Collection, Army Medical Museum, Fort Sam Houston, Texas, 1937.

Contey-Aiello, R. (ed.) *The 50th Anniversary Commemorative Album of the Flying Column 1945–1995.* Tarpon Springs, Florida: Marrakech Express, 1994.

Cooper, P. *Navy Nurse.* New York: McGraw-Hill Book Company, 1946.

Cooper, W. *Medical Department activities in the Philippines from 1941 to 6 May 1942, and including medical activities in Japanese prisoner of war camps.* Typewritten report. West Point, New York: Nininger Collection, United States Military Academy special collections, 1946.

———. *Roster of hospital personnel and correspondence, Fort Mills, P.I. Jan. 17, 1942–June 21, 1942.* National Archives, Philippine Archive Collection, Washington D.C. RG 407, Box 6.

"Corregidor finale." *Newsweek* 39(19), 21–24, May 18, 1942.

Cotton, J. "Civilian internment camps in the Far East." *Prisoner of War Bulletin* 2(2), 2–4, 1944.

Craighill, M. D. "Psychiatric aspects of women serving in the Army." *American Journal of Psychiatry, 104,* 226–30, 1947.

Crouter, N. *Forbidden Diary.* New York: Franklin, 1980.

Davis, D. M. "Processing and caring for prisoners of war." *American Journal of Nursing, 46,* 152–53, 1946.

Davis, D. S. "I nursed at Santo Tomas, Manila." *American Journal of Nursing, 44,* 29–30, 1944.

———. "Nursing in prison camps." *Military Surgeon, 100,* 42–46, Jan. 1947.

Davison, Maude C. Major ANC N700 404, date and author unknown. Army Nurse Corps Archives. Center for Military History, Washington, D.C.

Deacon, K. (no date). "Engineers in the Los Banos raid." Typed report from "The Military Engineer, No. 334." Limited circulation.

"Death in line of duty comes to *Life* correspondent Jacoby." *Life, 12,* 32, May 11, 1942.

Dorothy Davis Thompson '40, POW, Japanese Internment Camp, The Philippines, January 1942–December 1943. *The Alumni Magazine. Columbia University–Presbyterian Hospital School of Nursing Alumni Association.* 86(2), 7–10, 1991, Fall–Winter.

Duckworth, James (no date). *Official History of General Hospital #1 USAFFE at Camp Limay Bataan: Little Baguio, Camp O'Donnell, Tarlac, Philippine Islands, from Dec. 23, 1941, to June 30, 1942.* National Archives, Philippine Archive Collection, Washington, D.C., RG 407, Box 12.

"An Easter thought." *The Army Nurse, 2*(3), 2, 1945.

Engel, D. Davis. "I was married in battle." *American Magazine, 134,* 26–27; 112–16, Oct. 1942.

"The epic of Bataan." *Reader's Digest, 40,* 4–7, June 1942.

Espinosa, G. "Filipino nurses in Bataan and Corregidor." *American Journal of Nursing, 46,* 97–98, 1946.

Falk, S. *Bataan March of Death.* New York: Norton, 1962.

Fellmuth, F. "Nurse writes from Australia." *Army and Navy Journal, 79, 955,* April 25, 1942.

Flanagan, E. *Corregidor: Rock Force Assault 1945.* Novato, California: Presidio Press, 1988.

Flikke, J. *Nurses in Action.* Philadelphia: Lippincott, 1943.

"Foes rule the air over Philippines." *The New York Times,* 3, Dec. 29, 1941.

"Footnote to Bataan." *Newsweek, 19*(20), 20, May 4, 1942.

"For distinguished service." *Trained Nurse and Hospital Review, 109,* 38–39, July 1942.

"Former POW nurses feted at reunion." *Vanguard: Washington DC, 29*(9), 1; 3–4, 1983.

"Freed nurses reunited with men they aided on Bataan." *The San Francisco Examiner,* 3, March 1945.

Gammond, P. *The Oxford Companion to Popular Music.* New York: Oxford University Press, 1991.

Garen, E. "War terror in Philippines recalled." South Bend *Tribune*, no page, Spring 1992.

Geister, J. "Nurses stood by to the end." *Trained Nurse and Hospital Review*, 198, 343–46, 1942.

Gilligan, C. *In a Different Voice: Psychological Theory and Women's Development*. Cambridge: Harvard University Press, 1982.

Goldstein, G., van Kammen, W., Shelly, C., Miller, D., and van Kammen, D. "Survivors of imprisonment in the Pacific theater during World War II." *American Journal of Psychiatry*, 144 (9), 1210–1213, 1987.

Grashio, S., and Norling, B. *Return to Freedom: The War Memoirs of Col. Samuel C. Grashio USAF (Ret.)*. Tulsa, Oklahoma: MCN Press, 1982.

Gray, J. Glenn. *The Warriors: Reflections on Men in Battle*. New York: Harcourt, Brace, Jovanovich, 1959.

Guerrero, L. "Last days of Corregidor." *Philippine Review*, May 1943.

Gunther, J. *Inside U.S.A.* New York: Harper & Row, 1947.

Hafstrom, P. "Rescue of Army nurse brings joy to mother." *The Elkhart Truth*, 1; 8, Feb. 6, 1945.

Harries, M., and Harries, S. *Soldiers of the Sun: The Rise and Fall of the Imperial Japanese Army*. New York: Random House, 1991.

Harrison, G. *Mosquitoes, Malaria and Man: A History of the Hostilities since 1880*. New York: E. F. Dutton, 1978.

Hartendorf, A. V. *The Santo Tomas Story, Edited from the Official History of the Santo Tomas Internment Camp by F. H. Golay*. New York: McGraw-Hill, 1964.

Hartmann, S. *American Women in the 1940s: The Home Front and Beyond*. Boston: Twayne Publishers, 1982.

Hatchitt, E. C. "Bataan nurse." *Colliers*, 13; 50, Aug. 1, 1942.

"The heroic nurses of Bataan and Corregidor." *The American Journal of Nursing*, 42, 187–98, 1942.

Hewlett, F. "Quartermasters on Bataan performed heroic feats." *The Quartermaster Review*, 64; 92, May–June 1942.

Hibbs, R. "Beriberi in Japanese prison camp." *Annals of Internal Medicine*, 24, 270–82, 1946.

"Higher salaries to Army nurses—and nurses of cobelligerent countries may enlist." *Trained Nurse and Hospital Review*, 109, 44, 1942.

Hogan, R. "What did not happen to the Bataan nurses." *Liberty*, 19; 80–82, Nov. 17, 1945.

Home from Bataan. ASF Group, Bureau of Public Relations (no date). Army Nurse Corps Archives, Center for Military History, Washington, D.C.

Hurd, C. "Bataan defenders forced back again; enemy reserved exact heavy losses." *The New York Times*, 1, April 8, 1942.

———. "Corregidor surrenders under land attack. Troops half starved." *The New York Times*, 1; 5, May 6, 1942.

———. "Japanese capture Bataan and 36,000 troops." *The New York Times,* 1; 3, April 10, 1942.

"In the line of duty." *Time, 39,* 55–56, May 11, 1942.

Jacoby, M. "A handful of P-40s." In G. Carroll (ed.), *History in the Writing.* New York: Duell, Sloan & Pearce, 1945, 71–75.

———. "War hits the Philippines." In G. Carroll (ed.), *History in the Writing.*

James, D. (ed.) *South to Bataan, North to Murkden: The Prison Diary of Brigadier General W. E. Brougher.* Athens, Georgia: University of Georgia Press.

Jeffrey, B. *White Coolies: Australian Nurses Behind Enemy Lines.* Sydney, Australia: Angus & Robertson, HarperCollins, 1954. Reissued in 1995.

Jopling, L. Wilson. *Warrior in White.* San Antonio, Texas: The Watercress Press, 1990.

Jowers, K. "Together in peace." *Navy Times,* 38–41, April 13, 1992.

Karnow, S. *In Our Image: America's Empire in the Philippines.* New York: Random House, 1989.

Katz, C. J. "Experiences in a prison camp as a background for therapy." *Mental Hygiene, 34,* 90–94, 1950.

Keith, B. *Days of Anguish, Days of Hope.* Garden City, New York: Doubleday, 1972.

Kentner's journal: A daily journal of events connected with the personnel of the U.S. Naval Hospital Canacao, P.I. from 12-8-41 to 2-5-45, (no date). Unpublished manuscript. Washington, D.C.: Center for Military History.

Kerr, E. *Surrender and Survival: The Experiences of American POWs in the Pacific 1941–1945.* New York: William Morrow, 1985.

Kempf, O. V. Lt. Col. MAC. *Unit History Report of the Philippine Medical Depot December 8, 1941 to October 1942,* (no date). Washington, D.C.: National Archives, Philippine Archive Collection.

Knox, D. *Death March: The Survivors of Bataan.* New York: Harcourt, Brace and Jovanovich, 1981.

"The last days of Corregidor." *The Philippine Review,* May 1943.

"Last word." *Time 39,* 32, June 8, 1942.

Lifton, R. J. *Home from the War.* New York: Simon and Schuster, 1973.

Lutz, C. A., and Przytuski, K. R. *Nutrition and Diet Therapy.* Philadelphia, Pennsylvania: F. A. Davis, 1994.

"MacArthur in Australia." *The New York Times,* 1, March 18, 1942.

MacDonald, Florence. "Nursing the sick and wounded at Bataan and Corregidor." *Hospitals, 16,* 31–33, Dec. 1942.

Maxwell, LTC. P. *History of the Army Nurse Corps 1775–1948.* Unpublished typewritten manuscript. Washington, D.C.: U.S. Army Center of Military History, 1976.

McCall, J. *Santo Tomas Internment Camp, STIC in verse and reverse, STIC-toons and STIC-tistics.* Lincoln, Nebraska: Woodruff Printing Company, 1945.

McCance, K., and Huether, S. *Pathophysiology.* St. Louis, Missouri: C. V. Mosby, 1990.

McCarthy, F. "Raid rescues 2,146 from Luzon camp." *The New York Times,* 26, Feb. 23, 1945.

McCarthy, W. *The Angels Came at Seven.* New York: Maryknoll Fathers, 1980. Reprinted from April 1950 *Columbia* magazine.

Mellnik, S. (USAF ret.) *Philippine Diary 1939–1945.* New York: Van Nostrand, 1962.

"Messages on Philippines." *The New York Times,* 1, Dec. 29, 1941.

Miller, E. B. *Bataan Uncensored.* Long Prairie, Minnesota: Hart Publications, 1949.

Miller, E. S. *War Plan Orange.* Annapolis, Maryland: Naval Institute Press, 1991.

Miller, L. G. "Nurses free, going back to Pacific." *New York World Telegram,* 1, March 8, 1945.

"Missing in action." *The Trained Nurse and Hospital Review, 109,* 183, Sept. 1942.

Mitchiner, P. H., and MacManus, E. P. *Nursing in Time of War.* London: Churchill Ltd, 1943.

Mitchum, J. "Navy Medicine May–June 1942." *Navy Medicine, 83*(3), 30–35, 1992.

Monahan, E. "Women veterans woven into fabric of history." *Vanguard, 37*(3), 7, 1991.

Morison, S. E. *The Oxford History of the American People.* New York: Oxford University Press, 1965.

———. *The Rising Sun in the Pacific, 1931–April 1942. History of United States Naval Operations in World War II. Volume III.* Boston: Little, Brown and Company, 1948.

Morton, L. *The War in the Pacific: The Fall of the Philippines.* Washington, D.C.: Government Printing Office, 1962.

Motley, R. "Bataan and its aftermath." *Journal of the American Dietetic Association, 22,* 201–205, 1946.

Murphy, M. "A reporter at large: You'll never know." *The New Yorker, 19,* 46–56, June 12, 1943.

"The mysterious nurse of Manila," *RN Magazine 9,* 31, 68–74, 1946.

Nash, Frances. "Georgia nurse's own story . . . my three years in a Jap prison camp." *The Atlanta Journal Magazine,* 2–3, Sept. 1945.

"The Navy Nurse Corps." *American Journal of Nursing, 2,* 91–93, 1908.

"Navy nurse made history as a WWII POW." *The Red Rover 4*(13), 1; 3–5, Sept. 11, 1992.

Nesbit, J. *History of the Army Nurse Corps in the Philippine Islands, September 1940–February 1945.* Unpublished manuscript. Washington, D.C.: Center for Military History, 1945.

"News for nurses." *Trained Nurse and Hospital Review,* 199, 449, 1943.

"Nurse on Corregidor finds it 'not too bad,' " *The New York Times,* 3, March 17, 1942.

"The nurses' contribution to American victory: Facts and figures from Pearl Harbor to V-J Day." *American Journal of Nursing,* 45, 683–86, 1945.

"Nursing on Bataan." *The Pacific Coast Journal of Nursing, 38*(7), 398–401, July 1942.

Parker, T. C. "The epic of Corregidor-Bataan." *U.S. Naval Institute Proceedings, 69*(1), 9–22, 1943.

Parker, T. C. "Thirteen women in a submarine." *United States Naval Institute Proceedings, 76*(7), 716–21, 1950.

Parks, R. J. *Medical Training in World War II.* Washington, D.C.: Government Printing Office, 1946.

Pearson, E. "Morbidity and mortality in Santo Tomas Internment Camp." *Annals of Internal Medicine,* 24, 988–1013, 1946.

Petrillo, C. (ed.) *The Ordeal of Elizabeth Vaughn: Wartime Diary of the Philippines.* Athens, Georgia: University of Georgia Press, 1985.

Piemonte, R., and Gurney, C. (eds.) *Highlights in the History of the Army Nurse Corps.* Washington, D.C.: U.S. Center for Military History, 1987.

"Philippine epic: General MacArthur and his men make a Thermopylae of Bataan." *Life, 12*(15), 25–37, April 13, 1942.

"The Philippines: Ghostly garrison." *Newsweek 39*(19), 25, May 18, 1942.

POWs, nurses' list of names, (no date). Army Nurse Corps Archives, Center for Military History, Washington, D.C., File 383.6.

"P. T. Department: Lieutenant Brunetta Kuehlthau tells her experiences." *Army Nurse, 2*(6), 10, June 1945.

Quartermaster diary on Corregidor, 8 December 1941 to 12 March 1942. Author unknown. National Archives, Philippine Archive Collection, Washington, D.C., RG 407, Box 10, File #500–22.

Randolph, M. "What Army nurses expect from the profession." *American Journal of Nursing,* 46, 95–97, 1946.

Raymond, A. "War notes. Army nurses write an enduring chapter in fortitude and courage." *Trained Nurse and Hospital Review,* 109, 45–46, 1942.

Redmond, J. *I Served on Bataan.* Philadelphia: J.B. Lippincott Co., 1943.

"Reminiscences of a nurse POW." *Navy Medicine,* 36–40, May–June 1992.

Report No. 189, General Headquarters United States Army, Pacific, war crimes branch of mistreatment and imprisonment under improper condition of American prisoners of war at Corregidor, P. I., during summer 1942. National Archives, Suitland, Maryland. SCAP Collection, Box 1125.

Reuter, J. "The ball and cross: Tropical prison camp." *The Catholic World,* *162,* 159–63, 1945.

Roberts, M. *The Tradition and Destiny of the US Army Nurse Corps.* Washington, D.C.: U.S. Army Medical Department, 1949.

Romulo, C. P. *I Saw the Fall of the Philippines.* Garden City, New York: Doubleday and Co., 1943.

Rudin, E. "Memories of a World War II POW nurse." *U.S. Navy Medicine, 73,* 15–20, 1982.

Russell, M. *Jungle Angel: Bataan Remembered.* Brainard, Minnesota: Bang Printing Company, 1988.

Sanger, D. "Philippines orders U.S. to leave strategic Navy base at Subic Bay." *The New York Times,* 1–2, Dec. 28, 1991.

Sayre, E. "Submarine from Corregidor." *The Atlantic, 170,* 25–26, Aug. 1942.

Schaffter, D. *What Comes of Training Women for War.* Washington, D.C.: American Council on Education, 1948.

Schaller, M. *Douglas MacArthur.* New York: Oxford University Press, 1989.

Schedler, D., and Hampson, F. "Steel tank crashes gate of Japanese prison camp." *The San Francisco Chronicle,* 1, Feb. 6, 1945.

Schnurr, P. "The long-term course of PTSD." *Clinical Quarterly: The National Center for Post-Traumatic Stress Disorder,* 4(1), 15–16, 1994.

Scholl, Dorothy Belle (as told to Margaret Hamilton). "What I saw as army nurse on Bataan and Corregidor." *Kansas City Star,* Section C, 1; 3, March 18, 1945.

Seals, C. H. Typed message to Bataan commanders, Jan. 15, 1942. National Archives, Philippine Archive Collection, Washington, D.C. RG 407, Box 12.

Shacklette Haynes's diary, (no date). *Bataan, Corregidor, Santo Tomas 1942–1945,* Admiral Nimitz Museum Collection, State Historical Park, Fredericksburg, Texas. Microfilm.

Shields, E. *A History of the United States Army Nurse Corps (Female), 1901–1937.* Unpublished doctoral dissertation, Columbia University Teachers College, New York, 1980.

Smith, R. R. *The War in the Pacific: Triumph in the Philippines.* Washington, D.C.: Center for Military History, United States Army, 1963.

Speck, J. "Captured on Guam." *The Trained Nurse and Hospital Review, 109,* 414–16, Dec. 1942.

"So proudly we hail: Realistic story of nurses in the Philippines." *Life, 15,* 69–72, Oct. 4, 1943.

Sommers, S. (ed.) *The Japanese Story.* Packet #10. Marshfield, Wisconsin: American Ex-POW Inc., National Medical Research Committee, 1980.

Steinberg, D. *Philippine Collaboration in World War II.* Ann Arbor, Michigan: University of Michigan Press, 1967.

Steinberg, R. *Return to the Philippines.* New York: Time-Life Books, 1979.

Stevens, F. H. *Santo Tomas Internment Camp.* New York: Stratford House, 1946.

"Still holding." *Time, 39,* 17, March 2, 1942.

Stimson, J. A. "The role of American nurses in winning the war." *Canadian Nurse, 38,* 623–28, 1942.

Straub, Ruth (as told to Marcia Winn). "Nurse Ruth Straub's diary." *The Pittsburgh Post-Gazette,* nine-part series, Sept. 21–30, 1942.

"Stylish too." *The Trained Nurse and Hospital Review, 114,* 428, 1945.

Tennant, C., and Goulston, K. "The psychological effects of being a prisoner of war: Forty years after release." *American Journal of Psychiatry, 143*(5), 618–21, 1986.

"The texts of the day's communiques of fighting in various fronts." *The New York Times,* 2, Dec. 30, 1941.

"32 POW nurses honored, first reunion since WWII." *The American Nurse,* 10, July–Aug. 1983.

Thompson, D. Davis. *The Road Back: A Pacific POW's Liberation Story.* Lubbock, Texas: Texas Tech University Press, 1996.

Todd, C. E. "Nursing under fire." *Military Surgeon, 100,* 335–41, April 1947.

Toland, J. *But Not in Shame: Six Months after Pearl Harbor.* New York: Random House, 1961.

Ullom, M. "Heroines under fire: The U.S. Army Nurse Corps." *The Stars and Stripes, 106*(14), 6–7; 10–11, April 7, 1983.

———, (date not given). *The Philippine assignment: Some aspects of the Army Nurse Corps in the Philippine Islands, 1940–1945.* Unpublished manuscript. Washington, D.C.: Center for Military History.

Underbrink, R. L. *Destination Corregidor.* Annapolis, Maryland: Naval Institute Press, 1971.

Unit history and personnel rosters of General Hospital No. 2, December 41 to June 42. Author and date unknown. Washington, D.C.: National Archives, Philippine Archive Collection.

Unusual incidents at Hospital #2. Author and date unknown. Washington, D.C.: National Archives, Philippine Archive Collection, RG 407, Box 12, Folder No. 99.

U.S. Army. *Reports of General MacArthur: The campaign of MacArthur in the Pacific,* by the General Staff, Tokyo headquarters, Tokyo, Japan, vol. 1, part 1, 1950. West Point, New York: Nininger Collection, United States Military Academy special collections.

———. *Reports of General MacArthur: Operations of the South Luzon force,* by the General Staff, Tokyo headquarters, Tokyo, Japan, vol. 1, part II, 1950. West Point, New York: Nininger Collection, United States Military Academy special collections.

———. *Reports of General MacArthur: Japanese operations in the South West Pacific area,* by the General Staff, Tokyo headquarters, Tokyo, Japan, vol. II, part 1, 1950. West Point, New York: Nininger Collection, United States Military Academy special collections.

USS *Spearfish special mission. Forwards narrative account of evacuation of personnel from Corregidor, P.I. on 3 May 1942 during fourth war patrol*, June 3, 1942. Serial SA-115. Allied Naval Forces Based Western Australia. Operational archives, Naval Historical Center, Washington, D.C.

Valentine, C. "Nursing at Los Banos." *RN*, 8, 30–2; 66–8, 1945.

Valentine, E. R. "Our nurses on the world's fronts." *The New York Times Magazine*, 12; 53, Sept. 13, 1942.

Wainwright, J. M., edited by B. Considine. *General Wainwright's Story: The Account of Four Years of Humiliating Defeat, Surrender and Captivity.* Garden City, New York: Doubleday, 1946.

Ware, S. *American Women in the 1930s: Holding Their Own.* Boston: Twayne Publishers, 1982.

Wartime translations of seized Japanese documents: Allied translator and interpreter section reports, 1942–1945. Frederick, Maryland: University Publications of America, 1989.

Waymire, K. "11 navy 'angels' arrive home after 3 years at Cabanatuan." *The San Francisco Examiner*, 1; 3, March 11, 1945.

Weinstein, A. *Barbed Wire Surgeon.* New York: Macmillan Company, 1948.

Weintraub, S. *Long Days Journey into War.* New York: Truman Tally Books, Dutton, 1991.

"What Tokyo reports." *The New York Times*, 1, April 10, 1942.

White, W. L. *They Were Expendable.* New York: Harcourt, Brace and Company, 1942.

Whitman, J. *Bataan: Our Last Ditch.* New York: Hippocrene Books, 1990.

Williams, D. *To the Angels.* San Francisco: Denson Press, 1985.

Willoughby, A. *I Was on Corregidor: The Experiences of an American Official's Wife in the War-Torn Philippines.* New York: Harper, 1943.

Willoughby, Major General Charles (ed.). *Operations of the Intelligence Service in the SW Pacific Area: A brief history of the G-2 section, GHQ, SWPA, and affiliated units,* by the General Staff, Tokyo headquarters, Tokyo, Japan, 1948. Kruger Collection, United States Military Academy, West Point, New York.

Wright, Major B. C. *The 1st Cavalry Division in World War II.* Tokyo, Japan: Toppan Printing Company, 1947.

Young, E. F., edited by F. J. Taylor. "Three years outside this world." *Saturday Evening Post*, 217, 18–19+, May 5, 1945.

Zeiss, R., and Dickman, H. "PTSD 40 years later: Incidence and person-situation correlates in former POWS." *Journal of Clinical Psychology*, 45 (1), 80–87, 1989.

Endnotes

FULL CITATIONS IN BIBLIOGRAPHY.

Foreword

1. The Japanese attack on the Philippines occurred on December 8, not December 7, because the islands are across the International Date Line from Hawaii.
2. Bertha Dworsky Henderson, 1992 correspondence with author.
3. Doris Kehoe, 1992 correspondence with author.
4. Phyllis Arnold, 1992 correspondence with author.

Chapter One: Waking Up to War

1. Eleanor Garen letter to her mother, Lulu Garen, dated October 25, 1941. Eleanor Garen's letters, scrapbooks and notebooks are located at Northwestern Memorial Hospital Archives, Chicago, Illinois. Her great-nephew, Dennis Kennedy, and niece, Doris Sante, gave permission to quote from Garen's files. Future references abbreviated "Garen files."
2. Mary Rose Harrington Nelson, April 13, 1989, author interview.
3. Redmond, J. (1943), pp. 15–16.
4. Davis, Josephine Nesbit. Army Nurse Corps Oral History Program interview. Interviewed by Major Susan Graski, April 9, 1983, transcript.
     In 1983–85, the Army Nurse Corps conducted interviews with thirty former army nurse POW's and one former navy nurse POW as part of the Army Nurse Corps Oral History Program. Transcripts and audiotapes are on file at the Department of the Army, Center for Military History, Washington, D.C. References to information taken from these interviews abbreviated "1983 ANC interview."
5. Ruby Bradley, 1989 author interview. She unsuccessfully tried to locate the Dudleys after the war.
6. A lone radar technician at Iba Field, forty miles west of Clark Field and Fort Stotsenberg Hospital, saw dozens of blips on his screen. His radar was the only working unit in the islands. The planes were flying toward Clark, while the men and women were eating lunch at the officers club, the hospital or the nurses quarters. The Army Air Corps pilots planned to fly a mission that afternoon. Wainwright, J. M., pp. 20–23.
7. In August 1944, Cassie wrote an essay about her experiences on December 8, 1941, which she called "The Uncertain." Used with permission. This essay and notes she made about December 8 form the basis of this section.
8. Information about Helen "Cassie" Cassiani from a series of interviews with the author from 1990–97.
9. Ruth Straub. Straub's diary was serialized in seven installments from September 21 through September 30, 1942. All entries in this chapter from the September 21, 1942, installment, p. 1; 10.

Chapter Two: Manila Cannot Hold

1. Margaret Nash, 1991 telephone interview with author.

2. Cooper, W. E., pp. 47–53.

3. Ruth Straub diary.

4. Helen Cassiani Nestor, 1992 author interview. Quotations from this interview form the basis of this section.

5. Helen Cassiani, typed commendation. Used with permission. After the war someone told Cassie that she qualified for a Silver Star. She never received this medal or any additional recognition for her actions on December 24, 1941.

6. Beck, J. J., pp. 35–36.

7. Ullom, M., p. 22.

8. *Ibid.*

9. Williams, D., p. 6.

10. This menu with an accompanying poem was given to the military nurses working at Annex G, the Holy Ghost Convent and College at East Mendiola Street. Used with permission, Red Harrington Nelson.

11. Nesbit, J., p. 47. American nurses serving on Guam, Pearl Harbor, Hawaii and the Philippine Islands had been under fire since early December 1941 but the Philippine group was the first in the war to travel and set up hospitals in a combat area.

12. Ullom, p. 32.

13. Nesbit, p. 15.

In Josie Nesbit's 1945 unpublished report, she gives no hint of a deliberate plan to abandon the navy nurses. She never even mentions the navy group when she reports the details of the army nurses' evacuation from Manila, pp. 16–19.

In his 1946 official report, Colonel Wibb Cooper wrote, "The [navy] medical and nursing staff were merged with the Sternberg staff and assigned to appropriate duties" (p. 50). He does not say why the navy nurses and doctors were left behind.

14. As recollected in Red Harrington Nelson's 1989 author interview.

15. Information about Red Harrington Nelson from a 1983 ANC interview, 1989 author interview, Sharon Eifried interviews 1990–91. Although Harrington Nelson is a former navy nurse, she participated in the Army Nurse Corps Oral History Program. Also see Rudin, E., pp. 15–20.

16. "Army, Navy leave City," p. 1.

17. "Messages on Philippines," p. 1.

18. Mary Rose Harrington Nelson, 1989 author interview.

19. *Wartime translations of seized Japanese documents.* File 10-R-744.

20. "Missing in action," p. 183.

Chapter Three: Jungle Hospital #1

1. Whitman, J., p. 11.

2. *Ibid.*

3. Estimates of the numbers of refugees on Bataan vary from fourteen thousand to thirty thousand people. This estimate from the *Quartermaster Diary on Corregidor,*

8 December 1941 to 12 March 1942. The kilometer posts used on Bataan measured the distances from Manila.

4. Gastinger quoted in Knox, D., p. 35.

5. Scholl, D., Section C, C1; 3.

6. Helen Cassiani Nestor, 1990 author interview.

7. Duckworth, James, p. 9.

8. Second Lieutenant Alexander Nininger Jr. became the first World War II Congressional Medal of Honor recipient for his actions during this battle. *Newsweek, 19,* 22, Feb 9, 1942.

9. The Trendelenberg Position, as this angle was called, was the standard treatment for hemorrhagic shock. Researchers later discovered this position increased pressure on the brain and diaphragm and recommended it not be used in anyone suspected of head and chest injury.

10. Weinstein, A., pp. 20–21. Dr. Weinstein was a surgeon with Hospital #1.

11. Helen Cassiani (no date). Handwritten notes written during the war. Used with permission.

12. "By command of General MacArthur: Carl H. Seals, Colonel, A.G.D., Adjutant General" was written under MacArthur's name. From Seals, C. H.

13. Beck, pp. 61–62.

14. Beck, pp. 71–72.

Chapter Four: The Sick, the Wounded, the Work of War

1. Sally Blaine Millett, 1990 author interview.

2. H. C. Michie, Commander, Medical Corps. Hospital Memorandum #16, dated March 16, 1961, Camp Livingston, Louisiana. Garen files.

3. Sally Blaine Millett, 1990 author interview; Clara Mae Bickford wrote her recollections about the first days on Bataan in Shacklette Haynes's diary, p. 7. Used with permission.

4. *Unit History and Personnel Rosters of General Hospital No. 2, December 41 to June 42.* Author and date unknown, p. 2.

5. Sally Blaine Millett, 1990 author interview.

6. Mr. Calimbas, a local banana and coconut farmer who was loyal to the Americans, put together the carpentry crew.

7. Sally Blaine Millett, 1990 author interview.

8. When numbering the wards, the staff skipped the number thirteen.

9. *Unusual incidents at Hospital #2,* p. 1. From the command details and comments about the setting up of the facility, Major Jack Schwartz MC, who arrived with the first group from Sternberg on December 27 and who kept a roster of American nurses, officers and Philippine Army officers at Hospital #2 (RG 407, Box #4), was likely the author of this file.

10. Josie Nesbit Davis, 1983 ANC interview.

11. Josie Nesbit Davis, 1983 correspondence with Miss Dorothy Starbuck, Veterans Administration. Used with permission of Miss Starbuck.

12. Biographical information on Josie Nesbit from a letter she wrote to a Colonel

Nichols dated February 21, 1980. In 1993, this letter was uncataloged at the Center for Military History, Washington, D.C.

13. Josie Nesbit Davis, 1983 letter to Dorothy Starbuck.

14. The *Unit History* lists two different census numbers for late January. On page 12, the number given for January 25 is 2,160 patients. On page 19, for January 24 the census was reported as 1,205. The author used the higher number because Josie Nesbit's 1945 manuscript lists 2,000 patients in the hospital on February 6, 1942, p. 26.

15. Twenty-two American dentists, doctors and medical administrators came to Hospital #2 in January 1942. Seventeen Filipino doctors and one dentist also served at the hospital but the dates of their arrival are not known, *Unit History*, pp. 56–57. A total of 250 American enlisted men also served at Hospital #2. Their arrival and departure dates are unknown, *Unit History*, p. 19.

16. In 1940, Jimmie Davis composed "You Are My Sunshine."

17. *Unit History of Hospital #2*, p. 26.

Chapter Five: Waiting for the Help That Never Came

1. Harrison, G., p. 10.

2. Cooper, p. 35.

3. Nesbit, p. 28.

4. Bumgarner, J., p. 69.

5. Cooper, p. 35.

6. Cooper, p. 84.

7. Mr. Hewlett's poem is published in many primary and secondary sources. This version is from Wainwright, p. 54.

8. Redmond, p. 101; Williams, p. 61.

Although the women were later called the "Angels of Bataan," a literature search revealed that the term did not appear in print until 1945. Several of the women told the author they remembered General Wainwright and other men calling them "angels" on Bataan.

9. *Bacillus Welchii* is an obsolete term that was used during World War II to describe the gas gangrene bacteria. The causative agent is *Clostridium perfringens*, a member of the *Clostridium Bacillaceae* family. McCance, K., and Huether, S., p. 72.

10. Redmond, p. 56.

11. The surgeon who developed the new treatment for gas gangrene was Colonel Frank Adamo. "Jungle hospital," p. 58.

12. *Ibid.*

13. *Ibid.*

14. "Nurse on Corregidor finds it 'not too bad,' " p. 3.

15. Ruth Straub (September 23, 1942), p. 1; 5.

16. Nesbit, p. 29.

17. Redmond, p. 56.

18. "Jungle Journal," February 25, 1942. Miss Catherine Nau, Managing Editor. Army Nurse Corps Archives, Center for Military History, Washington, D.C. Uncataloged mimeographed file.

19. The first U.S. convoy of troops arrived in Northern Ireland on January 26, 1942. Army nurse Leona Gastinger Sutphin was quoted in D. Knox, "Everybody felt worst when we heard on the radio that a convoy of our troops had gone to Ireland instead of coming to us" (p. 86). Another army nurse supports this claim, but why government censors allowed this information to be broadcast is a puzzle.

20. Helen Cassiani Nestor, 1990 author interview.

21. *Ibid.*

22. Redmond, p. 79.

23. Weinstein, p. 30.

24. Engel, D. Davis, pp. 26–27; 112–16. In an October 1997 telephone interview, Dorothea Engel said that Lieutenant Emmanuel "Boots" Engel Jr. was captured by the Japanese and spent almost three years as a POW in the Philippines. He died in late 1944 on an enemy transport ship that was heading toward Japan when it was mistakenly sunk by an American submarine. According to Mrs. Engel, seven Americans survived the sinking to tell this story and list some of the dead POW's. Dorothea Engel never remarried. At the war's end in 1945, she "kept searching the newspapers for lists of survivors," but did not see her husband's name. "Gradually I came to see that he was never coming home," she recalled. Mrs. Engel remained in the army until 1947, serving a tour in Germany with the occupation forces. She eventually settled in her Midwestern hometown and worked at various nursing positions until her retirement in 1987. In the fall of 1997, Mrs. Engel was eighty-one years old and living alone.

25. Bumgarner, pp. 72–73.

26. Army nurse Blanche Kimball wrote the slogan in Eleanor Garen's spiral notebook titled "Nurses addresses, July 1942." Garen files.

27. From a handwritten, undated note Cassie wrote in Santo Tomas Internment Camp. Private collection. Used with permission.

28. Helen Summers's song was handwritten in Inez McDonald's diary, located in the archives at the U.S. Army Medical Museum, Fort Sam Houston, San Antonio, Texas. McDonald's diary had many pages ripped out; only songs, poetry and a few pages of dates remained in the back of the book.

29. Ruth Straub (September 24, 1942), pp. 1; 7; and (September 25, 1942), *The Pittsburgh Post-Gazette*, pp. 1; 9.

Chapter Six: "There Must Be No Thought of Surrender"

1. Eleanor Garen personal communication, February 7, 1942. Eleanor most likely got her letter off Bataan in one of the few remaining planes that allied pilots flew to Cebú for supplies. Garen files.

2. Eleanor Garen's 1941 letters to her mother in the Garen files.

3. *Wartime translations of seized Japanese documents*, File 40-B-17.

4. *Quartermaster Diary on Corregidor, 8 December 1941 to 12 March 1942,* March 3, 1941, entry.

5. "Battered Bataan," p. 17; "Still holding," p. 17; Bulosan, C., p. 20.

6. Sutherland, R. Typed message to Bataan troops. National Archives, Philippine Archive Collection, Washington, D.C. RG 407, Box 10.

7. Josie Nesbit Davis, 1983 ANC interview.

8. "MacArthur in Australia," p. 1.

9. Ann Mealor Giles, 1983 ANC interview.

10. The lyrics to "Dugout Doug" appear in many books including Karnow, p. 298, and Toland, p. 280.

11. Wainwright, J. Typed message to Bataan troops. National Archives, Philippine Archive Collection, Washington, D.C., RG 407, Box 10.

12. Carroll, G., p. 83.

13. Baldwin, H. W., p. 5.

14. Gray, J. Glenn, p. 122.

15. Shacklette quoted in Redmond, p. 100.

16. Josie Davis Nesbit, 1983 ANC interview.

17. Helen Cassiani Nestor, 1990 author interview.

18. Sally Blaine Millett, 1990 author interview.

19. Ruth Straub (September 26, 1942), pp. 1; 4.

20. The song was handwritten in Inez McDonald's diary, located in the archives at the U.S. Army Medical Museum, Fort Sam Houston, San Antonio, Texas. Used with permission of Mrs. Kennedy Schmidt.

21. In his June 21, 1945, War Department interview with a Judge Advocate Department agent, Duckworth said, "In my opinion it [the bombing] was not deliberate. I base that on two reasons, first that they had such ample opportunity to bomb us and had never done so. They knew they were winning and there was no reason for them to get angry. . . . Secondly I heard they were using inexperienced flyers and it is my opinion that it was just poor bombing on their part. When I was showing a Japanese general through the hospital after surrender he expressed his disapproval by gestures not words. He pointed to the holes and shook his head and gestured that it was too bad. All the bombings were either at the first or tag ending of a run." Transcript, Supreme Command for the Allied Forces in the Pacific (SCAP) collection, National Archives, Suitland, Maryland, pp. 3; 6.

22. Wainwright, p. 72.

23. Redmond, pp. 97–99.

24. Wainwright, p. 79.

25. Ruth Straub (September 28, 1942), p. 2.

Chapter Seven: Bataan Falls: The Wounded Are Left in Their Beds

1. Harries, M., and Harries, S., pp. 223–24.

2. *Ibid.*

3. Harries, p. 479.

4. Wainwright, pp. 78–80.

5. *Ibid.*

6. *Ibid.*

7. *Ibid.*

8. *Ibid.*

9. Helen Cassiani Nestor, 1990 author interview.

10. Edith Shacklette Haynes, 1983 ANC interview.

11. *Ibid.*

12. Weinstein, p. 49.

13. Redmond, p. 122.

14. Geneva Jenkins, 1983 ANC interview.

15. Josie Nesbit Davis, 1983 ANC interview.

16. *Ibid.*

17. Sally Blaine Millett, 1990 author interview.

18. Anna Williams Clark, 1983 ANC interview.

19. Lucy Wilson Jopling, 1990 author interview.

20. Minnie Breese Stubbs, 1983 ANC interview.

21. Redmond, pp. 123–25.

22. Keith, B., pp. 53–55. Chaplain Preston Taylor later became a major general in the U.S. Air Force.

23. *Ibid.*

24. In July 1944, Helen Cassiani wrote an essay called "Variation on an Evacuation." Quotations from this unpaginated essay. Used with permission.

25. Sally Blaine Millett, 1990 author interview.

26. Minnie Breese Stubbs, 1983 ANC interview.

27. Sally Blaine Millett, 1990 author interview.

28. Ruth Straub (September 28, 1942), p. 2.

29. Earlier, Josie Nesbit had left the docks with a sergeant to find a telephone to call Corregidor for help. Some sources state that Josie went back to Little Baguio but she does not specify where she went. They found the lines to Corregidor cut. An officer told her to go back to the pier and wait. "They'll be back," she remembered him saying. Before she left, he invited her and the sergeant to breakfast. They gobbled down eggs and food the men wanted consumed before the enemy got them. Then, Josie returned to the pier with her staff to wait. Josie Nesbit Davis, 1983 ANC interview.

30. Anna Williams Clark, 1983 ANC interview.

31. Williams, p. 82.

32. Gastinger quoted in Knox, D., p. 104.

33. Wainwright, p. 81. He incorrectly included the two wounded women, Rita Palmer and Rosemary Hogan, in his description. These two had arrived on Corregidor before the evacuation of the nurses.

34. Wainwright, pp. 84–85.

35. *Ibid.*

36. The speech written by Captain Salvador Lopez had been widely reproduced including Ullom, p. 75.

37. Historians agree there are no definitive mortality and morbidity statistics for the Death March or the years the Bataan veterans spent as POW's. The numbers and details used are from: Ashton, P., p. 165; Falk, S., p. 150; Kerr, E., p. 60.

38. Weinstein, p. 49.

39. Report no. 209, General Headquarters, United States Army Forces, Pacific. War Crimes Branch. National Archives, Suitland, Maryland. SCAP Collection, RG 331, Box 1118.

40. Information on Mrs. Mercado's rape taken from several war crimes testimonies on file at the National Archives, Suitland, Maryland. SCAP Collection. RG 331. Testimony from Ethyle Mae Taft Mercado, Major Herman Archer and Sergeant Norman Miller, patients in Hospital #2; and an unnamed testimony witnessed by Captain Carl Twitchell on June 25, 1945.

Mrs. Mercado survived the war and returned to the United States. Intelligence agents analyzed her testimony and wrote: "There is evidence that an American . . . named Mrs. Mercado was raped by Japanese but the evidence, much of which is hearsay, is very general and fails to identify the perpetrators. In view of these facts it is not believed that prosecution for this offense is justified." Page 3, Report No. 209, SCAP Collection, RG 331.

41. Duckworth, James, p. 26.

Chapter Eight: Corregidor—the Last Stand

1. Ullom, p. 44.

2. Information on Maude Davison from: Comeau, Genevieve K., (1961); *Davison, Maude C. Major ANC N700 404;* and Davison personnel file, obtained from the National Personnel Records Center, St. Louis, Missouri, under the Freedom of Information Act; and a 1993 interview with her stepson, Robert Jackson.

3. The term "Guam blisters" appears in Gwendolyn Henshaw Deiss's, Sallie Durrett Farmer's and Earlyn Black Harding's 1983 ANC interviews.

4. Russell, M., p. 28.

5. Hattie Brantley, 1983 ANC interview.

6. Ruth Straub (September 29, 1942), p. 2.

7. *Ibid.*

8. Guerrero, L., pp. 9–12. After conquering the islands, the Japanese published the *Philippine Review* as a literary propaganda journal. Its purpose was to persuade Filipino intellectuals to join the Japanese in forging a new government. The May 1943 issue was devoted to young men and women. "No one of its contributors is over 50, most of them are below 45. . . . You have been promised a down-to-earth issue and here you have it—in young, vigorous, multiloqeunt language" (p. 1). The journal was published from March 1943 through December 1944. Steinberg, D. (1967), and Dr. David Steinberg, October 1997 personal communication. L. Morton (1962) erroneously attributes "Last Days of Corregidor" to Mrs. Maude Williams, a civilian nurse-anesthetist who worked with the army nurses. Apparently Mrs. Williams copied Guerrero's essay into her diary without attribution. Duplicates of this essay also were found with Inez McDonald's memorabilia at the U.S. Army Medical Museum, Fort Sam Houston, San Antonio, Texas, and in Eleanor Garen's notebook, Garen files. It is the only collaborator's work found in the nurses' diaries. One possible explanation of why they included the essay in their personal notes may be that they found the piece accurately reflected their Corregidor experience.

9. Ruth Straub (September 29, 1942), p. 2.

10. Wainwright, p. 102.

11. Wainwright, p. 101. There is no mention in either Colonel Cooper's 1946 report or Maude Davison's records about the specific criteria used to choose the evacuees. The official story behind the list of names remains a mystery. What information exists was culled from the 1983 ANC interviews and 1989 through 1997 author interviews with army nurses who were stationed on Corregidor at that time.

12. Ann Mealor Giles, 1983 ANC interview.

13. A copy of Order No. 28, signed by Brigadier General Carl H. Seals, adjutant general with General Wainwright, was given to the author by Sally Blaine Millett.

14. Ullom, M., p. 7.

15. Eunice Hatchitt Tyler, 1990 author interview. Clara Mae Bickford Bilello died May 19, 1978. Mrs. Tyler said Bickie later told her, "I hated you that night."

16. Williams, p. 92.

17. Helen Cassiani Nestor, 1990 author interview.

18. Redmond, p. 150.

19. Josie Nesbit Davis, 1983 ANC interview.

20. Ann Wurts's story was published in Nesbit, p. 32, and Williams, pp. 93–94. According to Nesbit, "The name she [Wurts] suggested was not among the twenty who left" (p. 32).

21. Wainwright, p. 102.

22. This phrase appears in many references, including Rumolo, p. 306.

23. Anna Williams Clark, 1983 ANC interview.

24. Ruth Straub (September 29, 1942), p. 2.

25. *USS Spearfish Special Mission,* June 3, 1942, entry.

26. Dietitian Ruby Motley Armburst was interviewed in 1984 by Lieutenant Colonel Martha Cronin, USA. A transcript is located at Carlisle Barracks, Pennsylvania, under the title "Army Medical Specialist Corps POWs of the Japanese."

27. Ann Mealor Giles, 1983 ANC interview. Mrs. Giles never received a medal or commendation for her decision.

28. Wainwright, p. 109. Wainwright misspells her name as "Mieler."

29. Ruth Straub (September 30, 1942), p. 2.

30. Eleanor Garen personal correspondence, May 3, 1942. Garen files.

31. Ruth Straub (September 30, 1942), p. 2.

32. Among the fifty-four army nurses was Mary Brown Menzie, who joined the ANC in December 1942. And, there were two army nurses, Ruby Bradley and Beatrice Chambers, imprisoned in the northern Luzon town of Baguio. Twenty army nurses left Corregidor on two PBY's, eleven on the submarine and one had evacuated Manila on a hospital ship in January 1942.

Chapter Nine: A Handful Go Home

1. Sally Blaine recalls the aircraft were called the "Lead PBY" and the "Wing PBY." Lieutenant Pollock piloted the Lead PBY, which was damaged on Mindanao. Lieutenant Leroy Deede piloted the Wing PBY, which safely lifted off Lake Lanao and

landed in Australia. The ten army nurses on the damaged seaplane were: Earleen Allen, Louise Anschicks, Agnes Barre, Ethel "Sally" Blaine, Helen Gardner, Rosemary Hogan, Geneva Jenkins, Eleanor O'Neill, Rita Palmer and Evelyn Whitlow.

2. In 1991, Sally Blaine Millett, one of the nurses who was stranded on Mindanao, wrote a twenty-one-page paper detailing the ordeals of her group. According to her recollections, Rosemary Hogan removed her white terry-cloth jacket and tried to plug the hole in the fuselage. The water was soon ankle deep in the cabin. After quickly exiting the PBY and leaving their luggage behind, the group traveled to a hotel in Donsalan (now Malawi City). Colonel Stewart Wood, a Japanese-speaking assistant chief of staff to General Jonathan Wainwright, was also stranded. As senior officer, Wood took command of the nurses. He told the women that he believed the plane was unsafe to carry all of them. He wanted the group to stay together and find a place to hide until MacArthur could send another rescue plane. Everyone agreed with his assessment and plan.

3. Sally Blaine Millett never heard any criticism of the PBY crew for leaving Lake Lanao without them. The ten army nurses, three civilian women, a naval officer and Colonel Wood began an unsuccessful twelve-day odyssey traveling around Mindanao looking for a safe haven. The group surrendered on twelve noon, May 11, 1942. The nurses spent over three months interned in a hospital on Mindanao. On August 26, 1942, the Japanese moved them to a coastal town where they were confined with one hundred captured missionaries. On September 5, the women boarded a prison ship for a trip to Manila. Their Japanese captors had told them they were going to be repatriated. Instead, the group ended up imprisoned in Santo Tomas Internment Camp in Manila. Colonel Wood and the naval officer went to the Tarlac prisoner of war camp on Luzon with other high-ranking American officers. Colonel Wood survived the war.

4. *Reminiscences of Admiral Stuart S. (Sunshine) Murray, U.S. Navy (ret.), Volume 1* (no date), pp. 293–95. The ten army nurses who were passengers on the PBY plane that successfully landed in Australia were: Catherine Acorn, Dorothea Daley, Susan Downing Gallagher, Eunice Hatchitt, Willa Hook, Ressa Jenkins, Harriet Lee, Mary Lohr, Florence MacDonald and Juanita Redmond.

5. Redmond, pp. 160–61.

6. *Ibid.*

7. "Army nurses from the Philippines now in Australia," p. 820.

8. "News for nurses," p. 449.

9. Eunice Hatchitt Tyler, 1990 author interview.

10. Redmond, pp. 165–66.

11. Eunice Hatchitt Tyler, 1990 author interview.

12. Sue Gallagher to Mrs. Whitwell, dated June 19, 1942. Leona Gastinger to Mrs. Whitwell, dated November 9, 1942. Garen files.

13. Juanita Redmond to Mrs. Gates (no date). Ruth Straub to Mrs. Gates, dated August 15, 1942. The State Historical Society of Wisconsin, Madison, Wisconsin. Uncataloged scrapbooks of "Marcia Gates, Army Nurse Corps."

14. *Allied Naval Forces Based Western Australia. USS Spearfish Special Mission. Serial SA-115. 3 June 1942.* The eleven army nurses who left on the submarine were:

Leona Gastinger, Nancy Gillahan, Grace Hallman, Hortense McKay, Mary Moultrie, Mollie Peterson, Mabel Stevens, Ruth Straub, Helen Summers, Beth Veley and Lucy Wilson. The navy nurse was Ann Bernatitus.

15. Lucy Wilson Jopling, 1990 author interview.

16. Wilson Jopling, p. 50.

17. Parker, p. 719.

18. Both "poems" from Wilson Jopling, pp. 54–55.

19. Flikke, J., p. 192.

20. Eunice Hatchitt Tyler, 1991 author interview.

21. *Captain Ann Bernatitus, Nurse Corps, United States Navy, Retired,* p. 2.

22. White, W. L.

23. Redmond, J.

24. Valentine, E. R., p. 53.

25. *Cry Havoc,* MGM film, November 1943. Director, Richard Thorpe. Screenplay, Paul Osborne. Adapted from a play by Allan Kenward called *Proof Through the Night.*

26. *Since You Went Away,* United Artists film, July 1944. Director, John Cromwell. Screenplay, David O. Selznick.

27. *They Were Expendable,* MGM film, December 1945. Director, John Ford. Screenplay, Lieutenant Commander Frank Wead. Adapted from W. L. White's 1942 book with the same title.

28. *So Proudly We Hail,* Paramount film, June 1943. Director, Mark Sandrich. Screenplay, Allan Scott.

29. For a more detailed discussion about the making of this file see Baker, M. J., pp. 111–25.

30. Eunice Hatchitt Tyler, 1990 author interview.

31. In a September 1990 interview in her home, Mrs. Eunice Hatchitt Tyler told the author that after many years of letters, telephone calls and gatherings, the women finally accepted the fact that the misrepresentations in the movie were not of her making and were certainly beyond her control.

Chapter Ten: In Enemy Hands

1. Wainwright, p. 119.

2. Alice Hahn Powers, 1983 ANC interview.

3. On December 8, 1941, shortly after the Pearl Harbor attack, the Japanese assaulted the tiny Pacific island of Guam. At the end of the three-day battle, the captured American forces included five navy nurses. Chief Nurse Marion Olds and her staff, Doris Yetter, Leona Jackson, Lorraine Christiansen and Virginia Fogerty, spent one month as prisoners on Guam. In early January these POWs sailed for Shikoku, Japan, and prison camp. The women transferred to a detention house in Kobe. They returned home as part of a prisoner exchange in August 1942.

4. Hattie Brantley, 1983 ANC interview.

5. Inez McDonald Moore, 1983 ANC interview.

6. Mitchum, J., p. 32.

7. Bertha Dworsky Henderson, 1983 ANC interview.

8. Garen, E., the South Bend *Tribune*. Eleanor gave Susan Sacharski this article with no date or pagination.

9. Wainwright, pp. 122–23. Initially, General Wainwright wanted to surrender only the Luzon force and allow the troops under General Sharp in the southern Visayan and Mindanao islands to continue to fight. General Homma insisted the general surrender all forces. If he did not, General Homma promised he would continue to assault Corregidor. General Wainwright knew a massacre could occur. He signed the unconditional surrender of all Philippine forces at midnight.

10. This cloth is located in Inez McDonald Moore's files at the Fort Sam Houston Medical Museum archives, San Antonio, Texas.

11. Helen Cassiani Nestor, 1990 author interview.

12. Josie Nesbit Davis, 1983 ANC interview.

13. Jeanne Kennedy Schmidt, 1992 correspondence with author.

14. Madeline Ullom, 1983 ANC interview. The one existing photograph from this session does not include Ullom. She may have been present in other photographs, now missing or destroyed.

15. *Experiences of Major S. M. Mellnick from the Fall of Corregidor, May 6, 1942 to escape from a Japanese Prison Camp. Report No. 189.* (no date), pp. 1–2.

16. *Ibid.*

17. Sallie Durrett Farmer, 1983 ANC interview.

18. Eleanor Garen, 1991 interview with Susan Sacharski.

19. Ann Mealor Giles, 1983 ANC interview.

20. Helen Cassiani Nestor, 1990 author interview.

21. The "slapped" nurse was Marcia Gates. In her war crimes testimony, August 15, 1945, she stated, "I was talking to an officer and one of the Japanese officers in charge of the tunnel on Corregidor slapped me in the face." Mrs. Wingate, a civilian woman on Corregidor, was hit with the flat side of a soldier's bayonet. Army nurses Adolpha Meyer and Anna Williams witnessed this incident and provided war crimes prosecutors with details. National Archives, Suitland, Maryland. SCAP Collection, 1945, RG 153, transcripts.

22. Mary B. Menzie, Affadavit, April 1945, War Crimes Testimony, SCAP Collection, RG 153. Information on this incident also found in: Report 189, Case summary of attempted criminal assault on 1st Lieut. Mary B. Menzie, SCAP Collection, RG 153, Box 1125; and United States War Crimes Commission report February 12, 1946, SCAP Collection, RG 153, Case 40–155. Mrs. Menzie received a Purple Heart after the war for the injury to her wrist. Army nurse Beulah Putnam was the woman with her when the incident occurred. She provided war crimes testimony about the attempted assault. Maude Davison was skeptical about the occurrence. She said her "wrist looked as if it had been scratched, not cut." National Archives, Suitland, Maryland, SCAP Collection, RG 153.

23. Ann Mealor Giles, 1983 ANC interview.

24. Cassie's 1944 essay about the monkey provided the details used in this section. Rita Palmer and Eleanor Garen also mentioned the animal in various interviews.

25. Cooper, pp. 13–14.

26. Anna Williams Clark, 1983 ANC interview.

27. Madeline Ullom, 1983 ANC interview.

28. *Ibid.*

29. According to Nesbit, the Filipino nurses who had been with the army nurses were put on a truck and taken to Bilibid Prison with the men. The Filipino nurses remained in Bilibid from July 3, 1942, until July 22. The Japanese released the women after forcing them to sign loyalty papers. Two Filipinos, Maureen Davis and Betty Brian, were sent to the prison that held the American nurses because they were wives of American soldiers. Colonel Wibb Cooper spent one week at Bilibid Prison before being sent to the Tarlac POW camp to join General Wainwright and other high-ranking American officers. After a month in Tarlac, Cooper, Wainwright and others were sent to a POW camp in Formosa. Colonel Cooper felt that the Japanese wanted to separate the senior officers from the lower ranks. Colonel Cooper survived the war. In his 1945 report, he wrote, "Never in the history of war has medical personnel been called upon to perform their duties under such arduous circumstances and over such a long period. . . . It is with pardonable pride that I recall the supreme effort put forth by all the Medical Department personnel . . . in the years to come this group . . . can look back with great comfort and pride to the part they played during this grim period while upholding the finest traditions of the Medical Department, United States Army" (p. 149).

30. Madeline Ullom, 1983 ANC interview.

Chapter Eleven: Santo Tomas

1. Description of Santo Tomas Internment Camp from Hartendorp, A. V., pp. 33–35; McCall, J., plate XV; Stevens, F. H., pp. 12–78 (1946).

2. In November 1997, architect Andrew Attinson shared his thoughts and analysis of the Santo Tomas Main Building with the author.

3. Hartendorp, pp. 42–43.

4. The Ten Commandments of STIC (Stevens, pp. 169–70):

I. Thou shalt have no other interest greater than the welfare of the Camp.

II. Thou shall not adopt for thyself, or condone in others, any merely selfish rule of conduct, or indulge in any practice that injures the morale of the Camp. Thou shall not violate the procedures agreed upon by the authorities or by the majority, for punishment can surely be visited upon all—innocent and guilty alike—because of the misdeeds of a few.

III. Thou shall not betray the ideals and principles which thou wast taught, so that in the future thou wilt not be condemned for neglecting [thy] heritage.

IV. Remember the work of the Camp, to do thy share. Six days shalt thou labor and do all thy work assignments, and also, as on thy rest day, refresh thy mind and heart with worship. For thy work will be satisfying and effective only when it is done in the right spirit.

V. Honor thy forefathers by recalling vividly their struggle for better things, that thou mayest contribute now and in the days to come to the realization of their ideals.

VI. Thou shall not hinder the best development of the youth of the Camp.

VII. Thou shall not break down family relationships.

VIII. Thou shall not steal.

IX. Thou shall not injure thy neighbor's reputation by malicious gossip.

X. Thou shall not covet thy neighbor's shanty or his room space. Thou shall not covet thy neighbor's wife, nor his fiancée, nor his influential position, nor anything that is thy neighbor's.

5. Williams, pp. 123–24.

6. Peggy Greenwalt Walcher, May 1992 telephone interview with author. Peggy gave the 12th Regimental flag to the Quartermaster Museum in Fort Lee, Virginia.

7. Hattie Brantley, 1983 ANC interview.

8. Nesbit, p. 38. Ida Haentsche Hube was a contract nurse with the American army in 1898 during yellow fever and typhoid epidemics. In 1906, she signed with the newly formed U.S. Army Nurse Corps and served honorably until 1910. Mrs. Hube became the target of a G-2 investigation after the war. Government agents tried to determine why the Japanese had allowed her to remain free and living in the Manila Hotel, which became a Japanese officers' residence and club. They explored rumors that Mrs. Hube had helped German nursing sisters and Japanese nurses in Manila during the war and that she had spoken admiringly of Hitler's beliefs. In 1946, she attempted unsuccessfully to return to Switzerland, and an ANC public relations officer wrote, "Meanwhile she, [Mrs. Hube] hopes for the help of various nursing celebrities who have known her in the past." Mrs. Hube died in Manila in 1946 or 1947. Source: Louise Anschicks scrapbooks, Fort Sam Houston Medical Museum archives, San Antonio, Texas. "The mysterious nurse of Manila," RN Magazine.

9. Nesbit, p. 42.

10. Ibid.

11. Josie Nesbit Davis, January 15, 1983, letter to Miss Dorothy Starbuck, Veterans Administration, p. 4. Used with permission of Miss Starbuck.

12. Mr. R. Fitzsimmons, a Spanish-American War veteran and Manila shipping executive, offered the women interest-free loans. Five army nurses got together and borrowed several hundred dollars. The elderly gentleman asked them to promise to pay him back after the war, or to pay his estate if he did not survive. Earl Carroll, an executive with General Electric and a member of the Executive Committee, was another source of loans. Garen files.

Chapter Twelve: STIC, the First Year, 1942

1. Helen Cassiani Nestor, 1991 author interview. Quotations and information about Cassie in STIC come from a series of six interviews conducted by the author from 1990 through 1995.

2. Helen Cassiani Nestor loaned the author her notebooks from the classes she took in STIC. Quotations from class on "Interpretation of music, psychological and sociological," July 15, 1943.

3. Mimeographed baseball booklet titled "Baseball Program and Schedule, Baseball Committee Carroll Livingston–John McFie–Fred Sanger–Walter Schoening. Price

Twenty Centavos." The four women's teams were: the Manila Ladies, STIC Nurses, Hospital Kitchen and Bureau of Education. Helen Cassiani Nestor's private collection. Used with permission.

4. Terry Myers Johnson, July 1992 telephone interview. The author interviewed Helen Cassiani Nestor and Terry Myers Johnson in September 1993. All quotations from those interviews, unless otherwise noted.

5. In 1941, Mack Gordon wrote "Chattanooga Choo-Choo" with music by Harry Warren. It became a best-selling song for the Glenn Miller Orchestra.

6. Sommers, S. (ed.), *The Japanese Story*, p. 14.

7. Among others, navy nurse Red Harrington also took part in the underground. Before the war she had befriended a navy physician, Cecil "Cec" Welch, a fellow South Dakotan and a man who shared her impious sense of humor. The two often spent evenings drinking beer and eating green onion seeds at the Nutshell Bar outside Cavite Navy Yard. When the navy abandoned the bombed-out Cavite base in December 1941, Red and Cec found themselves in Manila and, after the enemy occupied the city on January 2, 1942, they ended up together again, working at Saint Scholastica Hospital under Japanese orders until March, when Red and the other navy nurses were sent to Santo Tomas and Cec and the other doctors and corpsmen were locked up in Bilibid Prison. Red and Cec kept in touch through the underground. Using tiny scraps of paper that could be swallowed if they were discovered, the two traded news and words of support.

8. Cassie's creative writing essay titled "The Uncertain," dated August 1, 1944.

9. Alice Hahn Powers, 1983 ANC interview.

10. Sallie Durrett Farmer, (no date) ANC interview.

11. Hattie Brantley, 1983 ANC interview.

12. Anna Williams Clark, 1983 ANC interview.

13. Bertha Dworsky Henderson, 1983 ANC interview.

14. Rose Rieper Meier, 1984 ANC interview. Mrs. Meier was interviewed in her Kansas home after the 1983 Washington, D.C., reunion when the other former POW's were interviewed. Her transcript is located in the Army Nurse Corps archive.

15. Anna Williams Clark, 1983 ANC interview.

16. Nash, Frances, p. 2.

17. Ann Mealor Giles, 1983 ANC interview.

18. Young, E. F., p. 92.

19. Helen Cassiani Nestor, 1983 ANC interview.

20. Earlyn Black Harding, 1983 ANC interview.

21. Ruby Motley Armburst was an army dietitian who lived and worked with the military nurses.

22. Eunice Young, 1983 ANC interview.

23. Gwendolyn Henshaw Deiss, 1983 ANC interview.

24. Young, E. F., p. 89.

25. Alice Hahn Powers, 1983 ANC interview.

26. Inez McDonald Moore, 1983 ANC interview.

Chapter Thirteen: Los Banos, 1943

1. *Talinum* is a spinachlike vegetable popular in the Philippines.

2. Hartendorp, p. 108.

3. Young, E. F., p. 90.

4. Stevens, p. 406.

5. Mary Rose Harrington Nelson, 1989 author interview. According to Hartendorp, pp. 151–53, Dr. Leach wrote a letter to the head of the internee Executive Committee stating he needed a "military order" to go to Los Banos. The STIC commandant sent him a letter stating, "You are requested to proceed." In May 1943, he was repatriated in a prisoner exchange. Dr. Dana Nance from the Baguio Internment Camp replaced him as medical director at Los Banos.

6. Mary Rose Harrington Nelson, 1989 author interview. Mrs. Nelson told the same story in her 1983 ANC Oral History interview.

7. Description of Los Banos from: Valentine, C., pp. 66–68; Investigation of Case B-89, Los Banos Internment Camp, Los Banos, Laguna, Philippines, National Archives, Suitland, Maryland. SCAP Collection, Box 1123, Report 155; Reuter, J., pp. 159–63.

8. Foot baths became a vital ritual since rampant fungus infections developed almost immediately in men who walked barefoot in the warm, humid climate. At first, the nurses treated the infection with potassium permangnate, a purple-colored antiseptic. When those supplies became exhausted, they used boric acid soaks, a mild antiseptic solution, and finally plain warm water baths and hot sun. If an infection became particularly painful, the nurses applied a mixture of alcohol, bichloride of mercury and salicylic acid.

9. Information about Miss Laura Cobb obtained from the National Personnel Records Center, St. Louis, Missouri, under the Freedom of Information Act. Her personnel records report two different birthdates, 1892 and 1896. The earlier date is closer to the age listed during her internment. Three navy nurses, Margaret Nash, Mary Rose Harrington and Dorothy Still Danner provided descriptions of Laura Cobb to the author in interviews and telephone conversations, 1990–92.

10. From the "Sweetheart of Sigma Chi." These lyrics were found with Mrs. Nelson's transcripts of her 1983 interview in the Army Nurse Corps Oral History Project, Army Nurse Corps archives, Center for Military History, Washington, D.C., Army archives. Used with permission. The original song is by Bryon D. Stokes, 1912, with music by F. Dudleigh Vernon.

11. Mary Rose Harrington Nelson, 1989 author interview. Quotations about her romance with Page Nelson from this interview.

12. Lyrics by Frank Loesser, music by Joseph J. Lilley, 1942.

13. Eleanor Garen's blue notebook with the imprint "Bureau of Education" on the cover. Henceforth referred to as "EG book." Garen files.

14. In a spiral pad titled "Eleanor Garen Nurses' Addresses," many women, including Josie Nesbit, Alice Hahn and Anna Williams, wrote their addresses and also mentioned how much they appreciated Garen's cheerful disposition. Garen files.

15. EG book, p. 1.

16. EG book, pp. 10–11. Socrates, "Apology."

17. EG book, p. 15. William Blake, "From Auguries of Innocence."

18. EG book, p. 54. Stephen Crane, "A Little Ink More or Less."

19. EG book, p. 68. A. E. Housman, "Yonder See the Morning Blink."

20. Pearson, p. 1012.

21. According to Hartendorp, pp. 180, 198–99, and Stevens, p. 420, the Japanese participated in the repatriation of imprisoned civilians in STIC because there was going to be a prisoner exchange of Japanese and Allied nationals in Goa, Portuguese India. On September 26, 1943, 127 STIC internees boarded the exchange ship *Teia Maru*. Twenty-four members of the American consular staff joined them. There were 131 Americans, 15 Canadians and 6 other nationals among the 151 people going home. At Goa, the repatriated Allies boarded the diplomatic ship *M. V. Gripsholm* for the journey to New York. Miss Dorothy Davis, a civilian nurse on board who had worked in STIC's hospital with the military women, had memorized the names of the army and navy nurses. She gave officials a full accounting. The management of the shipping company in Los Angeles sent form letters to the women's relatives.

22. Christmas card found in Inez McDonald Moore's files. Fort Sam Houston Medical Museum archives, San Antonio, Texas.

23. Ruby Bradley and Beatrice Chambers's experience had differed from that of the other army nurses on Bataan, Corregidor and, later, Mindanao. American military officers had decided to abandon Camp John Hay in Baguio in December 1941 after aerial attacks had devastated the post. Bradley and Chambers started out at Camp John Hay; then in April 1942 they moved to Camp John Holmes.

24. Nesbit, p. 45.

Chapter Fourteen: Eating Weeds Fried in Cold Cream, 1944

1. Hartendorp, p. 230. The Japanese also renamed the camps: STIC became Camp #1, Los Banos became Camp #2 and Baguio, Camp #3. The internees, however, still used the original names.

2. Nash, p. 1.

3. In the clinic, Louise Anschicks, an army nurse whose career began at the end of World War I, was responsible for the administration of vitamin injections, which the camp received in the 1943 Christmas shipment of Red Cross kits. In the twelve months of 1944, Anschicks recorded that 50,608 injections of thiamine, ascorbic acid, liver and chloride were given to STIC's prisoners. Source: L. Anschick's scrapbook, U.S. Army Medical Museum, Fort Sam Houston, San Antonio, Texas.

4. Every adult in STIC was ordered to sign an oath promising not to escape or conspire against the Japanese while they were internees. Initially, the army nurses returned the oath cards unsigned because they felt their jailers could interpret the wording broadly and begin to punish people on a whim. But after a lengthy discussion, the women finally signed the pledge. Many wrote statements in the margins indicating that they were signing under duress. Most, however, shrugged off the oath as meaningless. Only two men refused to participate in the process and, as a consequence, spent time in the camp jail. The oath read, "I, the undersigned, hereby

solemnly pledge myself that I will not under any circumstances attempt to escape or conspire directly or indirectly against the Japanese Military authorities, as long as I am in their custody." Hartendorp, p. 254.

5. Her diary reveals other details about the harassment and deprivations the prisoners endured and is located at the Admiral Nimitz Museum, Fredericksburg, Texas. Microfilm. Used with permission of her family.

6. The packages arrived in September 1943 on the exchange ship *Teia Maru,* but were not distributed to the prisoners until March 1944.

7. Hattie R. Brantley, May 9, 1945, war crimes testimony. Report 91. National Archives, Suitland, Maryland. SCAP Collection, Box 1118, transcript.

8. Nesbit, p. 43.

9. Sally Blaine Millett, 1990 author interview.

10. Mary Rose Harrington Nelson, 1989 author interview.

11. Stevens, p. 440.

12. Helen Cassiani Nestor, 1991 author interview. During the spring and summer of 1944, the Japanese allowed the first mail into STIC, and Cassie finally received news from home. In one letter, she learned that Louis, her older brother, who had taught her to play baseball, was dead from leukemia and that he had a daughter, Roberta, and had named Cassie as her godmother.

13. In 1992, the doll was on display in the Women's Corridor at the Pentagon in Washington, D.C.

14. Nash, p. 2.

15. Stevens, p. 350.

16. Williams, p. 196. Edith Shacklette's wartime diary, September 21, 1944, entry.

17. McCall, p. 133.

18. The average adult female, ages twenty-five to fifty, requires a daily diet of about 2,000 calories, 50 grams of protein a day for heat, energy and growth and repair of body tissues, 455–490 grams a day of carbohydrates to feed body and brain cells and 85 to 100 grams a day of fat for body fuel.

19. Hartendorp, p. 329.

20. Other authors cite twelve deaths that month (Hartendorp, p. 359; McCall, p. 145). The figure used here is from Marie Adams's Red Cross records. It was her job to record all deaths in STIC and organize burials. She turned over her records to the War Crimes Office in 1945. Her chronological list includes names, ages, nationalities, dates and causes of death. National Archives, Suitland, Maryland. SCAP Collection, 40-31-136.

21. Madeline Ullom, June 11, 1945, war crimes testimony. Report 91. National Archives, Suitland, Maryland. SCAP Collection, Box 1118, transcript.

22. Marie Adams, June 11, 1945, war crimes testimony. National Archives, Suitland, Maryland. SCAP Collection, 40-31-136.

23. Pearson, E., p. 998.

24. Helen Cassiani Nestor, 1990 author interview.

25. Mary Rose Harrington Nelson, 1989 author interview. Edith Shacklette's daily room-monitor notes provided more information about menstruation. Each woman had to reuse her fabric pads. An individual waited until her supply fell apart before

putting in a request for more. A woman's menstrual hygiene is usually private. In the camps, this privacy disappeared. Shack told her staff to "mark your sanitary pads well." In a 1990 interview, Mrs. Sally Blaine Millett said the nurses embroidered their initials on each cloth to keep their supplies separate. Every month, they rinsed out their bloody pads in sanitary napkin buckets kept in the communal bathroom. Wealthier internees could pay someone else to do this task. After they had washed them, the nurses had to lay the pieces outside on a lawn, in full public view, to dry. Often a woman sat next to her wash. Thus, there was no way to hide their sexual physiology.

26. McCall, p. 129.

27. Nash, p. 1.

28. Anna Williams Clark, 1983 ANC interview.

29. Edith Shacklette's Japanese diaries. No dates for recipes and menu entries.

30. Sally Blaine Millett, 1990 author interview.

31. Gwendolyn Henshaw Deiss, 1983 ANC interview.

32. Minnie Breese Stubbs, 1983 ANC interview.

33. Margaret "Peg" Nash, 1991 telephone interview with author.

34. Sally Blaine was twenty-nine years old in 1944; 1990 author interview. Edwina Todd (p. 340) mentions that the navy women also suffered from urinary incontinence.

35. *Ibid.*

36. McCall, p. 134

37. The four leaders were E. E. Johnson, C. L. Larsen, A. F. Duggleby and C. C. Grinnell, chairman of the Internee Committee, who lent money to the nurses. Two months later in 1945, friends identified their bodies in a mass grave. According to STIC historians and recorders, Hartendorp (pp. 424–25) and Stevens (p. 483), no reason was given for the executions.

38. The message appears in many sources, including Hartendorp (1964), Nesbit (1945) and Ullom (no date).

39. From January 1942 until July 1944, the average weight loss for men was 31.4 pounds, for women, 17.7 pounds (McCall, p. 96). Another survey taken in January 1945 indicated that men had lost twenty more pounds since August 1944, bringing their average weight loss since internment to fifty-one pounds. The women had lost fifteen more pounds, causing their average weight loss to climb to thirty-two pounds (Pearson, p. 1003).

40. Eleanor Garen, 1991 interview with Susan Sacharski.

41. EG book, p. 115, Shakespeare, "Merchant of Venice," and p. 111, Helene Martha Ball, "That Is All."

42. EG book, p. 121, April 28, 1944, entry.

43. Steven, p. 156.

44. Nash, p. 2.

45. Hartendorp, pp. 399–400. Dr. Stevenson survived his jail sentence.

46. Marie Adams, June 11, 1945, war crimes testimony. National Archives, Suitland, Maryland. SCAP Collection, 40-31-136.

47. Dorothy Still Danner, 1992 telephone interview with author.

48. Nash, p. 3.

Chapter Fifteen: And the Gates Came Crashing Down

1. Steinberg, R., p. 114. No doubt MacArthur's intelligence officers had told him that the city was starving and that the internees at STIC and the prisoners of war at the other stockades, down to one cup of food a day or less, were dying by the score.

2. *Ibid.*

3. Hartendorp, p. 405.

4. Eleanor Garen, 1991 interview with Susan Sacharski.

5. Rose Rieper Meier, 1984 ANC interview.

6. Hartendorp, p. 405.

7. Wright, Major B. C., p. 125. Other sources reported the contents as, "Roll out the barrel, Santa Claus is coming Sunday or Monday," and "Roll out the barrel. Christmas will be either today or tomorrow."

8. Scholl, p. C3.

9. Minnie Breese Stubbs, 1983 ANC interview.

10. Bertha Dworsky Henderson, 1983 ANC interview.

11. *Ibid.*

12. Hartendorp, p. 406.

13. In 1938, Irving Berlin wrote the music and lyrics to "God Bless America." Singer Kate Smith popularized the song, which became a kind of second national anthem during the war.

14. Ullom, p. 231.

15. Bertha Dworsky Henderson, 1983 ANC interview.

16. Rose Rieper Meier, 1984 ANC interview.

17. Time Inc. Picture Collection, Time Life Syndicate, Time Files 17030.

18. Scholl, p. C3.

19. Helen Cassiani Nestor, 1990 author interview.

20. Eleanor Garen, 1991 interview with Susan Sacharski.

21. Steinberg, p. 126.

22. Hartendorp, p. 406.

23. Hartendorp, p. 407.

24. Sally Blaine Millett, 1990 author interview.

25. Rita Palmer James, 1983 ANC interview. Sir Alexander Fleming discovered and named penicillin in 1929. Ten years later a research team at Oxford University succeeded in purifying the antibiotic drug, which allowed for large-scale production in time for clinical use with military casualties in the war.

26. Williams, p. 205.

27. Rose Rieper Meier, 1984 ANC interview. K-rations were lightweight, emergency food developed during the war for fighting units.

28. Sallie Durrett Farmer, (no date) ANC interview.

29. Time Inc. Picture Collection, Time Life Syndicate, Time Files 17030.

30. Edith Shacklette's Japanese diaries, February 7, 1945, entry.

31. Anna Williams Clark, 1983 ANC interview.

32. Jeanne Kennedy Schmidt, 1992 personal correspondence.

33. Sally Blaine Millett, 1990 author interview.

34. Edith Shacklette's Japanese diaries, February 8, 1945, entry.

35. Sally Blaine Millett, 1990 author interview.

36. Cassie quoted by Terry Myers Johnson, 1992 author interview.

37. Charlie Dworsky and John Henderson were married for twenty-five years and had one son, John R. Henderson. He died in 1991. She died in 1992. Information from her obituary in the *San Jose Mercury News* (February 28, 1992), p. 5B.

38. The 12th Regimental Quartermaster flag is now at the Quartermaster Museum in Fort Lee, Virginia. Peggy Greenwalt Walcher, May 1992 telephone interview with author.

39. Information about the plan and execution of the Los Banos rescue mission from: Calip, J., and Guerrero, J. (pp. 13–17) and Bailey, M. (pp. 57–66).

40. Mary Rose Harrington Nelson, 1989 author interview.

41. Todd, p. 340.

42. Margaret "Peg" Nash, 1991 telephone interview with author.

43. *Ibid.*

44. Edith Shacklette's Japanese diaries, February 12, 1945, entry.

45. In 1945, the death rate in Santo Tomas was 72.4 per thousand. The nurses served with 1,536 physicians and corpsmen on Bataan and Corregidor. Their mortality rate represents deaths from: battles leading up to surrender, the Death March, the brutal military prison camps, the labor battalions and the "hell ships" (overcrowded POW ships en route to Japan, which were accidentally sunk by Allied bombs and torpedoes).

46. Anna Williams Clark, 1983 ANC interview.

47. Edith Shacklette's Japanese diaries, February 12, 1945, entry.

48. *Ibid.*

49. *Ibid.*

50. Rita Palmer James, 1983 ANC interview.

51. Clarke, A. R., p. 345.

52. Repatriated Allied Prisoner Physical Examination Form. Garen files.

53. "Angels of Bataan saved—work on!" p. 1.

54. Miller, L. G., p. 1. Story appeared in March but the dateline was February 19.

55. Edith Shacklette's Japanese diaries, February 14, 1945, entry.

56. Edith Shacklette's Japanese diaries, February 16, 1945, entry.

57. Each woman received: the Bronze Star, the Asiatic-Pacific Theater Medal with two battle stars, a Presidential Unit Citation with two oak leaf clusters, the American Defense Medal with one battle star, the Philippine Defense Ribbon with one battle star, the Philippine Liberation Ribbon with one battle star and six hash marks for years of overseas military service. Information from Sally Blaine Millett, Josie Nesbit and Ruby Bradley's military records.

58. Several other evacuees met the POW's when they came home. Though few have discussed it, clearly there was tension in these reunions. Obviously, the evacuees had prospered during the war and some of the former POW's resented the lucky women who had been spared imprisonment. Redmond, for example, had jumped two ranks to major, and she had written a best-selling book about the nurses' part in the battle of Bataan.

59. Bertha Dworsky Henderson, 1983 ANC interview.

60. Telegram in Garen files.

61. "Rescue of Army nurse brings joy to mother," South Bend *Tribune* (no page). As it turned out, Lulu Garen did not make the trip to the coast. Instead, she was at a local airport when her daughter's cross-country flight touched down. Garen files.

Chapter Sixteen: "Home. We're Really Home."

1. "Bataan Angels sigh with joy as planes land in California," *Fresno Bee,* Feb. 26, 1945. This news article, and others cited in this chapter without page numbers, were compiled in a large scrapbook titled *Home from Bataan,* ASF Group, Bureau of Public Relations (no date). Army Nurse Corps archives, Center for Military History, Washington, D.C.

2. "Angels of Bataan," Associated Press, Feb. 22, 1945.

3. "Tough soldiers weep at return of 'angels,' " *San Francisco Chronicle,* 1945.

4. "Bataan nurses are honored during busy week at Letterman," p. 2.

5. "68 'Angels of Bataan' fly back to heaven after 3 years of prison camp hell," *Salt Lake City Tribune,* Feb. 25, 1945.

6. The two nurses awarded Purple Hearts for the wounds they received when the Japanese bombed Hospital #1 on Bataan in April 1942 were: Rita Palmer from Hampton, New Hampshire, and Rosemary Hogan from Chattanooga, Oklahoma. At an unknown date, Mary Brown Menzie, the army nurse who was assaulted by a Japanese soldier on Corregidor in May 1942, also received a Purple Heart.

7. Copies of the Roosevelt letter found in Inez McDonald Moore's files at Fort Sam Houston Medical Museum archives, Fort Sam Houston, Texas, and in the Garen files.

8. "Freedom: A lot of little things . . . to Angels of Bataan," *California Call,* Feb. 28, 1945.

9. Phyllis Arnold, 1983 ANC interview.

10. "The Bataan 'Angels.' " *The New York Times,* Feb. 28, 1945.

11. "Freed nurses reunited with men they aided on Bataan," p. 3.

12. Undated correspondence from Alice "Swish" Zwicker to Terry Myers. Terry Myers Johnson personal files. Used with permission.

13. Ullom, p. 276.

14. Excerpt drawn from two stories: "Two Georgia nurses of Corregidor run into arms of happy families," *Atlanta Constitution,* March 5, 1945, and "Bright jonquils and real bed spell nepenthe for Tomas nurse," *Atlanta Journal,* March 5, 1945.

15. "Philippine nurses return to homes of their dreams," *St. Louis Star Times,* March 2, 1945.

16. "Of all gifts Tupelo offers Bataan 'Angel' Lt. Inez McDonald chooses hair wave," *Clarion Ledger,* March 7, 1945.

17. Eleanor Garen, 1990 interview with Susan Sacharski.

18. Bertha Dworsky Henderson, 1983 ANC interview.

19. Hogan, R., pp. 80–82.

20. "Lieut. Garen home; 'Everyone looks fat,' " South Bend *Tribune,* March 1945.

21. *Ibid.*

22. The series ran in the the South Bend *Tribune* from March 6 to March 9, 1945.

23. Eleanor Garen, 1990 interview with Susan Sacharski.

24. Waymire, K., p. 1. The story appeared on the lower left corner of the front page. The navy nurses were never imprisoned in Cabanatuan, a military POW camp. The were freed from Los Banos Internment Camp.

25. Margaret "Peg" Nash used this term in a 1991 author interview.

26. Mary Rose Harrington Nelson discussed her wedding in a 1991 interview with Sharon Eifried.

27. Helen Cassiani Nestor talked about her homecoming in a 1990 author interview.

28. Ross, L., "Bridgewater Army Nurse, Freed at Jap Prison Camp, Comes Home." *The Boston Globe,* March 3, 1945.

29. Helen Cassiani Nestor, 1990 author interview.

Chapter Seventeen: Aftermath

1. According to her stepson, Maude Davison retired with the rank of lieutenant colonel. Official military biographies list her rank as captain and major.

2. Robert Jackson, 1993 author interview. His comments form the basis for this section. Maude Davison's husband, Charles, had two grown sons, Robert Jackson, a Red Cross field director, and Bill Jackson, a bibliographer at Harvard University. According to Robert, his brother, Bill, did not spend much time with his stepmother.

3. *Ibid.*

4. Robert Jackson said that Maude Davison suffered a massive stroke that eventually killed her. A September 1965 official army biography lists her death from a myocardial infarction due to arteriosclerotic heart disease.

5. On March 5, 1957, army officials dedicated a building in her honor—Davison Hall, a bachelor women's officers quarters at Brooke Army Medical Center in San Antonio, Texas.

6. In 1976, Lieutenant Colonel Pauline Maxwell, ANC (Ret.) wrote a multivolume history of army nursing. This unpublished typewritten manuscript, *History of the Army Nurse Corps, 1775–1948,* is filed at the Center for Military History, Washington, D.C. In Volume 14, page 57.1, Maxwell mentioned the dispute over Davison's award. The memoranda concerning Davison's award were found in 1993 after Maxwell's death. Lieutenant Colonel Iris West, ANC historian, was searching Maxwell's file cabinets when she discovered a folder with Maude Davison's name written on it. The memoranda were inside.

7. The Congressional Medal of Honor and the Distinguished Service Cross are the army's highest decorations.

8. Memorandum dated March 26, 1946, from Colonel Wibb Cooper to Awards and Decorations Board, Headquarters Fourth Army, Fort Sam Houston, Texas.

9. Memorandum dated June 19, 1946, from Brigadier General LeGrande Diller to the Awards and Decorations Board.

10. Memorandum dated July 26, 1946, from General MacArthur to the chief of staff, United States Army.

11. Memorandum dated April 24, 1946, from General Jonathan Wainwright to adjutant general, Washington, D.C.

12. Wainwright, p. 81.

13. Report of Awards and Decorations Board dated September 9, 1946.

14. Memorandum dated October 1, 1946, from General H. Bull to General Paul.

15. Memorandum dated January 14, 1946, from Captain K. E. Lowman to the secretary of the navy. Captain Lowman sent two proposed citations, one for a Bronze Star, another for the Legion of Merit. The memoranda about Cobb's awards are in her personnel file. Records obtained from the National Personnel Records Center, St. Louis, Missouri, under the Freedom of Information Act.

16. Memorandum dated January 25, 1945, from Dana Nance, M.D., medical director of Los Banos Philippine Military Internment Camp Number 2, to surgeon general, Bureau of Medicine and Surgery, Washington, D.C. Ann Bernatitus, the only navy nurse to be evacuated from the Philippines before surrender and the only navy nurse to serve on Bataan, was awarded the Legion of Merit for her service on Bataan. She was the lone navy nurse in World War II to receive the decoration. Like Davison, Cobb's award reflected her wartime military service during the early days of the war in 1941 to 1942. Her citation does not mention her leadership or work as a POW.

17. Davis, D. M., p. 153.

18. Bruhn, pp. 24–25. "Happy" Bruhn is Mina Aasen's niece. Used with permission.

19. Bruhn, p. 28.

20. Craighill, M. D., p. 226.

21. EG book, pp. 122–23.

Chapter Eighteen: Across the Years

1. Adams, J. T., p. 404.

2. All quotations from Sally Blaine Millett, 1990 author interview and a December 1993 correspondence. The stories of the twelve women that follow are in some ways representative of the group; that is, they are as diverse as the culture at large. For the most part these are the women on whom some detail was available.

3. Bertha Dworsky Henderson, 1983 ANC interview.

4. All quotations from Eunice Hatchitt Tyler, 1990 and 1991 author interviews.

5. Carolyn Armold Torrence, Dorothy Scholl Armold's daughter, gave the author the news clippings without an identifying newspaper or date. Quotations from Carolyn Armold Torrence, 1992 author interview.

6. Harold Armold Jr., 1992 author interview.

7. Biographical information from Madeline Ullom, 1993 correspondence with author. Speech excerpts from Ullom, pp. 6–7; 10–11.

8. Denny Williams, 1990 author interview.

9. All quotations from Terry Myers Johnson, 1992 author interview.

10. Helen Cassiani Nestor, 1994 author interview. After learning about Terry's death, Cassie made a donation to the University of Nevada women's softball team as a tribute to the days when the two of them played the sport in Santo Tomas Internment Camp.

11. Josie Nesbit Davis, 1983 ANC interview.

12. Nesbit's message appeared in a dinner booklet at the 1992 "Gala salute to all United States of America military women prisoners of war." Compiled by Ms. Alice Booher of the Southeast Business and Professional Women (SE/BPW).

13. Ruby Bradley wrote a paper in the early 1960s titled "Prisoner of War in the Far East." Uncataloged file, Army Nurse Corps archives, Center for Military History, Washington, D.C., pp. 22–23. Other quotations in this section from Ruby Bradley, 1989 author interview.

14. *Ibid.*

15. *This Is Your Life* aired live on NBC from October 1952 until September 1961. Host Ralph Edwards wanted his guests to have demonstrated charity, community spirit, conformity and patriotism. The show often ended with Edwards making a charitable donation or gift in honor of his guest. Ruby Bradley's military career made her a logical subject for a show, as did Edwards's establishment of a nursing scholarship in Bradley's name.

16. The other women awarded the permanent rank of colonel in the regular army were Inez Haynes, chief of the Army Nurse Corps, and Ruby F. Bryant.

17. A summary of Ruby Bradley's career was found in her 1983 ANC Oral History folder at the Army Nurse Corps archives, Center for Military History, Washington, D.C. Dates of service, promotion record and list of awards taken from this summary. Her military awards include: Bronze Star Medal; World War II Victory Medal; American Defense Service Medal with one Bronze Star and Foreign Service Clasp; Asiatic-Pacific Campaign Medal with two Bronze Battle Stars, Distinguished Unit Badge; Presidential Unit Emblem with two Oak Leaf Clusters on Blue Ribbon; Philippine Defense Ribbon with one Bronze Service Star; Philippine Liberation Ribbon with one Bronze Service Star; American Campaign Medal and American Theater Ribbon; Philippine Independence Ribbon; American of Occupation Medal with Japan Clasp; National Defense Service Medal; Korean Service Medal with one Silver Service Star (in lieu of five Bronze Service Stars); two Bronze Service Stars for participation in the UN Offensive, Chinese Communist Forces Intervention, UN Summer–Fall Offensive, Second Korean Winter, Korea-Summer-Fall 1952, Third Korean Winter and Korea Summer–Fall 1953; United Nations Service Medal; Legion of Merit with an Oak Leaf Cluster; Oak Leaf Cluster for Bronze Star Medal, Commendation Ribbon with Metal Pendant. She also received: the 1953 Virginia Distinguished Service Medal; the International Red Cross 1955 Florence Nightingale Medal; and an honorary Doctor of Science degree from West Virginia University.

18. Ruby Bradley, 1991 interview with Sharon Eifried.

19. All quotations from Mary Rose Harrington Nelson, 1989 author interview and a 1991 interview with Sharon Eifried.

20. "Queen for a Day" was a radio show that aired first in 1945 under the title "Queen for Today." The honoree received "feminine" merchandise, such as washing machines, clothes, underwear and hosiery. Host Jack Bailey continued with the show when it moved to NBC television in 1956.

21. Quotations from Eleanor Garen, 1991 interview with Susan Sacharski.

22. On December 31, 1945, there were 27,850 army nurses on active duty. By Sep-

tember 30, 1946, approximately 8,500 nurses remained in the Army Nurse Corps. Piemonte, R., and Gurney, C., pp. 19–20. After Congress passed the Army-Navy Nurse Act of 1947, the army upgraded nurses' military status by awarding them permanent commissions. Eleanor was one of 894 nurses who were integrated into the regular army at that time.

23. Eleanor Garen, 1992 correspondence with Susan Sacharski. Used with permission.

24. Eleanor Garen, 1993 correspondence with Susan Sacharski. Used with permission. In 1993, Eleanor's niece Doris Sante donated the possessions of the former army nurse to archivist Susan Sacharski at Northwestern Memorial Hospital, Chicago, Illinois.

25. Information about Helen Cassiani Nestor's postwar years from numerous interviews from 1990 through 1997 with the author. All quotations about her and her family in this section come from these interviews.

26. Helen Cassiani Nestor, January 21, 1997, personal correspondence.

Afterword

1. In October 1997, under the leadership of retired Air Force Brigadier General Wilma L. Vaught and "The Women in Military Service for America Memorial Project" (WIMSA), the massive stone arch at the entrance to Arlington Memorial Cemetery in Washington, D.C., was dedicated to honor servicewomen from the American Revolutionary War to the present day.

2. Oberst and Thor Nelson's quotations from the dinner booklet given to all participants at the 1992 gala. Compiled by Ms. Alice Booher, Southeast Business and Professional Women (SE/BPW).

3. "American military women prisoners of war," S5341.

Epilogue

1. Gilligan, (1982).

2. According to Bataan Death March survivor Sam Moody's personal communication (1998), five men, all veterans of the Bataan and Corregidor battles, retired to Florida and regularly met for lunch. At one of their gatherings, they decided to find a way to honor the nurses. Moody, who was once a patient in Hospital #2 on Bataan, said, "I always felt the nurses never got any credit and I wanted to do something. I feel like they are my sisters." The five men contacted other veterans from Bataan and Corregidor. "We got mostly $5 and $10 donations but we raised enough money." Moody and his friends designed the plaque and wrote the inscription. They were present during the dedication ceremonies at the Altar of Valor on Mount Samat, Bataan.

Index